Special Educational Needs

Special Educational Needs

A Guide for Inclusive Practice

Edited by

Lindsay Peer and Gavin Reid

SAGE

Los Angeles | London | New Delhi
Singapore | Washington DC

First published 2012

SAGE Publications Ltd
1 Oliver's Yard
55 City Road
London EC1Y 1SP

SAGE Publications Inc.
2455 Teller Road
Thousand Oaks, California 91320

SAGE Publications India Pvt Ltd
B 1/I 1 Mohan Cooperative Industrial Area
Mathura Road
New Delhi 110 044

SAGE Publications Asia-Pacific Pte Ltd
33 Pekin Street #02-01
Far East Square
Singapore 048763

Library of Congress Control Number: 2011926931

British Library Cataloguing in Publication data

A catalogue record for this book is available from the British Library

ISBN 978-0-85702-162-5
ISBN 978-0-85702-163-2 (pbk)

Typeset by C&M Digitals (P) Ltd, Chennai, India
Printed in Great Britain by TJ International Ltd, Padstow, Cornwall
Printed on paper from sustainable resources

CONTENTS

LIST OF TABLES AND FIGURES

FIGURES

TABLES

ACRONYMS AND ABBREVIATIONS

ABA	applied behaviour analysis
AD	autistic disorder
ADD	attention deficit disorder
ADHD	Attention deficit hyperactivity disorder (or hyperkinetic disorder)
APD	auditory processing disorder
AS	Asperger disorder
ASD	autistic spectrum disorder
ASHA	American Speech-Language-Hearing Association
ASL	additional support for learning
ASN	additional support needs
ASNTS	additional support needs tribunals for Scotland
BDA	British Dyslexia Association
BMI	Body Mass Index
BPS	British Psychological Society
BSA	British Society of Audiology
BSED	behavioural, emotional and social difficulties
CAMHS	Child and Adolescent Mental Health Services
CAPD	central auditory processing disorder
CBT	cognitive behavioural therapy
CDC	(US) Center for Disease Control
CHSS	Centre for Health Services Studies
CNS	central nervous system
CREID	Centre for Research in Education, Inclusion and Diversity
CSIE	Centre for Studies on Inclusive Education
CSP	co-ordinated support plan
CVI	cortical visual impairment
CWDC	Children's Workforce Development Council
DCD	developmental co-ordination disorder
DDA	Disability Discrimination Act 1995
DfES	Department for Education and Skills
DISS	Deployment and Impact of Support Staff
DSA	Disabled Students' Allowance
DSM	*Diagnostic and Statistical Manual of Mental Disorders*
EBD	emotional and behavioural difficulties
ECG	electrocardiogram
ESRC	Economic and Social Research Council
FM	frequency modulated
FTT	first-tier tribunal
HESC	Health Education and Social Care Chamber

HPC	Health Professions Council
ICD	International Classification of Diseases and Related Health Problems
IEP	individualized educational plan/programme
LEA	local education authority
MFL	modern foreign languages
MLD	moderate learning difficulties
NEAT	non-exercise activity thermo-genesis
NIMH	(US) National Institute of Mental Health
NOSI	non-obscene socially inappropriate (behaviour)
NPD	National Pupil Database
NRC	National Research Council
OCB	obsessive-compulsive behaviour
OCD	obsessive-compulsive disorder
ODD	oppositional defiant disorder
OME	otitis media with effusion
OT	occupational therapy (therapist)
PAIG	Paediatric Audiology Interest Group
PCHI	permanent congenital hearing impairment
PDD	pervasive developmental disorder
PDD-NOS	pervasive developmental disorder – not otherwise specified
PPS	Parent Partnership Service
PTA	pure tone audiometry
QTVI	qualified teacher of the visually impaired
RCSLT	Royal College of Speech and Language Therapists
RCT	randomized controlled trial
RNIB	Royal National Institute for the Blind
SaLT	speech and language therapy
SASC	SpLD Assessment Standards Committee
SEN	special educational needs
SENCo	special educational needs co-ordinator
SENDA	Special Educational Needs Disability Act 2001
SENDIST	special educational needs and disability tribunal
SENT	special educational needs tribunal
SIGN	Scottish Intercollegiate Guidelines Network
SLCN	speech, language and communication needs
SLI	specific language impairment
SLT	speech and language therapy (therapist)
SMD	sensory modulation difficulties
SpLD	specific learning difficulty
TA	teaching assistant
TS	Tourette syndrome
VA	value added
VI	visually impaired/visual impairment
VIS	Visual Impairment Scotland
VOCA	voice output communication aid

ACKNOWLEDGEMENTS

It was a privilege for us to be appointed as editors of this book and we would like to take this opportunity to thank all the authors for their excellent contributions. Each one leads a busy professional life and we recognized this when we invited them to contribute. We have therefore been overwhelmed by the enthusiasm and the quality of responses from each of the contributors. Each one is highly recognized in the field and is held in the highest esteem. We are therefore fortunate that they have been able to collaborate with us in developing the idea and the chapters for this book.

We are also delighted that, in many of the chapters, there has been a great deal of professional collaboration. It is this synthesis of ideas that makes the chapters rich and informative. We are also indebted to those who wrote single-author chapters. Given their professional schedule this is greatly appreciated.

We have tried to embrace a breadth of perspectives in this book although, as readers will appreciate, special educational needs is a large area with a range of views, principles and practices. We recognize that we have not covered every aspect of special educational needs; we have done the best we can in a book this size.

To this end we are indebted for the advice we received from the editorial team at Sage Publications and, of course, for the quality chapters we received from the authors. We are also grateful to those parents of children with special educational needs who shared their personal stories.

We are sure that the book will be widely appreciated. This will confirm that the efforts of all have been well worthwhile and we hope the book will serve as a valued reference and guide for practice for all professionals in a range of fields related to special educational needs. We are also indebted to Baroness Warnock for writing such a positive and insightful Foreword. We hope you will benefit from this book as much as we have enjoyed the editing process.

Lindsay Peer and Gavin Reid 2011

ABOUT THE EDITORS AND CONTRIBUTORS

THE EDITORS

Lindsay Peer, CBE, is an educational psychologist and chartered psychologist, speaker, author and expert witness, and is widely recognized as an expert in the range of specific learning difficulties, special needs and mainstream education. In 2002 she was appointed CBE for services to education and dyslexia. She has lectured extensively as a keynote speaker in the international arena since the late 1980s and further advises governments, trades unions, policy-makers, lawyers, schools, psychologists and parents. She has been a keynote speaker in the UK, USA, India, Sweden, Belgium, Finland, Israel, Iceland, Norway, Italy, Spain, Majorca, Greece, South Africa, Botswana, Swaziland, Cyprus, the Czech Republic and Holland. Lindsay an Associate Fellow and a Chartered Scientist of the British Psychological Society and a Fellow of both the International Academy of Research in Learning Disabilities and the Royal Society of Arts. She is a member of the Association of Child Psychologists in Private Practice. She is registered with the Health Professions Council. She is registered with the UK Register of Expert Witnesses. She held the posts of Education Director and Deputy CEO of the British Dyslexia Association until 2003 and has been a member of its Accreditation Board from 1992 to date. She has many years' experience as a teacher, teacher trainer and SENCo. Lindsay has published a considerable body of material, both theoretical and practical. She published the first groundbreaking book linking 'glue ear' with dyslexia. Lindsay assesses children, students and adults facing challenges in learning. She is authorized to assess for public examinations. She has experience with dyslexia, dyspraxia, AD/HD, Asperger's syndrome, speech and language difficulties, hearing impairment, moderate learning difficulties and cerebral palsy (http://www.peergordonassociates.co.uk/).

Gavin Reid is an independent educational psychologist, international author and leading seminar presenter. He is based in Vancouver, Canada. He also has consultancies in UK, Switzerland, Asia, Kuwait, Abu Dhabi and Cairo. He has been a visiting professor in the Department of Educational Psychology and Special Education at the University of British Columbia (UBC) in Vancouver, Canada. He is also a consultant to the Institute of Child Education and Psychology, Europe (ICEP), a director of the academy for Inclusion of Special Needs and Global Educational Consultants (http://www.globaleducational consultants.com/) and a consultant with the UN Development Programme in Kuwait. He has been a consultant for the Open University in the UK since 1999 and is on the course team for the 'Difficulties in literacy development' course. He is a co-founder and director of the Red Rose School for children with specific learning difficulties in St Annes on Sea, Lancashire and Educational Director of the Lighthouse School in Cairo, Egypt. He was formerly a senior lecturer in the Department of Educational Studies, Moray House School of Education, University of Edinburgh, 1991–2007. He has currently 25 books in print in the area of teacher education in the field of dyslexia, literacy learning styles and motivation, and classroom management (http://www.drgavinreid.com/index.html).

THE CONTRIBUTORS

Jane Abdullah qualified from the Newcastle-upon-Tyne School of Occupational Therapy in 1984. Following three years spent working in adult neurology, she specialized in paediatrics at the Manchester Children's Hospital before moving to Watford and then St Albans and Hemel Hempstead as Head of the Paediatric Occupational Therapy Services. In 1998 she left the NHS to work as an independent therapist. At present, she is actively involved in providing assessment and treatment to children with a variety of needs in both special and mainstream schools. She has been preparing independent reports for special educational needs and disability tribunals since 1999.

Elias Avramidis is a lecturer at the Department of Special Education, University of Thessaly (Greece) and honorary research fellow at the Graduate School of Education, University of Exeter. His research (covering primary, secondary and tertiary settings) mainly focuses on examining the theory and practice of inclusive education and the barriers to its implementation. He has published on topics such as teachers' attitudes towards inclusive education; the identification of and provision for children with difficulties in literacy; and the social impacts of inclusive education.

Judy Barrow has been a volunteer with Tourette Scotland since 2002 and has been employed as their Development Manager since 2009. She has direct experience of Tourette syndrome as well as a background in therapeutic care, community education and community development, and person-centred counselling.

Sheena Bell (Senior Lecturer in Special Educational Needs and Inclusion at the University of Northampton) is a member of the CeSNER team (Centre for Special Needs Education and Research) leading courses for specialist teachers and assessors of dyslexia/SpLD. She has taught in England and abroad, ranging from prisons to primary schools.

Daryl J. Brown has a first degree and doctorate in earth sciences from Oxford University and an MSc in the psychology of special educational needs from the University of Nottingham. He is head teacher and psychologist at the Maple Hayes Dyslexia School and Research Centre, Lichfield, specializing in the application of the dual-route processing model to literacy and, with Neville Brown, is co-author of *Meaning, Morphemes and Literacy*. He is currently working with Neville on a major work, *A Lexicon of Morphemes of the English Language*.

E. Neville Brown entered the teaching profession in 1958 and became head of English in 1960 in a Midlands' secondary school. His research has featured three times in the NATO Human Factors Program. After founding a unit in Birmingham for non-achieving school-leavers, he established the charity, The Foundation for the Education of the Underachieving and Dyslexic, then the Maple Hayes Dyslexia School and Research Centre in Lichfield in 1982, which received an award in 2008 for being the top school in the country for added value. An associate fellow of the British Psychological Society, chartered psychologist and scientist, Neville was elected to the International Neuropsychological Society in 1980 for his work in that field. Neville lectures worldwide on the theory and practice of literacy learning, and continues to be active in teaching children: he was ITV 'Teacher of the Year' in 2008.

Steve Chinn set up an award-winning secondary school for dyslexic boys which he ran for 19 years. He has researched and written extensively about dyslexia, and mathematics and dyscalculia. His current project is a book, complete with standardized tests, on assessing and diagnosing maths learning disorders. He lectures worldwide.

Margaret Crombie currently works part time for the Open University as an associate lecturer and consultant on the 'Difficulties in literacy development' module. She has previously worked as a teacher of children with specific learning difficulties in literacy, and in a management role for local authorities in Scotland. She has researched into language learning and dyslexia, and investigated dyslexia in the early years. She has contributed to many previous publications on literacy learning.

John Davidson first became known as having Tourette syndrome after a BBC documentary in 1989 highlighted his condition, bringing Tourette syndrome into the public eye. He has endeavoured to bring about better understanding and support for Tourette syndrome and ensuring that more is learnt about its traits and impacts. He lives and works in the Borders area of Scotland. He volunteers on a range of projects for those living with TS.

Jill Duncan is Head of Graduate Studies at the Royal Institute for Deaf and Blind Children's Renwick Centre for Research and Professional Education and Conjoint Senior Lecturer, University of Newcastle, Australia.

Janet Farrugia qualified as a speech and language therapist in 1980 and worked in The National Health Service from 1980 – 1987 in a variety of nurseries, specialist units and health centres specialising in paediatric speech, language and communication delays and disorders. In 1987 Janet established her independent practice and in 1996 opened a paediatric speech and language clinic called 'Say and Play' which is based at Edenside Clinic in Bookham, Surrey. She achieved a masters degree in Human Communication in 2001. Janet is a founder member and was Secretary to the Association of Speech and Language Therapists in Independent Practice (ASLTIP) and sat on the Working Party of the Royal College of Speech and Language Therapists (RCSLT) looking into Independent

Therapy. Since 1996 Janet has been involved in medico legal work for special educational needs tribunals and has provided over 500 reports and attended as an Expert Witness at SENDIST on numerous occasions. She has also completed a Bond Solon Witness Familiarisation Course and Excellence in Written Evidence (2010). She was involved in a joint venture with ASLTIP and RCSLT regarding Best Practice Guidelines in the SENDIST process. http://www.speechandlanguagetherapy.com

John Friel is a barrister recognized as a leader in the field of education rights for children with learning difficulties and disabilities. He is also recognized as having worked with Harry Chasty in the early days of recognition of dyslexia and other similar disabilities, to achieve legal recognition of the rights of dyslexia within the education system. He has won leading cases in the House of Lords, the Court of Appeal, the Upper Tribunal and the Special Educational Needs and Disability Tribunal. He has worked closely with psychologists for many years and contributes to professional training in various conferences every year. Currently he is a trustee of The Moat, a special school for severely dyslexic children, and SOS!SEN, a charity which helps parents on all aspects of learning difficulties and disability rights. He is a former trustee of Dyslexia Action and has in the past been Chair of Governors of the Advisory Centre for Education. In addition, together with his daughter, Charlotte Friel, he is a guest lecturer at University College London on the trainee psychologists' course. He is also the father of two boys with severe dyslexia and understands the system and the difficulties that arise very well indeed. He is the senior team leader of the specialist education section at the Hardwicke Building (http://www.hardwicke.co.uk/).

Neville Harris is Professor of Law at the University of Manchester. He specializes in welfare law, especially education law and policy, and his books include *Education, Law and Diversity* (Hart 2007), *Special Educational Needs and Access to Justice* (Jordans 1997) and, as co-author, *Challenges to School Exclusion* (Routledge Falmer 2000).

Keith Holland is an optometrist with a specialist interest in the visual and sensory problems that affect learning. With a specialist practice in Gloucestershire, Keith lectures worldwide and writes extensively on learning skills.

Sionah Lannen is an independent chartered educational psychologist and is registered with the Health Professionals Council in the UK. She is co-founder and Head Teacher of the Red Rose School for children and young people with specific learning difficulties in St Annes on Sea, Lancashire. She is currently involved in a number of European-wide school initiatives. She has been an educational psychologist in Scotland, Canada, the Middle East and Lancashire.

Bernadette McLean is Principal of the Helen Arkell Dyslexia Centre. She is a founder member of the Dyslexia Specific Learning Difficulties Trust, serves on the British Dyslexia Association Accreditation Board and the Board of the SpLD Assessment Standards Committee.

Brahm Norwich is Professor of Educational Psychology and Special Educational Needs at the Graduate School of Education, University of Exeter. He has worked as a teacher and professional educational psychologist, and he has researched and published widely in these fields. His books are *Moderate Learning Difficulties and the Future of Inclusion* (Routledge 2005), *Special Pedagogy for Special Children: Pedagogies for Inclusion* (with Ann Lewis, Open University Press), *Dilemmas of Difference, Disability and Inclusion: International Perspectives* (Routledge 2008) and *SEN: A New Look* (with Mary Warnock and Lorella Terzi, Continuum Publishers 2010).

Janet O'Keefe qualified as a speech and language therapist in 1985. She worked for the NHS in Kent and Suffolk before becoming independent in 1997. She has a special interest in children with autistic spectrum disorders, including Asperger Syndrome. She is a member of the National Deaf Children's Society and an accreditation team member of the National Autistic Society; and one of the honorary consultants in speech and language therapy for the Twins and Multiple Births Association (TAMBA). Janet was the RCSLT/ASLTIP Medico-Legal Representative from 1999–2002 and is now a full member of the Expert Witness Institute. Janet undertakes Independent Speech and Language Therapy Assessments and reports to be submitted as part of statutory assessments for children with Special Educational Needs or appeals to SENDIST across the UK and expert reports for Medico Legal cases in the High Court. She established Wordswell in 1999 to provide speech and language therapy services to children in both state and independent schools in the Eastern Region of England. Janet has written a book *Towards a Positive Future, Stories, ideas and inspiration from SEN children, their families and professionals* and established The Clarity Foundation, a multidisciplinary network of health, education and social care professionals who work with children with SEN. http://www.wordswell.co.uk

Adrienne Papendorf is a mother of two sons – one statemented with dyslexia. Her educational background is in history, and she works part time as a finance manager at a university for a group specializing in disabilities, especially blindness, in the developing world.

John Ravenscroft is the former Head of the Scottish Sensory Centre and Visual Impairment Scotland research project. His main research interest focuses around children with vision impairment and multiple disabilities.

Sheila Riddell is Director of the Centre for Research in Education, Inclusion and Diversity (CREID) at the University of Edinburgh. She is the author of *Policy and Practice in Special Educational Needs: Additional Support for Learning* (Dunedin Academic Press 2006) and co-author of *Improving Disabled Students' Learning in Higher Education* (RoutledgeFalmer 2009), *Disabled Students in Higher Education: Perspectives on Widening Access and Changing Policy* (RoutledgeFalmer, 2005) and *The Learning Society and People with Learning Difficulties* (Policy Press 2001).

Artemi Sakellariadis is the Director of the Centre for Studies on Inclusive Education (CSIE). She trained as a special educator and taught in special schools for many years, before committing her energy to the development of inclusive provision for all in mainstream schools.

Tony Sirimanna is a senior consultant audiological physician at the Great Ormond Street Hospital for Children, London, and an honorary senior lecturer at the Division of Neurosciences, Institute of Child Health, University of London. He has been a consultant audiological physician since 1994. He is the Lead Clinician for the Audiology, Audiological Medicine and Cochlear Implant Departments at Great Ormond Street Hospital. He is also the medical lead and a quality assurance consultant for the national Newborn Hearing Screening Programme in England, Chair of the Clinical Standards Committee of the British Association of Audiovestibular Physicians in the UK, Secretary of the Specialist Advisory Committee for Audiological Medicine at the Royal College of Physicians in London and Clinical Champion for Paediatric Audiology in London for the London Strategic Health Authority. He has over 15 years of experience in diagnosing and managing patients with auditory processing disorder (APD) in two major APD clinics in the UK. He was instrumental in setting up the UK APD steering group under the auspices of the British Society of Audiology in October 2003 and was the first Chair of the group. He currently runs the largest paediatric APD clinic in the UK based at Great Ormond Street Hospital.

Richard Soppitt is a consultant child psychiatrist and honorary senior research fellow at the Centre for Health Services Studies (CHSS), Canterbury and makes national media broadcasts, publishes and lectures in the areas of autism, depression, conduct disorder and ADHD.

Susan Strachan has two children with dyslexia and runs the local dyslexia support group (DyslexiaScotlandNorthEast.org.uk) in Aberdeen, Scotland. Her professional background is paediatric occupational therapy and additional support needs training (Sensationallearning.com). She also co-founded and leads TRAINsGrampian.org, which provides free local autism-related training to families and professionals.

Charles Weedon is a teacher and educational psychologist. He is an honorary fellow of the University of Edinburgh and his particular interest is specific learning difficulties.

Elisabet Weedon is Deputy Director of the Centre for Research in Education, Inclusion and Diversity (CREID) at the University of Edinburgh. Her main research interests are in the areas of lifelong learning and social justice. She has been involved in research into the experiences of disabled students in higher education, the use of restorative practices in education and dispute resolution in the area of additional support needs. Current projects include an investigation of the experiences and outcomes for Muslim pupils, research into lifelong learning in Europe and learning in the workplace.

Kevin Woods is Professor of Educational and Child Psychology at the University of Manchester, where he works as the Director of initial professional training in educational psychology. He has been a practitioner educational psychologist for 20 years and his research interests include the developing role of educational psychologists in public service, student assessment needs and attachment.

FOREWORD

This is a timely book. Thirty years on from the Education Act 1981, which set the framework for the education of children newly designated as having special educational needs, it is useful to have a review of the scene. As the editors say, a great deal has changed. However, there has been no radical rethink of the framework, something which I believe is a matter of urgency, and was strongly recommended by the House of Commons All-party Select Committee in 2005. But before this could be undertaken it would be necessary to look in detail at how things stand in the field today. This book will be essential reading for anyone interested in initiating further change.

One of the most useful aspects of the collection is that the educational system in Scotland is included in the survey. This system, comparatively new, has now had time to settle down, and there is undoubtedly much to be learnt from its emphasis on additional support, wherever it may be needed.

One of the inadequacies of many official pronouncements about special educational needs is the habit of treating all special needs as much the same, as if students' problems were capable of being tackled in the same way, the same outcomes expected. This is manifestly absurd: education for some children, even children with statements, can lead to a life of full employment, enjoyable activity and a proper awareness of the contribution they make to society. For others, sadly, this is not the case, and they can look forward only to a life of dependency. It does the concept of special educational needs no good to pass over this fact. One of the virtues of the present volume is that a large part of it is devoted not to general discussion of special educational needs as a whole, but to specific conditions and their appropriate recognition and the support that children need when the condition is identified. It is here perhaps that the Scottish model of provision is most illuminating.

Throughout the book the reader is made aware, in some chapters more than in others, of the tension that exists between a policy that recognizes the reality of the differences between different individual children and how the needs of each may be met, and one which seeks to regard all children as the same, as all parts of one society of school or college, their problems exacerbated by the failure of society to adapt. This is as it should be, for the tension is real. And on the whole ideological posturing is avoided. For in reality such tensions must be faced and, if possible, resolved not in the lecture room or the academic groves but in the classroom and the unit, practice backed up by research, but with pupils and teachers at the centre. The last chapter is devoted to that other aspect of reality, the parents who know their children best. Again this was a good decision. My only criticism of this chapter is that it, in a short space, can hardly do justice to the cries of frustration and despair that I hear through my postbag. Undoubtedly one of the changes that has come about in the last thirty years is a deterioration in the relation between parents and local authorities, and, sadly, matters can only get worse in the present economic climate. This is yet another reason for saying that this book is timely. I hope that it will be very widely read.

Mary Warnock

1 INTRODUCTION

Gavin Reid and Lindsay Peer

The field of special educational needs (SEN) has undergone significant changes in the last quarter of a century. These changes in policy, perception and practice have interwoven with national and international movements in inclusion, equity issues and social equality. It has been a vigorous and dynamic area for research. There is no doubt that the Warnock Report of 1979 and the subsequent legislation that followed the report paved the way for the subsequent developments that have had a considerable impact on policy and practice.

It is the intention of this book to discuss the many different strands of SEN from different perspectives – research, policy, practice, parents and the student themselves. It might be argued that one of the features of this field has been the polarization of perspectives: a continuum of views still exist on best practice for children with SEN. It is not the purpose of this book to become entrenched in this debate but, rather, to highlight the range of perspectives through the individual chapters included in the book. Some of the chapters strongly promote an inclusive perspective while others focus on the individual student and their individual needs. We are also mindful of the needs of parents – parents have been and will continue to be a crucial element in the development of practice and have also influenced policy. Parents are considered throughout and, indeed, the concluding chapter of this book is written from parents' perspectives.

The thrust of this book has therefore been to promote both inclusive provision and to highlight individual needs. Additionally we have attempted to be as comprehensive as possible and, although we have not been able to include individual chapters on all the existing syndromes, we hope that the general principles and strategies promoted throughout the book will in fact impact on serving the needs of all children whatever their specific needs.

The scenario of SEN is established in Chapter 2 with Riddell, Weedon and Harris discussing recent changes in England and Scotland and particularly the issues of categories and resources. The field of SEN has not been without tensions and these are also brought out in this chapter. The authors refer to the tensions as 'dilemmas of difference' – in particular, the tensions between parental expectations and education authority policy and practices. They pinpoint in particularly the broader definition encapsulated in the Education (Additional Support for Learning) (Scotland) Act 2004 (the ASL Act) and the tensions that have arisen from this. As they indicate:

> there continues to be a commitment to the overarching categories of SEN and ASN [additional support needs], with their implicit emphasis on the commonality of all pupils with difficulties in learning, but at the same time there are moves towards the use of fine-grained categories, suggesting a focus on pupil differences.

In many ways this encompasses the dilemmas practitioners have to deal with and parents try to work within. The authors of this chapter support their analyses with several excellent case studies.

This chapter is followed by Avramidis and Norwich who discuss the research implications of recent philosophical trends and developments in special education and who present the main research paradigms operating in the field along with their methodological implications. They also discuss the current trend towards evidence-based practice and the implications of this for policy and the perception of disability in society. They discuss the distinction between the medical and social models of disability and the implications of this for research methodology. They also discuss the trends towards inclusive education and the controversial view that inclusion is a product of social-political arguments rather than a product of empirical evidence. The agendas that drive research methodology have to be considered. They maintain that:

> more often than not, researchers in the field are firmly attached to particular theoretical and methodological positions, thus reproducing sterile debates about the supremacy of particular methodologies (e.g. the scientific/quantitative v. interpretive/qualitative divide). Many do not see value in asking different kinds of research questions about the same phenomena.

They argue that for research progress to take place a convergence and consensus about research methodologies and philosophical positioning is necessary.

The theme of inclusion is developed in Chapter 4 by Sakellariadis who discusses the issues and dilemmas that an individual with SEN experiences. She provides a rationale for inclusion and how it may benefit all people. The chapter questions many of the situations that many take for granted and raises the need to focus more on the support needs of people with SEN. She suggests that inclusion needs to be sufficiently resourced and effectively managed.

The potential impact of the social model of disability is also developed by Weedon in Chapter 5. Weedon, utilizing his practical experience, argues that:

> in the early years [of education] there is a deep-rooted and pervasive acceptance of the social model of disability, and with it an almost instinctive inclusivity. Each child is seen as a unique individual, and it is part of the teacher's craft to find ways for all the individuals in the class to share the learning. In the later years, where subject specialization and formal assessment gain increasing influence, there is an increasing dynamic towards a bio-medical categorization, an allocation of learners to categories in order that they might better fit the demands of the examination system.

This statement questions current thinking in areas of differentiation and in particular the examination system. Weedon argues that:

> to generate a dynamic that seeks continuously and imperceptibly to shift our perceptions a little further away from a bio-medical model whenever it is possible to do so, towards a socially constructed model; and continuously and imperceptibly away from a view that attributes a deficit to an individual, and to look instead at the barriers we construct within the environment.

This statement has considerable current relevance to the direction of SEN and has implications for all syndromes and support services.

This theme is followed in Part II of the book which focuses on perspectives from practice. In Chapter 6 Farrugia and O'Keefe highlight the importance of language for all areas of development – educational, social and emotional. They discuss the 'at risk' factors that predispose children to speech and language difficulties and highlight the path for assessment and access to professional services. They also provide pointers for teachers on what signs can reveal the possibility of speech and language difficulties but they also provide detailed analyses of diagnostic criteria and the range and different types of speech and language difficulties, including stammering and stuttering, voice disorders, attention, listening skills, receptive and expressive language and the cognitive factors associated with language learning. This is a practical chapter well grounded in current theory and has a host of useful ideas for teachers and other professionals.

Sirimanna in the following chapter looks at auditory processing difficulties, providing a detailed and comprehensive overview of this area, which is gaining increasing attention from parents and professionals. It is likely this attention will be heightened with the publication of DSM V in 2013 which appears to be promoting a co-morbid approach to the field of learning disabilities, with some categories being subsumed under a more general label (http://www.dsm5.org/ProposedRevisions).

Sirmanna's chapter is followed by a discussion on the role of occupational therapists by Abdullah. In this chapter Abdullah describes the role of the occupational therapist and focuses in some detail on developmental co-ordination disorders and dyspraxia. She provides some excellent practical examples and a range of theoretical explanations. She also discusses the very real issues that can be associated with development co-ordination disorder, such as attention difficulties, social difficulties and the challenges in behaviour and in acquiring academic skills.

In Chapter 9 Holland discusses vision and learning, explains the importance of visual aspects of learning and describes the nature of the visual difficulties that can prevent learning. There is a solid theoretical underpinning to his discussion and he discusses the research from a balanced and insightful perspective. Holland provides in this chapter some excellent suggestions for teachers. He also provides some words of caution when he says that 'these issues [visual difficulties] may well be misdiagnosed as being part of a specific learning difficulty, and thus treated through additional tuition, when what is really required is an appropriate visual assessment and treatment'.

The theme of dyslexia is tackled by Bell and McLean in Chapter 10, who focus primarily on good practice in training specialist teachers and assessors of people with dyslexia. This chapter is set against the backdrop of increased commitment for the training of dyslexia specialists (e.g. the Rose Report of 2009) and concern on the effectiveness of training in the field of SEN. They quote the comment from the national Lamb Inquiry in England (2009) which indicates that:

we cannot currently be confident that those who are charged with making a judgement about the quality of the education provided for pupils with SEN can do so on the basis of a good understanding of what good progress is or how best to secure it.

Bell and McLean provide an indication of the type of skills needed by specialist teachers in dyslexia, including training in assistive software. They indicate that 'crucial to any teaching programme for learners with dyslexia is that it should be individualized. Trainees learn how to direct learning programmes towards students' particular strengths and weaknesses (to develop individualized programmes)'. In this chapter the authors remind us of the importance of obtaining first-hand evidence from course participants themselves on their needs and how far the courses meet these needs. On a positive note the authors conclude by saying that 'this is an optimistic period for training dyslexia specialists,' but they also issue a concern indicating that 'as we move into the future it is vital that economic constraints do not prevent us from training the teachers and assessors who can make such a difference to the lives of people with dyslexia at all levels'.

The theme of dyslexia is followed up by Crombie in Chapter 11 on literacy. In this chapter Crombie looks at the current and the future context for literacy and literacy difficulties. She highlights the comments from a state-of-the-nation document (Jama and Dugdale for the National Literacy Trust, 2010) which indicates that one in six people in the UK are struggling with 'literacy' and have 'literacy levels below what would be expected of an eleven year old'. Crombie discusses different types of literacy and the nature of literacy difficulties and also highlights considerations for identifying literacy difficulties. She refers to both theory and practice and also highlights the importance of school/parent partnerships and the increasingly important role of technology in the digital age and its implications for the future of literacy.

One of the themes of literacy is the focus of the chapter on morphological approaches by Brown and Brown. In this chapter the authors present the morphological approach to literacy acquisition as a 'challenge to the underlying assumptions of current pedagogy'. They provide a range of practical examples to support their view and also look at the potential impact of this approach on schools.

In the following chapter Chinn focuses on mathematics difficulties and, in particular, dyscalculia. He utilizes research in effective learning to highlight the implications of this for students with mathematical difficulties. He explains the key factors that contribute to dyscalculia, the prevalence of dyscalculia, diagnostic criteria and strategies for intervention.

This is followed (in Part III on syndromes and barriers) by a chapter on attention deficit hyperactivity disorder (ADHD) by Soppitt. There is a great deal of information available on ADHD and much of this can present a confusing picture for professionals and parents. There are a number of entrenched theoretical positions and divergent views on intervention approaches. In this chapter Soppitt indicates that aetiology is usually multi-factorial, involving interaction between bio-psychosocial factors. He also outlines interventions, including educational, parenting, cognitive behavioural therapy and pharmacological. He also suggests that, although multi-agency working in relation to ADHD raises challenges, it must be fully considered as the way forward in order to prevent young people with ADHD becoming socially excluded.

The theme of visual impairment is addressed in Chapter 15 by Ravenscroft. In this chapter Ravenscroft presents an insightful overview of the field of visual impairment and discusses current research on the profile and prevalence of children with visual impairment living in the UK. He also discusses strategies to empower the mainstream teacher in relation to addressing the needs of children with visual impairments and explores the balance between academic attainment and independent daily living skills. As he indicates, it is important for children with visual impairment to fulfil their academic potential but, equally, it is crucial they can engage with the world around them!

The issue of sensory impairment is followed by Duncan, who summarizes the central issues related to students with a hearing loss, including hearing technology, communication modality, literacy and cognition. She also provides practical strategies for supporting classroom teachers with students with a hearing loss. Using a range of case studies she highlights how important transitional periods can be effectively handled and the struggles and challenges that parents, children and professionals face. As she indicates, 'students with hearing loss have diverse learning needs ... they, along with their families and classroom teachers, require specialist practitioner support in order to maximize learning potential'. This is in line with the other areas previously highlighted, such as visual impairment, attention difficulties, dyslexia and dyscalculia, which are, in many ways, priority areas for training agendas.

The current interest in autism and autistic spectrum is vast and diverse. It is challenging to incorporate the range of research and perspectives in this fast-changing and developing field into one succinct chapter. In Chapter 17 Reid and Lannen deal with this by focusing on the challenges and the issues. They provide a background to understanding autistic spectrum disorder (ASD), as well as an overview of the criteria for identification and assessment. They also note the main areas of research and provide a range of strategies for intervention. They also look at the characteristics and identification procedures of ASD as well as the impact of ASD on classroom learning. They comment on the range of programmes available for young people with ASD and provide pointers for consideration in relation to these programmes.

This chapter is followed by a chapter on Tourette syndrome by Barrow and Davidson, who provide a clear understanding of the nature and the impact of Tourette syndrome. Arguably this is one of the most misunderstood syndromes and there are educational as well as social implications to this. As Barrow and Davidson point out, in some cases the behaviours of the child with Tourette syndrome can be misunderstood as disruptive, attention seeking and mischievous. They provide a clear explanation of Tourette syndrome and also indicate the range of overlapping disorders. Barrow quotes Davidson, who says that:

> growing up with Tourette syndrome was very difficult. I believed I was different from everyone else due to the involuntary symptoms. I often felt unloved and unwanted by family and friends and felt that I was being a hindrance to the rest of my family.

Reading statements like this can be heart wrenching and it is this which should persuade educators to pursue educational and training programmes for all those who may have to deal with children and adults with Tourette syndrome. The authors indicate the range of current issues in relation to supporting people with Tourette syndrome. They explain that:

> the ability to explain and allow for the condition varies from school to school, and particularly at primary school level, where disruptive behaviour has more of an impact. Some schools prefer to leave it to the parents to resolve what they see as 'problems' with TS [Tourette syndrome]. Yet, practice shows that the school is the best place to explain the condition for teachers and pupils to resolve a way forward.

This is an important message for educators.

In the final part of the book the theme is 'working together', which follows on from many of the messages contained in the previous parts of the book. In Chapter 19 Woods focuses on the role of educational psychologists and particularly the wide-ranging and dynamic roles that now need to be adopted by educational psychologists. This is followed by a chapter by Friel on the legal issues which often gain prominence when working together is not possible, positive or effective. It is important to be aware of the legal implications.

The final chapter of the book is on parental perspectives, which have also been the subject of many of the individual chapters. In this chapter, Papendorf, Peer, Reid and Strachan indicate that 'the field of special educational needs can be a confusing one for professionals but can be fraught for parents'. All the contributors of this chapter are parents and have experienced the frustration and the anxieties of supporting their child through the educational journey and have had to deal with a range of circumstances and experiences in education and in society. The chapter also indicates the power of parents as advocates, advisers and people who can challenge the existing conventions and developing trends with conviction, insights and success.

It is perhaps fitting to end this book on SEN with parental perspectives. Parents have contributed a great deal to this book and, in fact, have contributed to the direction and impact of SEN in almost every country. They have a key role to play and, together with informed and trained educators, the future of dealing with the range of challenges associated with SEN can witness further positive changes in perceptions and working practices. This can lead to an enhanced understanding of the needs of children and their families which ultimately will benefit schools, society, families and individuals.

Part I

POLICY, PRACTICE AND PROVISION

2

SPECIAL AND ADDITIONAL SUPPORT NEEDS IN ENGLAND AND SCOTLAND – CURRENT DILEMMAS AND SOLUTIONS

Sheila Riddell, Elisabet Weedon and Neville Harris

Learning objectives

This chapter will help readers to:

- gain a greater understanding of current SEN/ASN (special educational needs/additional support needs) policy in England and Scotland and of recent policy changes;
- problematize SEN/ASN categories, since some may enable children to access additional resources while others have a stigmatizing effect; and
- understand the tensions between parental power and local authority accountability.

This chapter identifies a number of current issues stemming from policy and practice in the field of SEN (England) and ASN (Scotland). In particular, we focus on dilemmas in two particular spheres: 1) the use of categories and their implications for resourcing, inclusion and the curriculum; and 2) the balance of power between parents and professionals. The chapter is structured around the idea of dilemmas, involving a choice between a number of courses of action, none of which is entirely unproblematic (Norwich, 2008: 3). The first dilemma turns on tensions between a universalist approach, which involves treating everyone the same, and a recognition of difference approach, which may involve positive action for some groups with a view to rectifying existing inequalities. The upside of the universal approach is that it emphasizes common aspirations for all; however, the downside is that it may underplay the disadvantages faced by some children as a result of their impairment combined with their social, political and economic context. Additional resources to fund reasonable adjustments, as well as efforts to bring about attitudinal change, may be necessary in order to level the playing field. Similarly, an approach based on the recognition of difference has upsides and downsides, potentially justifying the allocation of additional resources, but also stigmatizing and justifying social marginalization. These tensions, referred to as dilemmas of difference (Minow, 1985; Phillips, 1999), are not peculiar to education but are common to many social policy arenas and equality strands.

Before looking more closely at particular areas where dilemmas of difference arise, we first describe changes within the SEN and ASN policy fields over the past three decades. The second broad dilemma which we highlight in this chapter concerns the balance of power between parents and professionals. While there has been a move towards the empowerment of parents with a view to delivering personalized services in education and other social policy fields, there are clearly both upsides and downsides to this approach. On the one hand, individual parents may argue that they are in the best position to determine their child's needs and appropriate provision, but on the other hand local authorities may argue that they should retain the ultimate power in decision-making since they can act as impartial arbiters in the allocation of scarce resources. These dilemmas are explored more fully below.

This chapter draws on findings from an ESRC-funded research project entitled *Dispute Resolution and Avoidance in Special and Additional Support Needs* (RES-062-23-0803). The research used a mixture of methods, including analysis of policy and official statistics; approximately 50 key informant interviews; a questionnaire survey of local authorities in England and Scotland; a survey of parents (Scotland only); a survey of Parent Partnership Services (England only); and case studies of 49 parents in dispute with the local authority in six authorities (three in England and three in Scotland).

SEN AND ASN POLICY IN ENGLAND AND SCOTLAND

For about a decade following the publication of the Warnock Report (DES, 1978) the English and Scottish systems moved along roughly parallel lines, both using the umbrella term 'special educational needs' to define those children having greater difficulty in learning than their peers. In both countries, local authority officers and education professionals retained major decision-making power with regard to resources and additional support, with a commitment to work 'in partnership' with parents. However, during the 1990s, there was increasing divergence as Conservative educational reforms were implemented more forcefully in England, promoting managerialism and consumerism. Following the Education Act 1993, all English state schools were obliged to have regard to the *Code of Practice on the Identification and Assessment of Special Educational Needs* (DfE, 1994) and publish information about their policies for children with SEN. This legislation also established the Special Educational Needs Tribunal (SENT) to resolve disputes between parents and the local authority.

Major reform of ASN policy and practice in Scotland took place a decade after the reforms of the English SEN system described above. The Education (Additional Support for Learning) (Scotland) Act 2004 (the ASL Act) broadened the definition of ASN to include children who had difficulty in learning as a result of social problems as well as disabilities, and put in place a raft of measures to increase parental rights and local authority accountability. Theoretically, this should have led to more children being identified as having ASN, but the predicted expansion did not take place. The legislation also abolished the record of needs and established a new document, the co-ordinated support plan (CSP), to record the needs of children with multiple, complex and enduring difficulties requiring significant multi-agency support. However, as we explain below, local authorities have been very reluctant to open CSPs, preferring to use their own non-statutory plans. Finally, the ASL Act put in place a number of new dispute resolution mechanisms, outlined in a new code of practice (Scottish Executive, 2005).

The operation of dispute resolution mechanisms in England and Scotland respectively are discussed below in the section on parents and accountability.

THE IDENTIFICATION AND CATEGORIZATION OF CHILDREN WITH SEN AND ASN: THE DILEMMA OF UNIVERSALISM VERSUS DIFFERENCE

Paradoxically, while the definition of ASN in Scotland is somewhat broader than that of SEN in England, only 5% of pupils in Scotland are identified as having such difficulties compared with 20% in England (see Figure 2.1).

In part, this is because the English statistics include children with a statement of needs as well as those on school action-plus programmes (i.e. receiving help from professionals outside schools) and school action programmes (receiving help from school-based practitioners such as teaching assistants, the class teacher and the learning support teacher). The official statistics gathered by Scottish government, by way of contrast, only include children with a record of needs (which is in the process of being phased out), a CSP or an Individualized Educational Programme (IEP). Many children in Scotland, including some of those with the most significant difficulties, receive a local support plan which does not have statutory status and is not counted in the official statistics.

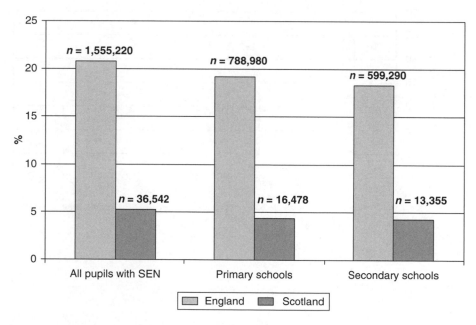

Figure 2.1 Pupils with SEN (England) and ASN (Scotland) in publicly maintained schools as a percentage of all pupils by type of school (2007) (The total includes all pupils with SEN/ASN, including those in special schools)

Source: Based on statistics from the DfES and the Scottish Government

As we noted above, while efforts have been made to replace individual categories of difficulty with one overarching category, this has proved very difficult for a variety of reasons. First, parents of children with particular types of difficulty, such as autistic spectrum disorder, and voluntary organizations representing these groups, have campaigned for official recognition of specific categories. Government has also found it useful to request local authorities to audit the incidence of particular types of difficulty, partly as an accountability mechanism, but also to inform funding decisions. In England, the practice of gathering data by type of difficulty, which was abandoned following the Warnock Report, was reinstated in the 1990s. In Scotland, despite official support for the broad conceptualization of ASN, local authorities have always been required to provide information to the government on numbers of children with particular types of difficulty. Figures 2.2 and 2.3 provide information on the categories of difficulty used in England and Scotland.

About three quarters of pupils identified with SEN come from four of the twelve categories included in the classification. The largest of these four categories includes young people with moderate learning difficulties (MLD) and the second largest group consists of pupils with behavioural, social and emotional difficulties (BSED). Pupils with speech, language and communication needs (14%) and those with specific learning difficulties (12%) account for just over a quarter of SEN pupils (see Figure 2.2).

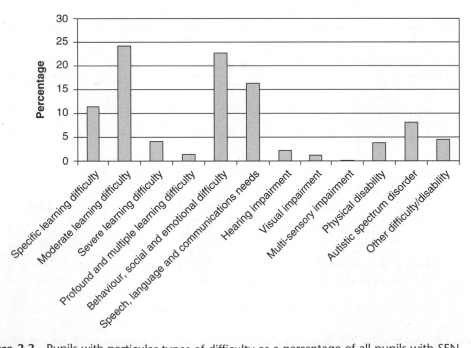

Figure 2.2 Pupils with particular types of difficulty as a percentage of all pupils with SEN (England)

Source: Based on statistics from the DES

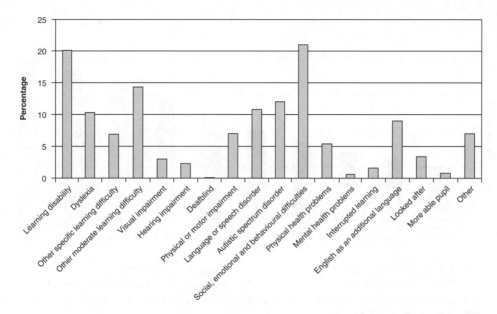

Figure 2.3   Pupils with particular types of difficulty as a percentage of all pupils with ASN (Scotland) (pupils with more than one support needs will have all support needs recorded and these figures should therefore be treated with caution)

Source: Based on statistics from the Scottish Government

A larger number of categories of difficulty (18 in total) are used in Scotland (see Figure 2.3). The largest category (learning disability) accounts for about a fifth of all pupils with ASN, while the second largest category, BSED, accounts for just over 15%. Together, these two include just over one third of the ASN population. Young people with autistic spectrum disorder, other moderate learning difficulties and language or speech disorder account for nearly another third. Dyslexia, other specific learning difficulties and physical and motor impairments each account for 7–9% of the ASN population. The remaining categories (including more able pupils, pupils who use English as an additional language, looked-after pupils and pupils with interrupted learning) came into use following the ASL legislation but are being very little used.

However, as noted above, recognition of particular types of difficulty is not necessarily an unalloyed good. As shown by Figures 2.4 and 2.5, there is a strong association between the identification of SEN/ASN and social deprivation, particularly for some types of difficulty such as BSED and MLD. These labels are rarely sought by parents, and are often applied by schools to children they find difficult to include. Tomlinson (1985) made a useful distinction between normative difficulties, such as sensory or physical impairments, which can be measured against an agreed norm, and non-normative difficulties, such as BSED, whose identification is much more reliant on professional judgement. Non-normative categories, which are also by far the largest, are very strongly

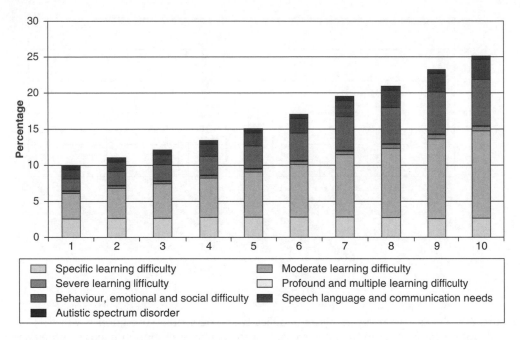

Figure 2.4   Percentage of English school population within each Income Deprivation Affecting Children Index (IDACI) decile by type of difficulty (category 1= least deprived, category 10 = most deprived)

Source: Keslair and McNally (2009)

associated with social deprivation, whereas lower-incidence normative difficulties are only loosely associated with social deprivation. These patterns of identification raise questions about whether children benefit from being identified as having SEN/ASN or whether, as argued by Armstrong (2003), this identification is a form of stigmatization which is used to justify their poor school attainment and exclusion from the labour market. It is worth noting that, in both England and Scotland, statutory plans, which provide stronger guarantees of additional resources and greater rights to challenge local authority decisions, are disproportionately allocated to children in more socially advantaged areas, again suggesting that, for children in more deprived areas, the disbenefits of being identified as having certain categories of need may outweigh the benefits.

Overall, the use of categorical systems illustrates tensions between discourses of sameness and difference. There continues to be a commitment to the overarching categories of SEN and ASN, with their implicit emphasis on the commonality of all pupils with difficulties in learning, but at the same time there are moves towards the use of fine-grained categories, suggesting a focus on pupil differences. Some of these categories have gained currency as a result of pressure from parents and voluntary organizations (e.g. autistic spectrum disorder and dyslexia), while others have entered the lexicon as a result of professional pressures (e.g. mental health problems). While normative

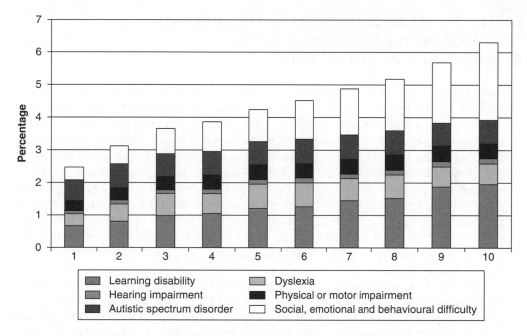

Figure 2.5 Percentage of Scottish school population within each Scottish Index of Multiple Deprivation (SIMD) decile by type of difficulty (percentages in each group in stacked bar) (category 1= least deprived, category 10 = most deprived)

Source: Based on statistics from the Scottish Government

difficulties are identified across the social spectrum, children identified as having non-normative difficulties are concentrated in socially deprived areas. This suggests a dilemma of categorization, where some labels may have negative educational consequences, while other labels may bring benefits in relation to releasing additional resources without social stigmatization.

The use of particular categorization systems has implications for placement of children with SEN/ASN and the type of curriculum provided. The dominance of generic terminology, with its implicit discourse of commonality rather than difference, means that in England and Scotland there has been a presumption of mainstream placement. Around 1% of the total school population in Scotland and England are placed in special schools and units. Similarly, the expectation has been for all children to access a common curriculum with appropriate modifications (Lewis and Norwich, 2005). In England the statutory requirement in relation to inclusion, in place since 2002, requires that provision is made in mainstream schools for all children without statements. However, the increasing use of fine-grained categories of details, and the growing influence of voluntary organizations representing particular categories of difficulty, such as autism, has led to growing pressure for more differentiated curricula and teaching methods, potentially increasing the emphasis on children's differences rather than their sameness.

PARENTS AND ACCOUNTABILITY: THE DILEMMA OF PARTICIPATIVE DEMOCRACY VERSUS BUREAUCRATIC ACCOUNTABILITY

As noted earlier, a recurring dilemma in the field of SEN/ASN concerns the balance to be struck between local authorities and parents in determining the distribution of scarce resources, particularly in the field of SEN/ASN when particular types of provision may be extremely costly, with consequences for other service users. A theme of the modernizing government agenda, which has been developed by successive governments, has been an emphasis on personalized rather than standardized services, in which consumers have a far greater say over the nature of services provided. This has partly been achieved by the growth of a mixed economy of welfare, with the voluntary and private sectors increasingly being funded by government to deliver services which were previously provided by the state, a move deprecated by some social policy critics (e.g. Ball, 2007), but sometimes welcomed by service users, such as the recipients of direct payments (Pearson, 2006).

The growth of consumerism through the exercise of voice has been a further element in the personalization agenda. In the field of SEN/ASN, along with many other spheres of education, parental power has traditionally been limited, with local authority and professionals retaining control over resource allocation decisions (Harris, 2005). The establishment of a number of dispute resolution mechanisms, since 1994 in England and 2004 in Scotland, was intended to increase opportunities for parents to challenge local authority decisions. Our recent ESRC-funded research project on dispute resolution in SEN/ASN (RES-062-23-0803), referred to earlier, explored the use and perceptions of different ways of resolving disagreements (tribunal, mediation and, in Scotland only, adjudication) and questioned whether these had succeeded in altering the balance of power between parents and local authorities. Tribunals exist to hear appeals from parents of children with SEN/ASN in cases of disputes between parents and local authorities (Scotland only) schools. The outcomes of the tribunals are legally binding unlike the outcomes from mediation; in Scotland, the remit of the tribunal is limited to children with CSPs.

A questionnaire survey conducted with all local authorities in England and Scotland found that they tended to hold negative views of the tribunal. In England, almost half of them did not think that the tribunal made a positive contribution to dispute resolution. They did not object to the right of appeal *per se*, but they believed that it encouraged parental challenges to decisions or intensified disputes. They regarded the process as irksome and likely to go against them. Some thought that the tribunal was overly generous towards parents in the degree of procedural flexibility it allowed them, for example regarding time limits, and in helping some secure a high level of resources for their child, skewing resource allocation. In Scotland, there were concerns about the tribunal's rather adversarial hearing and variable approach. Parents, on the other hand, whose views were explored through case studies, were generally positive about the tribunal, seeing the process as somewhat stressful but feeling that in general fair outcomes were achieved. Figures 2.6 and 2.7 illustrate the use of the SEN/ASN tribunal in England and Scotland.

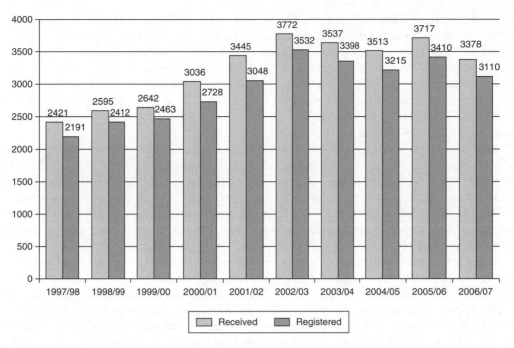

Figure 2.6 Total number of tribunal appeals received and registered annually between 1997/8 and 2006/7 the Special Educational Needs and Disability Tribunal (SENDIST) (England)

Source: Based on statistics from SENDIST

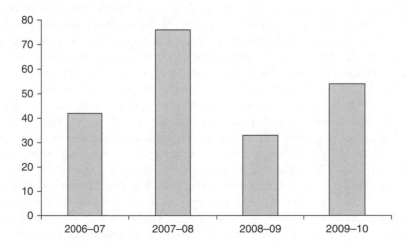

Figure 2.7 Reference to the Additional Support Needs Tribunal for Scotland (ASNTS) by local authority, 2006–10

Source: Based on statistics from the ASNTS

Since its inception, the use of the English tribunal[1] has exceeded expectations, although there have been fewer appeals from parents living in areas of social deprivation and those from minority ethnic backgrounds. In Scotland, the use of the Additional Support Needs Tribunals for Scotland (ASNTS) has been much lower (only 76 references were made in 2007/8, with fewer references in the subsequent years). This is partly because references must relate to a CSP, but only a tiny proportion of children with ASN are deemed to meet the qualification criteria for a statutory plan (see Riddell and Weedon, 2009, for further discussion of this point).

Mediation has been strongly supported by government in preference to court or tribunal on the grounds that it is a cheaper and less stressful means of resolving disputes between the citizen and the state. A duty was placed on English local authorities to provide access to independent mediation under the terms of Special Educational Needs and Disability Act 2001, and the ASL Act 2004 obliged Scottish local authorities to provide access to independent mediation and adjudication. In both England and Scotland, mediation has proved much less popular than hoped for by government (Riddell *et al.*, 2010). Although there are no national figures on SEN or ASN mediation, our local authority survey suggested that in England there was an average of little more than one mediation per authority, compared with an average (based on national statistics) of approximately eight appeal hearings per authority. More than half of authorities (60%) reported no mediations that year. In Scotland, three quarters of all authorities reported fewer than five mediations each. The reasons for the low uptake included a failure by local authorities to promote or publicize mediation, a reluctance to participate on the part of schools or local authorities, and suspicion by parents that mediation was a way of 'fobbing them off' rather than delivering justice, a view which was sometimes reinforced by parents' advisers and representatives. During the year 2006/7, there were only 12 cases of adjudication in Scotland, signalling parents' lack of knowledge of and confidence in this route.

Overall, the low uptake of alternative dispute resolution mechanisms (mediation and adjudication), and the apparent preference, at least in England, to take cases to the tribunal suggests that parents have little faith in less formal dispute resolution routes, which rely on trust between parties. However, it should be noted that the Parent Partnership Service (PPS) played a significant role in informal mediation. It was when this informal mediation failed that parents tended to opt for the tribunal rather than trying formal mediation. As noted above, Harris (2005) has argued that there has been little progress with regard to increasing parental participation in education decision-making, with local authorities and schools retaining control in many critical areas, including the field of SEN/ASN. This was reflected in the Lamb Inquiry which reported that parents lacked confidence in the system of decision-making and felt disempowered (DCFS, 2009). Findings from the research reported here also suggest that the bureaucratic decision-making continues to hold sway. While this is contrary to the rhetoric of parental empowerment, it must be acknowledged that there is a genuine dilemma in managing the balance of power between parents and professionals, since local authorities can legitimately claim that if the pendulum swings too far in the direction of allowing parents to act as the ultimate arbiters in resource allocation decisions, then their role as independent arbiters in the fair allocation of resources becomes compromised.

CASE STUDIES

So far we have discussed two particular dilemmas in the field of SEN/ASN. In the following section, we present two case studies drawn from the research project described above to illustrate that way in which these dilemmas are manifested in everyday life. The names used are all fictitious.

 Case Study

The McIntosh family lived in Sea City, an affluent Scottish city with a low use of CSPs and a high proportion of formal disputes. At the time of the research, Fraser McIntosh was 15 years of age and had a diagnosis of autistic spectrum disorder. His parents, both professionals, worked freelance in order to combine work and childcare. Fraser was placed in a special school but, during his teenage years, his difficulties became more apparent, with attendant stresses for his family and teachers. His mother became convinced that school staff did not have the specialist training to manage his behaviour effectively. She researched the options independently, and eventually decided that placement in a residential Steiner school would best meet her son's needs, although she knew the council was unlikely to agree because of the cost. Mrs McIntosh made a formal placing request, with a view to taking the case to tribunal as a last resort. Following advice from an advocacy organization, Mrs McIntosh took on the role of lead professional and, prior to a review meeting, had private meetings with all 13 professionals involved with Fraser. Each confirmed in writing that Fraser's current school could not meet his needs, and that a residential special school placement was required. The placing request was granted, although the senior officer continued to maintain that the local authority was able to meet the child's needs and that cost of the residential placement was unjustified and detrimental to other children's education because of its resource implications. This view was reinforced by the educational psychologist, who spoke of the danger of middle-class parents claiming more than their fair share of resources for their children.

 Case Study

Carole Redgrave, a single parent working as a care assistant, lived in Midshire, an English local authority spanning both urban and rural areas with a low use of statements. Her daughter, Lucy, was aged 10 at the time of the research and, from early on in her primary school career, had struggled with basic numeracy and literacy, leading to a diagnosis of 'non-specific special educational needs'. Lucy was placed on a school action-plus programme which delivered very little extra support, and still failed to make progress. On the advice of an educational psychologist, Mrs Redgrave asked if she could be assessed for a statement of needs, since this would deliver dedicated support, but a request for a formal assessment was turned down twice, despite support from a range of professionals. Mrs

(Continued)

(Continued)

Redgrave felt fobbed off by both the school and the local authority, but persisted in arguing Lucy's case because she was convinced that her daughter would thrive in mainstream with extra help. The local PPS was recommended by a friend, and they supported her through mediation, after which a statement of needs was issued guaranteeing ten hours of support from a teaching assistant. According to the PPS, the headteacher had wanted Lucy to be placed in a special school, since she thought this was the only place where additional support would be available, but according to the PPS worker, Lucy was 'nowhere near the criteria for special'. The additional support in mainstream was successful, with marked improvements in Lucy's behaviour, confidence and attainment.

SUMMARY

To summarize, a number of dilemmas characterize the field of SEN/ASN, in particular, the dilemma of whether to emphasize difference or sameness, and the dilemma of whether to accord greater power to parents or professionals in determining the type of appropriate education for a child with SEN/ASN. These dilemmas are interconnected, since they both have implications for resource distribution and identity. We noted that the educational reforms of the 1990s in England tilted the balance of power in the direction of parents, making professionals far more accountable and opening up accessible appeal routes. In Scotland, the ASL Act was implemented more than a decade after SEN reforms in England, with the aim of widening the pool of children eligible for additional support and boosting parents' power to hold professionals to account. In both England and Scotland, there has continued to be a commitment to an inclusive educational system, underpinned by the presumption that a child will be placed in mainstream unless there are compelling reasons for a special school placement. It is also worth noting that the judicial system, both internationally (the European Court of Human Rights) and domestically (the tribunals and courts in England and Scotland), has largely failed to uphold as a matter of human rights parental convictions as regards the type of placement their child should have (Harris, 2007). This has led to disputes focusing on resource issues rather than broader issues of principle.

The analysis of official statistics on the identification of children with SEN/ASN in England and Scotland underlined some of the ongoing tensions in the system. Low-incidence normative difficulties, such as physical and sensory impairments, are identified across the social spectrum, and the issuing of a statement of needs or a CSP releases additional resources, potentially helping the child to achieve their educational potential. By way of contrast, high-incidence non-normative difficulties, such as BSED, which carry with them the risk of stigmatization, are much more likely to be identified among children living in socially deprived areas. Children with SEN/ASN living in such areas are less likely to be allocated additional resources, which might outweigh the negative impact of a stigmatizing label.

The brief case studies presented above also highlight the central dilemmas and the way in which they are manifested differently in particular circumstances. Mrs McIntosh wanted her son to be identified as unequivocally different from other children, so that the significant cost of the residential special school could be justified. Mrs Redgrave, on the other hand, was not seeking a specific label for her child's difficulties, but an assessment which would release additional support to be delivered in mainstream rather than a special setting. Both parents were similar in wanting their voices to be heard and in being willing to use formal routes of redress if necessary, although Mrs McIntosh had greater social and cultural resources at her disposal. The response of the schools and local authorities was similar in both cases, as they expressed deep anxiety about the danger of preferential resource allocation to those who were most willing to fight their corner. Over the next five years, as governments in England and Scotland struggle to deal with the squeeze in public sector funding in the aftermath of the recession, it is likely that such dilemmas will intensify.

 Discussion Points

- What are the upsides and downsides of the broad definition of ASN employed in Scotland compared with the much narrower definition of SEN used in England?
- The English green paper published in March 2011 argues that too many children with non-normative difficulties are being identified as having SEN in England. What are the pros and cons of including such children under the SEN umbrella?
- Mediation has been promoted in England and Scotland as a better way of resolving SEN disputes compared with the tribunal. What are the advantages of judicial and non-judicial forms of dispute resolution and how can mediation be promoted?
- What can be done to help parents of children with SEN/ASN in their efforts to ensure that their children get the support they need?

Further Reading

Harris, N. (2007) *Education, Law and Diversity*. Oxford: Hart. This book provides a critical account of educational legislation and regulation in England, although with reference to the jurisdictions of the UK, with a particular focus on implications for equality.

Harris, N. and Riddell, S. (2011) *Resolving Disputes about Educational Provision: A Comparative Perspective on Special Educational Needs*. Farnham: Ashgate. This book discusses the nature of grievances and disputes in the field of SEN and the pros and cons of various dispute resolution mechanisms. It also focuses on SEN systems and approaches to dispute resolution in England, Scotland, the Netherlands and the USA.

Weedon, E. and Riddell, S. (2009) 'Additional support needs and approaches to dispute resolution: the perspectives of Scottish parents', *Scottish Educational Review*, 41: 62–81. This paper provides an overview of provision for children with additional support needs in Scotland. It draws on survey findings which reveal parents' responses to the new additional support for learning legislation and the opportunities for dispute resolution which they afford.

Note

1. In England, the jurisdiction held by the Special Educational Needs and Disability Tribunal (SENDIST) is now with the Health, Education and Social Care Chamber (HESC) of the First Tier Tribunal (FTT), which hears special educational needs and disability discrimination cases. In Scotland, the Additional Support Needs Tribunals for Scotland (ASNTS) deal with references relating to CSPs only, although the Equality Act 2009 extends its remit to disability discrimination cases.

References

Armstrong, D. (2003) *Experiences of Special Education*. London: RoutledgeFalmer.

Ball, S.J. (2007) *Education plc: Understanding Private Sector Participation in Public Sector Education*. London: Routledge.

DCSF (2009) *Special Educational Needs and Parental Confidence* (the Lamb Inquiry). London: HMSO.

Department for Education (DfE) (1994) *Code of Practice on the Identification and Assessment of Special Educational Needs*. London: DfE.

Department for Education and Science (DES) (1978) *Special Educational Needs* (the Warnock Report). London: HMSO.

Department for Education and Skills (DfES) (2001) *SEN Code of Practice on the Identification and Assessment of Pupils with Special Educational Needs*. London: DfES.

Harris, N. (2005) 'Empowerment and state education: rights of choice and participation', *The Modern Law Review,* 68: 925–7.

Harris, N. (2007) *Education, Law and Diversity*. Oxford: Hart.

Harris, N. (2009) 'Playing catch-up in the schoolyard? Children and young people's "voice" and education rights in the UK', *International Journal of Law, Policy and the Family,* 23: 331–66.

Harris, N. and Smith, E. (2009) 'Resolving disputes about special educational needs and provision in England', *Education Law Journal,* 10: 113–32.

HMIe (2007) *Report on the Implementation of the Education (Additional Support for Learning) (Scotland) Act 2004*. Livingston: HMIe.

Keslair, F. and McNally, S. (2009) *Special Educational Needs in England. Final Report for the National Equality Panel*. London: Government Inequalities Office.

Lewis, A. and Norwich, B. (eds) (2005) *Special Teaching for Special Children? Pedagogies for Inclusion*. Maidenhead: Open University Press.

Minow, M. (1985) 'Learning to live with the dilemma of difference: bilingual and special education', in K.T. Bartlett and J.W. Wegner (eds) *Children with Special Needs*. Boulder, CO: Transaction Books.

National Equality Panel (2010) *An Anatomy of Economic Inequality in the UK*. London: Centre for Analysis of Social Exclusion, London School of Economics.

Norwich, B. (2008) *Dilemmas of Difference, Inclusion and Disability: International Perspectives and Future Directions*. London: Routledge.

Pearson, C. (ed.) (2006) *Direct Payments and Personalisation of Care*. Edinburgh: Dunedin Academic Press.

Phillips, A. (1999) *Which Equalities Matter?* Cambridge: Polity Press.

Riddell, S., Harris, N., Smith, E. and Weedon, E. (2010) 'Dispute resolution in additional and special educational needs: local authority perspectives', *Journal of Education Policy*, 25: 55–71.

Riddell, S., Stead, J., Weedon, E. and Wright, K. (forthcoming) 'Additional support needs reforms and social justice in Scotland', *International Studies in the Sociology of Education*.

Riddell, S. and Weedon, E. (2009) 'Approaches to dispute resolution in additional support needs in Scotland', *European Journal of Special Needs Education*, 24: 355–69.

Scottish Executive (2005) *Supporting Children's Learning: Code of Practice*. Edinburgh: HMSO.

Scottish Office Education and Industry Department (SOEID) (1998) *A Manual of Good Practice in Special Educational Needs*. Edinburgh: HMSO.

Tomlinson, S. (1985) 'The expansion of special education', *Oxford Review of Education*, 11: 157–65.

Weedon, E. and Riddell, S. (2009) 'Additional support needs and approaches to dispute resolution: the perspectives of Scottish parents', *Scottish Educational Review*, 41: 62–81.

3

THE STATE OF THE RESEARCH – COMPROMISE, CONSENSUS OR DISARRAY?

Elias Avramidis and Brahm Norwich

Learning objectives

This chapter will help the reader to:

- understand some recent philosophical trends and policy developments in special education and their implications for research;
- appreciate the methodological implications of adhering to particular paradigmatic orientations and the impact of recent trends, such as the evidence-based policy and practice movement; and
- understand the challenge of reaching consensus in the field through tolerance and mutual exchange between different traditions.

RESEARCHING SPECIAL AND INCLUSIVE EDUCATION

The education of children with learning difficulties and/or disabilities has changed dramatically over the last 30 years, resulting in new ways of understanding their needs and organizing appropriate provision in most Western countries. Such changes have undoubtedly influenced the focus of research and, by extension, the methodologies employed by the research community. This chapter aims to review critically the various methodological approaches utilized and to appraise the current state of research in the field. Although the emphasis is largely placed on research developments in the UK, the issues discussed here have relevance to other national contexts.

It is important to understand that the term 'special educational needs' itself reflects a particular construction of how education for children with learning difficulties and disabilities is organized. Historically special education was associated with separate special schooling and class teaching. Placements in specialist settings were based on the identification of specific kinds of difficulties, and research tended to focus on analyses of the difficulties and their implications for specialist teaching. Much of the special education research focused mainly on a deficit perspective that located 'learning difficulty' or 'disability' within the individual, while ignoring the immediate teaching and wider institutional contexts. This research was within a particular kind of scientific style of psychological research based on abilities and dispositions, which ignored other theoretical approaches, such as functional and contextual ones. The introduction of the term 'special educational needs' (SEN) in the early 1980s reflected a functional and contextual psychological model, which viewed children experiencing difficulties in learning as 'special' within a particular educational context. In other words, this implied that other contextual factors (i.e. classroom organization, teaching processes and teacher attitudes) also contributed to a child's underachievement.

One of the developments in research in the field of special needs and inclusive education over this period has been the turn towards more sociological analyses. These analyses tended to reflect a critique of psychological ones, especially the abilities/dispositional analyses, reflecting critical perspectives on schooling for children identified as vulnerable and having SEN. It is also important to be clear that just as there are different traditions of psychological research relevant to this aspect of education, so there are different traditions within sociological approaches (Thomas, 2004). But within the sociological tradition there was also a development of theories about disability – disability studies – which drew on the critical or emancipatory tradition to represent disability as produced by an oppressive and exclusive society and not as reflecting impairment located in the person (Barnes *et al.*, 1999). The field of disability studies was associated with the disability movement which fought for the rights of disabled people, and in so doing set itself in opposition to the sociology of health and medicine (Bury, 1991).

In the disability movement the medical model is represented as not only locating 'impairment' in the individual but also as requiring a cure or alleviation that involves the intervention of medical and other professionals. By contrast, in the social model people with impairments are seen as disabled by society's failure to accommodate their needs. Though the social model does not deny the presence of impairment in disabled people's lives, it denies that impairments have implications for disability. In this respect, the social model views disability as socially created and the explanation of its changing character is located in the social and economic structure of the society in which it is found (Mertens and McLaughlin, 2004). The significance of the origins of the social model is that it underpinned the development of ideas about inclusive education and critiques of what were portrayed as deficit models of SEN. Research relevant to the education of children with learning difficulties and disabilities came therefore to be undertaken within a social model based on inclusive education assumptions. Associated with these assumptions were emancipatory and participatory research approaches (Clough and Barton, 1998) that influenced research methodologies and specific research methods.

The international endorsement of inclusive education has resulted in substantial educational reforms, thus opening up new lines of research. Indeed, many studies in school settings sought to identify organizational structures and practices which may be associated with facilitating or impeding the development of inclusion. This body of work reflected an 'organizational paradigm' of research in SEN (Skidmore, 2004). Having been influenced by the school effectiveness tradition, these researchers saw special needs as arising from deficiencies in the way schools are currently organized, leading to moves to school restructuring. Accordingly, rich descriptions of exemplary inclusive schools were provided (Rouse and Florian, 1996) alongside recommendations for developing inclusive school cultures. However, the factors identified as conducive to inclusion were expressed in very broad terms that did not capture the ambiguity, tensions and complexity of schooling. As descriptions of inclusive schools, it remained unclear whether these factors were causal of inclusive development or simply defining characteristics of inclusive schools. In this respect, despite the proliferation of descriptive studies of inclusive schools the need for rigorous evaluation studies which shed light on the academic and social outcomes of the process remained. These considerations have led authors such as Farrell (2000) and Lindsay (2007) to conclude that inclusion has been advanced on the basis of sociopolitical arguments rather than empirical evidence.

RESEARCH PARADIGMS AND THEIR APPLICATION TO SPECIAL EDUCATION

Special needs research has traditionally utilized scientific-style quantitative research designs. One reason for such designs has been the concern for 'hard facts' based on reproducible measures of the impact of interventions (Mertens and McLaughlin, 2004). Moreover, special needs research in the UK has tended to use explanatory quantitative research strategies, such as predictive surveys based on the statistical analysis of large samples, and experimental designs to establish causal relationships.

Some educational researchers see scientific-style quantitative research as rooted in a positivist/post-positivist paradigm, where the purpose of research is to test empirically knowledge claims about educational phenomena. Positivists are often characterized in educational research as adopting a realist-external ontology, with the social world existing 'out there' independently from the inquirer, and committed to practising an objectivist epistemology, in which 'truth' can be captured by approximation. However, scientific-style methodologies do not have to adopt any ontological assumptions about reality; they need only assume that theories can be constructed to predict effects that operate in education. Such a pragmatic philosophy judges scientific research in terms of its predictive usefulness not its realistic ontological assumptions. Whether scientific-style research in special education is positivist or pragmatic, there is still the common assumption that knowledge claims can be confirmed or refuted by rigorous scientific procedures. However, it is arguable that scientific-style research cannot always be applied to special education. For example, in low-incidence conditions such as deaf-blindness or cerebral palsy it is hard to find appropriately sample sizes. Further, the categories of disabilities often used in such research cover a diversity of differences (e.g. dyslexia, Down syndrome, autism, etc.) and individual children often have a pattern of difficulties that goes across different categories (e.g. a child may have dyslexia and specific motor co-ordination disorder). However, there are other traditions using scientific-style research approaches which do not sample by diagnostic categories, but in terms of lower-level functional categories (e.g. below-age expected reading levels; Solity *et al.*, 2000). The functional approach corresponds in special education practice to each student's programme being designed uniquely to satisfy that student's needs. In the UK context, this is reflected in the formulation of an Individual Education Plan (IEP) for each pupil identified with difficulties in learning, resulting in a diversity of programmes and associated practices. This rich contextual information needs to be taken into account when applying certain kinds of scientific-style research to educational practice.

These considerations about scientific-style research have led some researchers away from this approach to research towards qualitative research designs rooted within what is often called the interpretive/constructivist paradigm. However, the turn away from scientific quantitative research designs was not only because of the limitations of scientific-type designs, but also reflected a widespread move towards more relativist and sceptical assumptions about the social sciences. Some researchers argued that the ontological and epistemological assumptions of interpretivism rendered this paradigm more appropriate for the study of special education. In its more radical relativist version, the interpretive paradigm purported that there was no one 'reality' that is waiting to be 'discovered', as the positivist paradigm was said to assume. Instead, realities were said to be multiple and socially constructed, so recognizing that many interpretations can be made – a subjectivist epistemology. Following these assumptions, the concept of 'SEN' was viewed largely as a socially constructed phenomenon, which was relative and context specific. Accordingly, the interpretivist researcher did not accept psychological categories and classifications (e.g. disorders and syndromes). Instead, the perceptions of teachers, parents and children-young adults themselves were sought, with a view of enhancing understanding about the individual and their needs.

There have been several problems with a relativist interpretivist style of research. Radical interpretivist assumptions undermine logically any claim that can be made for the research conclusions, if the findings of such research are open to many interpretations. However, as with scientific-style research, there are different versions of interpretivist research: some versions recognize that some interpretations have priority over others because they fit the evidence better. However illuminating the findings produced by these interpretivist qualitative studies, the application of these research designs to special needs research has also been criticized on two further counts. First, most such studies are small scale and highly context specific (i.e. case studies) and so not easily generalizable in other settings. Secondly, these studies are by nature inappropriate for testing the effectiveness of interventions and, therefore, of limited value in terms of influencing policy-making and professional practice in the field. This need for evaluating and disseminating effective practices was further strengthened by the so-called evidence-based policy and practice movement to be discussed next.

THE EVIDENCE-BASED POLICY AND PRACTICE MOVEMENT

In the mid-1990s educational research in the UK was criticized for being idiosyncratic, sometimes ideologically driven and irrelevant to practitioners and policy-makers alike. David Hargreaves (1999) argued that educational research needed to be redirected towards the systematic development of an accumulating body of knowledge that is capable of informing the practical judgement of teachers. Accordingly, the purpose of research was seen as the development of evidence-based practice in education settings. Such a research agenda requires scientifically based research designs such as experimental studies and randomized controlled trials (RCTs) in search of 'what works' in practice to produce the necessary improvements in educational outcomes (Slavin, 2002).

The evidence-based practice movement, which has a longer history and had much influence in health services, was quickly espoused by the UK government. The DfES Centre for Evidence-informed Policy and Practice in Education (EPPI-centre) was established to facilitate the carrying out of systematic reviews in education and the dissemination of such findings. The purpose of such reviews was to identify effective practice in educational settings so that practice could be based on sound evidence of effectiveness. For example, Evans and Benefield's (2001) review of interventions to support primary-aged pupils with emotional and behavioural difficulties (EBD) in mainstream primary classrooms aimed to describe and explain current knowledge about effective classroom practice related to EBD. Similarly, Dyson *et al.* (2002) conducted a systematic review of the literature on school-level actions conducive to promoting the participation of all pupils. These 'systematic' reviews involved an exhaustive and transparent search of the literature, the setting of strict criteria for including or excluding studies, and the adoption of clear criteria for assessing the quality of the reported findings; by contrast, the more common 'narrative' or 'academic' reviews tend to be more wide ranging in their scope, less clear in reporting their search strategies or their criteria for including or excluding studies, and have less explicit criteria for assessing the quality of the identified studies.

Notwithstanding the merits of adopting a systematic approach to research synthesis, systematic reviews have been criticized for assuming the superiority of what can be referred to as oversimplified assumptions about scientific-style research (Hammersley, 2001). Indeed, such reviews value above all other research designs the randomized experimental research designs, which are considered to be the gold standard of research. Such a preference, coupled with the application of strict criteria for selecting and subsequently evaluating the research designs of the reviewed studies, results in a very limited account of the literature. For example, in Evans and Benefield's (2001) review, from the 265 articles, books, chapters and conference papers initially identified, only 33 fell within the scope of the review. Closer examination of these 33 studies resulted in the exclusion of another 22 studies, which failed to meet the criteria that had been set, thus bringing the final number of reviewed studies to 11. Similarly, in Dyson *et al.*'s (2002) systematic review, from the 325 reports initially identified only 6 studies were eventually maintained in the review. These systematic reviews can be interpreted differently depending on one's philosophical position. For those with interests in a cumulating body of knowledge about effective practices, the reviews can be seen to require more use of controlled trials (e.g. Gorard and Cook, 2007). For those who recognize the practical limits of such designs or with an interpretivist orientation, the reviews show that there is more to educational research than seeking knowledge about evidence-based practice. It is also worth noting that there are certain epistemological problems in establishing a simple evidence base for classroom practice (Bridges, 2008;

Issitt and Kyriacou, 2009). Without going into these in detail here, these critiques imply that there are contextual, relational and judgemental factors involved in classroom teaching which are not open to systematic and randomized controlled designs.

Leaving such philosophical debates aside, the particularities of the special education field outlined earlier (small sample sizes, diversity across categories of disabilities as well as within them, and the difficulty of matching and contrasting samples from different mainstream and special sectors) led most researchers in the field to resist adopting the experimental designs advocated by the evidence-based movement. It is notable that in the few systematic reviews of classroom practices relevant to including pupils with SEN (Davis and Florian, 2004; Nind and Wearmouth, 2006) that very few involved sophisticated randomized control designs. Instead, a range of diverse methodological approaches currently coexist and could be said to characterize the state of research in the field in the UK as in some disarray.

THE CURRENT STATE OF RESEARCH: FROM 'DISARRAY' TO 'CONSENSUS'

In considering the state of research in the field of special and inclusive education two important observations should be noted. First, mixed or contradictory findings are often reported, thus perpetuating ambiguity and debate among researchers in the field. For example, while one of the main arguments for inclusion relates to the social benefits that pupils with SEN gain from their increased interaction with typically achieving peers, the results emerging from relevant empirical studies are very mixed. Indicatively, Lindsay's (2007) review on the social effects of inclusion on children with SEN found few differences between children educated in special schools and those in mainstream provision. Of the 16 different studies identified, 2 were positive, 2 were positive with some caveats, 8 showed no differences and 4 were negative. We contend here that such discrepancies arise primarily because of the methodological limitations inherent in the research designs utilized in these studies and, to a lesser extent, because of socio-historical or contextual differences between these studies.

Equally mixed is the empirical evidence about the academic outcomes of inclusion for children with SEN and their peers. As Ruijs and Peetsma (2009) note in their comprehensive review, most studies examining academic effects are descriptive and concern children with mild to moderate learning disabilities, mild mental retardation, mild to moderate behavioural difficulties, and mild psychosocial problems (these are the terms they use). While the majority of these studies found positive or neutral results, some studies reported adverse effects on the achievement of children with mild SEN. A key limitation in most of these studies, however, was the absence of a 'control' group, which made impossible a comparison between the effects of an inclusive versus a special placement. Further, there was wide variation in the way inclusion was practised in these studies (i.e. some investigated the effect of full-inclusion projects; others investigated the effect of inclusion programmes in which children are only included for some lessons during the day).

A second important observation about the current state of research in the field concerns the prevalence of single methodological research designs, which provide only a partial understanding of the phenomenon under study. Indeed, more often than not, researchers in the field are firmly attached to particular theoretical and methodological positions thus reproducing sterile debates about the supremacy of particular methodologies (e.g. the scientific/quantitative versus interpretive/qualitative divide). Many do not see value in asking different kinds of research questions about the same phenomena. In this way, far from drawing upon a range of methodologies and methods, many researchers are limited to a narrow repertoire of methods emanating from their basic attachments. For example, scientific quantitative researchers can limit themselves to the collection of decontextualized data using experimental and large-scale explanatory survey designs without undertaking any fieldwork in the organizations they study; interpretivist qualitative researchers can utilize ecological methods (participant observations) without making any effort to access what is available about the performance or characteristics of the setting or organization in which they research. We would recognize that there are different research orientations and interests and that it is contradictory for research to be designed to produce scientific-style explanations or interpretivist illuminations in the same study. However, researchers can be flexible in their design and research orientations in different studies or different parts of their studies. We argue here that the field would benefit from the judicious blending of diverse methodologies and methods. We now examine briefly two such recent studies along these lines.

Rouse and Florian's (2006) multi-method study compared the progress of pupils from secondary schools with high SEN numbers with the progress of pupils from schools with low SEN numbers. The study was conducted in one local authority and involved combining assessment data from the English National Pupil Database (NPD) with demographic data (such as socioeconomic status, ethnicity, first language spoken and SEN designation) from the pupil-level annual school census data. To investigate the effect of inclusive education, the progress of students at three schools with more than 25% students with SEN on their register was compared with similar schools with less than 12% students with SEN. Specifically, the study investigated the academic progress of these children in literacy, numeracy and science through comparing their grades at Key Stage 2 – just before secondary education – with national tests at the end of secondary school. The quantitative analysis revealed that the three case-study schools with higher proportions of pupils with SEN performed better (as a whole) than the schools where the proportion was lower, thus leading the researchers to conclude that the presence of large numbers of children with SEN does not have a negative impact on the achievement of children who do not have this designation. However, two important caveats need pointing out here. First, it is debateable whether one can generalize from such a small sample. Secondly, drawing such firm conclusions by comparing the mean scores across groups of schools (i.e. calculating one mean score for the three schools with high proportion and comparing it with a mean score for the three with low proportion) can be misleading. Indeed, further statistical analysis by school provided a more complex picture: performance in one case-study school was similar to performance in the comparison schools; in the second case-study school it was significantly higher; and in the third case-study school it was significantly lower. The quantitative analyses were supplemented with qualitative evidence 'in order to explore the "stories" behind the numbers' (Rouse and Florian, 2006: 483). Fieldwork involved regular visits in two schools and consisted of observing lessons, interviewing key stakeholders and reviewing official documentation such as the school prospectus, inclusion policy and Ofsted inspection reports. According to the authors, these activities resulted in eliciting rich data about the schools' policies, practices and values (overall ethos) and provided possible explanations for the differences in achievement between the three case-study schools. Specifically, it was concluded that the obtained differences in achievement could be attributed to the ways learning support provision and additional resources were deployed in the three settings. Again, reaching firm conclusions from such limited fieldwork (eight research days in two schools) can be risky. In conclusion, although the researchers' choice to mix methods in this study appears at first sight to be promising, closer inspection reveals limitations in both methodological approaches, thus rendering the firm conclusions reported questionable. Perhaps the absence of funding meant that the researchers could not achieve the 'breadth' and 'depth' of data collection and analysis they envisaged.

Another study by Blatchford *et al.* (2009) examined the impact of support staff on SEN pupils' learning and academic progress. Specifically, the Deployment and Impact of Support Staff (DISS) project represents a systematic attempt to determine the impact of different amounts of support provided by teaching assistants (TAs) on SEN pupils' attitudes to learning and their attainment outcomes. However, instead of adopting a traditional experimental design contrasting groups with and without support, the researchers opted for an alternative 'naturalistic' design that sought to measure support received by pupils under normal circumstances and then examine relationships with academic and behaviour outcomes. In this study, attitudes to learning were operationalized as a set of eight different dimensions, measured on the basis of teacher ratings near the end of the school year: distractibility, task confidence, motivation, disruptiveness, independence, relationships with other pupils, completion of assigned work and the following of instructions from adults. Academic progress, on the other hand, was assessed by analysing effects on end-of-year attainment controlling for start-of-year scores and SEN status. Accordingly, the design involved correlations between the main predictor variable (in this case, TA support) and the academic and behavioural outcomes. Although correlational analyses cannot establish causation, the longitudinal assessment of the academic progress and the controlling of prior attainment and SEN status meant that the effects of adult support on pupils' attainment could still be established. Additionally, the research involved the collection of a wide range of qualitative data including observations of lessons and interviews, thus enabling the research team to gain rich insights into the deployment of support staff in schools and the nature of their interaction with pupils. In this way, the DISS project represents a large-scale multi-method design that is innovative and has wider significance for policy-makers and practitioners. It is our contention that the field of special needs research would benefit from the increased utilization of coherent multi-methodological research designs of the type described here.

CONCLUDING COMMENTS

To sum up, our critical appraisal of the state of research in the field has revealed a rather unsatisfactory picture. While there has certainly been some notable research studies, it could be suggested that any progress has at best been moderate. Indeed, one of the main conclusions of Lewis and Norwich (2004) in their work on SEN pedagogy was about the lack of rigorous pedagogic research. The lack of rigorous empirical research capable of addressing the 'big questions' in the field such as how best inclusive practice can be promoted or what the future of special schools could be may be partly attributed to insufficient research funding. But the lack of research is also a matter of consensus about appropriate research methodologies. Interestingly, even areas which were considered of key importance a decade ago (e.g. effective in-class support, teachers' views and training needs, parental attitudes to inclusion, etc. – see Farrell, 2000), today still remain lacking in conclusive evidence and clarity.

The current disarray in the field is, in our view, largely due to the clash of different research orientations reflecting uncompromising positions about what counts as knowledge and understanding in educational research. Being firmly entrenched within particular paradigmatic camps, researchers tend to utilize only methods that directly emanate from their basic attachments, thus achieving only a partial understanding of the phenomena they study. It is therefore vital that a convergence and consensus about research methodologies and philosophical positioning be reached. This includes reaching consensus about the value of different kinds of research questions and maintaining flexibility on how best to go about addressing them. In this respect, research approaches from diverse disciplinary and philosophical backgrounds could be combined within the same research project in a complementary manner. For example, although nothing is more basic in the delivery of special education services than the manner and content of instruction provided to children with SEN, there is a scarcity of empirical evidence to support the effectiveness of particular teaching strategies with particular student populations. Filling this gap in the literature would require the implementation of systematic, controlled, intervention-based studies that compare various teaching strategies for their effectiveness with clearly defined samples of pupils with learning difficulties or disabilities. Such a research emphasis would lead some researchers to employ quantitative explanatory designs. At the same time, qualitative approaches are also needed in order to provide the richness of detail that would furnish a picture of the complexity of the intervention programme under evaluation, the contextual factors influencing its success and the individuals involved.

The clash between scientific and interpretivist approaches can thus be avoided if researchers respect and value theory and research approaches from diverse research traditions and are open to employing coherent multi-method research designs. This requires some humility about the exclusive value of preferred methodologies and philosophical assumptions, what could be seen as a theoretical and methodological triangulation. It becomes, therefore, essential to convince those researchers who are firmly attached to specific paradigmatic stances to abandon their adherence to particular methodological positions; and, more importantly, to move towards finding creative ways to address the key issues in the field through synthesizing diverse approaches within the same large-scale collaborative project. This is not an easy or comfortable task as researchers cannot be forced to alter their research practices; nevertheless, the expansion of mixed-method research could be encouraged in the journals' editorial policies and facilitated through the careful channelling of research funds. We contend that this is a route from disarray to tentative research progress.

SUMMARY

- Recent philosophical developments have undoubtedly affected the design and conduct of research in the field.
- Researchers in the field are often firmly attached to particular theoretical and paradigmatic positions, thus reproducing sterile methodological debates.
- The overall state of research could be seen as being in some disarray, thus failing to provide the empirical evidence needed to address the current issues.
- Research progress requires openness and mutual exchange between different traditions leading to the increased utilization of mixed-method research designs, which would be guided by a stronger focus on key issues (encouraged by journal policies and engineered through a more careful channelling of research funds).

Further Reading

Mertens, D. and McLaughlin, J.A. (2004) *Research and Evaluation Methods in Special Education.* London: Sage. An excellent introduction to the ways research and evaluation methods are applied in special education and a step-by-step guide to planning, conducting and reporting research.

References

Barnes, C., Mercer, G. and Shakespeare, T. (1999) *Exploring Disability: A Sociological Introduction.* London: Polity Press.

Blatchford, P., Bassett, P., Brown, P., Martin, C., Russell, A. and Webster, R. (2009) *The Impact of Support Staff in Schools. Results from the Deployment and Impact of Support Staff (DISS) Project. Research Report 148.* London: DCSF.

Bridges, D. (2008) 'Evidence-based reform in education: a response to Robert Slavin', *European Educational Research Journal*, 7: 129–33.

Bury, M. (1991) 'The sociology of chronic illness: a review of research and prospects', *Sociology of Health and Illness*, 13: 451–68.

Clough, P. and Barton, L. (eds) (1998) *Articulating with Difficulty. Research Voices in Inclusive Education.* London: Sage.

Davis, P. and Florian, L. (2004) Teaching Strategies and Approaches for Pupils with Special Educational Needs: A Scoping Study. *Research report 516*. London: DfES.

Dyson, A., Howes, A. and Roberts, B. (2002) *A Systematic Review of the Effectiveness of School-level Actions for Promoting Participation by All Students*. London: EPPI-centre, Social Science Research Unit, Institute of Education.

Evans, J. and Benefield, P. (2001) 'Systematic reviews of educational research: does the medical model fit?', *British Educational Research Journal*, 27: 527–41.

Farrell, P. (2000) 'The impact of research on developments in inclusive education', *International Journal of Inclusive Education*, 4: 153–62.

Gorard, S. and Cook, T. (2007) 'Where does good evidence come from?', *International Journal of Research and Method in Education*, 30: 307–23.

Hammersley, M. (2001) 'On "systematic" reviews of research literatures: a "narrative" response to Evans & Benefield', *British Educational Research Journal*, 27: 543–54.

Hargreaves, D. (1999) 'Revitalising educational research: lessons from the past and proposals for the future', *Cambridge Journal of Education*, 29: 239–49.

Issitt, J. and Kyriacou, C. (2009) 'Epistemological problems in establishing an evidence base for classroom practice', *Psychology of Education Review*, 33: 47–52.

Lewis, A. and Norwich, B. (eds) (2004) *Special Teaching for Special Children? Pedagogies for Inclusion*. Maidenhead: Open University Press.

Lindsay, G. (2007) 'Annual review: educational psychology and the effectiveness of inclusive education/mainstreaming', *British Journal of Educational Psychology*, 77: 1–24.

Mertens, D. and McLaughlin, J.A. (2004) *Research and Evaluation Methods in Special Education*. London: Sage.

Nind, M. and Wearmouth, J. (2006) 'Including children with special educational needs in mainstream classrooms: implications for pedagogy from a systematic review', *Journal of Research in Special Educational Needs*, 6: 116–24.

Rouse M. and Florian, L. (1996) 'Effective inclusive schools: a study in two countries', *Cambridge Journal of Education*, 26: 71–85.

Rouse, M. and Florian, L. (2006) 'Inclusion and achievement: student achievement in secondary schools with higher and lower proportions of pupils designated as having special educational needs', *International Journal of Inclusive Education*, 10: 481–93.

Ruijs, N.M. and Peetsma, T.D. (2009) 'Effects of inclusion on students with and without special educational needs reviewed', *Educational Research Review*, 4: 67–9.

Skidmore, D. (2004) *Inclusion: The Dynamic of School Development*. Buckingham: Open University Press.

Slavin, R. (2002) 'Evidence-based education policies: transforming educational practice and research', *Educational Researcher*, 31: 15–22.

Solity, J., Deavers, R., Kerfoot, S., Crane, G. and Cannon, K. (2000) 'The early reading research: the impact of instructional psychology', *Educational Psychology in Practice*, 16: 109–28.

Thomas, C. (2004) 'How is disability understood? An examination of sociological approaches', *Disability and Society*, 19: 569–83.

4

INCLUSION AND SPECIAL EDUCATIONAL NEEDS – A DIALOGIC INQUIRY INTO CONTROVERSIAL ISSUES

Artemi Sakellariadis

Learning objectives

This chapter will help readers to:

- bring to light the people behind the label of special educational needs (SEN);
- explain the rationale for including all children and young people in their local neighbourhood school;
- demonstrate the benefits of inclusion for all;
- explore controversial issues from a range of perspectives; and
- challenge conventional forms of academic writing.

'I still don't understand what all the fuss is about,' Sophia sneers at me. 'If you ask me, it's quite simple. Inclusion is all right for some, but there will always be those for whom it can never work. I wish you would accept that and spare us all the provocation.' I bite my lip and walk in silence, trying to conjure up a constructive response. She does not mean to be curt, I am sure. She probably thinks she understands obvious and insurmountable difficulties, therefore assumes there is no merit in my position and no reason to discuss it. Sophia nudges me out of my thoughts. 'Well?' she raises an eyebrow expectantly.

'Well…' I formulate my answer as I speak it. 'This brings back memories. Years ago, when I was a teacher in a special school, a school adviser had said that a mainstream school would have been better for my pupils. Thinking he was being deliberately unreasonable in order to provoke, I had refused to engage in conversation. And here I am now, making a similar claim and hoping you will discuss it with me.'

'Are you seriously telling me…' she pauses and casts me an inquisitive look. 'No, come on, you are teasing again. Let's not waste our time. Can't we talk about something else?'

'Sophia, I promise you, I have never been more serious about this. I really do think that the rationale behind everyone going to their local neighbourhood school is not yet widely understood. Please let us have this conversation now. You know that others are listening in, which makes this all the more important.'

Discussion Point

Controversy continues to surround the issue of whether disabled children, or those said to have special educational needs, should go to their local mainstream or separate special school. Where do you stand? Take a few minutes to articulate what you see as the main advantages of mainstream and what of special schooling.

'OK, let's go for it. It shouldn't take long anyway. Just tell me, what makes you think staff in mainstream schools are well equipped to teach children with profound and multiple learning difficulties?'

She is evidently thinking about young people with high level support needs, the preferred term put forward by disabled people (Alliance for Inclusive Education, 2001), but I decide not to challenge her choice of words. She is clearly embarking on this conversation determined to prove me wrong swiftly, so I must pick my words carefully to help her acknowledge her assumptions and explore alternative perspectives. 'Who do you think *is* well equipped to teach those with the most complex needs and what is it that equips them?'

'Well, specialist SEN staff, of course. They've had all the necessary training.'

'Are you saying that it is only their training that equips them to do a good job?' I ask, knowing that this lets her assume that 'training' is a matter of initial teacher education.

'And their experience, naturally. Knowledge and experience make a good teacher. What are you getting at?'

I say nothing, allowing time for the circularity of her argument to dawn on her. We walk on in silence, hearing the sound of our own footsteps, staying firmly on the beaten track. There is a small path running almost parallel to this road, which I would prefer us to be on but which Sophia seems oblivious to. We carry on walking in silence, while I ponder on her last statement. Surely it takes more than knowledge and experience to be a good teacher, but this is beside the point. I remember something I wrote many years ago, attempting to expose how the availability of experts can disempower those who have yet to engage with a new experience: at the dawn of the twenty-second century a mother and her pregnant daughter are debating who will look after the baby. The daughter is adamant that, in line with current practice, her baby will be placed in a Baby Monitoring Institution (BMI) for at least one year. She argues that BMIs provide expert staff trained to attend to all health, nutritional, social and educational needs of babies and toddlers, whereas she is inexperienced and ill-equipped even to pacify a crying baby (Sakellariadis, 2003). Is there a parallel here? Does the availability and marketization of 'specialist' special educators adversely impact on mainstream school staff's confidence to support the learning and development of young people with high-level support needs? I make a mental note to suggest this as a discussion point for students considering how inclusion policies are put into practice.

'Are you going to tell me what you are getting at?' Sophia repeats her question, reminding me that she is not sufficiently engaged in this conversation to notice any discrepancies.

'I am just thinking that any teacher can access continuing professional development and no teacher can become experienced in anything, unless they are afforded the experience in the first place.'

'Surely you are not suggesting that we all need to become specialists so that any of us can teach any child with any disability!' she presses on, apparently still oblivious to the circularity of her earlier statement. I bite my lip. If she had known what Richard Rieser (2000) says about the social model of disability, she would have probably chosen a different form of words. Some people may have one or more impairments (long-term loss of physical or mental function) but that does not make them disabled. According to the social model, disability is an experience; people only become disabled when society fails to make adjustments or remove barriers. In this sense, a wheelchair user is not disabled by their physical impairment (they are able to move around, albeit by different means to most people) but may become dis-abled by an absence of ramps or by other physical barriers. I choose to say none of this to Sophia, who I sense is getting a little impatient. We need to wrap up on this issue of the perceived competence of staff.

'No, Sophia, I am not suggesting that at all. All we need to do as teachers is realize that the basic pedagogic principles are the same, no matter what we are helping young people to learn; from how to make friends to how to solve complex mathematical equations. We are well equipped to help young people learn and should not freeze in the headlights of relative inexperience. Plus, of course, we should remember that 'we are all ignorant; just about different things' (attributed to Mark Twain). When the time is right, we can seek knowledge about how some children learn or seek advice on how to support the learning and development of a particular child. So, yes, maybe not everyone in the profession feels well equipped at the moment, but staff do not lack the skills; if anything, some people lack confidence that they already have sufficient skills to support any child's learning, alone or with the support of others.'

I choose to leave it at that, aware this may be a lot for her to process right now. Even though she may find this to make sense at face value, it probably represents a considerable shift in how she perceives the capacity of ordinary local schools to respond to the full diversity of learners. I hope she will engage with this sufficiently to realize the shift. If we had more time, I would have explained why seeking support is not an indication of weakness or inadequacy. I would also have reminded her of Gandhi's words that our ability to reach unity in diversity will be the beauty and test of our civilization. I wonder if I should mention the recent Salt Review. The final report (DCSF, 2010) confirmed that many teachers feel ill-prepared to teach learners said to have severe or profound and multiple learning difficulties and suggested that this highlights a gap in initial teacher education. It also revealed a widespread perception that this group of learners requires 'carers' rather than educators. Sophia seems ready to pick up the conversation from where we left it and move us in a new direction:

'And why should teachers have to make time to gain more skills which only duplicate the expertise already available in separate special schools?'

I could raise the issue of human rights and explain why segregated education is discriminatory. Or I could mention national and international legislation or policies calling for the development of inclusive education for all. But our time is limited, so I try something different. 'Did you enjoy your holiday in Portugal last year?'

'I beg your pardon?' she gives me a baffled look, understandably surprised at the question's apparent irrelevance.

'Please answer me. Did you enjoy your holiday in Portugal last year?'

'Yes, thank you, as a matter of fact I did. Now what has that got to do with anything?'

'Well, I was just wondering why you chose a new hotel in Portugal, when there are other well established resorts all over the Mediterranean.'

'Ah, now you are being ridiculous. You know I was visiting my sister who lives there. It wasn't just a holiday – I was catching up with family and friends.'

'And would you say that going to school is just education? Shouldn't every child be spending their school days with their brothers, sisters, friends and potential friends from their local community?'

I think of my good friend, Eva, a school friend whom I am still in touch with. Longstanding friends are so precious! We have been there for one another in so many different ways over the years. I wonder if Sophia is still in touch with any of her school friends.

'But they need the specialist provision, you know they do.' Sophia interrupts my thoughts. I had intended to ask her how she might feel if she were to lose her sight, or her hearing, or the use of her legs and her employer transferred her to another site, bussing her a long distance every day, so that she could be with others who have lost their sight, hearing or use of their legs. But now the conversation is moving in a different direction.

'And just because they might need something in addition to what most children do, you think it is all right to take something away from them? How come a perceived need for adult specialists is allowed to trump children's need to be with their peers and to belong in their local community?' I stop short of saying that this is like putting a child in hospital without allowing family or friends to visit, on the grounds that the child needs the medical intervention.

'Well, you've got to be realistic. You either deprive them of their peers or of the tailor-made provision. What would you rather do?'

'Neither, Sophia. Neither.' I am unable to conceal a hint of impatience. I take a deep breath, then add in a calmer tone: 'With today's emphasis on personalized learning, there is no reason why tailor-made provision has to be offered in a separate place' (CSIE Staff and Associates, 2009). I am painfully aware that many children and young people have been included in their local school without appropriate support and, consequently, have found the experience neither pleasant nor beneficial. Did anyone suggest that including everyone in ordinary local schools is easy, or that effective provision can be developed overnight? We know there is a tendency in organizations and systems to resist change, but does that mean that we stop trying? I remember recently hearing Peter Farrell (2010) responding to parents who were praising special schools following their children's unpleasant experiences in mainstream. 'We have good evidence that there are many children with a range of disabilities who are marginalized in mainstream schools, who are bullied in mainstream schools, who feel uncomfortable in mainstream schools. That is not to say that inclusion is not a good thing, it's just to say that we haven't actually got it right yet.'

'Well that's a lovely rhetoric but we both know that the provision is not there. Children with severe learning difficulties simply cannot access the curriculum. What would they do all day in a mainstream school?'

I stop dead in my tracks. I lean against a tree, take off my right shoe and shake out a stone. I put my shoe back on, take it off again and shake it some more. Sophia seems ready to move on but I stay put. I take off my glasses and slowly clean both lenses. Without uttering a word, I hold them up to the light then clean them some more. With the corner of my eye I notice Sophia adjusting her hair band. Her eyes are focused at some point in the distance and she seems to be thinking. Good. She needs to make a mental leap that my words alone cannot engineer for her. She needs to realize that the proposal is not simply to place children in local schools as we know them; they have been set up with a narrower population in mind. What is called for is a critical examination of how we see disability, a radical reconsideration of how we organize teaching and learning in ordinary local schools and an innovative mindset allowing us to perceive pupil progress in the light of 'measuring what we value', if we must measure anything, instead of 'valuing what we can measure' (Ainscow, 2005). I look at my friend tenderly. She sounded impatient a few minutes ago. She probably thinks that parents who want their sons or daughters with high-level support needs to go to their local school are unrealistic and that their choices are more sentimental than rational. One day she might understand that lived experience has led some parents to expand their sense of what is normal; not in the sense of what is average or what is shared by most people, but more in a sense of what is a natural expression of our shared humanity. For the time being she, like so many others, is focusing on differences between disabled and non-disabled people and overlooks all of what we share in common. Sophia still seems absorbed in her thoughts. I wait patiently. A cat is sitting on a wall nearby, leisurely licking its paws. A welcome breeze brings the fresh scent of spring. We stay like this, almost frozen in time. Eventually Sophia glances at me, her earlier look of concern gradually changing to a smile, as she sets us off walking again.

'I think I see what you are getting at. You are saying that whatever learning opportunities are available to children in special schools, could be made available to them in their local school. The option is not there … not because it cannot be done but because the capacity has not been developed–'

'Yet', I interrupt, 'the capacity has not been developed yet.' If only I could take her to Canada, show her the provision at the Hamilton-Wentworth Catholic District School Board, where they closed all their special schools in 1969 and have been educating all children and young people in mainstream schools ever since (Hansen *et al.*, 2006). Sophia is oblivious to my thoughts.

'OK, so the capacity has not been developed yet in mainstream schools. However …' She takes a deep breath and I can sense there is something else troubling her. 'Even if we agree that this is what we'd like in principle, surely in practice concentrating resources in one place makes more sense financially.'

I knew this would come up sooner or later. Should I explain this or shall I let her work it out for herself? How difficult can it be to figure out that paying for staff to travel to mainstream schools is cheaper than paying for pupils to travel to special schools, often very long distances twice a day by taxi with a paid escort? Millions are spent each year for the sole purpose of getting children from home to a special school and back again. A recent report maintains that children's services rarely keep records in a way that enables them to evaluate the total cost of supporting an individual child. Transport costs and the costs of monitoring provision are identified as expenditure not being combined with the charges made by providers, since they come from separate budgets. The report suggests that without this financial information it is not possible to make informed judgements about the most cost-effective placement for a particular child (Audit Commission, 2007). Transport costs aside, how hard can it be to realize that for every special school that closes, funds needed to run the school and maintain the buildings could enable the same staff to help develop more inclusive provision in ordinary local schools? Sophia would probably say that the resources she had in mind are more than the human resources of my argument. That might not stand to scrutiny either. For a start, as Micheline Mason has said (pers. comm.), what better resource to support disabled children's learning and development than their non-disabled peers? An invaluable resource always available, and free, in ordinary local schools. Yes, there is something to be said about physical resources, but my hunch is that Sophia's understanding would be different from mine. Am I ready to subject myself to the discourse of care and to assumptions about *Snoezelen* rooms or hydrotherapy pools as essential resources of unique benefit to disabled children alone? No, not now. I let her assumption about financial benefit lie and decide to explore another thought.

'Are you saying that financial considerations alone should dictate decisions that affect the quality of people's lives?' I am aware that articulating a vague concern can serve to clarify it and, occasionally, to expose it as unsound.

'Well, no, not exactly. I am not saying that finances should dictate where children are educated, only that cost should be taken into account.'

'So how should that impact upon a decision, if appropriate provision was available in either type of setting? Even if it was cheaper to send children to separate special schools, and therefore this question arose, would you see cost-cutting as sufficient justification for uprooting young people and keeping them apart from their local community, sometimes throughout their school lives?' I stop short of asking her how she might feel if cost-cutting measures were affecting her own children. How would it seem if, responding to funding cuts, her local school removed art or chemistry from the curriculum?

 Discussion Point

Making available to disabled people facilities and services that most people take for granted, often necessitates additional expenditure (for example, the cost of providing hearing loops, accessible toilets, Braille signs or inclusive education for all in ordinary local schools). What weight do you think such financial implications should carry? Who do you think should decide, and on what grounds, what facilities and services are made available to whom?

'But some may not benefit from being in their local community. Some of them are not in a position to make friends, are they?' Sophia naïvely questions the merits of togetherness and overlooks young people's emotional well-being.

'What? Of course they are! With all due respect, might you be finding such friendships hard to imagine because you don't have any disabled friends yourself?'

'Well, no, but ...'

'Or is there a particular mould in your mind that a friend has to fit in, in order to be called a friend?'

I had promised myself to remain calm throughout this conversation and I am not doing too well right now. But what is a friend, if not someone who loves you for who you are? And how are non-disabled youngsters to get to know and appreciate their disabled peers, if they are purposely and consistently separated? Sophia has remained silent and I feel I owe her an apology:

'Look I am sorry, I didn't mean to sound terse. Let us go back to my earlier question: would you see cost-cutting as sufficient justification for uprooting young people and keeping them apart from their local community?'

'I'm not sure. Why is it suddenly so bad to be away from your local community? Lots of children go to boarding school and that's not frowned upon, is it?'

'Well in many ways it is, but I cannot see a sustainable comparison. Removing a young person from their local community to situate them within a homogeneous smaller community of perceived privilege is hardly comparable to landing young people together in a disparate assemblage of ostracized youngsters, don't you think? Are you really trying to compare eliticism with dismissal?'

'Whoa, you've said too much there. Why do you say disparate? They have their disability in common, don't they?'

She is confusing experience with impairment again. I let that go.

'Sophia, would you choose to work in a school purposely staffed entirely by brunettes?'

'Now you are being flippant; we are talking about responding to children's needs. Children who share a disability also share similar special educational needs. What is wrong with organizing provision around those needs?'

'It would be like making all people with curly hair go to the same hairdresser.' She is making sweeping assumptions again. If she has not yet grasped the full range of diversity, I cannot explain it here and now. But suggesting that everyone who has, for example, Down's syndrome should be treated in the same way is as naïve as suggesting that everyone who lives on the same street learns in the same way. To think that people with a particular impairment have more in common with others who have the same impairment than with their peers who do not, is also an assumption that might not stand up to scrutiny.

'No, no. Let's explore this.' It is she who is pursuing the logic in the argument now, I am pleased to notice. 'Don't you think that children themselves would prefer to be in a school with others like them, rather than being thrown in a place where they are for ever standing out as being different?'

'They might do. But what would this mean for them in the long term? Most children would rather eat sweets than vegetables, but would you raise them on a strict diet of nothing but sweets?' If we had more time, I would have tried to deconstruct the notion of what is best for the child. Sophia may not have been seduced by the perception of a cosy bubble if she realized the extent of discrimination disabled people face. This is often unintentional and unacknowledged, yet does not happen in countries where all children go to the same schools and grow up understanding the full range of diversity. The reciprocal link between ignorance and prejudice simply has to be broken. We also know that separate special schools have lower expectations of children; diversity tends to get pathologized and young people are often destined for a life in day centres. If Sophia chose to engage with the bigger picture, would she still opt to commit people to a life of social isolation?

'Come on, let us be serious. Let us take children who suffer from autism, for example.' I flinch, but say nothing. To suggest that anyone 'suffers' from autism, or Down's syndrome for that matter, is little more than a projection of our own assumptions upon their lived experience. I smile at the fleeting memory of Ros Blackburn (1998) saying that she considers herself to be 'blessed with autism'. To mention this now could spark off a long debate on individual perceptions of disability, which we do not have time for. Sophia is already halfway through her next sentence: 'What is wrong with putting them all in the same school with staff who really understand their needs and have developed appropriate provision? They would be in a happy, friendly and absolutely appropriate environment that fosters their development without the pressure of being different.'

I could tell her about a number of adults with autism who fully support inclusive education in ordinary local schools. With Ros Blackburn still on my mind, I remember her describing her parents' fight to get her in a mainstream school and saying that 'autism doesn't need to see autism' (1998). I pick my words very carefully. 'At first glance the thought of a pressure-free environment may appear seductive. But if you think about it, a pressure-free environment is not a priority for everyone else, is it? Most children are subjected to the pressure of learning tough subjects and/or taking stressful exams; we justify this on the grounds that they are gaining knowledge and skills that will serve them well in adult life. Why should it be any different for disabled children? What exactly would we be protecting them from, by removing the pressure of being different, and how long do we think we can protect them for?' She could have chosen to challenge me with the issue of schooling for deaf children and the need to respect deaf culture but, at the end of the day, I believe the same argument still holds. Surely in the twenty-first century everyone's right to belong in an inclusive society is no longer contested. If we want to live together as adults, we have to go to school together as children. When the London Borough of Newham was redesigning its provision in the wake of the Education Act 1981, it sought an innovative solution to this challenge. Following extensive consultations and deliberations, the council decided to 'build, develop and preserve deaf culture within the mainstream' (Jordan and Goodey, 2002): a primary and a secondary school were set up to offer resourced provision for deaf children, while every child had the choice of attending their local or one of the resourced schools.

Discussion Point

- Do you believe that every child or young person should have the opportunity to spend time with other young people similar to them? If yes, who should be the best judge of which similarities between young people are significant?
- Do you believe that every child or young person has a right to be part of the local community in which they live?
- If you have answered yes to both the above, how would you suggest that both considerations can be honoured?

Sophia has been walking in silence for a brief while, potentially thinking about what I have just asked her. She now takes a deep breath and seems ready to resume our conversation: 'I'll tell you what we need to protect them from. Bullying. Children can be so cruel, why subject children with special needs to it?'

I make a mental note to return to her choice of words but, for now, respond to her question directly: 'Yes, children can be cruel and so can adults, if they think they can get away with it. Are you saying that bullying only happens in mainstream schools and, therefore, those who attend separate special schools are in a bully-free environment?'

'How do you mean?'

I wonder if she has ever set foot in a special school, but don't want to embarrass her by asking. We seem to be dealing with a large number of assumptions here, so I decide to deal with them quickly, one at a time: 'Well, first of all, let me tell you this: researchers have found that young adolescents said to have moderate learning difficulties were bullied just as much in either type of school. I can give you the reference if you like.' In fact this research put forward a far more disturbing picture. 'A notable emergent theme from the study was the high incidence of "bullying" that was experienced. Though experienced in both settings, those in special schools experienced far more "bullying" from children in other mainstream schools and from peers and outsiders in their neighbourhood' (Norwich and Kelly, 2004). 'But even if we thought that bullying only happens in mainstream schools, are you seriously suggesting that we should send disabled children away rather than tackle the bullying? Is this what you would do about other forms of bullying?'

'What are you smiling at?'

'Nothing, sorry. The thought of removing children to protect them from bullying could be rather amusing in the context of other young people at risk of discrimination.' I manage to stifle a little giggle. 'What do you suggest we do about homophobic bullying, for example? Take all lesbian, gay, bisexual and transgender children and adults out of ordinary local schools and secure them somewhere else to keep them safely protected?'

'OK, I guess you are right. You'd have to tackle the bullying, wouldn't you?'

'M-hm.'

'Yes, OK, I'll give you that. Protection from bullying is not really a reason to turn children with special needs away from mainstream.' Now is a good a time as any.

'Actually, Sophia, can we just stop and think for a moment whom you might mean when you refer to children with special needs?' She takes a few moments to think.

'Well I can't give you a definition, but we both know whom we are talking about, don't we?'

'We may or may not do. The point is, the words that we use serve to shape our thinking, and vice versa. I'm just wondering what we are doing to young people's sense of identity and what power structures we are supporting, by referring to a potentially undefined group of people as "children with special needs". Can you try to put into words for me who it is you think we are talking about?'

Sophia walks on in silence, squinting her eyes and tightening her lips. I am not surprised that she cannot come up with an easy answer. In the words of Baroness Warnock (2005):

> The definition, as you probably know, which comes in the 1981 Education Act is the purest vicious circle you will ever know. A special need is defined as *'any need that the school needs to take special measures to meet'*. Well, that is not much of a definition but it is the only definition there is.

I am also reminded of the words of Alan Dyson (1990): 'Special educational needs are needs that arise within the educational system rather than the individual, and indicate a need for the system to change further in order to accommodate individual differences.' As I have written elsewhere, the difference between whether a child 'has' or 'experiences' difficulties is similar to whether a child 'brings' or 'finds' difficulties at school. To many this might seem like a futile word game; to others such differences are of paramount importance, not least because they can have a strong impact on young people's sense of identity (CSIE Staff and Associates, 2009).

'Look, sorry, I can't and I am beginning to worry that we are running out of time. Just tell me this: I can see the logic for inclusion for all, but we've got a system that works well. It has worked well for years. If it isn't broken, why fix it?'

'Because it doesn't serve us well. Not all of us. Disabled adults have been saying for years that being sent to separate special schools leads to adult lives at the margins of society.' The absence of disabled people's voices in debates about inclusion for all has been heavily criticized. Derrick Armstrong (2003: 116) says these voices need to be taken seriously because 'they challenge both the homogeneity of experience and the social relations that have constructed difference as "abnormal"'.

'So the people who designed this system were wrong?' She says this in a quiet voice, which might suggest that her steadfast support for the current system is beginning to be called into question.

'Well, yes and no. For a start, please don't imagine designers of education systems sat around a drawing board conjuring up the idea of mainstream schools for some and separate special schools for others. Far from it, this system of dual type of provision is more the product of evolution than of conscious and deliberate planning.' On another day I might have preferred to say happenstance.

'What do you mean, yes and no?' She seems troubled by the suggestion that we have arrived here more by chance than judgement.

'Only that it is a system that reflects the moral values of its time. I wrote about this recently. Current ideas about schooling were established over 100 years ago, when disabled people were not expected to ever have a place in mainstream society. Although cultural norms have significantly shifted and disabled people are being increasingly valued as rightful members of mainstream society, current educational practice has yet to embrace these changing attitudes (CSIE Staff and Associates, 2010). Inclusion for all is a fundamental human rights question, to which education is called upon to find an answer (Sakellariadis, 2007).'

'But what can we do? We are talking about the need for massive change here. How can we begin to bring that about?'

'We don't need to begin anything; change is already underway. We simply need to embrace the transformation and use every opportunity to explore our assumptions and reflect on our practice.' I stop short of referring to a need to address our 'collective indifference' (Slee, 2010). 'We also need to share examples of good practice as widely as possible and remember that where there's a will there's a way.' I remember a recent report on the quality of provision for pupils said to have learning difficulties and disabilities, which concluded: 'Effective provision was distributed equally in the mainstream and special schools visited, but there was more good and outstanding provision in resourced mainstream schools than elsewhere' (Ofsted, 2006).

 Case Study

Emersons Green Primary School in South Gloucestershire is a mainstream school with a resource base for pupils with physical and/or visual impairments. Purpose built and first opened in 2000, the school has been set up so that provision in the resource base (which opened in 2001) forms an integral part of the school, intentionally moving away from earlier models of locating a 'unit' in a particular space of the school building, separate from the mainstream classes.

The school ensures that everyone is welcome and feels valued. Learning is organized in ways that are meaningful and relevant to every learner, while the school ensures that academic, social, physical and other forms of learning are all celebrated.

There is a high adult:child ratio at break times. Over and above supervising the children, adults facilitate co-operative play and other interactions in constructive ways. They often model ways for disabled and non-disabled children to play together, then gradually stand back and let the young people develop their own play and friendships.

Developing inclusive provision is seen as an ongoing process. Anywhere you look, you can find evidence of diversity being embraced. Situations which another school may have found challenging, if not impossible, here appear commonplace and ordinary. I was particularly struck by the 10-year-old peer mentor who fulfilled his duties with the help of an assistive communication device.

'That makes perfect sense, thanks. Are there any resources that you would recommend?'

We have now reached the station and are walking towards the platform. Are there more resources I would recommend? I certainly know of some excellent resources (Pearpoint *et al.*, 1992; Alderson, 1999; Hayes, 2004; DfES and DRC, 2006; Tashie *et al.*, 2006; Booth and Ainscow, 2011) but I hesitate to go through them now.

'At the danger of sounding too simplistic, you don't need great big manuals lining your shelves. Developing inclusive provision is not so much about what you do, as about how you do it. We are talking about a process, not a method.'

'What a wonderful note to finish our conversation on.' Sophia stops by the station entrance and turns to bid me farewell. We both understand the need to bring our conversation to an abrupt close; I wish her a constructive journey, the editors check her ticket and she is on her way. My trusted writing partner, albeit a figment of my imagination, has served her purpose. No doubt she will be conjured up again when I next choose to write something as a dialogue, attempting to be both scholarly and engaging. Walking away, I try to remember something I recently wrote (CSIE, 2010).

No battle for human rights has ever been fought without setbacks. There are bound to have been some who, steeped within an older frame of mind, vehemently opposed the abolition of slavery, or child labour, or … one day we may say segregated education. I look forward to the day when our society is collectively appalled at the memory of young people being ostracized from their communities, in the name of their own good.

SUMMARY

Disabled adults and their allies understand that children who are sent to separate special schools often end up living adult lives at the margins of society. They insist that, if we are to live our lives together in an inclusive society, every child should go to their local neighbourhood school. All young people should learn and develop alongside their brothers, sisters, friends and potential friends from the local community.

Others maintain that special schools are needed, on the grounds that they offer specialized provision not available in ordinary schools and provide a better environment for the pupils who attend them. Instances where inclusion has been insufficiently resourced and/or poorly managed are sometimes cited as examples to support this claim.

These positions are not mutually exclusive. The former represents a moral position, the latter a reflection on existing provision. The fact remains that inclusion for all is possible and can benefit all young people. If real choice is to be extended to all parents, as current and previous UK governments have pledged, the choice of mainstream has to exist, therefore the capacity to provide for all must be developed in ordinary schools. The effectiveness of this will depend, among other things, on the extent to which staff embrace the rationale for including all children and young people in their local school.

Further Reading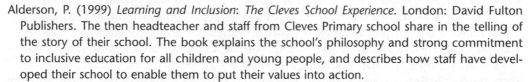

Alderson, P. (1999) *Learning and Inclusion: The Cleves School Experience.* London: David Fulton Publishers. The then headteacher and staff from Cleves Primary school share in the telling of the story of their school. The book explains the school's philosophy and strong commitment to inclusive education for all children and young people, and describes how staff have developed their school to enable them to put their values into action.

Booth, T. and Ainscow, M. (2011) *Index for Inclusion: Developing Learning and Participation in Schools* (3rd edn). Bristol: Centre for Studies on Inclusive Education. Booth, T., Ainscow, M. and Kingston, D. (2006) *Index for Inclusion: Developing Play, Learning and Participation in Early Years and Childcare* (rev. edn). Bristol: Centre for Studies on Inclusive Education. The *Index* is a set of materials to support schools and early years settings through a self-review of the setting's cultures, policies and practices. It offers a clear framework for a thorough exploration of every aspect of school life as part of the process of inclusive school development. The *Index* can help schools identify barriers to learning and participation, determine priorities for school development and put into place action plans to build supportive communities which foster high achievement for everyone. Very popular with school practitioners throughout the world, the *Index* has so far been translated into 37 languages.

DfES and Disability Rights Commission (2006) *Implementing the Disability Discrimination Act in Schools and Early Years Settings: A Training Resource for Schools and Local Authorities.* Nottingham: DfES Publications. Excellent resource with inspirational examples of inclusive education for disabled children and young people in ordinary local schools. The resource pack was introduced when the disability equality duty first came into force and has been made available to schools free of charge (schools need to request this through the teachernet website).

Hansen, J., Leyden, G., Bunch, G. and Pearpoint, J. (2006) *Each Belongs: The Remarkable Story of the First School System to Move to Inclusion.* Toronto: Inclusion Press. A fascinating book which charts the story of one local authority in Canada that chose to close down all its separate special schools in 1969 and has been educating all children and young people in ordinary local schools since then. For anyone who has ever wondered how inclusive education for all can be made possible, this is bound to be an interesting read.

Hart, S., Dixon, A., Drummond, M.J. and McIntyre, D. (2004) *Learning Without limits.* Maidenhead: Open University Press. Accessible and engaging, this book tells the story of a project bringing together classroom teachers who had rejected ideas of fixed ability and were developing teaching practices in line with their values and beliefs. The practices that each participating teacher developed are clearly described and explained. An inspirational read for teachers wanting to enthuse all learners while organizing teaching and learning in ways that avoid labelling by perceived ability.

Rieser, R. (2000) 'Disability discrimination, the final frontier; disablement, history and liberation', in M. Cole (ed.) *Education, Equality and Human Rights: Issues of Gender, 'Race', Sexuality, Special Needs and Social Class.* London: RoutledgeFalmer. In this chapter Richard Rieser clearly and unambiguously explains the medical and social models of disability. A must read for people who want to understand alternative ways of perceiving disability, this chapter will help readers apply these insights in their explorations of the ethical, political, social and educational challenges of inclusion for all.

Rustemier, S. (2002) *Social and Educational Justice: The Human Rights Framework for Inclusion.* Bristol: Centre for Studies on Inclusive Education. This report puts forward the substantial and persuasive international human rights principles supporting inclusive education. It reveals a catalogue of uncomfortable facts about segregated education in the UK and challenges traditional assumptions sustaining segregation.

Thomas, G., Walker, D. and Webb, J. (1998) *The Making of the Inclusive School.* London: Routledge. Like other books before it (e.g. Jupp, 1992), this book tells the story of closing a special school on the grounds of principle. The book is organized into two parts: Part I provides a clear and compelling case for inclusion for all and explores why this may be slow to achieve. Part II charts the fascinating process of a special school that decided to close on grounds of principle.

Useful Websites

www.csie.org.uk The website of the Centre for Studies on Inclusive Education. It provides up-to-date information and a wide range of resources for students, parents and professionals who want to reduce barriers to learning and participation and promote equality for all.

www.worldofinclusion.com The website of Richard Rieser Disability Equality. It offers a comprehensive guide to meeting statutory equality duty with regard to disability and many examples of how to raise awareness and promote disability equality in the curriculum.

References

Ainscow, M. (2005) 'Developing inclusive education systems: what are the levers for change?', *Journal of Educational Change*, 6: 109–24.

Alderson, P. (1999) *Learning and Inclusion: The Cleves School Experience.* London: David Fulton Publishers.

Alliance for Inclusive Education (2001) *The Inclusion Assistant: Helping Young People with High Level Support Needs in Mainstream Education. London:* Alliance for Inclusive Education.

Alur, M. and Bach, M. (2009) *The Journey for Inclusive Education in the Indian Sub-continent.* New York, NY: Routledge.

Armstrong, D. (2003) *Experiences of Special Education: Re-evaluating Policy and Practice through Life Stories.* London: Routledge Farmer.

Audit Commission (2007) *Out of Authority Placements for Special Educational needs.* London: Audit Commission.

Blackburn, R. (1998) 'Logically illogical' in *Proceedings of the National Portage Association Conference.* Northampton: National Portage Association.

Booth, T. and Ainscow, M. (2011) *Index for Inclusion: Developing Learning and Participation in Schools* (3rd edn). Bristol: Centre for Studies on Inclusive Education.

Chapman, L. and West-Burnham, J. (2010) *Education for Social Justice: Achieving Wellbeing for All.* London: Continuum.

CSIE (2010) Some more equal than others? Retrieved 24 May from http://www.csie.org.uk/news/index.shtml#200510.

CSIE Staff and Associates (2009) *The Welcome Workbook: A Self-review Framework for Expanding Inclusive Provision in your Local Authority.* Bristol: Centre for Studies on Inclusive Education.

CSIE Staff and Associates (2010) *Developing a Single Equality Policy for your School: A CSIE Guide.* Bristol: Centre for Studies on Inclusive Education.

DCSF (2010) *Salt Review: Independent Review of Teacher Supply for Pupils with Severe, Profound and Multiple Learning Difficulties (SLD and PMLD).* Nottingham: DCSF Publications.

DfES and Disability Rights Commission (2006) *Implementing the Disability Discrimination Act in Schools and Early Years Settings: A Training Resource for Schools and Local Authorities.* Nottingham: DfES Publications.

Dyson, A. (1990) 'Special educational needs and the concept of change', *Oxford Review of Education,* 16: 55–66.

Farrell, P. (2010) BBC 'The Big Questions' programme Sunday 9 May 2010. Retrieved 12 May from www.bbc.co.uk/programmes/b007zpll.

Hansen, J., Leyden, G., Bunch, G. and Pearpoint, J. (2006) *Each Belongs: The Remarkable Story of the First School System to Move to Inclusion.* Toronto: Inclusion Press.

Hart, S., Dixon, A., Drummond, M.J. and McIntyre, D. (2004) *Learning Without limits.* Maidenhead: Open University Press.

Hayes, J. (2004) 'Visual annual reviews: how to include pupils with learning difficulties in their educational reviews', *Support for Learning,* 19: 175–80.

Jordan, L. and Goodey, C. (2002) *Human Rights and School Change: The Newham Story.* Bristol: Centre for Studies on Inclusive Education.

Jupp, K. (1992) *Everyone Belongs: Mainstream Education for Children with Severe Learning Difficulties.* London: Souvenir Press.

Norwich, B. and Kelly, N. (2004) 'Pupils' views on inclusion: moderate learning difficulties and bullying in mainstream and special schools', *British Educational Research Journal,* 30: 43–65.

Ofsted (2006) *Inclusion: Does it Matter where Pupils are Taught?* London: Office for Standards in Education.

Oliver, M. (1993) 'Disability and dependency: a creation of industrial societies?', in J. Swain *et al.* (eds) *Disabling Barriers - Enabling Environments.* London: Sage.

Pearpoint, J., Forest, M. and Snow, J. (1992) *The Inclusion Papers: Strategies to Make Inclusion Work.* Toronto: Inclusion Press.

Rieser, R. (2000) 'Disability discrimination, the final frontier; disablement, history and liberation', in M. Cole (ed) *Education, Equality and Human Rights: Issues of Gender, 'Race', Sexuality, Special Needs and Social Class.* London: RoutledgeFalmer.

Rustemier, S. (2002) *Social and Educational Justice: The Human Rights Framework for Inclusion.* Bristol: Centre for Studies on Inclusive Education.

Sakellariadis, A. (2003) 'Confusion or inclusion? A comparative case study of individual perceptions of inclusion.' Unpublished thesis (MEd), University of Bristol.

Sakellariadis, A. (2007) 'Voices of inclusion: perspectives of mainstream primary staff on working with disabled children.' Unpublished PhD thesis, University of Bristol.

Sakellariadis, A. (2010) 'The challenge of supporting the supporters in the inclusive school', in F. Hallet and G. Hallet (eds) *Transforming the Role of the SENCO: Achieving the National Award for SEN Coordination.* Maidenhead: Open University Press.

Sapon-Shevin, M. (2007) *Widening the Circle: The Power of Inclusive Classrooms.* Boston, MA: Beacon Press.

Slee, R. (2010) *The Irregular School: Exclusion, Schooling and Inclusive Education.* London: Taylor & Francis.

Swain, J., French, S. and Cameron, C. (2003) *Controversial Issues in a Disabling Society.* Buckingham: Open University Press.

Tashie, C., Shapiro-Barnard, S. and Rossetti, Z. (2006) *Seeing the Charade: What we Need to Do and Undo to Make Friendships Happen.* Nottingham: Inclusive Solutions.

Thomas, G., Walker, D. and Webb, J. (1998) *The Making of the Inclusive School.* London: Routledge.

Warnock, M. (2005) Select Committee on Education and Skills: minutes of oral evidence taken on 31 October 2005. Retrieved March from http://www.publications.parliament.uk/pa/cm200506/cmselect/cmeduski/478/5103103.htm.

5 THE POTENTIAL IMPACT AND INFLUENCE OF THE SOCIAL MODEL OF DISABILITY

Charles Weedon

Learning objectives

This chapter will help readers to:

- recognize the ways in which disabilities may be socially constructed and how this might impact within education;
- be aware of how socioeconomic status interacts with the ways in which we respond to disabilities; and
- understand how these factors may impact upon assessment and examination arrangements, and of how issues of institutional and administrative convenience lead us sometimes to impose disabled identities upon individuals who have no functional impairments other than those imposed by the examination hall.

BACKGROUND – THE CONTEXT

In schools such as the one where I work, support-for-learning staff brace themselves for a perceptible surge of referrals at the start of the exam season each year. Almost continuous assessment is the hallmark of the exam years in schools: learners are subjected to a relentless diet of learning outcomes, practice exams, 'prelims', national assessment bank tasks and, finally, the 'real' exam. It tends to commence when a learner is 14 or 15 years of age – and it continues until formal education is complete.

This sharp increase in the tempo of assessment has one inevitable and recurring consequence: experienced subject teachers report barriers to achievement that had apparently escaped detection until this point:

"Jamie may be a scatty and disorganized lad, but he's up there with the best of them in his grasp of plant reproduction/historical bias/subtle use of extended metaphor (or whatever). But he never performs at anything like the right level in formal exams …

The referral process leads, usually, to some formal assessment. The already over-assessed learner is subjected to a barrage of further assessment, standardized tests and data gathering – and to be sure, quite often some subtle but well defined barrier to achievement *is* identified, and compensatory examination arrangements are put in place so that true levels of attainment may now be demonstrated in all these tests and examinations.

How did this happen? Had we been remiss in not identifying the difficulty earlier, much earlier? Or is it some kind of late-onset developmental difficulty that manifests itself in the mid-teens, then fades in the mid-twenties?

Or can it be argued perhaps more plausibly that educational institutions, driven by a bio-medical model of disability in combination with the demands and dynamics of the assessment industry, are *creating* these disabilities and barriers: have institutional imperatives habituated us into creating and accepting barriers that, for some learners, simply need not be there at all? For example, should the mildly dyslexic student who needs to use a word-processor and is allowed extra time in formal examinations be regarded as, or categorized as, 'disabled'? They certainly *are* categorized as such but only because of our assumption that we should measure mastery of a 'corpus of knowledge' by means of handwritten examinations that have to be completed in a limited period of time. To access the necessary accommodations, we are compelled to label the exam candidate as 'dyslexic'. Where the difficulty is a modest one, often the individual will need this label under *no* circumstances other than the examination hall. In doing this, we are causing these individuals to adopt a disabled persona, and for reasons it might be argued of doubtful validity. Crucially, if we were to dispense with that one assumption about the mode of assessing student competencies then – for some individuals with dyslexia – we will have dispensed with the label of 'disability'.

WHAT IS A 'SOCIAL MODEL OF DISABILITY'?

The social model of disability (e.g. Oliver, 1990; Barnes, 1991) suggests that many of the barriers faced by disabled people are environmental and societal – that certain individual characteristics and impairments that need not necessarily be disabling actually become disabling only because of the ways in which society responds to them. The barriers are therefore within the environment, not within the individual.

In contrast, a bio-medical model of disability will view those same characteristics, traits or impairments as disabling features intrinsically rooted within the individual, and which cause clear disadvantage to that individual. Our responses therefore focus upon the individual, rather than the context within which that individual is immersed.

It can be argued that many of the key professionals involved with barriers to learning at school level are still quite strongly influenced by a bio-medical model: while we may recognize and applaud the concept of lessening the environmental barriers, we find it hard to see just *how* it applies to our field – and for some of us, perhaps for most of us, the bio-medical concept of disabling individual differences influences much of our thinking and responses.

MacDonald (2009: 348), referring specifically to dyslexic students in higher education, captures the tension between the two models and challenges our thinking by stepping back from education. He quotes C. Wright Mills' reflections on unemployment: that when just one man in a city of 100,000 is unemployed, then 'that is his personal trouble … But when in a nation of 50 million employees, 15 million are unemployed, the very structure of opportunity has collapsed'.

Removed in this way from the context of education, the conflict between two contesting explanatory paradigms is immediately evident. Do the roots of an individual's difficulty lie primarily within that individual? Very few of us, if any, would be comfortable with such an assertion about unemployment – it clearly belongs to a long-gone era. Or do they lie, at least in part, in the structures within which that individual exists? For unemployment, this is clearly the case. MacDonald (2009: 347) argues that our perceptions of dyslexia are rooted firmly within the 'his personal trouble' paradigm; and that 'social class positioning and institutional discrimination … shape the experiences of people living with this condition'.

In our teaching and learning in schools, we have come some way towards accepting a social model. We accept completely the need to differentiate and individualize learning so that the classroom is as truly inclusive as is possible, so that each learner, whatever their characteristics and individual traits, can learn and develop according to their own needs and attributes.

But in our formal assessment practice, that premise changes: we revert to thinking of learning difficulties as if they are intrinsic to the individual; and accordingly, in our attempts to help, we focus on those individuals rather than the context within which they function. We do this by assigning people to *categories* of disability (about which we often disagree, sometimes passionately); and then we make compensatory arrangements for those in our assigned categories with the intention that their 'disability' should not constitute a barrier to their achievement.

BARRIERS TO LEARNING

My work involves identifying and responding to different kinds of barriers to learning within the rather privileged context of an all-through, co-ed independent day school. It is privileged in terms of the socioeconomic status of the service users. But it is privileged too in the opportunity it offers to engage with specific learning difficulties in a context that is supportive and, importantly, longitudinal. For example, a difficulty identified in Year 3, and our responses to that difficulty, may be monitored and considered within a stable educational environment over a period of, perhaps, ten years.

In such an environment, the more evident barriers to learning are likely to be understood relatively early in a learner's school life, and classroom practice is adapted to allow for them. It is the more subtle (and often later-emerging) barriers that are being considered here, barriers that have been allowed for effectively enough in the earlier years for them not to be 'disabling', in classrooms where differences between children are accepted and seen as the norm. Through their own efforts as well as an inclusive environment, a number of learners who will later be categorized as disabled compensate for their differences with some success in the earlier years (though often with considerable and unacknowledged effort).

Over time, though, two factors combine to change this. One is the lessening of the extent to which all learners are seen as unique, as being different each in their own way. Instead, as learning and teaching shifts from being child centred to subject centred, there emerges a sense that there is a 'normally learning' majority; and that in comparison with this majority there is a minority who are seen as not 'normally learning' – they come to be seen as being *categorically* different. The second factor may be the way that the effectiveness of a learner's compensating and masking strategies steadily diminishes as they encounter increasing thresholds of demand, and learning characteristics that have not been barriers until now become barriers. Often this may be at the onset of the 'exam years'; sometimes it may not be until the undergraduate years.

During those first ten years of a child's education, then, there is arguably a perceptible and continuous shift in professional thinking. In the early years there is an almost instinctive inclusivity, and acceptance of a social model of disability. Each child is seen as a unique individual, and it is part of the teacher's craft to find ways for all of the individuals in the class to share the learning. In the later years, where subject specialization and formal assessment gain increasing influence, there is an increasing dynamic towards a bio-medical categorization, an allocation of learners to categories in order that they might better fit the demands of the examination system.

CATEGORIZATION, COMPLEXITY AND SUBTLETY

Categorizing is what the human brain *does*, arguably what it is *for*. Learning is about packaging up all our accumulating experiences into usable schemata that allow us to respond to the seething and potentially overwhelming complexity that comprises any one moment of our lives. We categorize or we crash – and this drive to categorize can account for some of the challenges we experience in responding to learners with a specific learning difficulty (SpLD) (dyslexia) .

The categories utilized in learning may be too crude to be fully fit for the purpose, and this seems specially true of our attempts to respond to SpLDs. It is an enormous, dynamic and complex area of study; and we simultaneously comfort and delude ourselves by organizing our limited understandings into deceptively tidy categories. There are at least five potential sources of confusion when we set out to categorize a specific learning difficulty (Weedon and Reid, 2008):

- *Overlap of characteristic features:* pupils who present in the same ways in the classroom may have underlying needs that are very different.
- *Co-morbidity:* there is likely to be more than one SpLD present in the same pupil.
- *Meanings attached to labels:* even when we decide upon a label, it may mean quite different things to different people. There is a continuing lack of consensus about definitions.
- *Different professional perspectives:* the difficulties are compounded still further by the range of different professionals who may be involved with an SpLD child, each approaching the child from the standpoint of their own professional perspective.

- *A description, not a diagnosis*: lastly, there is a spurious precision in our use of these labels. Affixing a label implies some kind of certainty about just what causes the difficulty, what it stems from. Yet the most rigorously derived label for a specific learning difficulty may still be no more than 'a description dignified as a diagnosis' (Whitmore and Bax, 1999).

Despite quite longstanding recognition of all this, practice is changing only slowly. Research from Reading University (by Riddell and Cruddace, reported in *The Times Educational Supplement, Scotland,* 5 March 2010) estimates that 1 in 10 children have a dyslexic or reading disorder, of whom 50% have an overlapping speech and language disorder, 25% have an attention deficit disorder, and 25% a movement disorder. With an increased focus upon and funding for 'dyslexia' training in England, there is real concern that the simplistic use of labelling is going to increase the extent to which co-morbid difficulties may be overlooked, co-morbid difficulties that may in some cases be a primary source of difficulty.

We categorize, then, and seem set to continue to categorize – but we are doing so in a way that we know to be sometimes disorganized, imprecise and too narrowly focused.

BARRIERS TO LEARNING – FOR WHOM ARE THEY LIKELY TO BE IDENTIFIED, AND WHEN?

Schools are instrumental in creating barriers. We are complicit in the social construction of disability – but we have to be. Inevitably, the early school environment places much emphasis on the acquistion of core literacy and numeracy skills – and for the children we are thinking about, this may be something that they cannot do quite as easily as would be expected. The happy pre-schooler becomes perhaps less happy in early primary. Edwards (1993) asks 'if a person's ability to draw is extremely poor, why do we not call this "dyspictoria"?'; then answers his own question: because 'reading and writing are culturally esteemed skills'. Early schooling is profoundly instrumental in the social construction of disability – but arguably it has to be, if it is to help individuals develop skills that are socially valued.

The evidently bright and extroverted child whose literacy is lagging behind the expected levels is likely to attract attention fairly early in their school career, and appropriate action taken. The underlying difficulties will be identified, and addressed; and any residual barriers will be known and allowed for as the child moves up the school. Focused extra tuition will be provided. If residual barriers persist, readers and scribes may be provided. Probably wordprocessing with spellcheck will be encouraged – and the learner understands their own strengths and weaknesses, and develops as a confident and reflective learner who is achieving at an appropriate level.

The child is encountering a socially constructed disability, and a category-driven response is proving effective. The two paradigms are working together harmoniously and symbiotically. But for others, whose individual learning characteristics and traits form less of a barrier during the earlier years, no such intervention is needed, and the child-centred and inclusive nature of early schooling allows learning to proceed appropriately and successfully. For these children, it will be some years before this changes, and the remorselessly increasing demands of the examination hall start to make themselves felt.

THE ROLE OF SOCIAL CLASS POSTIONING

Whether or not the barrier is later identified and acknowledged will depend on a number of factors – but one is likely to be social class positioning. Where teacher and parent expectations are high, and other masking factors are absent (deprivation, poor diet, lack of exposure to complex language, lack of books in the home, etc.), then the barrier may well come to light. The biology teacher may recognize that Sam has an excellent grasp of plant reproduction, but always underperforms in written tests; the English teacher may be impressed by the way Ahmed can talk about the ideas being explored in a poem, but not write about them nearly as well. Parents will share ideas with other parents about the kaleidoscope of sometimes competing therapies and programmes that aim to improve performance and lessen their children's difficulties. These dynamics are there in all schools and families, but they are arguably closer to the surface among more affluent communities and families than among the less socially advantaged.

It is suggested, then, that there may be a 'Matthew effect' in our responses to SpLDs ('For to all those who have, more will be given'; Matthew 25:29). If so, the implications for increasing educational inequity are evident: those with economic or social capital will leverage those resources to enhance their children's academic success.

Scotland views itself as a country characterized by collectivisim and commitment to social justice, with its education system playing a key role in promoting the tradition of democratic intellectualism (Devine, 2006) – but there appear to be indubitable links between the identification of additional support needs and social deprivation, and children identified as having learning difficulties in more socially advantaged schools have higher achievement levels than those so identified in less socially advantaged schools (Riddell *et al.*, 2010).

Dyslexic students now form the largest single group of disabled students in higher education (Weedon and Riddell, 2007) – the proportion of dyslexic students in relation to those with other disabilities has risen from 15% in 1994/5 to 54% in 2004/5 (first-degree full-time students).

Weedon and Riddell found, too, that the highest proportion of dyslexic students were to be found in the more affluent, ancient and prestigious universities, and the lowest number in post-1992 institutions that served a lower socioeconomic catchment. Interestingly (and perhaps part of the same dynamic of expectation and outcome), the first group of students were the most critical of the support they had been given. Disproportionately from independent rather than state schools, supported by families with high educational expectations, financially more likely to be able to pursue an independent identification of a dyslexic difficulty, well supported throughout their school years, students from the higher socioeconomic groups appear more likely to be recognized as dyslexic; and then to make rigorous and demanding use of the support available.

In looking at dispute resolution procedures in Scotland, Riddell *et al.* (2010) found that parents from middle-class backgrounds appeared to use their social and cultural capital more effectively to challenge local authority decisions, and that these same parents were generally more successful than others in persuading professionals to provide additional resources. These students, from more advantaged backgrounds, are likely to have had enhanced experiences of support during the school years, and this in turn enhances their expectations of support through higher education.

Riddell and Weedon argue too that the situation is complex, in that certain categories of difficulty tend to be more stigmatized than others, and these tend to be assigned disproportionately to children living in the most socially disadvantaged neighbourhoods (2009). The converse seems likely also to be true – that other categories of disability, perceived as less stigmatizing, will be disproportionately monopolized by those more socially advantaged. Dyslexia and attention deficit hyperactivity disorder (ADHD) are easier concepts to cope with and respond to than the broader categories of learning and/or behavioural difficulties.

The data and research for higher education are fairly clear, and in the public domain. The same insights for school-age children, and the public examinations through which they must go, appear not to be easily available at the time of writing. But there seems no reason to assume that a similar pattern does not exist, and it seems plausible that any inequities may be more pronounced during the years of compulsory schooling than they are among the smaller, self-selected and socially more uniform population that continues into higher education.

ENCOURAGING A SOCIAL MODEL OF DISABILITY – HOW MIGHT IT HELP?

Riddell *et al.* (2005), writing about higher education, recognize the extent to which our understandings of disability *are* moving towards a socially constructed model – but recognize too the extent to which it remains the case that 'currently disabled students are forced to operate within a system which understands disability in terms of mental or physical deficit' (p. 17), perpetuated by 'a range of bureaucratic and administrative arrangements which promote a medicalised concept of disability'.

Simpson (2005) noted the extent to which, in schools, assessment is a process which is largely separated from teaching and learning. In the daily process of teaching and learning, practitioners are not faced by an 'either/or' choice, between a bio-medical or socially constructed response to learning difficulties. Most practitioners will, justifiably, draw upon a blend of constructs in responding to a learner's needs. For most of us, most of the time, a wise response seems to lie (sometimes rather fluidly) somewhere in between the two. But that flexibility of choice terminates most abruptly when learning is formally assessed.

The Disability Discrimination Act (2005) (DDA) defines a 'disabled person as someone who has a physical or mental impairment that has a substantial and long term adverse effect on his or her ability to carry out normal day-to-day activities'. Clearly this cannot be wholly categorical, and a learner's characteristics might be considered in terms of a continuum, with placement depending upon the extent to which every-day function is impaired: Everyday function impaired significantly ↔ Everyday function impaired to some extent ↔ Everyday function not impaired. Equally clearly, the critical factor in locating an impairment along this continuum must be the extent to which an individual's impairing difference is modest, or may be realistically compensated for.

With this in mind, it is easy to see how we may be comfortable with a social construction under some circumstances, where postioning on the continuum determines in a most obvious way whether or not an individual's characteristics might be regarded as a disability: *(Bio-medical model dominates and categorizing is helpful)* Blind ↔ Partially sighted ↔ Dependent on prescription glasses *(Socially constructed model dominates, and categorizing not needed).* A social construction of disability will be no help towards the left of the continuum – even the most evangelical supporter of inclusive practice will recognize the practical difficulties of teaching everyone Braille, and a bio-medical categorization is clearly helpful. Equally no one would regard the use of prescription glasses as disabling for most wearers. Somewhere along the continuum we have shifted paradigm, enabled to do so by our acceptance of wearing glasses.

But consider for a moment an absurd scenario where the wearing of spectacles was seen to confer an unfair advantage in exams, and all candidates were expected to be spectacle-free unless certified by an optician to have needs that could be met only by allowing the candidate to wear glasses in exams. Suddenly, we create a whole new population of disabled learners, exactly as we do where a learner has, perhaps, weak spelling, slow reading and poor handwriting. For these learners, we have allowed individual differences to be institutionally transformed into disabling factors: Severe dyslexia and consequent functional illiteracy ↔ Clearly defined dyslexic difficulty ↔ Accurate but relatively slow reader with poor handwriting and spelling. Some impairments are arguably self-evidently disabling and sit fairly uncontroversially towards the left of any bio-medical/social construction continuum. But towards the right of the continuum, why accept spectacles and not word-processors?

The answer must be sought primarily among issues of institutional convenience … and in an era where examination boards are commercial concerns, subject to market-place pressures, among issues of user-convenience and marketability. A mass education system has led to a mass assessment system. Examination boards compete for customers, and product marketability is likely to depend upon factors such ease of administration. The logistical imperatives are undeniable: where several hundreds of candidates have to be processed through crowded examination halls to a remorselessly tight schedule, a single desk with pen, question paper and answer booklet comprises a formidably efficient process. It makes no difference if 20% of the candidates are wearing prescription glasses. It would make a lot of difference if large numbers chose to word-process their answers, or if an invigilator could not call out, at the scheduled time, 'Stop writing now. Please pass your completed answer papers …'

This chapter does not argue that one or another model of disability is *better*. It argues instead that both have relevance and value; but that it can only be helpful to generate a dynamic that seeks continuously and imperceptibly, to shift our perceptions a little further away from a bio-medical model whenever it is possible to do so, towards a socially constructed model; and continuously and imperceptibly away from a view that attributes a deficit to an individual, and to look instead at the barriers we construct within the environment.

Fuller and Healey (2009: 76) note the way in which 'the higher education establishment has defended the need for clear qualification criteria based on disability status in order to determine which students should be entitled to alternative forms of assessment' and go on to note the way in which this 'binary divide between disabled and non-disabled students' means that universities force students at some level to 'adopt a disabled identity to obtain the support for learning to which they are entitled'.

Educational practice *is* moving in the right direction. But there is some way to go, and the argument here is that a shift away from institutionally convenient assessment practices towards practices that are more genuinely inclusive would aid that 'paradigm-creep', to the advantage and gain of all concerned:

> If it is valid to assess one student in a certain way, why should it not be equally valid for all? If the quality of the thinking about biology may be validly assessed where candidates A, B and C have someone to read the questions, or have extra time, why should it not be equally valid for candidates D through to Z, should they opt to do so?
>
> It makes every sense. Fine judgments no longer have to be made, by people like me, about which candidates should receive such arrangements (and only the most passionate psychometrician would argue that the instruments used to quantify these difficulties are other than very approximate). It would also be inclusive in the best sense – it changes underlying structures in a way that militates against exclusion (Weedon, 2006).

For policy-makers, the issue is clear: for a number of our pupils and students, we are creating disabilities for no other reason than our own administrative convenience. In itself, this does not seem defensible; and by default seems likely to compound educational inequity, with all the social and economic correlates that such inequity must bring.

At the practitioner level, there is little direct action we can take, other than to be aware of what we are doing, and to broadcast that awareness to all concerned – to colleagues, students, parents, university and college admission staff, potential employers:

> Yes, I am describing this individual as 'disabled' – but really only for the administrative convenience of the assessment industry, and because it is the only way to access fair examination arrangements. In *no* other way at all is there any 'disability'.

We can, too, seek to encourage the uptake of the compensatory arrangements more widely across the social spectrum. Exam boards do their best (and in the context of the Scottish Qualifications Authority it is a very effective best) to make available whatever compensatory arrangements are needed for every individual to demonstrate their true level of attainment. But exam boards can do no more than receive and respond to requests from schools and presenting centres. It is for staff within those schools and presenting centres to make full and assertive use of the available arrangements, so that no longer are they dominated by sectors of society already disproportionately empowered. Easier said than done – but worth trying to do.

SUMMARY

- The continuing debates about the usefulness or existence of specific barriers to learning (such as dyslexia) are a function of our tendency to *categorize* the barriers experienced by learners; and then to seek to *compensate* for those barriers.
- This may be most true of those learners whose specific barriers are not of a severity that has led to early identification/categorization.
- Learners from more advantaged sectors of society are more likely to have such modest difficulties identified/recognized by secondary schools and HE institutions, and to have appropriate accommodation made for them.
- Failure to recognize such barriers among less advantaged learners impacts negatively upon those learners as individuals, as well as upon the economic well-being of the wider community.
- Emphasizing a social model of disability should allow the development of more inclusive educational and assessment practices, thereby reducing the current social inequities of response.

 Discussion Points

- Do you think that your school or institution successfully identifies all those students who might validly request special examination arrangements?
- If so, is it conferring further advantage upon an already privileged section of society?
- If not, what steps might you take to make more rigorous use of the special examination arrangements that are available?

Further Reading

Burr, V. (2003) *Social Constructionism*. London: Routledge. An in-depth but accessible introduction to the ways in which a broad range of personal experiences will in part be socially constructed. Burr considers too some of the limitations of this approach.

Lock, A. and Strong, T. (2010) *Social Constructionism: Sources and Stirrings in Theory and Practice*. Cambridge: Cambridge University Press. Considers how contemporary social constructivism has developed and become a practical tool in understanding the everyday world.

Rapley, M. (2004) *The Social Construction of Intellectual Disability*. Cambridge: Cambridge University Press. Explores in some depth the ways in which apparently individual problems of all kinds are in effect interactional and social products, at least in part.

Trevino, A.J. (2011) *The Social Thought of C. Wright Mills*. Newbury Park, CA: Pine Forge Press. An examination of the beginnings of social constructivist thought. It focuses on Mills' interest in the interactions between personality and social structure, and on how bureaucratization affects power relationships.

References

Barnes, C. (1991) *Disabled People in Britain – the Case for Anti-discrimination Legislation*. London: Hurst & Co.

Devine, T.M. (2006) *The Scottish Nation, 1700–2007*. London: Allen Lane.

Disability Discrimination Act (2005) http://www.opsi.gov.uk/acts/acts2005/ukpga.

Edwards, B. (1993) *Drawing on the Right Side of the Brain*. London: HarperCollins.

Fuller, M. and Healey, M. (2009) 'Assessing disabled students – student and staff experiences of reasonable adjustments', in M. Fuller *et al.* (eds) *Improving Disabled Students' Learning*. London and New York, NY: Routledge.

MacDonald, S.J. (2009) 'Windows of reflection: conceptualising dyslexia using the social model of disability', *Dyslexia*, 15: 347–62.

Oliver, M. (1990) *The Politics of Disablement*. Basingstoke: Macmillan.

Pollak, D. (2005) *Dyslexia, the Self, and Higher Education*. Stoke-on-Trent: Trentham Books.

Rasmussen, P. and Gillberg, C. (1999) 'AD(H)D, hyperkinetic disorders, DAMP, and related behaviour disorders', in K.Whitmore *et al.* (eds) *A Neurodevelopmental Approach to Specific Learning Disorders*. London: MacKeith Press.

Riddell, S., Stead, J., Weedon, E. and Wright, K. (2010) 'Additional support needs reforms and social justice in Scotland', *International Studies in the Sociology of Education*.

Riddell, S., Tinklin,T. and Wilson, A. (2005) *Disabled Students in Higher Education*. London and New York, NY: Routledge.

Riddell, S. and Weedon, E. (2009) 'Managerialism and equalities: tensions withing widening access policy and practice for disabled students in UK universities', in M. Fuller *et al.* (eds) *Improving Disabled Students' Learning*. London and New York, NY: Routledge.

Simpson, M. (2005) *Assessment: Policy and Practice in Education*. Edinburgh: Dunedin.

Singleton, C. (ed.) (1999) *Dyslexia in Higher Education: Policy, Provision and Practice. Report of the National Working Party on Dyslexia in Higher Education*. Hull: University of Hull.

Singleton, C. (2000) 'Recent developments in the identification of dyslexia.' Lecture, De Montfort University.

Tomlinson, S. (1982) *A Sociology of Special Education*. London: Routledge & Kegan Paul.

Tomlinson, S. (1985) 'The expansion of special education', *Oxford Review of Education*, 11: 157–65.

Weedon, C. (2006) 'Exams, disabilities and natural justice', *The Times Educational Supplement, Scotland,* 13 January.

Weedon, C. and Reid, G. (2008) *Special Needs Assessment Profile – Specific Learning Difficulties v. 3 (SNAP-SpLD)*. London: Hodder & Stoughton.

Weedon, E. and Riddell, R. (2007) 'To those that have, shall be given? Differing expectations of support among dyslexic students', in M. Osborne *et al.* (eds) *The Pedagogy of Lifelong Learning*. London and New York, NY: Routledge.

Whitmore, K. and Bax, M. (1999) 'What do we mean by SLD? A historical perspective', in K. Whitmore *et al.* (eds) *A Neurodevelopmental Approach to Specific Learning Disorders*. London: MacKeith Press.

Part II

PERSPECTIVES FROM PRACTICE

6 SPEECH AND LANGUAGE

Janet Farrugia and Janet O'Keefe

Learning objectives

This chapter will help readers to:

- understand what speech, language and communication needs (SLCN) are and how to refer school-aged children for an assessment;
- appreciate, through case histories, the positive impact that speech and language therapy (SLT) can have on a child's ability to make progress, access the curriculum and reach their potential; and
- explore a range of strategies that can support children with SLCN at school and at home.

One in ten children has SLCN. This is equivalent to three children in every primary school classroom (Law *et al.*, 2000). SLCN is the most common type of special educational need (SEN) in children below 7 years of age, and half of all children with SEN have SLCN (the Lamb Inquiry – DCSF, 2009a). Everyone living and working with children and young people enhances communication skills. As a result of this several recent government-commissioned reports have commented on the support for pupils with SLCN in schools and emphasized the need for parents and professionals to work together to improve the educational and life attainments of this group.

The Bercow Report (2008) identified five key themes:

- Communication is crucial.
- Early identification and intervention are essential.
- A continuum of services designed around the family is needed.
- Joint working is critical.
- The current system is characterized by high variability and lack of equity.

Bercow (2008) concluded that the support for pupils with SLCN is highly variable and therefore inequitable. The year 2011 was the National Year of Speech, Language and Communication. It was lead by Jean Gross, Communication Champion in England, to raise awareness and understanding of SLCN, share effective strategies for stimulating and strengthening language and leave, as its legacy, meaningful, long-term benefits. Royal College of Speech and Language Therapists (RCSLT) Chief Executive Officer, Kamini Gadhok, said, in September 2007 at a Speech, Language and Communication Provision Review:

> SLCN needs are the most common disability presenting in early childhood. We know many children are not currently receiving the services they need. Some areas have very long waiting lists and children and families struggle without crucial support. If left untreated, SLCN have a huge impact on the education achievement and the health of a child. The human costs can be devastating with up to a third of children with diagnosed communication problems developing mental illness if untreated.

Conti-Ramsden *et al.* (2002b; 2009) summarized the findings of the Manchester Language Study regarding the educational outcomes of young people with SLCN. This study has been following the progression of children who have attended language units since the age of 7.

The positive findings of the report relating to educational outcomes for language-disordered children are as follows:

- Some 44% obtained at least one GCSE equivalent at the end of secondary education.
- On average, language disordered pupils were taking one more GCSE than they did in the 1990s.
- Around 60% were provided with some type of support during their core examinations.
- Some 90% remained in education post-16 with support
- Some 40% had part-time employment in addition to their studies.

The results indicate that significant progress has been made in the educational outcomes for language-disordered pupils in the last ten years because SLTs are working with teachers and parents to help them differentiate their language and carry out SLT programmes at regular intervals throughout the school week, but more progress is needed. The critical period for progress for children with SLCN is 7–14 years (Botting *et al.*, 2001). The data speak strongly for increased support for these young people and their families into adulthood and specific education and SLT support being available at both primary and secondary-school levels. In summary, social, emotional and behavioural risks seem to be associated with a history of communication impairment but a causal link should not be assumed (Botting and Conti-Ramsden, 2000). The increased risk seems to be related to the quality and quantity of education and therapy support received rather than the fact that the individual has a diagnosis of SLCN. The needs of young people with SLCN should be recognized and provided for in a wider range of ways as they reach adulthood too (Conti-Ramsden and Botting, 2008).

Pupils with SLCN may present in the classroom as:

- off-task;
- intolerant of loud sounds;
- not able to follow instructions;
- not able to conform;
- having poor discrimination of sounds (may show in spelling);
- 'in a world of their own' and often needing messages repeated;
- copying peers and the last to carry out instructions;
- continuously asking for help (if they are aware of their problems) or never asking for help (if they are unaware of their difficulties or are too embarrassed);
- having difficulty understanding the meanings of concepts such as 'more/less', 'same/different' or 'before/after', which can affect lessons such as maths, science, history and geography;
- using the wrong word;
- having poor grammar – often more obvious in written form;
- having sequencing difficulties;
- having difficulty categorizing and grouping information;
- having poor social skills;
- very literal – getting hold of the wrong end of the stick;
- having unclear speech and poor spelling;
- dysfluent (stammering);
- having a continuous hoarse voice.

In order to obtain a diagnosis of a child's SLCN, the child must be assessed by an SLT who is registered with the Health Professions Council (HPC). All SLTs must be registered with the HPC as it is a protected professional title.

SLTs work with children with feeding, eating, drinking and swallowing difficulties; speech difficulties (pronunciation); verbal comprehension difficulties (understanding what is said); expressive language difficulties (using words to express themselves in meaningful and well structured sentences verbally); and/or social communication difficulties (difficulties understanding and using the rules of communication, such as how to start, maintain and finish conversations appropriately). They may also work on written language difficulties (dyslexia).

SLTs may be employed by NHS Trusts, LEAs, schools, charities, independent services or be sole traders. There is open referral to all speech and language therapy (SLT) services in the UK which means that any parent, carer, health education or social services practitioner can, with the parents'/carers' consent, refer a child of any age for a SLT assessment if they have concerns about any aspect of a child's ability to understand spoken language, express themselves or use language socially. This can be done via the local NHS SLT service or an assessment can be commissioned privately by a parent/carer, school or LEA from an independent SLT. The earlier in a child's life that SLCN are identified, the earlier appropriate intervention and therapy can start, and the more effective it can be (Bercow, 2008). This is more likely to prevent educational and social difficulties in the future (Conti-Ramsden *et al.*, 2001).

Assessment by an SLT typically involves a combination of the following:

- *Case history*: to ascertain any contributing medical, educational or social issues (such as hearing loss, family history, non-verbal cognitive skills).
- *Observation*: for example, symbolic development, attention, eye contact, functional use and understanding of language.
- *Formal standardized assessments*.
- *Information from all relevant professionals and carers*.

Children with statements of SEN may have their SLT provision funded by the LEA as part of their statement and this may be provided by an NHS or independent therapist or by the school as part of their fees for attendance. It is the integration of SLT with education that is the most effective in progressing children with communication disorders where therapy can inform teaching and teaching can inform therapy (Conti-Ramsden *et al.*, 2009; Durkin *et al.*, 2009). Parents and professionals report that pupils benefit when SLT is integrated into the curriculum (Reid *et al.*, 1996).

SLCNS WHICH AFFECT A CHILD'S ACCESS TO THE CURRICULUM

Poor Attention and Listening Skills

If children are not paying attention, they cannot listen fully, and if they are not listening their understanding will be compromised. However poor attention and listening can sometimes be the result and not the cause of comprehension difficulties. This can be appreciated if we put ourselves in the position of having to listen to someone speaking a foreign language or somebody discussing a complicated topic. When we don't understand we lose concentration and switch off.

Receptive Language/Comprehension/Understanding Difficulties

This includes understanding what others say (receptive language or comprehension). If a child is slow with understanding but is following normal developmental patterns then this is called delayed receptive language. If a child's language development is unusual and not following normal patterns, then it is described as disordered. This could be due to the following.

Auditory processing difficulties

Auditory processing difficulties affects the ability to recognise and interpret sounds and impacts on the efficiency and speed of processing the meaning of spoken language.

This can result in misinterpretation and/or the speed of understanding. Consequently they are unable to retain and understand everything that is said. Auditory processing disorders impact significantly on a child's ability to process language and to focus on what is being said against background noise. There is evidence to suggest that background noise levels in the average classroom are higher than optimal conditions for understanding speech (Picard and Bradley, 2001).

Poor short-term auditory memory

This impacts on children's ability to process and retain lengthy verbal instructions/information. This difficulty can sometimes lead to the child seeming disobedient or stubborn when in fact they have not understood because too much information has been given to them at one time. As a consequence messages need to be repeated and chunked into smaller units.

Often this difficulty can be overlooked as many children learn to watch and follow what their peers are doing in the classroom and therefore are the last to carry out an instruction. As they grow older their difficulties become more apparent as they cannot continue to 'get by' through copying their peers. Others may be continuously asking for help or conversely may never ask for help. They are likely to have difficulties transferring information from short-term auditory memory into working memory. This may result in inconsistencies in understanding and learning, so a child may appear to have grasped something and understood it one day, but have completely forgotten it the next day.

Limited receptive vocabulary

This occurs when a child finds it hard to learn new words. Learning vocabulary is more complex than it may at first appear. The child has to be certain to what a new word is referring. When it is an object which is present and being pointed at, this difficulty is minimized. However, when more abstract words are used within a sentence, it can be much more difficult for a child to work out what the word refers to and consequently its meaning (for example, 'The polar bear is an *endangered* species'). Many children, might think that this means that the polar bear is dangerous because 'en*danger*ed' and '*danger*ous' sound similar. A child who has no language difficulties is likely to revise this opinion if they then hear, 'They therefore need protection'. This is because they will realize that their first interpretation of the meaning of the word 'endangered' is not consistent with this second sentence. They may ask the teacher to explain the meaning of the word 'endangered' or deduce it from the context. However a child with a receptive language disorder may not have understood the second sentence ('They therefore need protection') either because they would still have been trying to process the first sentence and/or because they also do not know the meaning of the word 'protection'.

Vocabulary deficits become cumulative: the less a child understands, the less they are going to understand: conversely if the child learns new words easily and has a good vocabulary, they are therefore in a very good position to be able to extend this.

It is also important to appreciate that understanding a new word is of limited benefit to a child if they do not recognize it when they hear it again. Children with language disorders find it hard to hold the phonological composition of words within their memory store. The normally developing child can usually repeat a new word quite accurately and recognize it after hearing it several times. However a child with a language disorder may need to hear the word repeated many more times before they can recognize it. If they also had a speech difficulty they will be unable to repeat the word in order to consolidate the sound patterns within it. This then makes it harder for them to remember it.

Speech Difficulties

It is useful to be aware of the different stages that children commonly pass through on their route to full intelligibility, in order to judge the relative maturity of a child's speech compared with others of their age and whether a particular child's development is typical or not.

Delayed speech

Many children have immaturities with speech which can be considered part of normal development (such as 'th' pronounced as 'f' or 'r' as 'w'). Children with difficulties pronouncing sounds may be following normal developmental patterns but later than normal – this is delayed speech. Most children with delayed speech will have grown out of this by the time they start school.

Children with disordered speech

Such children do not follow the typical pattern of normal speech development. Even though they may 'hear' a word correctly, they are unable to retain the correct phonological composition of the sounds within the word in order to lay down an appropriate motor pattern so they can repeat the word accurately. In its most severe form a child can be virtually unintelligible. This is called a 'phonological disorder'.

The child with verbal dyspraxia

This child has normal muscle development in the oral area, but the neural connection from their brain to their oral muscles (tongue, lips and palate) is impaired so they have difficulty pronouncing sounds and/or saying them at speed, particularly in complex words. Some children may also have difficulty moving their lips and tongue for non-speech activities such as licking, chewing and sucking. In its most severe form a child may be unable to say an isolated sound at will and therefore effectively be unable to speak; in its milder form a child may struggle to pronounce complex combinations of sounds like 'str' or multisyllabic words such as 'hippopotamus'.

Unfortunately there are some children who have such a severe form of dyspraxia (often referred to as *apraxia*) that they require alternative or augmentative communication systems. This can be in the form of signs/gestures (such as Makaton) and sign languages such as Signalong, Sign Supported English or Paget Gorman Signed Speech. Some children need the use of a voice output communication aid (VOCA) which is a computer-type device whose primary function is to use electronically stored speech as a means of communication.

 Case Study

Fred was diagnosed with verbal dyspraxia when he was at his infant school. He received blocks of SLT in his local clinic as well as within school but only made limited progress. When he was 9 years old his parents became increasingly concerned as he was struggling within school both academically and socially as he still could not communicate intelligibly. This was brought home to them on a school trip when his mother witnessed Fred raising his hand to ask a question to a museum guide and his teacher indicated that she should choose another pupil as she would not understand Fred. He was assessed by an educational psychologist as having average cognitive ability and an SLT carried out a detailed assessment making recommendations for a minimum of three sessions of SLT a week delivered within a specialist school environment for children with specific speech and language disorders. His mother reports: 'Fred is now a happy and confident child who is starting to talk clearly and achieve the potential that he clearly has. At the end of Year 6 Fred achieved a Level 4 in SATs in science.'

Expressive Language Difficulties

The development of syntax or grammar is the structure of language of which speakers are often unaware. The learning of grammar does not come to an end until late childhood. Children learning language use simplified grammar which becomes increasingly complex as the child matures. Expressive language difficulties will impact on written language too. There may or may not be an identifiable cause. Difficulties with expressive language include the following:

Delayed language

A child with delayed language speaks in an immature way like a younger child, and can nearly always be understood. Errors may include confusion with pronouns, immature forms and simplification of grammar and generally short sentences with little evidence of complex clauses, beyond those joined with 'and' (e.g. 'Mummy driving car. He gone to shops and buyed some Christmas things like a Christmas Tree').

Disordered language

A child with disordered language does not follow the normal patterns of language development and can produce some very unusual sentences which often do not follow regular grammatical rules and as such cannot easily be understood. These are some examples of sentences from children with disordered language produced when trying to retell a simple story:

> Come here but he didn't pull his drivers and then he got in there and then he pushed him off (child aged 6).
>
> When she ... when monkey couldn't remember he have to find this treasure at once. That's a good idea thought the ... she said. She thought ... she find a pineapple. When she found there's a baraver she found a red long skirt and ... and acourse there in things – the cage (child aged 10).

A child with a very severe language disorder may fulfil the diagnosis of specific language impairment.

Word-finding difficulties

These are when a child recognizes a word if it is said to them, but is unable to recall it effectively. Word-finding difficulties may be due to a semantic error in that a child may call a 'banana' an 'orange' or a phonological error when they would say a nonsense word which often sounds like the target word. Phonological errors refer to when a child is unable to remember the exact sounds and/or sequences of sounds within a word. This is more likely to happen with lengthy words and/or phonologically complex words (such as 'anemone', 'statistics' or 'binoculars'). However, for children with really severe word-finding difficulties, they may struggle to retrieve relatively simple words. Children with word-finding difficulties will be very hesitant when talking as they struggle to find the right words to use, which can cause them immense frustration.

 Case Study

Sophie was always a happy child but, when she was about 2, her mother noticed that she wasn't putting words together as she should, and that she often couldn't understand Sophie. She couldn't really talk in sentences and also found it hard to follow other people's conversation. Sophie always struggled in school as she found it hard to follow the teacher. She also found making friends very hard because she couldn't follow their conversations and so became very isolated, and by the time she was 15 she came very close to a breakdown. Sophie's parents obtained reports from an SLT, an educational psychologist and a child psychiatrist as part of a statutory assessment. Her mother stated:

> I still remember the emotion of finally having my worries confirmed and explained – Sophie was *not* just shy, she *didn't* have learning difficulties, she had a severe expressive speech and language disorder and moderate difficulties with her receptive language including auditory recall and speed of processing – no wonder she couldn't follow the teacher or keep up in class.

Sophie now has a statement of special educational needs providing her with intensive SLT as part of her educational curriculum.

Speech and language disorder/specific language impairment may be associated with dyslexia/written language disorder and may not be noticed until a child is at school. They may appear to have developed language and speech quite adequately but then teachers notice that they may find it difficult to understand certain things such as complex grammar, certain concepts or non-literal language. They may also find it hard to express themselves when trying to convey more complicated ideas and thoughts. These children may also have word-finding difficulties.

Developmental written language disorder/dyslexia refers to difficulties with reading, writing and spelling. A child may be considered to have dyslexia if, in spite of adequate teaching, the child has specific persistent difficulties with reading and writing in comparison with their abilities in other spheres, to a degree sufficient to prevent school work from reflecting their true ability and knowledge. Early identification of dyslexia is essential in order to ensure the child receives appropriate help. The earlier the difficulties are identified, the greater the likelihood of successful remediation. The case history of a dyslexic child may reveal early previously undiagnosed language difficulties that only become of recognized significance in the light of emerging reading and writing difficulties.

Snowling *et al.* (2006) state that 'Children with Dyslexia and Specific Language Impairment typically share a continuity of risk for decoding deficits in reading that can be traced to phonological problems, whereas children who have wider language problems are at risk of reading comprehension deficits'. From available evidence they proposed:

> that the probability of a child with oral language difficulties developing reading problems (and the nature of these problems) depends on a complex interaction of risk and protective factors. From the clinical perspective, an important protective factor is the availability of appropriate intervention, delivered at the right time, to foster oral and written language skills.

Social communication and pragmatic language difficulties

 Case Study

James was diagnosed with autism (at the more severe end of the scale) at the age of 22 months. Following lots of appointments with various different professionals James's parents were getting no further forward with making sense of anything. James was 'spiralling' out of control and it seemed as though there was absolutely nothing that his parents could do! James had weekly SLT over quite a substantial period of time and his parents carried out activities daily in between therapy sessions following a speech and language programme which they could share with his nursery and primary school teachers. The SLT devised a 'list' of ten or so items/activities each week that his parents were to work on. Using these 'positives' they worked forwards with a programme that once they had completed a few weeks, James could successfully complete most of the items on an A4 sheet.

(Continued)

(Continued)

With all this success James's parents became much more motivated than they had been in the months previous. When James went to school he had a statutory assessment and his LEA issued a statement of special educational needs and James's therapy transferred to his mainstream primary school with his teaching assistant attending SLT sessions with him and carrying out the daily programme activities.

Children with social communication/pragmatic language difficulties have problems using language to communicate effectively with others. They struggle to appropriately use language (such as requesting, informing and persuading) and to adapt their language appropriately in different situations and to different audiences. They find it difficult to provide relevant background information to unfamiliar listeners and may make inappropriate or off-topic comments. They generally understand things very literally so struggle with sarcasm and idioms. They may appear to be rude or manipulative. For example when told, 'we know that we don't push when waiting in line don't we?' they may reply 'yes' or 'no' without changing their behaviour. They struggle to follow conversational rules such as turn taking (they often monopolise conversations on a favoured topic), to use appropriate facial expressions and eye contact and to maintain appropriate physical distance when communicating. This all has a significant impact on their social communication skills and their ability to make and maintain friends. They are at increased risk of bullying.

Children with pragmatic comprehension difficulties can have a good understanding of semantics (the meaning of words and language). However, they will have difficulty inferring from context which meaning is intended. For example, most children of 10 years of age, upon hearing expressions such as 'You'd better pull your socks up' or 'It's raining cats and dogs', are able to deduce that a literal interpretation is not plausible in the context in which it has been said. However, children with pragmatic comprehension difficulties may not.

Semantic-pragmatic language disorder refers to the child who has difficulties with both understanding the meaning of words (semantics) and the development of the appropriate social use of language in different contexts (pragmatics). Many children with a diagnosis of semantic pragmatic disorder have a diagnosis of autistic spectrum disorder.

EDUCATIONAL PROVISION FOR CHILDREN WITH SLCN

Children who have SLCN which are preventing them from accessing the curriculum need to be assessed and their needs described in a statement of special educational needs so that SLT can be quantified and specified as an educational provision.

Direct SLT, no matter how intensive, is of limited benefit unless it is carried over into the child's school and home. This is because communication is something that goes on throughout the child's day and cannot be restricted to a few hours a week, when in the company of a SLT. Therefore a great deal of any SLT's time will involve training teachers and parents to ensure the child is helped to practise their therapy techniques and strategies at various times throughout the day in a variety of different contexts as an educational provision. Law *et al.* (2000) have stated:

> The emphasis is the embedding in the curriculum. It is important to ensure that therapists frame their intervention such that it is relevant to the student's educational experience and not something 'other' as has often been the case with clinic based models of delivery. This is not implying that the therapy should be indirect.

Children who have good speech and language skills are at an advantage when they learn to read and spell as the development of both spoken and written language skills is closely linked. Conversely, children who are having difficulties with speech and language development are at risk of having associated literacy difficulties. Frustration and evasion are understandable sequallae to the educational problems and daily ordeal of school work for these children.

 Discussion Points

The following discussion points arise from the case studies:

Fred

- Fred's verbal dyspraxia was so severe that his blocks of SLT were insufficient for him to make significant progress. A child like Fred often needs to practise speech sounds or words up to 1,000 times before they are firmly established as motor engrams.
- Fred needed such intensive SLT that it became impossible for him to remain in a mainstream school for many reasons, including his consequential loss of self-esteem, limited friendships and the amount of time he needed out of the classroom in order to be able to work on his speech.

Sophie

- Despite her severe expressive speech and language and moderate receptive language disorders Sophie 'managed' in mainstream and obtained five low-grade GSCEs. However, does this academic achievement constitute success when she was unable to go into a shop, use public transport, make a phone call, establish friendships or go out socially with her peers? Consideration needs to be given to a child's functional communication and life skills. Consequently, Sophie required a specialist post-16 placement that offered her this as well as intensive SLT as an integral part of her curriculum.

James

- James's SLT, teachers and family worked closely together as part of a multidisciplinary team and, as a result, he had a successful mainstream placement for his primary school education.

Children with severe and significant receptive language disorder may need direct SLT as an educational provision focusing on specific areas, such as the development of the understanding of grammar, vocabulary and semantic knowledge and helping the child to learn strategies, such as visualization, to support poor auditory memory. A great deal of the SLT's time should focus on training teachers in ways to simplify their language and provide visual support to enable children to understand the lesson delivery more effectively.

Children with severe dyspraxia and disordered speech generally require direct SLT as an educational provision. In order for this to be effective the SLT needs to carry out a very detailed analysis of the child's speech in order to reach a hypothesis as to where the breakdown in speech development has occurred. Following this the SLT should put together a very structured programme and work with the child on an individual basis, the frequency of which will depend on the severity of the child's difficulty. In order for this therapy to be effective and generalized into the child's everyday speech, it will be necessary for a teaching assistant, learning support assistant, SLT assistant or the parents to sit in on at least one session each week. A child with a severe speech disorder or dyspraxia will be affected in many ways in relation to their access to the curriculum.

Research has shown definite benefits for direct therapy for children with expressive language disorders as an educational provision (Law *et al.*, 2003). The frequency of therapy depends on many factors, including the severity of the child's language disorder, the knowledge of their teachers and the educational environment in which the child is educated. However, as with all SLT, it has to be accompanied by educating the child's teachers and parents and ensuring the generalization of the skills and strategies taught.

In therapy for written language disorders the therapist must be aware of the relationship between spoken and written language disorder. The SLT's knowledge and skills (such as linguistics and phonetics) mean that they are ideally placed to contribute to the management of children with dyslexia. When providing therapy to children with a spoken language disorder, the SLT will consider written language skills as part of the overall intervention programme. The discharge of a child who is speaking but not reading or writing or showing age-appropriate prerequisite skills cannot be seen as a successful discharge. Intervention should be offered utilizing the skills of teaching staff at all times.

To conclude, we agree with John Bercow that children with SLCN need to be identified early and SLT provision integrated across home and school settings by parents, therapists and teachers working together as part of the multidisciplinary team supporting the child to achieve their potential because communication is crucial to every child's development for both educational attainment and successful life outcomes. (Table 6.1 lists some suggested strategies to help children with SLCN.)

Table 6.1 Suggested strategies to help all children with SLCN and which impairments they specifically target

Activities	Attention and listening	Receptive language	Speech	Expressive language	Dyslexia	Pragmatic language
1. Familiar routines with a beginning, middle and end so children always know where they are meant to be, what they are doing, for how long and what they will do next. Give plenty of notice of any planned changes (visual timetables)	✗	✗			✗	✗
2. Sit the child away from distracting areas (not facing windows/door/other children with attention problems) and keep the environment as quiet as possible/position child near teacher, away from outside noise	✗	✗			✗	✗
3. Say the child's name to ensure attention. Use a physical prompt if necessary and wait until the child is looking at you before speaking	✗	✗			✗	✗
4. Keep language simple and clear. Give instructions in the order in which they should be carried out avoiding 'before' and 'after'. Keep language relevant and concise. Make everything explicit for the child. Use key words	✗	✗			✗	✗
5. Break up longer paragraphs into shorter ones and then ask children to 'para-phrase' them in their own words before proceeding to the next part	✗	✗			✗	✗
6. Do not rely on verbal communication alone for expression or reception. Use and encourage visual aids or physical prompts wherever possible. Put instructions in writing or use pictures/symbols. Use and encourage body language and gesture	✗	✗	✗	✗	✗	✗
7. Speak slowly, clearly and loud enough	✗	✗			✗	✗
8. When teaching, explain the main content of the lesson before the teaching begins and refer back to previous associated lessons	✗	✗			✗	✗

(Continued)

Table 6.1 (Continued)

Activities	Attention and listening	Receptive language	Speech	Expressive language	Dyslexia	Pragmatic language
9. Allow time for the child to process what has been said and give them time to respond (30 seconds as an average)	×	×	×	×	×	×
10. Encourage the child to ask for help/repetitions (e.g. 'Please can you repeat that') or a visual means of communicating this request (symbol or picture)	×	×			×	×
11. Teach concept words in pairs (e.g. 'big' in contrast to 'small')	×	×			×	×
12. Introduce new vocabulary beforehand and practise use	×	×	×	×	×	×
13. Question with real interest, comment on what the child is doing and encourage emphatically			×	×		
14. Actively stimulate conversation beyond the here and now			×			×
15. Try not to finish the sentence for them/interrupt while they are speaking … and try to stop others in the class from doing so			×	×		
16. Rephrase correctly what the child has said by saying it back to them (modelling)			×	×		
17. Use 'scaffolding' (for verbal and written) (e.g. who/what/where/when/how; beginning/middle/end)			×			×
18. Have discreet signals for when to stop talking (e.g. 'stop' gesture with hand)						×
19. Run social communication skills groups (explicit teaching programme)			×			×
20. Introduce a buddy system (with a socially able child)	×		×			×

SUMMARY

- The SLCN difficulties that occur in school-aged children and that affect access to the curriculum are attention and listening; receptive language/verbal comprehension/understanding; speech (pronounciation); expressive language; and social communication.
- SLT should be an integrated educational provision to enable the child with SLCN to achieve their potential.
- There are key strategies for the home and school that can help support a child with SLCN.

Further Reading

Attwood, T. (2006) *The Complete Guide to Asperger Syndrome.* London: Jessica Kingsley. This is a fully comprehensive, must-have and easy-read text for anyone living or working with individuals with Asperger syndrome.

Birnbaum, R. (2010) *Choosing a School for a Child with Special Needs.* London: Jessica Kingsley. This gives advice to parents of children with all sorts of SEN on how to choose a school for their child.

Bowen, C. (2010) *Children's Speech Sound Disorders.* Oxford: Wiley-Blackwell. An exceptionally practical book.

Hatcher, C. (ed.) (2011) *Making Collaborative Practice Work: A Model for Teachers and SLTs.* Guildford: J. & R. Press; Hilari, K. and Botting, N. (eds) (2011) *The Impact of Communication Disability across the Lifespan.* Guildford: J. & R. Press; Trott, K., Stackhouse, J. and Clegg, J. (2011) *Children's Language and Literacy Groups: A Practical Resource for Students and Staff in Nurseries and Schools.* Guildford: J. & R. Press; Roulstone, S. and McLeod, S. (eds) (2011) *Listening to Children and Young People with SLCN.* Guildford: J. & R. Press. These are the most up-to-date and pertinent books for SLCN.

Kersner, M. and Wright, J.A. (2001) *Speech and Language Therapy: The Decision-making Process when Working with Children.* London: David Fulton. This book helps the reader to understand the decision-making process in the assessment and management of children with speech and language problems. It also illustrates how decision-making can change within different environments and with different client groups. It also describes ways in which speech and language therapists work with other professionals. This book is relevant to speech and language therapy students and NQTs, specialist teachers in training and SENCOs in particular.

Logue, M. and Conradi, P. (2010) *The King's Speech: How One Man Saved the British Monarchy.* London: Quercus. This book, of course, epitomizes why speech and language therapy is so important as a profession. It truly makes a difference to the educational and life outcomes of individuals for ever.

Row, S. (2005) *Surviving the Special Educational Needs System: How to be a Velvet Bulldozer.* London: Jessica Kingsley. This book gives a parent's perspective on having a child with SEN and accessing the help and support they need in school.

Wells, B. and Stackhouse, J. (1997) *Children's Speech and Literacy Difficulties: A Psycholinguistic Framework*. Oxford: Wiley-Blackwell. This book is useful to show how a psycholinguistic approach can be used in assessing speech processing in children. It uses case studies to interpret a child's performance within a psycholinguistic model and, at the end of each section, it has questions to test the reader's understanding of what they have read. It will be of interest to all professionals working with children with speech and language difficulties to help them understand the importance of detailed assessment to ensure appropriate therapeutic intervention.

Useful Websites

www.ican.org.uk
www.afasic.org.uk
www.wordswell.co.uk
www.speechandlanguage-therapy.com
www.talkingpoint.org.uk
www.thecommunicationtrust.org.uk
www.comunicationsforum.org.uk
www.rcslt.org
www.helpwithtalking.com

References

Bercow, J. (2008) *A Review of Services for Children and Young People (0–19) with Speech, Language and Communication Needs*. London: DCSF.

Botting, N. and Conti-Ramsden, G. (2000) 'Social and behavioural difficulties in children with language impairment', *Child Language Teaching and Therapy*, 16: 105–20.

Botting, N., Faragher, B., Simkin, Z., Knox, E. and Conti-Ramsden, G. (2001) 'Predicting pathways of specific language impairment: what differentiates good and poor outcome?', *Journal of Child Psychology and Psychiatry and Allied Disciplines*, 42: 1013–20.

Conti-Ramsden, G. and Botting, N. (2008) 'Emotional health in adolescents with and without a history of specific language impairment (SLI)', *Journal of Child Psychology and Psychiatry*, 49: 516–25.

Conti-Ramsden, G., Botting, N., Knox, E. and Simkin, Z. (2002a) 'Different school placements following language unit attendance: which factors affect language outcome?', *International Journal of Language and Communication Disorders*, 37: 185–95.

Conti-Ramsden, G., Botting, N., Simkin, Z. and Knox, E. (2001) 'Follow-up of children attending infant language units: outcomes at 11 years of age', *International Journal of Language and Communication Disorders*, 36: 207–19.

Conti-Ramsden, G., Durkin, K., Simkin, Z. and Knox, E. (2009). 'Specific language impairment and school outcomes. I. Identifying and explaining variability at the end of compulsory education', *International Journal of Language and Communication Disorders*, 44: 15–35.

Conti-Ramsden, G., Knox, E., Botting, N. and Simkin, Z. (2002b) 'Educational placements and National Curriculum Key Stage 2 test outcomes of children with a history of specific language impairment', *British Journal of Special Education*, 29: 76–82.

DCSF (2009a) *Special Educational Needs and Parental Confidence* (the Lamb Inquiry). London: HMSO.

DCSF (2009b) *Independent Review of the Primary Curriculum* (the Rose Report). Nottingham: DCSF Publications.

Durkin, K., Simkin, Z., Knox, E. and Conti-Ramsden, G. (2009) 'Specific language impairment and school outcomes. II. Educational context, student satisfaction, and post-compulsory progress', *International Journal of Language and Communication Disorders*, 44: 36–55.

Easton, C., Sheach, S. and Easton, S. (1997) 'Teaching vocabulary to children with word finding difficulties using a combined semantic and phonological approach: an efficacy study', *Child Language Teaching and Therapy*, 13: 125–42.

Hirschman, M. (2000) 'Language repair via metalinguistic means', *International Journal of Language and Communication Disorders*, 35: 251–68.

Law, J., Garrett, Z., and Nye, C. (2003) 'SLT interventions for children with primary speech and language delay or disorder', *Cochrane Database of Systematic Reviews*, issue 3 (art. no. CD004110; DOI 10.1002/14651858.CD004110).

Law, J., Lindsay, G., Peacey, N., Gascoigne, M., Soloff, N., Radford, J., Band, S. and Fitzgerald, L. (2000) *Provision for Children with Speech and Language Needs in England and Wales: Facilitating Communication between Education and Health Services*. DfES Publications (http://www.dfes.gov.uk/research/).

Locke, A., Ginsborg, J. and Peers, I. (2002) 'Development and disadvantage: implications for early years', *International Journal of Language and Communication Disorders*, 37: 3–15.

Picard, M. and Bradley, J.S. (2001) 'Revisiting speech interference in classrooms', *Audiology*, 40: 221–44.

RCSLT (1996) *Communicating Quality 2: Professional Standards for Speech and Language Therapists*. London: RCSLT.

RCSLT (2005) *Clinical Guidelines by Consensus*. London: RCSLT.

RCSLT (2006) *Communicating Quality 3: Guidance on Best Practice in Service Organisation and Provision*. London: RCSLT.

Reid, J., Millar, S., Tait, L., Donaldson, M., Dean, E.C., Thomson, G.O.B. and Grieve, R. (1996) *Pupils with Special Educational Needs: The Role of SLTs., Interchange* 43. Edinburgh: SOEID.

Snowling, M.J. and Hayiou-Thomas, M.E. (2006) 'The dyslexia spectrum: continuities between reading, speech, and language impairments', *Topics in Language Disorders*, 26: 110–26.

7 AUDITORY PROCESSING DISORDER

Tony Sirimanna

Learning objectives

This chapter will help readers to:

- understand auditory processing disorder (APD) and its diagnosis and management;
- appreciate its prevalence and pathophysiology, and its presentation and co-morbid conditions; and
- understand how a child with suspected APD is assessed.

INTRODUCTION

In the UK over the last decade, there has been an increasing awareness of APD among professionals as well as the public. This has led not only to an increase in the demand on a handful of services providing APD diagnosis but also a significant burden on the already overstretched educational services for children with additional needs. On the other hand, disagreement among professionals, a lack of good-quality research on evaluating diagnostic and especially remediation approaches, and the unavailability of comprehensive service models in the UK have led to confusion among professionals and frustration among the public, especially parents. The response to this demand from UK professionals has been slow, although the British Society of Audiology has made some attempt to resolve these issues through its APD Interest Group (www. thebsa.org.uk). While recognizing the fact that there is still a lot more work to be done, this chapter provides an overview of the current understanding of APD children from a UK perspective.

DEFINITION OF APD

Over the last ten years there has been considerable scrutiny of the definition of APD, with attempts to increase the clarity and to remove ambiguity. The Bruton Consensus Conference in April 2000 (Jerger and Musiek, 2000), convened for agreeing on the 'diagnosis of APD in school-aged children', was probably the first such attempt, and the group defined APD as 'a deficit in the processing of information that is specific to the auditory modality'. The conference agreed that there are other conditions with a similar presentation such as ADHD (attention deficit hyperactivity disorder) or ADD (attention deficit disorder), ASD (autistic spectrum disorder), SLI (specific language impairment) and cognitive impairment, and therefore the tests that were available at that time may not diagnose APD unless a minimum battery of tests was used.

In early 2002 the author raised APD as an important developing area in paediatric audiology in the UK at a British Society of Audiology (BSA) Paediatric Audiology Interest Group (PAIG) meeting that led to establishing an APD Interest Group in October 2003 under the auspices of the BSA. One of the first actions of this group was to discuss, debate and agree on a definition for APD. This led to the working definition 'Hearing disability resulting from impaired brain function and characterized by atypical recognition, discrimination, segregation or ordering of non-linguistic auditory stimuli', thus dissociating auditory from language processing.

In 2005 the American Speech-Language-Hearing Association (ASHA) released a position statement that defined APD as:

> difficulties in the processing of auditory information in the central nervous system (CNS) as demonstrated by poor performance in one or more of the following skills: sound localisation and lateralisation; sense of movement of sound, auditory discrimination; auditory pattern recognition; temporal aspects of audition, including temporal integration, temporal discrimination (e.g. temporal gap detection), temporal ordering and temporal masking, auditory performance in competing acoustic signals (including dichotic listening), and auditory performance with degraded acoustic signals (www.asha.org).

Thus, the complex auditory functions were described beyond what is determined by pure tone audiometry (PTA), reiterating the fact that PTA does not really examine a person's ability to hear in normal listening conditions. The association went on to state that the 'diagnosis of APD requires demonstration of a deficit in neural processing of auditory stimuli that is not due to higher order language, cognitive, or related factors'.

More recently, the BSA APD steering group has reviewed its definition of APD and has agreed that APD is due to impaired neural function involving the auditory pathways leading to poor perception of speech and non-speech sounds. The reader is encouraged to visit the BSA website for an update and to follow the latest publications by the UK APD steering group.

PREVALENCE OF APD

In 1997 Chermak and Musiek estimated prevalence in children to be 2–3%. This rises to 10–20% in adults, probably due to neurological and neuro-degenerative disorders, suggesting that prevalence may increase with age (Cooper and Gates, 1991). Prevalence of APD in children in the UK is unknown, but it is likely to be many times more frequent than permanent congenital hearing impairment (PCHI).

PROCESSING OF AUDITORY INFORMATION

Hearing difficulties are often associated with a measurable deficit (impairment) on pure tone audiometry. The incidence of permanent hearing impairment in children increases from 1 per 1,000 at birth to 1.6 per 1,000 in 9–16-year-olds (Fortnum *et al.*, 2001), with a larger number having temporary hearing loss due to middle ear effusions ('glue ear') or acute middle-ear infections during the first 5–7 years of life. As pure tone audiometry, the main measure of hearing impairment, is carried out in a sound-treated or sound-proof room, it does not reflect the child's functioning in a normal day-to-day listening environment. There is a comparatively large number of children, as indicated by the prevalence studies, who have significant difficulties with hearing in such adverse acoustic conditions, and these children may have disabilities similar to those experienced by children with permanent or temporary hearing loss.

The processing ability of the human brain is unimaginable and the complexity of the sensory systems in place to sense the world we live in is enormous. At any given time the human brain receives multiple information through various sensory systems, including hearing and vision. Each sensation is physically different and therefore requires to be transformed into a language that the brain can understand before being processed (see Figure 7.1).

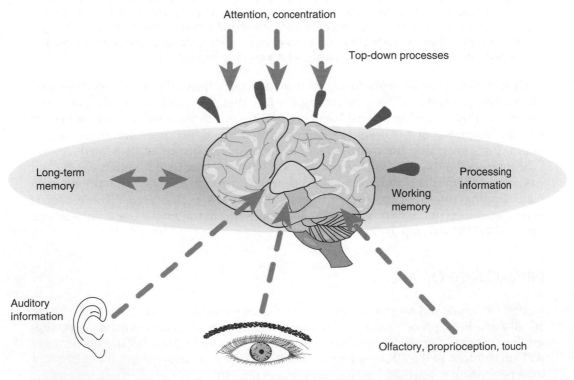

Figure 7.1 Sensory processing: simplified model and top-down influences

Every word we hear has a three-dimensional pattern consisting of loudness (intensity), and pitch (frequency) that changes in time. Each word therefore has a unique pattern and we store these patterns in our long-term memory through repeated exposure for future use along with associations, such as pictures, experiences, etc. The auditory system should have the capability of transporting these patterns from the ear to the place in the brain where pattern matching takes place without distorting this three-dimensional relationship. Any distortion or gaps in the pattern will lead to the 'processor' taking a longer time to find a match, thus leading to a processing delay. Such a delay in processing auditory patterns will lead to significant difficulties in hearing and understanding, especially with longer strings of information.

Poor temporal resolution ability (i.e. not been able to track acoustic changes in a word) leads to 'gaps' in what is heard, again requiring extra time to achieve a correct pattern match. Sensing loudness and pitch changes in time is vital for recognizing prosodic characteristics, such as rhyme, rhythm, stress and intonation that can give a different meaning to the same word.

Extracting speech from background noise occurs at different levels within the auditory pathways. The inner ear has a sophisticated arrangement where the outer hair cells act as an 'amplifier' for quieter sounds and a 'damper' for louder sounds, while the inner hair cells transform the mechanical energy (pattern) reaching the inner ear into an electrical pattern. The brain scans information that comes through the auditory channel continuously, identifying relatively static sounds as 'noise', as opposed to sounds that change as 'speech', and it uses the outer hair cells to dampen down noise through a neural feedback pathway called the 'olivo-cochlear bundle'. This mechanism acts as the first level of filtering background noise.

Further filtering of background noise occurs with the processor (brain) using binaural information (dichotic listening). The binaural functions are therefore extremely important in helping individuals to extract speech from background noise. Those children with a unilateral hearing loss have significant difficulties with hearing in background noise as they have lost the binaural function. Noise within a speech signal leads to gaps in what the individual hears and therefore those who have difficulties in 'filling the gaps' will struggle with hearing, in spite of normal pure-tone audiometric thresholds. Often static noise in the background is easy to ignore or discard compared with fluctuating noise (e.g. multi-talker babble noise; Fergusson et al., 2010) that has significant variation in the acoustic characteristics (i.e. 'speech-like noise').

There are other mechanisms that play a part in a child's ability to hear and, of these, top-down processes, such as attention and concentration, are extremely important. These lead to creating gaps in what is heard, thus producing a similar delay in processing auditory information. This often results in a vicious circle, making it even more difficult to focus, listen and therefore understand (see Figure 7.2).

Attention and the ability to sustain concentration on complex sounds such as speech are an essential part of hearing (i.e. listening). Often children are able to have sustained concentration on tasks they are fond of or like doing (e.g. playing a computer game) yet will not have the same focus in class. Such auditory attention is vital for understanding spoken instructions and verbal information and therefore some believe that these children have attentional APD (Moore et al., 2010).

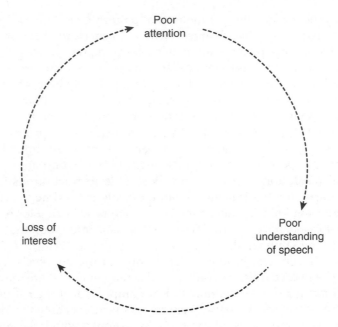

Figure 7.2 Relationship between attention and the ability to understand speech

Attention thus forms an important part of a child's ability to hear auditory information and therefore poor attention leads to difficulties in hearing. Other factors described above can augment these difficulties, highlighting the importance of understanding the complexity that plays a part in a particular child's inability to hear and understand in adverse listening conditions.

A past history of otitis media with effusion (OME), or 'glue ear' is commonly found in children referred for APD assessment. Moore *et al.* (2003) studied a cohort of children and found that those who have had OME have poor binaural release from masking (a test of binaural function) and therefore the likelihood of experiencing difficulty in hearing in background noise. These difficulties continue into the latter half of the first decade and the first half of the second decade before beginning to improve in most children. It is now considered that in this group APD is a secondary phenomenon due to periods of auditory deprivation.

Maturation of the auditory pathways starts from the periphery. Although the inner ear is fully developed at birth, the auditory nerve may take four to six weeks to mature fully (myelinate), but the synaptic function of the auditory brainstem fibres improves until about 3 years of age (Cox, 1985). The central auditory pathways take considerably more time to mature, with myelination of inter-hemispheric auditory pathways in the corpus callosum spanning into the teenage years. This means the central (or more complex) auditory functions are not fully developed in the first decade and are still developing in the second, a period when children start pre-school nursery and go through their primary and secondary education. Maturation of the auditory pathways

(Jiang, 1998; Pronton *et al.*, 2002 Ribeiro *et al.*, 2002) can be physiologically delayed in some children, and in a small number the delay could well be due to some pathological reason (Starr *et al.*, 2003). It is therefore quite possible for some children to have rather immature or delayed auditory functions in spite of normal sensitivity to sounds in acoustically optimum conditions.

The brain has the ability to change through stimulation (i.e. neuroplasticity), and this is greatest when individuals are younger. Various environmental factors lead to establishing new neural networks and shutting down those unwanted during this period. This can be used for remediation, especially using auditory training.

The ability to hear an unknown language, or non-sense syllables or words, and to repeat this correctly requires just the initial processing of auditory information, while making a correct pattern match and attaching meanings to what is heard requires language processing. Once the auditory patterns are recognized, matched and labelled, and meanings are attached, these are passed on to the next stage for processing in the language domain, along with other sensory information. This level of processing is dependent on language and cognitive abilities. Once the auditory information is processed in the language domain and integrated with processed information coming through other sensory modalities (i.e. sensory integration), a learned (as opposed to reflex) response can be made by the individual.

CLINICAL PRESENTATION

A child with APD may present with a range of symptoms and at least some of these are common to a number of other neurodevelopmental disorders, such as ADD/ADHD, dyslexia, specific language disorder and autism. Further, it is also possible for these conditions to co-exist with APD (Dawes and Bishop, 2010; Moore *et al.*, 2010) and, therefore, it may not be possible to differentiate on the basis of presenting features. A percentage of children will give a past history of fluctuating hearing loss due to 'glue ear' and most will present with hearing difficulties when there is background noise. They may also show other symptoms of hearing difficulties, such as asking for repetition, or 'day dreaming', and some may even show phonological difficulties. A small percentage of children present with acquired APD from various neurological conditions, such as a certain form of epilepsy and vascular events involving the brain (e.g. hypoxia or haemorrhage, brain trauma following accidents and intracranial tumours).

In a cohort of 350 children seen by the author for APD assessment, 84% had difficulty in hearing when there is background noise as the main presenting complaint. Of the same cohort, 32% had difficulty in understanding verbal instructions (especially sequential information), 22% had a diagnosis of dyslexia and 22% SLI. In the same cohort 18% had increased sensitivity to loud sounds and 41% gave a past history of otitis media with effusion ('glue ear'). This cohort clearly illustrates the commonest presenting feature (i.e. difficulty with hearing in a noisy environment). It also shows the co-morbidity that exists between APD and conditions such as dyslexia, and the relationship between significant periods of auditory deprivation during the early years of life and auditory processing.

Children with APD may behave like those with a peripheral hearing loss, in spite of normal pure-tone audiometry. The difficulties experienced by children with APD include not being able to hear when there is background noise, asking for repetition, taking a longer time to respond to verbal instructions, an inability to attend or focus on instructions that may result in disruptive behaviour in class, distractibility and sensitivity to loud sounds.

It is important to separate true APD from similar symptoms due to poor auditory memory, attention, concentration, and language and cognitive difficulties. Those with poor short-term auditory memory may have a limited ability in remembering sequential auditory information while those with language and cognitive difficulties may show poor understanding of verbal as well as non-verbal information. In addition to language impairment there are other co-morbid conditions, such as reading disability (Sharma *et al.*, 2006, 2009).

 Case Study

Sam, aged 10 years, presented with parental concerns about his ability to cope with secondary education. He admitted having difficulties in hearing spoken information, especially when in a noisy environment, and also not being able to understand speech. He was struggling with reading and comprehending what he read. His short-term auditory memory was very limited to an extent where he could remember only two sets of sequential information. This was confirmed by a short-term auditory memory test, with his score falling at the second centile. APD tests showed that he was able to hear clear speech in a quiet environment but his ability to hear clear speech in background noise (multi-talker babble noise) and degraded (low redundancy) speech (filtered words) in a quiet environment were both at the fifth centile (borderline). His temporal processing, pattern recognition and binaural integration functions were all within the normal range. Speech and language assessment showed significant receptive and expressive language deficit with cognitive abilities at the low average range.

Sam's auditory difficulties therefore were minimal compared with the language and cognitive problems, although the presenting features were similar to what can be expected in APD.

Recent research has highlighted poor auditory attention as one of the main reasons for deficits in auditory processing (Moore *et al.*, 2010). Lack of attention leads to poor listening ability and therefore not being able to hear and understand spoken instructions. The work by Facoetti *et al.* (2002) has also shown the importance of auditory attention in phonemic perception in a group of dyslexic children.

SCREENING FOR APD

There are a number of questionnaires and a few audiological tests used for screening children for APD. These include Fisher's Auditory Problems Checklist, the Children's Auditory Performance Scale (Smoski, 1990) (CHAPS), the SCAN (Keith, 2000) test (C & A) and the Test of Auditory Perceptual Skills-Revised (Wilson *et al.*, 2010) (TAPS-R). Some of these tools have been validated (e.g. SCAN C (Amos and Humes, 1998) and CHAPS), albeit using a small number of normal subjects, but none of these can be used with reasonable specificity to identify those who might have APD, although the sensitivity is reasonably high.

ASSESSMENT OF A CHILD WITH APD

Multidisciplinary Assessment

Often a careful history of the difficulties faced by the child will point the clinician in the right direction. Clarity of speech, pronunciation, receptive and expressive verbal and non-verbal language abilities, cognitive abilities, attention and concentration, and short-term and sequential auditory memory will help the clinician to understand the area of difficulty the child has. Finding out whether the child has other neurodevelopmental conditions, a family history of similar difficulties and pre- and perinatal problems (including a detailed description of past health issues) are all useful components of the initial assessment, thus requiring neurological, cognitive and language assessments.

Audiological Assessment and Diagnosis of APD

Hearing difficulties, in spite of normal pure-tone audiometry and middle-ear function, are due to the dysfunction of complex auditory processes, such as binaural resolution (separation, fusion and integration), temporal processing, frequency and intensity coding difficulties leading to poor auditory closure (ability to fill in the gaps in speech), difficulties with localization, lateralization and sensing the direction of the movement of sounds and filtering speech from background noise. None of these functions is measured by pure tone audiometry and therefore the assessment of APD requires a range of specialized tests that help us to examine these processes.

There is a vast range of audiological tests available that claim to assess auditory processing. Although reviewing and comparing these is not the aim of this chapter, understanding the principles would be beneficial. Therefore some of these are described as examples of the tests used to examine a particular function.

Before the various auditory-processing tests are used it is extremely important to confirm that the peripheral auditory mechanisms are functioning well. This includes examination of the ears and other relevant anatomy, assessing the middle-ear function and the functioning of the outer hair cells within the inner ear. Although it is possible for APD to occur in individuals with a permanent peripheral hearing loss it may not be easy to examine this further unless specific tests are used (Singh *et al.*, 2004).

Ideally, non-linguistic tests should be employed to test for APD in order to minimize the effect of any language deficit on the outcome. If linguistic tests are used it is important to understand the subject's language abilities before interpreting the results. Further, as all behavioural functions are dependent on top-down processes, it is extremely important to ensure that the child is attending fully during testing.

Most audiological tests used for the assessment of APD have a lower age limit of 7 years, but a few can be used for 6–7-year-olds. However, as normal younger children have very variable abilities, the normative dataset for tests at this age group usually has large confidence intervals, making it difficult to diagnose APD unless the scores (for the tests) are well below the mean score. Auditory tests currently available for APD can be grouped as shown in Table 7.1

There are a number of objective tests that are used in a selected number of patients:

- Auditory brainstem responses.
- Transient evoked otoacoustic emissions (outer hair cell function).
- TEOAE contralateral suppression test (test of the cochlear feedback mechanism – i.e. olivo-cochlear pathways).
- Mismatch negativity (event-related potential, objective evidence of processing sound at sub-cortical level).

The aim of the assessment of a subject with suspected APD is to exclude the dysfunction of the peripheral auditory system and to identify deficits in complex auditory functions so that appropriate measures can be put in place. This should only be carried out by those with sufficient audiological experience and access to a team of professionals who would be able to provide medical, cognitive and language assessments when required.

Table 7.1 Auditory tests for APD

Test group	Test	Function assessed
Monoaural low-redundancy speech tests	Filtered words	Auditory closure
	Speech in noise/auditory figure ground	Auditory decoding
	LiSN (listening in spatialized noise*)	Auditory decoding
Dichotic tests	Dichotic digits	Binaural integration
	Competing sentences	Binaural separation
	Staggered spondaic words	Binaural integration
	Binaural fusion test	Binaural interaction
	Rapid alternating sentence test	Binaural interaction
	Masking level difference	Binaural interaction
Temporal processing tasks	Random, gap detection test	Temporal resolution
	Gaps in noise test	Temporal resolution
	Pitch pattern sequence test	Frequency discrimination, temporal ordering +/– linguistic labelling
	Duration pattern sequence	Duration discrimination, temporal ordering +/– linguistic labelling

Note

*Cameron *et al.* (2006).

MANAGEMENT OF APD

There are no universally agreed criteria for the diagnosis of APD at present, although some services use their own. Often the diagnosis of APD is made when there is more than one abnormal test result. When the results are clearly abnormal in only one area (e.g. auditory closure), the term 'auditory processing issues' or 'auditory processing difficulties' is used.

The purpose of identifying conditions or areas of difficulty is to help the child to achieve their best potential and to maximize their life chances, so that the child can make an optimum contribution to society. Class sizes are ever increasing in the UK, with a reduced pupil-to-teacher ratio and diminishing discipline within the classroom, leading to disruption and poor attention to the detriment of the child achieving the best unless identified early. Auditory attention is extremely important and distractions, either auditory or visual, would affect the child's ability to concentrate and grasp essential information during lessons. Often acoustic conditions in the class are suboptimal for most children, with a high level of background noise generated within or from external sources and also sometimes with an unacceptable level of reverberation (echoing). Although normal children might be able to cope with these adverse conditions, those with APD will struggle. Most professionals look for diagnostic labels before help is provided, to the detriment of those who have difficulties with hearing and/or understanding when in a specific educational environment.

 Case Study

Elton was a 12-year-old who has just started being home educated. He was referred to the APD clinic by the community paediatrician (audiology) with a history of unexplained behavioural difficulties. His teachers suspected hearing loss when he was in primary school but a screening hearing test by the school nurse showed normal hearing. The suspicions continued, and a referral to a local ear, nose and throat specialist was made by his GP at the request of his parents. Audiological tests (including pure tone audiometry, middle-ear function tests, transient otoacoustic emissions and speech audiometry in quiet) were all normal and therefore he was discharged from the clinic with a diagnosis of 'normal hearing'. However, he continued to have difficulties with his educational progress and was disruptive in class. He was often seen disturbing those seated next to him, leading to him being seated at the front.

Elton's educational progress and behaviour in class further deteriorated and, after several meetings with his parents and an assessment by the local second-tier audiology and community paediatric services, he was excluded from class. APD tests clearly highlighted his difficulty, with an extremely poor ability to hear when there was background noise and marginal temporal processing difficulties. (Speech in noise test score at 0.1 percentile, filtered words at the first centile and a gap threshold of 20 ms.) His cognitive abilities were excellent, with superb non-verbal skills and an above-average IQ. He also had poor auditory memory with good memory for visual events. His language scores were below average and thought to be secondary to his auditory difficulties. When asked, Elton said that he often could not understand instructions and therefore had to ask his friends for clarification.

(Continued)

(Continued)

Various recommendations were made, including those for improving memory and attention, placing him in a better educational environment with better acoustics (background noise and reverberation), preferential seating, smaller classes and, eventually, a personal frequency modulation (FM) system. He continued to make significant progress with close supervision and additional help and passed his GCSEs with excellent grades, thus enabling him to continue with his education.

The commonest deficits seen in those with confirmed APD are with auditory closure and auditory decoding functions. These children struggle to hear when there is background noise and also with low-redundancy (poor-quality) speech (e.g. someone talking in a different accent). Very few children with APD have temporal processing difficulties and it is important that these are identified as specific auditory training may have to be considered. There is a proportion of children with coexisting conditions (Witton, 2010), such as dyslexia, ADD, ADHD and autism (Bellis, 2007). Language-processing difficulties may coexist but can also be secondary to APD. Top-down processes, such as attention (specifically auditory attention), are of paramount importance in understanding spoken language. Poor attention could be due to a primary attention disorder or secondary to auditory difficulties. It is therefore important to understand every aspect of the child's difficulties and take a holistic approach to management (Bamiou *et al.*, 2006). It must be remembered that, although individually not reaching significant levels, these multiple difficulties acting together can significantly affect a child's performance. The following section discusses the auditory aspect of the management but, as noted before, this should be implemented with recommendations for managing other disorders, deficits, difficulties and impairments in areas such as memory, attention, language and cognition.

Managing a Child with Poor Auditory Closure and Decoding Deficit

Not being able to fill in the gaps created by poor hearing, poor-quality speech or poor auditory attention, and an inability to extract speech from background noise make it difficult for children to understand speech. Such difficulties will lead to the child taking longer to process spoken instructions (i.e. processing delay).

Improving the acoustic environment

The aim here is to improve the speech-to-noise ratio so that the teacher's voice is heard fully by the affected pupil. As it is impractical and unsustainable to raise the teacher's voice throughout the lesson it is extremely important to make every effort to minimize the background noise. This should be achieved by a combination of classroom discipline, identifying the source(s) of the noise and dealing with it, and improving the acoustics in the classroom by using sound-absorbing material (employing softer material and avoiding hard surfaces that reflect sound). These measures will also minimize reverberation in the classroom.

Improving the speech-to-noise ratio

This can be achieved by sound-field systems or personal FM systems in combination with the above. Children are more likely to listen and therefore stay quiet during lessons if they are able to hear and follow the teacher. With the former the child benefits as long as they remain in the class, but a personal FM can be carried with the child to be used in most places (e.g. in the playground or on field trips). These systems require the teacher to wear a microphone and a transmitter system and, in group discussions, it is possible to use an additional roving microphone that could be passed around for individual speakers to use, so that the APD child is never left out of a discussion. If a personal wearable FM device (e.g. iSense; www.phonak.com) is used, a trial period before purchasing a system is recommended.

Getting the child to sit nearer to the teacher will also improve the loudness of teacher's voice over the background noise, but this helps only if the teacher stands at the front and does not move around.

Clarity of voice and accents

An individual's auditory system is programmed to identify the voice of familiar people, such as their parents, with the greatest ease. Although most individuals will manage to understand different accents by drawing in functions such as increased attention and lip reading, those with APD are unlikely to cope. These factors do have a synergistic effect. For example, if the teacher has a different accent, the child with APD is unlikely to manage with levels of background noise a normal child is able to.

Managing a Child with a Temporal Processing Disorder

The ability to sense changes in loudness and pitch is extremely important for identifying complex sounds such as speech. Not being able to do so will lead to an unacceptable number of 'gaps' in the speech sound, making it difficult for the child to understand speech or to take longer to process. These children may present with dyslexic features and be diagnosed as having dyslexia (Facoetti *et al.*, 2002). However, the number of children who have a temporal processing disorder in those presenting with a diagnosis of dyslexia is small (personal experience from over 600 children with suspected APD).

Although temporal processing disorders are not very common it is important to identify these because auditory training (Moore *et al.*, 2001) (both formal and informal) can make a significant improvement in a relatively short period of time (Depeller *et al.*, 2004). However, the sustainability of such improvements has been questioned. More research is needed to investigate further the effectiveness of these programmes.

Case Study

Barry was in the first year at secondary school when he was referred for assessing his auditory processing function. He had significant difficulties in junior school for years and had been on school-action plus but, in spite of this, he was a few years behind his peers in a number of areas by the time the secondary transfer took place. He had cognitive and language assessments as a part of community paediatric evaluation, which showed concerns in both areas with a strong suspicion of auditory factors playing a major role, while excluding dyslexia, ADD, ADHD and autism. Audiological assessment showed a picture compatible with a temporal processing disorder (phonological difficulties, poor auditory decoding and closure, and gap thresholds of 80 ms). Formal auditory training was recommended, with a choice of auditory training packages in addition to measures for managing some of the other difficulties in the short term. A commercially available auditory training package was used by the school with direct support from a specialist for overseeing the programme. Significant improvement was noted by three months and Barry continued to improve over the next year to 18 months to a point where he was performing at an age-appropriate level.

Informal auditory training also has a place in managing a child with APD, but administering this requires a good knowledge of the methods and experience.

Managing Poor Auditory Attention

As mentioned earlier, attentional deficits can be primary or secondary to auditory deficits (or a combination). It is crucial to identify these and manage them appropriately. At one extreme primary attentional deficits may require medication for the control of poor attention; at the other extreme, methods and tactics to sustain the child's attention for longer periods of time (e.g. didactic or interactive teaching, visual material to aid understanding, simple language, breaking down information into smaller chunks and pre-teaching) may be required. Listening programmes with enhanced music (e.g. The Listening Programme that claims to improve auditory processing abilities; (Esteves *et al.*, n.d.)) have been recommended by some professionals with a varying degree of success, but these can help to improve the child's ability to listen and sustain concentration.

Managing Auditory Short-term Memory Difficulties

In order to understand spoken instructions (for that matter, any sensory information that changes in time) it is essential that an individual has the ability to retain these auditory events in the working memory sequentially so that meaningful interpretation can take place. Those with limited working memory could take longer to process information. Improving the sequential short-term auditory memory could be attempted using various memory games, such as Simon game, mind maps and attaching visual imagery.

SUMMARY

Our understanding of APD is improving, and research is leading us to a clearer definition, a better understanding of its effects, the co-morbid conditions and interactions, and the methodical approach to managing the affected individual in order to give them the best opportunity for achieving the optimum from the educational and life chances point of view. As professionals we have a responsibility to understand the complexity of this condition, diagnosis and recommendations and to find the optimal solution for a particular child. It is important to realize that a proactive approach pays off much more than waiting for a child to fail before help is provided. Initial signs of APD (or any other neuro-developmental condition) should be recognized, and early diagnosis and appropriate management advice should be sought in order to achieve the best for the child, their family and society as a whole.

Further Reading

Bellis, T.J. (2003) *Assessment and Management of Central Auditory Processing Disorders in the Educational Setting: From Science to Practice* (2nd edn). New York, NY: Thompson Delmar Learning.

British Society of Audiology (2011a) *Position Statement – Auditory Processing Disorder (APD)* (www.thebsa.org.uk).

British Society of Audiology (2011b) *Practice Guidance – An Overview of Current Management of Auditory Processing Disorder* (APD) (www.thebsa.org.uk).

MRC Institute of Hearing Research (2004) *Auditory Processing Disorder* (available in portable document format on the BSA/APD special interest group web pages: http://www.thebsa.org.uk/apd/APDPamphletOct04.pdf).

Musiek, F.E. and Chermak, G. (2006) *Handbook of Central Auditory Processing Disorders: From Science to Practice* (vols 1 and 2). San Diego, CA: Plural Publishing Inc.

These books should provide further information about APD. The publication by the MRC Institute covers the management of APD, especially where there are auditory closure and decoding deficits.

Useful Websites

American Speech–Language–Hearing Association   www.asha.org
Australian APD   www.auditoryprocessing.com.au
British Society of Audiology – APD Steering Group   www.thebsa.org.uk
MRC Institute of Hearing Research (APD Research in the UK)   www.ihr.mrc.ac.uk
UK APD consumer website   www.apduk.org

References

Amos, N.E. and Humes, L.E. (1998) 'SCAN test-retest reliability for first- and third-grade children', *Journal of Speech, Language, and Hearing Research*, 41: 834–45.

Bamiou, D., Campbell, N. and Sirimanna, T. (2006) 'Management of auditory processing disorders', *Audiological Medicine*, 4: 46–56.

Bellis, T.J. (2007) 'Treatment of (central) auditory processing disorders', in M. Valente *et al.* (eds) *Auditory Treatment*. New York, NY: Thieme.

Cameron, S., Dillon, H. and Newall, P. (2006) 'Development and evaluation of the listening in spatialised noise test', *Ear and Hearing*, 27: 30–41.

Chermak, G.D. and Musiek, F.E. (1997) *Central Auditory Processing Disorders: New Perspectives*. San Diego, CA: Singular Publishing.

Cooper, J.C. Jr and Gates, G.A. (1991) 'Hearing in the elderly – the Framingham cohort, 1983–1985. Part II. Prevalence of central auditory processing disorders', *Ear and Hearing*, 12: 304–11.

Cox, L.C. (1985) 'Infant assessment: developmental and age related considerations', in J. Jacobsen (ed.) *The Auditory Brainstem Response*. San Diego, CA: College Hill Press.

Dawes, P. and Bishop, D.V.M. (2010) 'Psychometric profile of children with auditory processing disorder and children with dyslexia', *Archives of Disease in Childhood*, 95: 432–6.

Depeller, J.M., Taranto, A.M. and Bench, J. (2004) 'Language and auditory processing changes following Fast ForWord', *Australian and New Zealand Journal of Audiology*, 26: 94–109.

Esteves, J., Stein-Blum, S., Cohen, J. and Tischler, A. (n.d.) 'Identifying the effectiveness of a music-based auditory stimulation method on children with sensory integration and auditory processing concerns: a pilot study' (http://www.thebsa.org.uk/apd/APDPamphletOct04.pdf).

Facoetti, A. *et al.* (2002) 'Auditory and visual automatic attention deficits in developmental dyslexia', *Cognitive Brain Research*, 16: 185–91.

Fergusson, M.A., Hall, R.L., Riley, A. and Moore, D.R. (2010) 'Communication, listening, speech and cognition in children diagnosed with auditory processing disorder (APD) or specific language impairment (SLI)', *Journal of Speech, Language, and Hearing Research*, 5 August (e-publication).

Fortnum, H.M., Summerfield, A.Q., Marshall, D.H., Davis, A.C. and Bamford, J.M. (2001) 'Prevalence of permanent childhood hearing impairment in the United Kingdom and implications for universal neonatal hearing screening: questionnaire based ascertainment study', *British Medical Journal*, 323: 536–40.

Jerger, J. and Musiek, F. (2000) 'Report of the Consensus Conference on the Diagnosis of Auditory Processing Disorders in School-aged Children', *American Academy of Audiology*, 11: 467–74.

Jiang, Z.D. (1998) 'Maturation of peripheral and brainstem auditory function in the first year following perinatal asphyxia: a longitudinal study', *Journal of Speech, Language, and Hearing Research*, 41: 83–93.

Keith, R.W. (2000) 'Development and standardization of SCAN-C test for auditory processing disorders in children', *Journal of the American Academy of Audiology*, 11: 438–45.

Moore, D.R., Fergusson, M.A. and Edmondson-Jones, M. (2010) 'Nature of auditory processing disorder in children', *Pediatrics*, 126: e382–e390.

Moore, D.R., Hartley, D.E. and Hogan, S.C. (2003) 'Effects of otitis media with effusion (OME) on central auditory function', *International Journal of Pediatric Otorhinolaryngoly*, 67 (suppl 1): S63–7.

Moore, D.R., Hogan, S.C., Kacelnik, O., Parsons, C.H., Rose, M.M. and King, A.J. (2001) 'Auditory learning as a cause and treatment of central dysfunction', *Audiology and Neuro-otology*, 6: 216–20.

Pronton, C. *et al*. (2002) 'Maturation of human central auditory system activity: separating auditory evoked potentials by dipole source modelling', *Clinical Neurophysiology*, 113: 407–20.

Ribeiro Fuess, V.L., Ferreira Bento, R. and Medicis Da Silveira, J.A. (2002) 'Delay in maturation of the auditory pathway and its relationship to language acquisition disorders', *Ear, Nose and Throat Journal*, 81: 706–12.

Sharma, M. *et al*. (2006) 'Electrophysiological and behavioral evidence of auditory processing deficits in children with reading disorder', *Clinical Neurophysiology*, 117: 1130–44.

Sharma, M., Purdy, S.C. and Kelley, A.S. (2009) 'Comorbidity of auditory processing, language, and reading disorders', *Journal of Speech, Language, and Hearing Research*, 52: 706–22.

Singh, S. *et al*. (2004) 'Event-related potentials in pediatric cochlear implant patients', *Ear and Hearing*, 25: 598–610.

Smoski, W. (1990) 'Use of CHAPS in a children's audiology clinic', *Ear and Hearing*, 11: 53S–56S.

Starr, A. *et al*. (2003) 'Pathology and physiology of auditory neuropathy with a novel mutation in the MPZ gene (Tyr145Ser)', *Brain*, 126: 1604–19.

Wilson, W.J. *et al*. (2010) 'The CHAPS, SIFTER and TAPS-R as predictors of (C)AP skills and (C)APD', *Journal of Speech, Language, and Hearing Research*, 54: 278–91.

Witton, C. (2010) 'Childhood auditory processing disorder as a developmental disorder: the case for a multi-professional approach to diagnosis and management', *International Journal of Audiology*, 49: 83–7.

8

DEVELOPMENTAL CO-ORDINATION DISORDER AND DYSPRAXIA FROM AN OCCUPATIONAL THERAPIST'S PERSPECTIVE

Jane Abdullah

Learning objectives

This chapter will help readers to:

- understand the role of a paediatric occupational therapist (OT);
- understand the difference between the terms developmental co-ordination disorder (DCD) and 'dyspraxia' from an OT's perspective;
- gain a general overall view of the many difficulties a child with DCD can present with; and
- appreciate how some of these difficulties can impact on daily function.

Note

For ease of reference, the terms 'child' or 'children' will be used throughout this chapter to refer both to children and young people.

OTs

OTs are health and social-care professionals. Paediatric OTs aim to develop, restore and maintain the skills and strategies needed for safe, functional and dignified independent living which are part of daily life for children aged 0 to school-leaving age (e.g. the ability to learn and retain new skills, 'to be part of a family, play, look after themselves, make friends and go to school'; Dunford and Richards, 2003). OTs aim to help children develop, restore and maintain the skills, behaviours and relationships necessary for independent living. They use standardized and non-standardized assessments, clinical observations and task analysis to identify specific difficulties. They will then offer treatment, strategies, advice and information as deemed necessary. They work as members of a team and play a key role in educating parents and professional colleagues concerning the functional challenges a child may have.

DCD AND DYSPRAXIA

Imagine what it would be like if you could not dress yourself or wear fashionable clothes because you couldn't manage the fastenings on them. How would it feel to find holding and using a pencil painful and difficult, and that, despite trying with every ounce of energy available to write neatly, the work you produce always looks messy and is usually illegible? How would it feel to be consistently chosen last for team games, or ostracized from playground activities because you can never get to the ball on time? How would you concentrate on the teacher when the sound of a lawn-mower outside the window keeps distracting you, the feeling of the collar on your school shirt is continually irritating you or you are unable to sit still on your chair? How would you manage to participate in out-of-school clubs when you are completely exhausted and drained by the end of the school day? How do you make and sustain friendships when you cannot keep up with your peers?

These children may be identified as having:

- clumsy child syndrome;
- perceptual-motor dysfunction;
- minimal brain dysfunction;
- motor-learning difficulty;
- sensory-integrative dysfunction;
- spatial problems;
- visuo-motor difficulties;
- dyspraxia; or
- developmental co-ordination disorder.

In the UK such difficulties are often referred to as dyspraxia, although in other countries the term Developmental Co-ordination Disorder (DCD) is more commonly used. Despite having been a recognized childhood condition for the better part of a century, researchers and clinicians are still developing a consensus on methods of identification and effective approaches for remediation (Sugden *et al.*, 2006). Although the terms DCD and dyspraxia are often used interchangeably in the UK, to OTs they are not the same. OTs use DCD as an umbrella term, and dyspraxia is seen as a subcategory within this.

DCD is now the favoured term among clinicians and researchers as it describes the range of symptoms experienced by the child.

DIAGNOSTIC CRITERIA FOR DCD

DCD (DSM IV and ICD 10 criteria) can be defined as an impairment in the development of motor co-ordination that interferes significantly with the activities of daily living at home and at school (e.g. dressing, holding a pencil), which is not explained by a medical condition (e.g. cerebral palsy), learning difficulties (e.g. Down's Syndrome) or adverse environmental factors. The four criteria can be summarized as follows:

1   Movement and co-ordination skills are substantially delayed, and performance in daily activities that require motor co-ordination is substantially below the level expected given the child's

chronological age and measured intelligence. This may be demonstrated by significant delays in achieving motor milestones (e.g. sitting, crawling or walking) or with problems in areas such as gross and fine-motor skills that affect efficient and effective balance, performance in sports, handling small items, handwriting, etc.

2   The difficulties stated in 1) significantly affect the child's educational progress and/or activities of everyday life (daily living) (e.g. washing, dressing, feeding).

3   The difficulties demonstrated cannot be explained by a general medical condition (e.g. cerebral palsy, muscular dystrophy) and do not meet the criteria for a pervasive developmental disorder which is closely associated with movement and co-ordination difficulties.

4   If learning difficulties are present, the problems with movement and co-ordination are in excess of those usually associated with the level of learning difficulty identified.

DCD is one of the most common disorders among school-aged children (Wann, 2007). Between 5 and 10% of school-aged children are thought to be affected, with 2% being severely affected. International studies suggest that DCD is present in 6% of children between the ages of 5 and 12 which equates approximately to one child in every class at primary-school level (Willoughby and Polatajko, 1995; Blondis, 1999). Boys are more affected than girls (Kadesjo and Gillberg, 1998).

DCD can severely limit school performance, self-esteem and the age-appropriate activities of daily living. Long-term follow-up studies have shown that these children do not 'grow out of it' (Losse *et al.*, 1991; Hellgren *et al.*, 1993; Soorani-Lunsing *et al.*, 1993; Schoemaker *et al.*, 1994). Consequently, early diagnosis and intervention are important for both child and family. These children are commonly referred to OTs for assessment, treatment and advice.

DYSPRAXIA

Unlike DCD, there is no formal diagnostic criteria for the term dyspraxia. It has often been used by the media, teachers and health professionals to mean *all* children with co-ordination difficulties regardless of whether any diagnostic criteria had been applied. There are surprising differences between the various definitions of dyspraxia.

OTs use the term dyspraxia to describe a specific aspect or symptom associated with DCD (i.e. the child has particular difficulties in the ability to plan (ideation) and carry out (execute) sequences of movement (motor planning)). OTs consider that dyspraxia is 'an inability to carry out non-habitual interaction with the environment in the correct sequence due to problems in formulating the plan of action' (Fisher *et al.*, 1991). This means that many children who fulfil the criteria for DCD do not have 'dyspraxia' in its true sense. Dyspraxia is therefore seen as a subcategory within the much wider group of children with DCD.

Dyspraxic children may be of high, average or low intelligence. Some children may be very mildly affected while others are badly disabled. It affects between 6 and 10% of the population. It is four times more common in boys. Dyspraxia is a very real, albeit often hidden, disability which impacts on many areas of daily life.

PRAXIS

In order to understand the OTs perspective of dyspraxia, it is important to have an awareness and understanding of the term 'praxis'. Dyspraxia derives from the words *dys* (indicating impaired ability) and *praxis*, which is 'the ability to interact successfully with the physical environment, to plan, organise and carry out a sequence of unfamiliar actions and to do what one needs and wants to do' (Kranowitz, 1998). Praxis describes the ability by which an individual determines how to use their body in skilled tasks – e.g. playing with toys, using a pencil, building a structure, straightening up a room or engaging in many other activities and occupations (Ayres *et al.*, 1987). It affects every aspect of life (i.e. behaviour, language, daily living skills, learning and movement).

Praxis includes three components:

- *Ideation* – forming ideas and knowing what to do.
- *Motor planning* – organizing the sequence of movements.
- *Execution* – carrying out movement (plan) in a smooth sequence.

In order to be regarded as having dyspraxia by an OT, a child must present with difficulties with ideation or motor planning.

SOMATODYSPRAXIA

This is a term used when applied to sensory integration, which is a model of practice used by many OTs when both assessing and treating children. Bundy *et al.* (2002) describe sensory-integrative dyspraxia as 'difficulty with planning unfamiliar movements' and somatodyspraxia as a 'relatively severe form of sensory-integrative based dyspraxia characterised by difficulty with both feedback (simple) and feed forward (difficult) motor tasks'. These children have difficulty leaning new tasks, but can with sustained practice become quite skilful, although their ability remains highly specific to that learnt task.

CO-CONCURRING DEVELOPMENTAL DIFFICULTIES AND DISORDERS

Children with DCD may have other difficulties that are not due to dyspraxia itself, but often coexist with it. This is referred to as co-morbidity. These problems impact on the child's everyday function and capacity for learning and include:

- attention difficulties (ADD and ADHD);
- autistic spectrum disorders (ASD);
- specific language difficulties;
- dyslexia;
- poor short-term and working memory;
- poor emotion self-regulation;
- sensory processing disorders; and
- visual-motor difficulties.

CHARACTERISTICS OF DCD

DCD is not really a single disorder with a known cause, a typical developmental pathway or a known outcome. Children with DCD and/or dyspraxia are often accused of not trying though, in fact, they are usually trying very hard. They are fully capable of understanding that, despite their best efforts, their work is not comparable with the work of other children. Due to the myriad underlying difficulties they face on a daily basis, many aspects of daily living are affected. Each child with movement difficulties has their own set of strengths and weaknesses when it comes to performing everyday, school and sporting activities. They may therefore present with many or only some of the following difficulties.

Hypermobile Joints

About 20% of people have joints that are more mobile than usual. Joint hypermobility affects the way children learn to move and often results in them developing inefficient patterns of movement and posture. Hypermobility can affect sitting posture, agility and balance tasks. Poor endurance and low stamina often result in fatigue.

Low Muscle Tone (hypotonia) and Poor Postural Control

Muscle tone describes the level of activity within muscles. Low tone can result in reduced strength, endurance and poor postural control. Fatigue is common because so much energy is expended when trying to execute physical movements correctly.

Impaired Movement and Co-ordination

Evidence of soft neurological features (e.g. unusual postures of the hands, arms or face when moving or concentrating) can occur. There is often an early history of delayed gross and fine motor skills and impaired or delayed language.

Gross motor skills

These are large movements using the arms and legs (e.g. jumping, running, climbing, throwing, skipping). Difficulties vary from child to child and can include poor timing;

poor balance; slow saving reactions; tripping over their feet; difficulty combining movements into a rhythmic sequence; or difficulty moving (transitioning) from one body position to another.

Fine motor skills

These are small movements made with the hands/fingers (e.g. using a pencil, knife and fork, tying shoelaces or fastening buttons). Fine motor problems cause difficulty with a wide variety of other tasks, such as constructive or manipulative play, art and craft activities, using utensils or tools, brushing teeth, opening jars and packets, handling coins, using keys, applying cosmetics, styling hair or shaving.

Dyspraxia

If such problems exist new movements and actions are harder to learn and undertake when planning, organising and executing a movement response due to problems with ideation and motor planning. Difficulties occur in forming and following through a plan of action, and sequencing and timing the movements required to produce an environmentally appropriate response. Often step-by-step instruction is needed, with additional extended practice, before a movement sequence can be learnt.

Poor Body Awareness (proprioception) and Spatial Awareness

Proprioception is the internal sense we have of body position and movement. This is the perception a child has about their own body. Children with poor proprioception may misjudge the distance between themselves and items in the environment due to difficulty in relating their bodies to physical objects, and they may have difficulty imitating the actions of others. They may have trouble knowing how much force to use, so may have a 'plodding' walk, inadvertently break toys, hold on to their pencil too tightly or alternatively use a flaccid, weak grasp. They can demonstrate poor tactile discrimination and have difficulty with feeling or localizing a touch stimulus. Problems with spatial awareness, difficulty with the perception of speed, distance and direction, knocking things over, bumping into people accidentally or moving in crowded places can occur.

Laterality and Bilateral Integration

Some children have difficulty in determining left from right. They may demonstrate a poor sense of direction, cross-laterality, ambidexterity or have a poorly developed hand dominance. Difficulties with bilateral integration can create poor sequencing of movements when using two hands to produce different but complementary movements e.g. when cutting out with scissors, fastening buttons or learning to swim.

Perceptual Functions/Visual Perceptual/Visual Motor Difficulties

Children with visual perceptual problems may have trouble with visual memory, discriminating the difference between similar shapes/letters, difficulty screening out non-relevant visual information or difficulties with spatial organization. There can be poor registration and interpretation of the messages that the senses convey, and consequent difficulty in translating those messages into appropriate actions. Children with dyspraxia are seven times more likely than typically developing students to achieve very poor scores in visual-spatial memory (Alloway, 2007).

Eye Movements

Difficulty co-ordinating both eyes together can occur causing blurred/double vision or poor tracking and scanning. Difficulty with controlling the movements of the eyes to follow a moving object, or looking quickly and effectively from object to object may occur. Problems with eye/hand co-ordination or scanning and tracking skills will impact on reading and writing skills when crossing the body midline or copying from the board.

Organizing and Sequencing Tasks

Difficulty in planning and organizing thoughts, ideas and responses occur. Constant disorganization (e.g. forgotten books or lost items of PE kit) is common, and difficulty with memory, especially short-term memory, with consequent problems in remembering instructions, organizing time, remembering deadlines, an increased tendency to lose things or problems carrying out tasks which require remembering several steps in sequence can occur.

Specific Learning Difficulty

Some children may have dyslexia or problems with numbers (e.g. rote learning, reading, writing, spelling, poor formation of numbers/letters or reversed order of letters in words). This can impact on common strategies used to help organize and sequence daily activities.

Sensory Integration Dysfunction

Children with DCD often have difficulty processing the information they receive from their senses. Sensory processing, or sensory integration, is the ability to register, organize and interpret sensory information from the sensory systems of sight, sound, smell, taste, touch and movement. There are also three other senses:

- *Tactile* (somatosensory), which primarily receives and interprets information received through the skin.
- Vestibular, which interprets and processes information related to movement, balance and gravity, which is received through the inner ear.

- *Proprioceptive* that interprets and processes information about body position and parts of the body. It receives information through the muscles, ligaments and joints.

The development of sensory integration is an on-going process that is connected to a child's maturation, because these senses develop and refine as the child grows. Efficient and effective sensory processing has an essential role to play in the ability to regulate arousal and attention levels, and in controlling emotional and behavioural control. If sensory information is perceived inaccurately, faulty sensory integration occurs. Some children may be oversensitive to some stimuli and undersensitive to others.

Common difficulties include the following:

- *Hyper(over)sensitivity* (e.g. distress at loud noises, discomfort with textures, fear response on swings/roundabouts). Tactile defensiveness can cause an aversive response to tactile experiences, such as craft materials, food, clothing and bathing. Hypersensitive children will often avoid a variety of activities, may become easily overwhelmed or react aggressively at times.
- *Hypo(under)sensitivity* (e.g. under-responsiveness to pain; unawareness of temperature; not tuning into their name being called). Decreased discrimination of vestibular (movement) and proprioception (sense of body position and movement) can result in poor posture, frequent falling, clumsiness, poor balance, constant moving and fidgeting, and poor attention. Decreased discrimination of tactile information can result in a poor body scheme, difficulty with praxis and poor hand skill development. These children may crave touch input.
- *Somatodyspraxia*, due to poor tactile and proprioceptive processing, can result in clumsiness; frequent tripping, falling and bumping into objects; difficulty with fine motor and manipulation skills; and poor organization (Cermak, 1991).
- *Gravitational insecurity* is caused by a fear of movement that is out of proportion to the movement being undertaken. Limited participation in gross motor play, avoidance or fear of escalators, or resistance to their feet being off the ground may occur.

Independence

Many aspects of daily living are a struggle and independence skills are often immature. Increased help, support and assistance that are in excess to that expected for their age is often needed. As DCD children grow and move through school the ability to ask for help with basic skills (e.g tying laces and writing down homework) no longer becomes acceptable, and this can lead to frustration, demoralization, behavioural difficulties and social isolation.

Poor Attention and Concentration

Children with DCD need to put in far more effort than other children to achieve seemingly simple motor tasks and they frequently have trouble sustaining on-task attention and maintaining the level of concentration needed throughout the day. Trouble tuning out the non-relevant stimuli (e.g. a truck outside) and tuning into the relevant stimuli (e.g. the teacher's voice can be challenging). Dividing attention between two tasks (e.g. listening to the teacher while writing down homework) can be especially difficult.

Social Difficulties

Difficulty interacting with other children of their age can occur. Gross and fine motor problems, poor motor planning and sensory integration dysfunction can affect the ability to engage in an activity or game. Speech and language difficulties may make communicating with others or understanding the rules of a game problematic, thereby further excluding them from play. They often prefer to talk rather than do. Older children may converse well with adults but they may be ostracized by their own age group because they do not 'fit in'.

Behavioural Difficulties

Behaviours reflecting underlying poor attention and concentration, a high level of frustration and reduced motivation can be displayed (e.g. non-compliance, whining, tantrums or aggressive behaviour). They may be restless and lacking in control, and/or demonstrate unhappiness, loneliness, poor self-esteem, lack of confidence and social isolation. They may become adept at avoiding or 'opting out' of tasks or may use strategies such as 'clowning around' to draw attention away from their problems.

Variability

This is one of the most frustrating and demoralizing aspects of DCD for both the parents and child as ability can vary from day to day and even from hour to hour. These children have 'good days and bad days'. They may be able to manage an activity well one day but the next will have forgotten how to do it. This can be confusing, frustrating and demoralizing for the child and inexplicable to parents or teachers who can wrongly label the child as being lazy, stubborn or as 'having attitude'. Such problems may lead to 'opting out' or difficult behaviours.

Not all children demonstrate all these difficulties, but it can be seen that problems associated with both DCD and dyspraxia have a direct impact on living and learning in many areas of a child's life, at home, school and play and an in-direct impact on siblings, parents, the wider family, friends and teachers.

THE IMPACT OF DCD AND DYSPRAXIA ON DAILY LIFE

Many of the difficulties mentioned above are found combining together to hinder function and independence in many aspects of daily life. Consequently, the activities of daily living, independence and efficient and effective function can be severely affected as illustrated in the following case studies.

Self-care

 Case Study

Alex has poor balance and struggles to stand on one leg to put on trousers. His fine motor difficulties impact on him fastening buttons, etc. His poor motor planning affects his ability to put clothes on in the correct order and his reduced poor body awareness affects his ability to know when clothes are pulled down or tucked in correctly. His difficulties with bilateral integration, where one hand does one movement and the other a different but complimentary movement, affects tying shoelaces, and poor attention and concentration impact on him staying focused. He knows he needs far more help and assistance than other children his age which he finds demoralizing and frustrating.

 Case Study

Joe has a poor awareness of internal body rhythms and a difficulty in registering and responding to the signals that indicate the need to use the toilet. This is causing constipation and overflow problems and affecting socialization at school. Due to poor body awareness, he cannot locate the correct part of his bottom to wipe and he struggles to manage the fastenings on clothes due to poor fine motor ability.

In such situations the OT can offer advice, strategies and specific activities following a thorough task analysis to help develop the skills necessary for efficient and effective functioning.

PE, Sports and Physical Fitness

In order to be efficient and effective at sport a child needs to have balance control, agility, the ability to run fast, upper limb (hand and arm) strength and the ability to combine all these skills at once. Most children develop fitness through everyday activities such as climbing, running and jumping, and these contribute to the development of strength, power and endurance. Children with DCD find movement hard, so are less likely to be physically active, which results in low strength, stamina and lower levels of physical fitness.

 Case Study

Serena has poor motor planning and difficulties with gross motor skills, so she has difficulty participating in PE and sport, particularly ball sports. Her low muscle tone and reduced postural control affect balance, strength and stability. She needs supportive insoles and struggles with barefoot tasks such as dance. Her poor motor planning impacts significantly on sport, as extra time is needed to plan, organize and execute her movements and, during team sports, she cannot do this quickly enough which leads to her hindering rather than helping her team. Her reduced upper limb strength and weak hand and finger muscles cause problems when throwing and catching a ball, or holding a bat or racket. Due to poor eye movements, she struggles to track a ball and her reduced hand/eye co-ordination impacts on catching or hitting it.

Finding sports and hobbies that encourage an active lifestyle, participation and enjoyment in physical leisure activities is important for children with DCD. Less competitive sports/hobbies, an emphasis on non-team sports or on socially based activities (e.g. swimming, wall climbing, sailing, orienteering, scouts, drama or music) should be explored.

Handwriting

Handwriting is a complex skill with perceptual, cognitive and motor components, which all combine together to produce efficient and effective writing ability. Different writing tasks require a differing emphasis on these components (e.g. simple copying tasks are less cognitively demanding than dictation). DCD children frequently struggle with handwriting as it involves motor control, praxis and visual-motor integration. In addition, difficulty in learning basic movement patterns, developing a desired writing speed, the acquisition of the letters of the alphabet, establishing the correct pencil grip and an aching hand while writing can occur.

 Case Study

Sam has poor postural control and difficulty holding his body upright when writing or sitting at a table. His weak shoulder stability affects holding his arm, hand and fingers in a steady position. Fine motor problems holding and controlling the pencil, and motor planning difficulties impacting on the ideation and execution of the writing, mean that, due to the physical effort needed to write, his train of thought is interrupted. Sam has additional difficulties remembering which movements are needed to form letters (motor memory).

The OT can trial different shapes and weights of pen, provide activities to develop muscle strength and stability, develop strategies to help with motor planning and advise teachers on how best to present and refine written work.

Academic Skills

Due to underlying problems with sensory processing, praxis, perceptual function and motor co-ordination, problems can occur in acquiring the expected academic skills at the same speed as classmates.

 Case Study

Ali's motor planning difficulties make it difficult for him to follow multiple part directions and to remember regular routines. Due to handwriting and processing difficulties he is slower to take down written material and due to the concentration required for writing, he often misses instructions. Because many tasks require increased effort, he frequently has difficulty completing set tasks within the allocated timeframe.

OT INPUT

OTs assess, treat and provide advice and information as part of their input to children with DCD and dyspraxia. Therapeutic techniques and activities involving purposeful activity and play are used to help children achieve as good a quality of life as possible.

Assessment

To identify specific areas of difficulty, the OT observes the quality of movement and the manner in which the child performs motor and functional tasks, during both standardized and non-standardized tests. Supplementary information is gained via questionnaires, interviews with parents/school and through observation of the child, ideally within different settings.

Treatment

When treating, many OTs favour a 'top down' approach based on the assumption that required skills are developed as a result of the interaction between the child, the task and their environment (Mandich *et al.*, 2001). More traditional process-orientated approaches concentrate on remediating underlying problems, so that improvements in occupational performance can occur (Coster, 1998).

OTs use a combination of different models of practice and, depending on the needs of the child, different formats of intervention may be provided. Therapy input can include:

- a cognitive goal-directed approach;
- sensory integration treatment;
- sensory diet;
- a sensorimotor approach;
- a perceptual motor approach; and
- compensatory skill development.

Treatment may be offered through face-to-face sessions; through a programme of graded tasks/skills undertaken on a daily basis at home/school; regular monitoring sessions; or by a list of activities to practise at home or school, with access to an OT when needed.

Advice and Consultation

OTs provide advice and consultation to parents, schools and other agencies and often provide additional training regarding the implementation of activities, skills and strategies outlined in OT programmes.

Through treatment and intervention, the OT aims to increase the child's ability to access and participate in personal independence and functional tasks within home, school and leisure settings.

SUMMARY

- Children with DCD have difficulties with everyday tasks that require motor co-ordination.
- Due to the myriad underlying difficulties faced on a daily basis, many aspects of living are affected.
- OTs can help these children develop their abilities through different treatment interventions and they can provide strategies to enable them to engage efficiently and effectively in daily tasks.

Further Reading

Addy, L. (2004) *How to Understand and Support Children with Dyspraxia*. Hyde, Cheshire: LDA.

Boon, M. (2000) *Helping Children with Dyspraxia*. London: Jessica Kingsley.

Cermak, S.A. and Larkin, D. (2002) *Developmental Motor Co-ordination*. Albany, NY: Delmar.

Colley, M. and the Dyspraxia Foundation Adult Support Group (2000) *Living with Dyspraxia*. Hitchin: DF.

Dyspraxia Foundation (1998) 'Occupational therapy for children at secondary school', in *Praxis Makes Perfect. Part II*. Hitchin: DF.

Kirby, A. (2003) *The Adolescent with DCD*. London: Jessica Kingsley.

Kirby, A. (2007) *100 Ideas for Supporting Pupils with Dyspraxia and DCD*. London: Continuum.

Kirby, A. and Drew, S. (2003) *Guide to Dyspraxia and Developmental Co-ordination Disorders*. London: David Fulton.

Lee, M. and Portwood, M. (2004) *Co-ordination Difficulties: Practical Ways Forward*. London: David Fulton.

Portwood, M. (2000) *Understanding Developmental Dyspraxia*. London: David Fulton.

Useful Websites

Alert Program – How Does Your Engine Run   www. alertprogram.com
Brain Gym   www.braingym.org.uk
Canchild Centre for Disability Research   www.canchild.ca/en
Dyscovery Centre   www.dyscovery.newport.ac.uk
Dyspraxia Foundation   www.dyspraxiafoundation.org.uk
The Listening Program (TLP)   www.thelisteningprograme.com

References

Alloway, T.P. (2007) 'Working memory, reading and mathematical skills in children with developmental coordination disorder', *Journal of Experimental Child Psychology*, 96: 20–36.

American Psychiatric Association (2000) *Diagnostic and Statistical Manual of Mental Disorders: DSM-IV. International Version with ICD-10 Codes* (4th edn). Washington, DC: APA.

Ayres, J., Mailloux, Z. and Wendler, C. (1987) 'Developmental dyspraxia: is it a unitary function?', *Occupational Therapy Journal of Research*, 7: 93–110.

Blondis, T.A. (1999) 'Motor disorders and attention-deficit/hyperactivity disorder', *Pediatric Clinics of North America*, 46: 899–913.

Bundy, A., Lane, S. and Murray, E. (2002) *Sensory Integration Theory and Pratice*. Philadelphia, PA: F.A. Davis.

Cermak, S.A. (1991) 'Somatodyspraxia', in A. Fisher *et al*. (eds) *Sensory Integration: Theory and Practice*. Philadelphia, PA: F.A. Davis.

Coster, W. (1998) 'Occupation-centred assessment of children', *American Journal Occupational Therapy*, 52: 337–45.

Dunford, C. and Richards, S. (2003) *Doubly Disadvantaged: Waiting lists for Children with Developmental Co-ordination Disorder* (fact sheet and survey). Cardiff: University of Wales College of Medicine.

Fisher, A., Murray, E. and Bundy, A. (eds) (1991) *Sensory Integration: Theory and Practice*. Philadelphia, PA: F.A. Davis.

Hellgren, L. *et al*. (1993) 'Children with deficits in attention, motor control and perception (DAMP) almost grown up: psychiatric and general health at 16 years', *Developmental Medicine and Child Neurology*, 35: 881–92.

Kadesjo, B. and Gillberg, C. (1998) 'Attention deficits and clumsiness in Swedish 7-year-old children', *Developmental Medicine and Child Neurology*, 40: 796–804.

Kranowitz, C.S. (1998) *The Out of Sync Child*. New York, NY: Penguin Putnam.

Losse, A., Henderson, S.E., Elliman, D., Hall, D., Knight, E. and Jongmans, M. (1991) 'Clumsiness in children – do they grow out of it? A 10-year follow-up study', *Developmental Medicine and Child Neurology*, 33: 55–68.

Mandich, A., Polatajko, H., Macnab, J. and Miller, L. (2001) 'Treatment of children with developmental coordination disorder: what is the evidence?', *Physical and Occupational Therapy in Pediatrics*, 20: 51–68.

Schoemaker, M.M. and Kalverboer, A.F. (1994) 'Social and affective problems of children who are clumsy: how early do they begin?', *Adapted Physical Quarterly*, 11: 130–40.

Soorani-Lunsing, R.J., Hadders-Algra, M., Olinga, A.A., Huisjes, H. and Touwen, B.C.L. (1993) 'Is minor neurological dysfunction at 12 years related to behaviour and cognition?', *Developmental Medicine and Child Neurology*, 35: 321–30.

Sugden, D., Chambers, M. and Utley, A. (2006) *Developmental Coordination Disorder as a Specific Learning Disorder: Leeds Consensus Statement* (http://www.dcd-uk.org/consensus.html).

Wann, J. (2007) 'Current approaches to intervention in children with developmental coordination disorder', *Developmental Medicine and Child Neurology*, 49: 405.

Willoughby, C. and Polatajko, H.J. (1995) 'Motor problems in children with developmental coordination disorder: review of the literature', *American Journal of Occupational Therapy*, 49: 787–94.

VISION AND LEARNING

Keith Holland

Learning objectives

This chapter will help readers to:

- understand the role played by visual processing in learning;
- appreciate the view that issues with vision can impact enormously upon learning;
- explore issues relating to research, identification and intervention for visual difficulties; and
- recognize support strategies and resources that can be used to minimize the impact of visual difficulties.

INTRODUCTION

Mention vision in the context of learning difficulties and these days most people will immediately think 'colour' – coloured lenses or coloured overlays. But visual problems have a much larger role in special educational needs than most people realize, with 'colour' being but a very small – but currently rather popular – part of this. Almost 100 years ago, the first description of dyslexia was of a 'congenital word blindness', described by a Scottish eye surgeon, James Hinshelwood in 1917, and the literature on dyslexia has had a close – and at times controversial – association with vision ever since. Many children suffer from subtle visual difficulties which can affect learning, sometimes coexisting with other learning difficulties.

There is perhaps no other area in special needs where more confusion exists than that of vision. This arises partly because there are several professional groups involved in assessing visual difficulty, approaching the area from very different perspectives. The child, who passes a standard eye test, being able to read clearly at distance with healthy eyes, may be regarded as having no visual difficulty. The same child may, however, experience difficulties with convergence and tracking that make reading difficult and tiring. Identifying and taking appropriate corrective action can have a significant impact on this child's educational progress, and make a big difference to their quality of life. To complicate the situation further, this same child may cope with a visual difficulty through some periods of their education, but be symptomatic and experience difficulties at other times. This visual difficulty may be caused by 1) a structural or physical issue (refractive error of sight); 2) a visual efficiency problem relating to eye movement, focus and binocular vision issues; or 3) a visual perceptual problem (what we do with the information provided by the eyes) – or indeed any combination of the three. How, then, should these difficulties be identified? How should they be assessed? How should they be treated?

THE VISUAL SYSTEM

Light enters the eye through the cornea, a clear fixed membrane which provides much of the refractive or focusing element of the eye, before passing through a variable aperture (known as the pupil) and thence through a flexible lens that can alter focus to produce a focused image on the rods and cones of the retina.

The rods and cones convert incoming light into electrical signals which are transmitted via the optic nerve to an area of the brain known as the occipital cortex. This is located at the rear of the brain, but has links to every other area of the brain – indeed, visual information is represented in over two thirds of the brain area. Thus, vision is intimately linked with other sensory systems, such as balance and audition.

The two eyes are each controlled by six muscles, which can move the eyeballs up, down and to either side, and can also rotate the eyeballs relative to head tilt. These muscles themselves are controlled by 3 of the 12 cranial nerves that leave the brain – highlighting the importance of eye movement control. A complex mechanism exists to ensure that both eyes are looking at the same point in space (this is known as convergence), and that the lens inside the eye is focused to that same point or distance (this process is known as accommodation). This focus/convergence relationship is crucial for efficient visual function, but is impacted on by stress – an important point to realize in children with learning difficulties, who are often under undue stress in learning situations, and whose visual efficiency may consequently be reduced.

Of late, much attention has been paid to visual information processing, and what has become known as the 'dual-channel' or 'parallel pathway' theory. To understand this best, it is important to realize that the retina is not only a light receptor but also an extension of the central nervous system with a great deal of processing of visual information occurring at the retinal level. There are several pathways conducting information from the retina to the visual cortex, the two main pathways known as the parvocellular (p) and magnocellular (m) pathways.

Table 9.1 illustrates the main differences between these two pathways. The magnocellular system is the rapid visual-awareness system, picking up change in the visual environment at a subconscious level and directing the attention of the slower parvo system for detailed analysis. There is so much visual information in the world that we would not be able to process everything we can see, all the time, all at once, without massive overload! On entering a room, a brief magnocellular survey of the room builds a virtual model of the space, while the parvocellular system acts to fill in detail. Any

Table 9.1   Key features of the magnocellular and parvocellular pathways

Magnocellular pathway (*m* system)	Parvocellular pathway (*P* system)
Responsible for peripheral and background awareness	Detail/speech-grabbing system
Response to change – responds when something alters in the visual field	Analytical – what is it? System responsible for interpretation of what we are attending to
Subconscious	Conscious awareness
Fast, instictive response to stimulus (takes less than 150 ms)	Slow response (takes 600 ms–2 s to respond)
Stimulus processing – takes in our entire space world at once	*Awareness of specific items in our world at any moment*

change in the environment is detected by the *m* system, attracting attention, that then directs the *p* system for detailed analysis. In this way, we can subconsciously be aware of our visual world all the time, but only directing attention to the interesting bits, or where change occurs.

VISUAL SYSTEM ANOMALIES

Researchers have identified anomalies in the relationship between these two systems, and have related these to dyslexia. A team at Oxford University has identified significant anomalies in the magnocellular system in particular, and has identified a genetic basis for this centred around chromosome 6 (Stein, 2001). Stein's hypothesis (known as the dual-channel hypothesis) has met with widespread acceptance, and goes some way to explain the visual issues seen by many dyslexics. Sensory information transmitted by the *m* and *p* channels needs to remain in synchrony with each other, and Stein has identified a mis-timing in the relationship between the two channels in many dyslexics, due to a fault in the magnocellular pathway.

Stein has demonstrated that changing the relationship between the two channels is possible through the use of colour (light of differing wavelengths at opposite ends of the spectrum can increase or decrease the response speed of the magnocellular channel), and this provides one explanation for the effect of coloured lenses in enhancing reading skills. Stein's team has shown that blue or yellow tints can significantly improve visual stability (Ray *et al.*, 2005) – in one study one third of dyslexic students improved their reading age by two months for every month in which coloured filters were worn.

For many years, many optometrists have recognized inefficient visual skills as a major cause of reading difficulty, and have found that improving visual dysfunction through a combination of lenses and eye exercises (known as vision therapy) can have a significant impact on reading and learning. From an optometric perspective, assuming a child has appropriate spectacles in place for any significant long or short-sightedness, there are three main areas of visual difficulty that can affect learning.

Convergence

First, a child needs to maintain stable convergence over time and in an effortless way in order to attend to near-vision activity. The convergence mechanism really only kicks in within a 1 m range, and children can have excellent visual skills beyond this distance (for instance, excelling in sport) yet have major difficulties at near, affecting their learning. Children with convergence problems complain of eyestrain and discomfort associated with close work, impacting on concentration and leading to distractibility. One study has shown 25% of children diagnosed with attention deficit disorder (ADD) have poor convergence control (Granet, 2005). In the light of this, it is good clinical practice for all children with attention difficulties to undergo careful testing for convergence difficulties before a formal diagnosis of ADD is made.

Poor convergence may not be obvious in young children where reading demands are of short duration and text size is large with good spacing. They may only start showing up as reading demands increase, with text becoming smaller and reading taking place over longer periods of time. Children with good verbal skills avoid reading by talking or asking questions, thus masking their difficulty. It is possible for convergence difficulties not to have a great impact on reading until a child is at secondary school, if they are able to use other strategies in compensation.

Some children can adopt unusual head postures and tilts, or even resort to allowing their hair to cover one eye as a form of patching to prevent double vision! As many children can be confused over the meaning of 'double vision', it is helpful to be able to demonstrate this. A simply made tool for the classroom teacher or assessor can consist of a passage of text photocopied on to two acetate sheets, which are precisely laid over each other. By moving the sheets apart very slightly or rotating one relative to the other by a few degrees it is possible to demonstrate the effect of convergence breakdown to a child, and to see the variability of the effect with different typefaces and sizes. Affirmation that this occurs should lead to referral for specialist visual investigation (see Figure 9.1).

Convergence difficulties respond well to appropriate spectacles that stabilize visual control, and this would normally be an initial treatment to provide immediate relief. Vision therapy exercises usually provide excellent longer-term correction and stabilization but do require concentration and skilled direction over some months to take effect. A recent series of studies has shown vision training to be the best long-term solution to convergence difficulties and to impact significantly on reading abilities (Scheiman *et al.*, 2005).

Focusing

Poor focus control will similarly impact on reading and can take two forms. Children can show a significantly reduced range or amplitude of focus, making it difficult to sustain accurate focus at a normal working distance – and it should be remembered that young children will tend to be working much closer to their paper than teenagers or adults! Children may also experience difficulties in switching focus rapidly and effortlessly

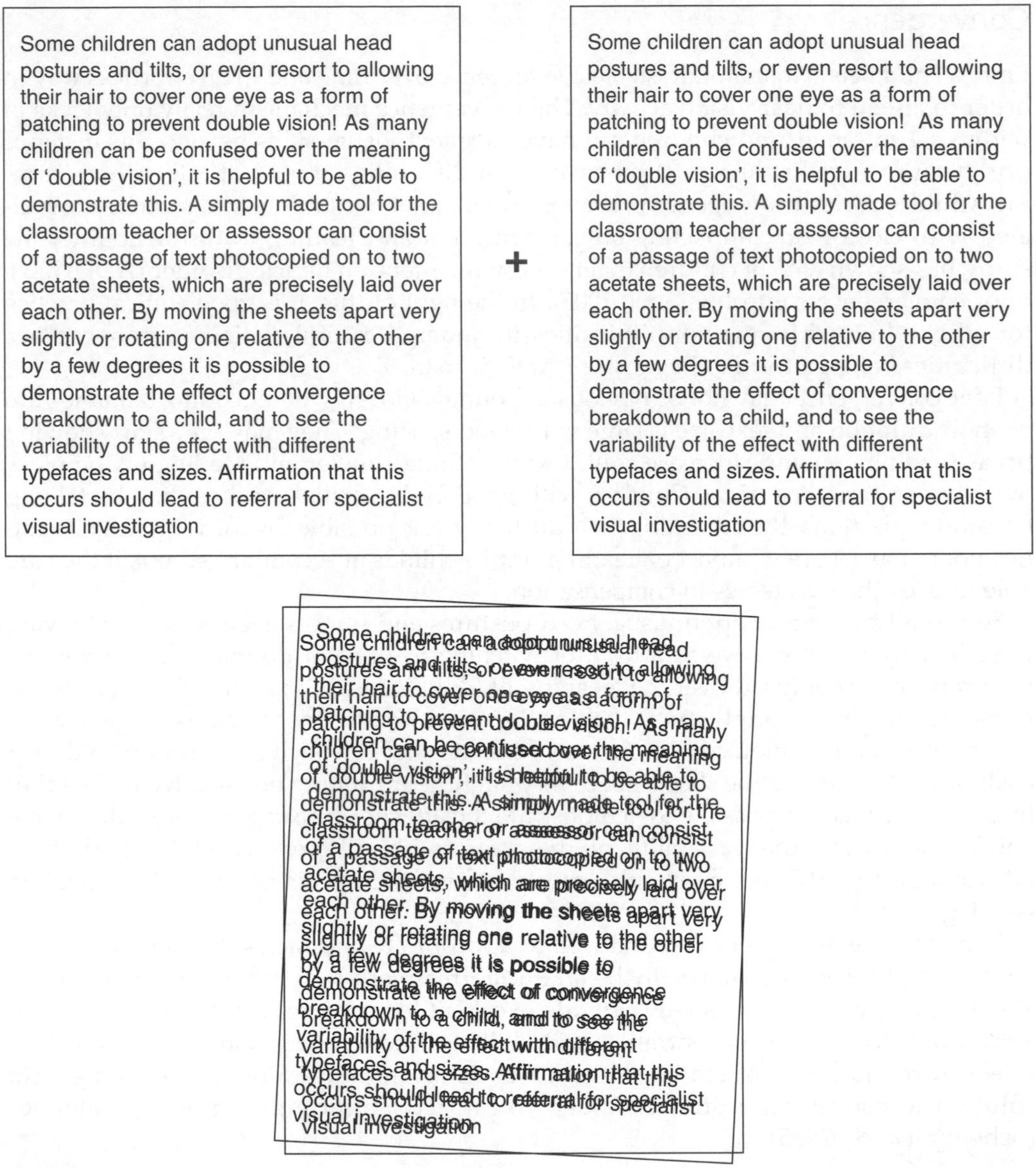

Some children can adopt unusual head postures and tilts, or even resort to allowing their hair to cover one eye as a form of patching to prevent double vision! As many children can be confused over the meaning of 'double vision', it is helpful to be able to demonstrate this. A simply made tool for the classroom teacher or assessor can consist of a passage of text photocopied on to two acetate sheets, which are precisely laid over each other. By moving the sheets apart very slightly or rotating one relative to the other by a few degrees it is possible to demonstrate the effect of convergence breakdown to a child, and to see the variability of the effect with different typefaces and sizes. Affirmation that this occurs should lead to referral for specialist visual investigation

+

Some children can adopt unusual head postures and tilts, or even resort to allowing their hair to cover one eye as a form of patching to prevent double vision! As many children can be confused over the meaning of 'double vision', it is helpful to be able to demonstrate this. A simply made tool for the classroom teacher or assessor can consist of a passage of text photocopied on to two acetate sheets, which are precisely laid over each other. By moving the sheets apart very slightly or rotating one relative to the other by a few degrees it is possible to demonstrate the effect of convergence breakdown to a child, and to see the variability of the effect with different typefaces and sizes. Affirmation that this occurs should lead to referral for specialist visual investigation

Figure 9.1   Overlaying two identical photocopy acetates allows a demonstration of how text can double when convergence breaks down.

from far to near, and back again, and this can impact on copying skills in the classroom. If a child also has reduced short-term memory skills, this issue can become a major problem in a very didactic learning environment. The typical symptoms of focus difficulty include eyestrain and visual discomfort with close work, transient blurred vision at near and fatigue. The solution is often similar to that for convergence problems – and indeed it is very common to see reduced focusing associated with poor convergence. Spectacles to ease focusing at near and vision training exercises to increase focus flexibility both work well and can easily be carried out at home.

Children experiencing difficulties with focus and convergence will often find close work effortful and uncomfortable and not unnaturally will 'switch off', losing concentration and becoming disinterested in the learning process. They may compensate by relying on listening and verbal skills, and on television and other visual means of learning. Thus, they can often present a puzzle in the classroom, working well within the class yet underachieving when it comes to paper-based activity and learning. This should be a warning sign that further investigation is needed.

Eye Movement

The eyes also need to be able to move around, tracking and scanning their visual world. In the context of reading, a very specific pattern of eye movements is required to enable sequential movements in a left-to-right direction and on a line-by-line basis for efficient cognition. This type of movement, known as saccadic eye movement, is distinct from the pursuit eye movements required when following moving targets.

Pursuit eye movements involve locking on to a target that is moving and maintaining fixation on the target, even when the rest of the visual world appears to be moving relative to the target (try looking at your thumb and moving it about and you will see that the world behind the thumb seems to move in the opposite direction and is ignored while you are concentrating on the thumb). Pursuit eye movements are therefore all about ignoring the periphery while maintaining attention on the central target. This is important when we are moving about in the world and following targets such as a ball in sport. Problems with pursuit eye movement can affect spatial awareness and co-ordination, and can also have social implications, such individuals sometimes finding it difficult to interact with the moving world around them.

Saccadic eye movement requires an individual who is fixing one point to use their peripheral awareness to gauge where to move to for the next fixation. As we read, this involves moving from the point we are looking at to an appropriate point some way ahead in order for cognition of the next word or words to occur – an efficient adult reader will typically move between 12 and 15 letters forward at a time, while a 9-year-old child will typically move only 5 or 6 letters forward at a time. A characteristic pattern of saccadic eye movements is desirable in reading, with occasional regressions or backward movements taking place to double check what we have read (see Figure 9.2).

During the 1970s and 1980s, it was suggested by Pavlides that disorders with saccadic eye movement control were the likely cause of reading difficulties, and thus the possible cause of dyslexia. While there is no doubt that many children with

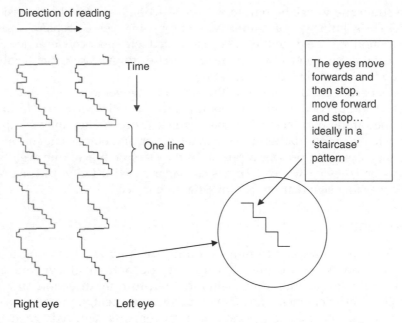

Direction of reading

Time

One line

The eyes move forwards and then stop, move forward and stop... ideally in a 'staircase' pattern

Right eye   Left eye

Figure 9.2 The horizontal, or saccadic, eye movements of a competent reader, recorded with an infrared eye-tracking device

reading problems have poor-quality saccadic eye movements, it is not likely that this is the cause of dyslexia. However it is important to recognize poor eye movement skills and to investigate these further. Typically, children with poor-quality saccades are also likely to have issues with convergence and focusing skills, and these areas all need to be treated in an integrated fashion. Technological advances have meant that it is quite possible to analyse the eye movements required for reading in a clinical setting and to compare these with established norms. This also means that treatment can be monitored and progress measured objectively (see Figure 9.3).

VISUAL PROBLEMS AND LEARNING

The existence of visual issues affecting convergence, focusing and eye movement skills can have a significant impact on visual perception. Children with such difficulties may show reduced skills in the way they assess visual information. Most commonly, poor visual figure-ground skills and poor visual-closure skills are seen. Visual figure-ground skill is the ability to analyse detail (the figure) in a busy background, and this affects the ability rapidly and effortlessly to find detail on a 'busy' page. Visual closure refers to

Trace 1 taken December 2008
(before intervention)

Trace 2 taken May 2009
(after intervention)

Figure 9.3   Two examples of eye movement recordings taken for the same child, aged 14 for trace 1, showing the dramatic changes possible after stabilizing visual problems through spectacles and vision therapy

the ability to 'fill in' incomplete detail that is seen and is an essential component of reading and scanning information. The two skills are intimately linked, and difficulties here will affect both comprehension when reading and the acquisition of information quickly and accurately when scanning through pages. These problems are also likely to reduce visual processing speed. While there can be other causes for this, reduced visual perceptual skills of this nature can often contribute to lower-than-predicted results in the subtests of some intelligence testing (for example, in the coding and block design subtests of the Weschler intelligence scale).

Early and persistent visual difficulties can impact on how well we rely on visual recall or visualization skills, and this in turn can affect the way we choose to learn spellings. Children with visual problems will often find it hard to recall spellings as visual images and rely heavily on phonetic spelling. They may be able to learn by rote and use this to achieve success in spelling tests, but this often fails to transfer well to long-term memory, and they may appear to make 'careless' and inconsistent errors soon after.

Problems with visual perceptual abilities can be quite fluid, and stabilizing visual input, either through appropriate spectacle lenses or following a course of visual training, can sometimes have an immediate and dramatic impact on visual perception, making it easier for a child to acquire visual information and to maintain attention on near

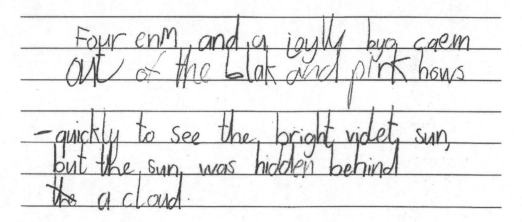

Figure 9.4 A handwriting sample before, and immediately after, insertion of lenses to stabilize poor convergence control

tasks. This can sometimes be seen in a child's handwriting, with almost immediate increased fluency and consistency when visual factors are eliminated (see Figure 9.4).

INCIDENCE AND INDENTIFICATION OF VISUAL PROBLEMS

The incidence of visual problems that affect learning is quite variable in the research literature, but a good estimate would be of between 10 and 15% of the child population having visual inefficiencies that are impacting on learning. This translates to between one and two children in every average classroom, with a significantly higher figure in groups of children with learning difficulties. It is essential, therefore, that class teachers and parents work together to recognize these children and that appropriate mechanisms exist for referral, analysis and treatment.

Once a visual issue has been initially identified, appropriate referral for specialist investigation needs to be arranged. There is no longer any national school eye-examination service in the UK and, where screening does take place, it does not normally involve visual skills for learning. One should therefore not assume that because a school 'eye test' has been carried out – and probably passed – that appropriate testing has taken place.

In the UK, all children under the age of 16, and under the age of 19 if in full-time education, are entitled to a basic sight test paid for by the National Health Service. Unfortunately, this service is essentially geared around the need for spectacles to correct refractive error, and there is no guarantee that an eye examination will investigate the visual factors that affect learning. Restricted funding of the service over many years has meant that there are considerable time pressures on optometrists when examining children, and subtle issues with binocular vision control and eye movement skills are unlikely to be looked at.

More detailed investigation of the visual factors that affect learning is available on a private basis. One group of optometrists who specialize in this work is the British Association of Behavioural Optometrists, and their website identifies practitioners who have completed considerable additional training in this specialism and offer expert evaluation and treatment (www.babo.co.uk). Binocular vision anomalies are also investigated by orthoptists working within the hospital eye service, and referral for such investigation can normally be arranged through a child's GP.

Before undergoing a specialist eye examination, it is useful to complete a checklist that allows identification of the symptoms relating to visual difficulties, and this may be carried out by either teachers or parents (ideally, by both), and it provides a useful overview of the child's difficulties. It should be remembered that parents do not necessarily see their children in a normal learning environment in order to identify many of these issues and, in a classroom setting, children may sometimes hide symptoms from their teacher for fear of the response, or being thought of as being 'stupid'. None the less, questionnaires are probably the most useful initial screening approach. A suitable questionnaire which can be used in the classroom or by parents is shown below. This is used by the author to identify children with possible visual difficulties. Any positive responses should lead to referral for visual investigation:

- Often lose place when reading.
- Misses out words or rereads the same word.
- Needs to use a finger or marker to keep their place.
- Quickly becomes tired when reading.
- Experiences transient blurred or double vision during close work.
- Complains of words 'moving about', 'shimmering' or 'dancing' when reading.
- Has difficulty copying from board down on to paper.
- Complains of headache (usually around the temples) after close work.
- Has poor concentration for close work.
- Short and often decreasing working distance.
- Continuous reading is inaccurate, yet can read single words quite easily.
- Has difficulty 'taking in' what is reading, and has to read something several times for meaning.

In addition, the following more general symptoms may also suggest visual problems:

- Poor co-ordination at near, typically shown as bumping into, or knocking things over, yet may be good at sports (this may be identified as 'dyspraxia', but may simply be a vision problem).
- Reluctance to play with jigsaws and similar puzzles.
- Difficulty with spatial concepts in maths.
- Irregular and untidy handwriting.
- Travel sickness.
- A strongly phonetic pattern to spelling.

VISUAL CORRECTION

Glasses and Contact Lenses

It is normal for adults with poor focusing skills (which typically occurs from the mid-40s onwards) to wear bifocal or varifocal spectacles, in order to provide optimum correction at both distance and near. It is perhaps surprising, therefore, that children, who will frequently have the same need for different prescriptions at near and far, are rarely prescribed bifocals.

Once optimum visual correction is in place with glasses or contact lenses, there is a need to develop underlying visual skills through vision-training exercise programmes, and these have been proven to be very effective in improving convergence, focusing and eye movement difficulties. Vision training can be somewhat time-consuming and does require dedication from both child and parent. Some optometrists overcome this by offering in-practice training programmes where much of the work is done by the optometrist or a vision therapist working in conjunction with the child. Some computer-based training programs are also available which can be particularly useful for children in boarding school situations – especially as these computer programs often have Internet links which allow an optometrist to monitor progress remotely, but there are limitations to what can be trained via a computer. One study has shown that regular use of a computer-based tracking program typically produces a six-month improvement in reading age with a six-week intervention programme CME of 15 minutes' computer-based training a day (Hoover and Harris, 1997).

Coloured Lenses

There has been much talk and hype about the use of coloured lenses in treating dyslexia and, as noted at the beginning of this chapter, they are perhaps now the most well-known 'treatment' for visually based reading difficulties. There is certainly a place for the use of judiciously tinted lenses to stabilize the magnocellular/parvocellular anomalies described earlier, and the work of Stein has shown how blue or yellow tints can be beneficial (Ray *et al.*, 2005). The first person to recommend the use of tints was Helen Irlen, an American psychologist, and her programme of tinted spectacles included many claims of dramatic cures when introduced in the late 1980s. Further work by Arnold Wilkins (Wilkins and Neary, 1991), at the time Professor of Applied Psychology at Cambridge University, led to a more systematic and structured approach to the use of tints, and a device (the intuitive colorimeter) was developed to formalize the testing and prescribing of tints. Wilkins, together with Bruce Evans who co-operated in his research, coined the term 'Meares–Irlen' syndrome to describe the visual difficulties they felt benefited from coloured lenses. Wilkins also developed several tools which allow screening with simple coloured overlays to see if colour may be beneficial (Wilkins, 1994).

The research on coloured lenses is, however, arguable as to the long-term impact they have on reading. Although many studies have been carried out showing the short-term benefits of coloured lenses on reading, very few have adequately allowed for the presence of other visual difficulties. Indeed, in one major review of the literature it was found that 95% of patients considered appropriate for coloured lenses had significant undetected and uncorrected vision disorders that were ignored within the studies (Blaskey *et al.*, 1990). There is little information on the longer-term impact of coloured lenses, and their use is certainly not straightforward.

Modifications to Books and Computers

Children with visual difficulties often have increased sensitivity to glare and to repetitive patterns, such as may occur with many lines of text on a page. Reducing contrast may aid this, and the use of off-white paper may be particularly helpful to such individuals (a cream colour is used by Barrington Stokes for their range of dyslexia-friendly books). Similarly, modifying the background colour on computer monitors may reduce glare problems for screen users. A useful computer program can be downloaded without cost, allowing modification of screen background colour, and many students report this to be helpful (the program can be downloaded from www.thomson-software-solutions.com).

Modifications to the Classroom

Within the classroom or work environment, there are several modifications that can be made to reduce visual stress. First the use of a slightly sloping desk surface (to approximately 20 °) has been shown to lead to an increased working distance which, in turn, can reduce visual demands. We typically angle material to match the plane of our face and older-style sloping desks are ideal for this, encouraging both good posture and working distances. The more recent use of horizontal desk surfaces can lead to moving forward and dropping the head down towards the desk, in turn leading to a reduced working distance – as well as increasing stress on the neck muscles. Portable desk slopes that sit on the desk and angle text to an appropriate 20 º are becoming widely available and can be carried from classroom to classroom by students who need them.

The surroundings of classrooms are often overlooked, but children with visual difficulties are often more sensitive to peripheral distractions. Excessive amounts of brightly coloured material displayed in front of and to the side of children, with objects hanging from the ceiling around the classroom, can be the cause of major distraction. Studies have shown that subdued, plain-coloured backgrounds are conducive to better study and do minimize distraction effects for children, as well as having a calming effect on the class as a whole.

Lighting in the classroom can also play an important role and should be even and flicker-free, ideally using high-frequency fluorescent lighting rather than conventional fluorescent lights, which will often produce flicker at the end of tubes for a considerable part of the lights' life. While this may not be a big issue for many children, those with visual difficulties – and particularly those with magnocellular dysfunction – will be unduly sensitive to this, and can find them a source of irritation and distraction.

High-frequency fluorescent tubes do not normally produce any flicker of this nature. Optimal lighting for a classroom would involve the use of halogen up-lighting, thus producing the closest lighting to natural daylight; however, the energy requirements of these lights preclude their use in these environmental and energy-conscious times (but they are ideal in the home).

Recent work has been carried out on typefaces and type layouts to reduce visual demands, and several typefaces have been designed specifically for individuals with dyslexia and other reading problems (such as the Sassoon font). As long ago as 1878, researchers postulated that poor typography could cause visual difficulty, and the use of serifs has been shown to diminish legibility of text. Some researchers have also suggested that ragged margins are easier for poor readers to cope with than fully justified text, providing greater reference as to where you are on the page. Text size would also appear important, and many children, particularly those with tracking difficulties, avoid 8 or 10-point text wherever possible, preferring instead 12 or even 14-point material which reduces visual demands.

It is important to ensure when photocopying material in a classroom that copies are clear and sharp, and not reduced in size to get more on the page. Copying coloured material into black and white can also cause problems of reduced legibility and contrast.

The increasing use of display screens, both from a teaching perspective and from home use in computer games and on the Internet, is a controversial area. Studies point to both the benefits and pitfalls of excessive screen use, and the research is really not clear on the overall impact. The quality of screens has improved enormously in the last three to four years, and some of the early negative research carried out with monochrome CRT computer displays is perhaps no longer valid. However, there is increasing evidence that excess screen use can both impact on perceptual development and restrict time that could otherwise usefully be spent on more motor-based activity and play. It is perhaps beyond the scope of this chapter to expand into motor training, but the role of motor activity in developing the skills needed for learning is well documented, and anything that detracts from this is regarded by the author as being detrimental to well rounded learning.

Most classrooms now make use of interactive whiteboards, allowing the use of computer-projected material and PowerPoint slides alongside free writing on the board itself. There would appear to be very little work carried out on the potential risks and difficulties associated with the interactive whiteboard, but children frequently complain to their optometrist of glare problems and visual discomfort due to the very high light levels of the screen compared with the surroundings. Contrast on the screen itself can often be poor and causes difficulties with copying. Teachers should regularly check the clarity of screens themselves from different areas of the classroom and ensure that all children are comfortable in using such screens. One very practical aspect to the use of technology is with the simple task of copying – in the days of roller blackboards, children who were slow at copying could keep going as the board rolled around. This is not possible with the interactive board where, at a touch of a button, material changes. This can be a cause of considerable stress to some children who struggle with copying, and should be borne in mind by the teacher! Children with focusing difficulties, who also have problems with short-term memory, are likely to find copying off boards particularly difficult, and it is important to ensure that printed copies of material are available for them.

SUMMARY

- It is important to appreciate the huge role played by visual processing in learning and to recognize that issues with vision can impact enormously on learning.
- All those working with children should be aware of the role that vision plays in learning, what happens when it goes wrong and what can be done, both in class and professionally, to alleviate these difficulties.
- A small survey by the author of teenagers excluded from schools in a Gloucestershire town during one year because of poor behaviour identified visual problems in a remarkable 85% of the sample.
- Vision problems are truly a 'hidden handicap': they cannot be seen or felt by others and are often not recognized by the sufferer themselves but do require careful investigation and handling. Only then can a child go on to reach their true potential.

Further Reading

Hellerstein, L. (2010) *See it, Say it. Do it! The Parent's and Teachers Guide to Creating Successful Students and Confident Kids*. Denver, CO: Hi Clear Publishing. This is a bang up-to-date guide for parents and teachers on how to develop visual skills in children – both at home and in the classroom.

Scheiman, M. and Rouse, M. (2006) *Optometric Management of Vision Related Learning Problems*. ST Louis, MO: Mosby. This is the leading textbook in the field and, although designed for eye-care professionals, contains a wealth of information that would benefit other professionals.

References

Blaskey, P. *et al.* (1990) 'The effectiveness of Irlen filters for improving reading performance: a pilot study', *Journal of Learning Disability'*, 23: 604–12.

Granet, D.G.C. (2005) 'The relationship between convergence insufficiency and ADHD', *Strabismus*, 13: 163–8.

Hoover, D. and Harris, P. (1997) 'The effects of using the readfast computer programme on eye movement abilities as measured by the OBER2 eye movement device', *Journal of Optometric Vision Development*, 28: 227–34.

Pavlides, G.T. (1981) 'Do eye movements hold the key to dyslexia?', *Neuropsychologia*, 19: 57–64.

Ray, N. *et al.* (2005) 'Yellow filters can improve magnocellular function: motion sensitivity, convergence, accommodation and reading', *Annals of the New York Academy of Science*, 1039: 283–93.

Richardson, A.J. and Montgomery, P. (2005) 'The Oxford–Durham study: a randomised, controlled trial of dietry supplementation with fatty acids in children with developmental coordination disorder', *Paediatrics*, 115: 1360–6.

Scheiman, M. *et al.* (2005) 'A randomised clinical trial of treatments for convergence insufficiency in children', *Archives of Ophthalmology*, 123: 14–24.

Stein, J. (2001) 'The magnocellular theory of developmental dyslexia', *Dyslexia*, 7: 12–36.

Stein, J., Fowler, S. and Richardson, A.J. (2000) 'Monocular occlusion can improve binocular control and reading in dyslexics', *Brain*, 123: 164–70.

Wilkins, A.J. (1994) 'Overlays for classroom and optometric use', *Ophthalmic and Physiological Optics*, 14: 97–9.

Wilkins, A.J. and Neary, C. (1991) 'Some visual, optometric and perceptual effects of coloured glasses', *Ophthalmic and Physiological Optics*, 11: 163–71.

GOOD PRACTICE IN TRAINING SPECIALIST TEACHERS AND ASSESSORS OF PEOPLE WITH DYSLEXIA

Sheena Bell and Bernadette McLean

Learning objectives

This chapter will help readers to:

- understand the current climate in the training of dyslexia specialists in England;
- explore the key skills needed by specialist teachers;
- appreciate the knowledge and skills needed to support people with dyslexia across all phases of education and employment;
- understand the value of evaluation as a crucial element in training courses; and
- appreciate the support needed for teachers undertaking specialist training.

TRAINING FOR DYSLEXIA SPECIALISTS: WHERE ARE WE NOW?

The field of training specialist teachers and assessors is evolving both in terms of our understanding of dyslexia and literacy difficulties, and in systems and protocols of teaching and learning for people with special educational needs (SEN) within the school system and beyond. In England, although the network of specialist teachers and assessors is expanding, government policy states clearly that *every* teacher is a teacher of children with SEN (Department for Education and Skills, 2001). A recent national report in England warned that:

> we cannot currently be confident that those who are charged with making a judgement about the quality of the education provided for pupils with SEN can do so on the basis of a good understanding of what good progress is or how best to secure it (Lamb, 2009).

This report reinforces the need for the English school inspection body to report specifically on the quality of the education provided for children with SEN and disabilities. Dyslexia training in England is regulated by bodies which include expert representatives of national dyslexia organizations that are currently developing a national qualifications framework in order to ensure that all trained and qualified specialist teachers and assessors have the necessary competences to carry out their roles effectively.

While demanding that the needs of students with dyslexia and other SEN are met in mainstream schools and classrooms alongside their peers, the inclusion agenda nevertheless requires institutions to respond to the individual learning styles of learners with dyslexia who may need individualized teaching and support. Definitions of dyslexia are not internationally agreed although there are common characteristics. In England, the British Psychological Association (BPS) has been widely used as a baseline for intervention, focusing specifically on a failure to read and spell single words despite appropriate teaching (British Psychological Society, 1999). For over ten years there have been constraints on identifying people with dyslexia because of the narrow focus of this definition. Rose's report into dyslexia teaching (2009) effectively widened this by proposing a working definition that embraced a number of other dyslexic characteristics, such as verbal memory and processing speed.

Although all teachers should be equipped to teach the wide range of learners they encounter in their classrooms (Department for Education and Skills, 2001), there is a need to train expert teachers who can respond on an individual level to learners with dyslexia. A structure of dyslexia support is proposed to schools and local authorities in England which is based on a pyramid of support (Rose, 2009). At the first level, classroom teachers should develop core skills for recognizing children with risk factors of dyslexia and put in appropriate interventions immediately. At the second level, more experienced or qualified specialist teachers should assess the child's difficulties and use assessment to plan focused teaching programmes. At the third level, specialist teachers with appropriate qualifications or other professionals should carry out a full diagnostic assessment to decide if the child has dyslexia, and make recommendations for teaching and support. In England, teachers trained to this level may now hold professional practising certificates which require an appropriate qualification and evidence of continuing professional development and practice to ensure national standards are met.

Students with dyslexia may not need pedagogical approaches that are essentially different from other learners, but they will need individually focused programmes of learning involving 'greater planning and structure, more time for reinforcing learning and more continuous assessment' (Lewis and Norwich, 2001: 2). This attention to very specific individual needs necessitates training specialist teachers and providing opportunities for them to work with individual students. Specialist teachers require still more complex knowledge, understanding and skills to carry out diagnostic assessments for learners with dyslexia. In England, in recent years, a range of training courses has been developed to equip specialist teachers to fulfil both the role of specialist teacher and diagnostic assessor:

> The course has opened my eyes to the particular difficulties faced by dyslexic children and particularly to how many pass through their school days with no recognition and no support (experienced SENCO (special educational needs co-ordinator) 2010).

However, specific one-to-one provision for individual students with dyslexia may not be available in all schools, or delivered by practitioners with little or no specific training. Many schools who manage to support their teachers and teaching assistants in completing training courses report immediate feedback:

> After only one term, the course has helped teachers to build up a bank of useful resources in their schools. It has enabled trainees to develop evaluative thinking and self-evaluation, informing their current practice. Already this new learning is impacting — it's like a ripple effect! (Local Authority Inclusion consultant, 2010).

Regrettably, financial constraints may prevent schools from investing in specialist training for their teachers. Once trained there may also be issues over deploying specialists across the institution. Schools may not have sufficiently large SEN budgets to allow for individual or small-group teaching programmes with specialist practitioners and, if such teaching is carried out at all, it may be with teaching assistants whose qualifications, experience and expertise are highly variable. It is imperative that teachers with specialist qualifications are prepared to disseminate their knowledge and competence with others. Communication and presentation skills should be embedded in the training now offered to specialists (Rose, 2009):

> I have led teacher and support assistant training to highlight how best to support dyslexic children in the classroom. We are now better able to identify children and to use appropriate strategies to give them the support they need (experienced SENCO, 2010).

Courses should equip and inspire trainees to pass on their newly acquired knowledge and skills:

> I want to cascade as much information as I can to colleagues so that everyone realizes how students can be affected by the difficulties they have and how something simple, like a worksheet on coloured paper, can make a big difference to their achievements and subsequently self-esteem (experienced SENCO, 2010).

Despite recognition of the need for early identification and intervention (Rose, 2009), there is inconsistency of provision across educational phases. For example, in the higher-education phase in England, a Disabled Student Allowance (DSA) provides funding directed towards the individual with dyslexia after a rigorous process of assessment and identification of individual need (Jamieson and Morgan, 2008). The DSA can supply finance for a range of aids (for example, assistive software) and also 1:1 support from specialist teachers, according to the individual's learning profile. At present, no such funding stream exists in the school system and provision of specialist tuition is highly variable.

The contrast between protocols for dyslexia assessment and support in schools and higher education may contribute to the fact that most students with dyslexia in higher education are not formally diagnosed until after entry into higher education training (Singleton, 2008). Across the compulsory education sector there are many excellent teachers and schools but, without clear legislative requirements and targeted, ring-fenced funding, identification and provision for dyslexia are likely to remain inconsistent. In addition, the current global recession is probably not conducive to increasing funding for these vulnerable learners. It was recognized by the last English government that there was a need for a specialist dyslexia teacher in every school and funding for a limited period was allocated to train such teachers, using existing, high-quality training courses (DCSF, 2009). If and when such targets for specialist teachers are achieved, each English school must decide on priorities for the use of their SEN funding in relation to dyslexia, and this will depend on the school pupil population and their diverse needs.

KEY SKILLS NEEDED FOR SPECIALIST TEACHERS

Even in primary school settings, where literacy acquisition is a key over-riding target, specialist teachers are different from classroom teachers: classroom teachers are trained to deliver a national curriculum, but specialist teachers need liberation from this to respond to the individual needs of children.

Teachers need to develop the confidence to use their imagination to 'pick and mix'. For children with dyslexia, there is no one programme which can fulfil the needs of every individual; therefore, evaluation of what works for a particular learner is essential. Learners who access support will have struggled with the learning environment of a mainstream classroom. Some learners with dyslexia have floundered by being placed in remedial settings and given more of the same style of teaching which led to their failure in their mainstream class.

Learners with dyslexia require far more repetition and over-learning than other students; therefore, specialists need to have a vast repertoire of attractive and engaging activities which can be adapted to focus on particular learning preferences and key targets, while tapping into own interests and goals. Courses for specialist teachers must show participants how to make teaching more multi-sensory. 'Death by worksheet' can be a dire fate; specialist teachers learn to teach in a much more creative and three-dimensional manner. Multi-sensory methods require teachers to use all the sensory channels to help their students acquire literacy. For example, letter shapes do not have to be learnt simply by writing them. Teachers can plan lessons where a range of senses are used to enable the participant to maximize their strengths and scaffold weaker channels. The list in Table 10.1 is by no means exhaustive, but shows how course participants may be encouraged to respond to the needs of learners.

Naturally, not all the activities will be suitable for all phases. However, even adults can respond well to multi-sensory activities when there are developed in a suitably non-childish way. For example, many adult learners respond well to using three-dimensional letters, small whiteboards with large felt-tip pens, highlighters and image association.

In the mainstream classroom, it can be easy to miss signs of specific learning difficulties, particularly when students disguise these with bad behaviour, or by keeping a low profile enabling them to remain undetected in a busy classroom. Many adults with dyslexia are well practised at concealing weaknesses at work and therefore do not receive the appropriate support and possibly simple adjustments to their working practice which would help them carry out their roles more efficiently, and reduce stress and anxiety about exposure.

For many trainees, training courses challenge the way they assess their learners. In early stages of courses, some teachers make comments such as *careless mistake* and *read more slowly and carefully* on students' scripts, showing that even motivated and interested teachers need to understand how dyslexia can affect reading and writing behaviours.

Table 10.1   Multi-sensory teaching methods

Sensory channel	Teaching points	Activities to combine sensory channels
Auditory (oral)	Say the letters (sounds or names, depending on target)	Drawing picture with memory cues to associate letter
Visual	Use colour, shape associations (such as S for snake), images	Saying letter sounds/phonemes/words
Kinaesthetic/ tactile	Use three-dimensional letters Making the letters	Painting
		Sticking string shapes
Taste/smell (olfactory)	Although more unusual, associations can be made for students with difficulties in other channels e.g. J with JAM	Writing in sand
		Alphabet arc activities
		Finger writing in modelling clay
		Make biscuits
		Write on playground in water
		Fernald methodology (Doveston *et al.*, 2006)
		Matching games
		Acting
		Making shapes with the body/dance

Even specialist teachers can make assumptions that learners are careless, simply reading too fast and therefore stumbling on words. They may, however, be exhibiting errors symptomatic of the underlying difficulties of dyslexia.

 Discussion Point

On a training course for specialist teachers, one of the participants is teaching a secondary school-level learner who is having difficulty sequencing ideas for an essay. He is unable to plan by using headings and subheadings. Multi-sensory methods, such as mind mapping, using Post-its to brainstorm ideas and sticking these on a large piece of paper, moving them around to form logical sequences, have been used. What other ideas might be suggested to help this teacher respond to the learner's needs?

SKILLS CAN BE TAUGHT TO TEACHERS ACROSS EDUCATIONAL AND OTHER PROFESSIONAL CONTEXTS

Course providers should consider the context of their participants, but should also ensure that teachers understand the challenges that people with dyslexia face throughout their lives. Teachers need to be aware of the implications of legislation and policy at national and local levels for trajectories of students with dyslexia in the education system. People with dyslexia must deal with highly complex twenty-first century social structures combined with increasingly mobile populations on national and international levels. Choices in terms of education and employment are rapidly evolving. Students with dyslexia and their families should be informed and included in decisions about support structures and transition planning, so that they can fulfil their potential in the long term. For some students with intractable dyslexic difficulties, integrated settings may not provide the most suitable environment either for skills acquisition or the development of a positive self-concept. Nevertheless, the opportunity to choose a specialist setting may be available only to students whose parents have the financial means to pay for private education.

Teachers must look ahead to facilitate the students' future progression through the education system and employment. Thus, teachers in primary schools need to be aware of the direct challenges presented to the dyslexic learner in a wide secondary curriculum.

Assistive technology is potentially enormously helpful to students with dyslexia as they move into secondary education and the information technology-driven workplaces of the twenty-first century. Many would benefit from learning to touch type as early as possible, to provide easy access to computer technology:

> From this course I have also learnt of the benefits of making sure learners are competent in basic ICT skills. I can also now see the benefits of encouraging them to learn to touch type (specialist teacher, 2010).

Technical problems need technical solutions; such solutions can ease the lot of people with dyslexia and their families but this is not all. People with dyslexia tend to have adaptive problems requiring them or the people and environment around them to devise adaptive solutions. Technical solutions may not allow people with dyslexia to listen and process oral information more quickly, but teachers and other presenters of oral information can adjust the speed at which information is delivered. Such adjustments can be used alongside digital recorders and other technological solutions to increase the accessibility of all learners, not just those with dyslexia.

The affective needs of children moving from a supportive primary school with one key teacher into the more challenging world of the secondary school can put additional strains on those who may have hitherto been able to cope with academic work. In all phases of education, and employment, the specialist teacher may need to play the role of advocate for learners with dyslexia, explaining their issues to non-specialists to ensure that their needs are met through 'reasonable adjustments' enshrined in English disability legislation (DfES, 1995).

Similarly, specialist teachers in secondary schools should be aware of possible funding for support and access as students move into higher education. Transition planning for students is a long-term project, to be addressed before the final year and before moving into post-compulsory education or the workplace, and teachers have a key role to play in this process. Specialist teachers must be prepared to discuss issues of disability disclosure and enable students to assess the range of factors involved in choosing dyslexia-friendly institutions. In England, higher education students with dyslexia must accept the label of disability to access funding, which may not sit comfortably with their self-concept (Armstrong and Humphrey, 2009).

High-quality training in assistive software should be available before the student with dyslexia progresses into higher education with its high demands on organization skills and novel learning formats such as lectures (involving note-taking, a huge challenge to dyslexic learners with information-processing difficulties) and seminars (which may involve reading aloud or quick responses to written information, often highly stressful for the learner with dyslexia).

It is an advantage for courses to attract trainees from a range of backgrounds to bring a variety of perspectives to the course. This can be exploited within the training group in discussions and information sharing. Teachers in primary schools must understand how to prepare dyslexic learners for the change of teaching style they will encounter in secondary school. Conversely, a support teacher from a university setting needs to understand how previous educational experience may have affected learners in terms of motivation and skills acquisition, as well as self-esteem.

Teachers can bring a wealth of experience of working with learners. They need opportunities during and after the course to practise their skills as part of their personal development as specialist teachers. Although they have a role in the dissemination and training of other non-specialist professionals, it is important that dyslexia specialists are given the opportunity to work with individuals or small groups where they are able to use their skills. Increasing pressures on resources in schools may be a barrier to this taking place.

TEACHING – WHAT TRAINEES NEED TO KNOW

Crucial to any teaching programme for learners with dyslexia is that it should be individualized. Trainees learn how to direct learning programmes towards students' particular strengths and weaknesses. They should be based on a clear view of what students can do already, taking into account progression and relating clearly to their individual learning contexts, which can be as diverse as a primary school classroom, a university, a business enterprise or a prison. Course tutors must respond to the demands of these contexts and should also ensure that the skills and needs of trainees are carefully audited to ensure responsive individualized teaching.

 Discussion Point

Many existing courses for specialist teachers and assessors train teachers across age ranges. Dyslexia may be mitigated by good teaching and the environment in which a learner develops their skills, but the underlying difficulties remain the same. An understanding of learner context and motivation is key to developing a teaching programme. How far should specialist teachers be open to experiencing support with learners outside their normal educational sphere, and what might be the advantages of doing so?

On courses for specialist teachers, trainees are the 'piggy in the middle': they are both receiving and giving teaching (see Figure 10.1).

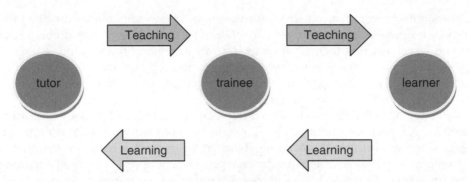

Figure 10.1 Teaching and learning on specialist teacher courses

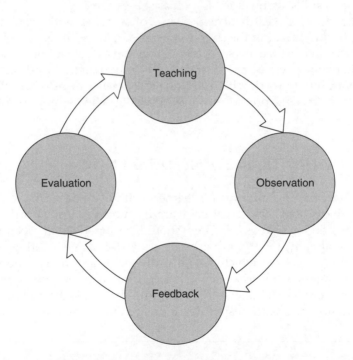

Figure 10.2 The cycle of training for observations

Course tutors can model good teaching in the way they work with their trainees (for example, giving them manageable targets). It is essential that any specialist courses integrate observations of the participants teaching in their own settings. Ideally more than one observation should be included so that teachers are given the chance to develop skills as they extend knowledge. Positive feedback and reflection on feedback are highly beneficial, as they help develop a habit of self-evaluation, an important part of the one-to-one teaching process (see Figure 10.2):

In the light of a recent observation, I now have many more ideas of how to incorporate multi-sensory teaching into lessons (support teacher, 2010).

Detailed records of this process enable trainees to track back and review progress, just as they do with their own students. Continuing to use this process of critical evaluation and adapting teaching as they gain more experience develops professional competences:

I also understand that my own learning in this specialist field will not stop. I will have to continue to update my reading and learning to stay in touch with changes and new techniques. I felt confident in most areas of assessment and I do recognise that this will improve, again with practice, as my tutor informed me 'you wouldn't expect to know everything by the end of this course – that comes with experience' (teaching assistant, 2010).

BUILDING A KNOWLEDGE AND SKILLS BASE FOR ASSESSMENT

Trainees need a clear understanding of the underlying processing difficulties which are causal factors in dyslexia. If students are not learning, it is essential for teachers to have a hypothesis of where difficulties lie in order to offer appropriate support:

I had not fully realized how important working memory and processing speed is in those learners with traits of dyslexia or how important phonological processing is (teaching assistant, 2010).

Although teachers do not need detailed knowledge of medical research, an awareness of current advances in neuroscience and genetics is important because of its applications to practice. For example, the fact that there are genetic links for dyslexic traits (Pennington and Olson, 2005) has implications for how teachers approach the families of students with disabilities; parents may not offer literacy support as they themselves have similar difficulties. Similarly, a specialist teacher's awareness of issues such as visual processing difficulties (Singleton, 2008) may affect not only the nature of support offered but also generate recommendations for referrals. Such intervention can have a huge effect on a learner's progress.

Courses must include the normal development of literacy skills, an area which is now not generally included in teacher training, even at primary level. Teachers should also be taught simple, qualitative assessments for working memory, sequencing and phonological awareness and how to observe and comment on the functional expressive and receptive language skills of learners. Specialist teachers should be trained to administer detailed individual assessments including the mastery of non-standardized tests. They should be equipped to devise and use questionnaires and checklists to collect relevant background information. They need to understand and interpret the results of screening tests and reports. All teachers and supporters should be aware of the language of statistical standardized tests and the implications for learners to prevent common misunderstandings of the significance of age equivalents and problems with the misinterpretation of percentiles. Initial teacher training does not generally provide training in this area and yet the English education system appears to rely increasingly on the results of such tests both to classify students and justify educational support. Specialist teachers should share this knowledge with colleagues:

> I have always been in the habit of reading dyslexia reports and educational psychologist's reports prior to working with a learner if at all possible. However, in the past I had only looked at the recommendations as I had not understood many of the other areas. But now I can understand percentiles and scores which are considered 'normal' and those scores able to receive access arrangements (specialist teacher, 2010).

While the development of literacy skills is not the remit of this chapter it is important to stress that effective literacy skills specialists experienced in teaching synthetic phonics may not be successful in teaching those skills to those dyslexics whose phonological difficulties make them unreachable by this approach:

> I want to learn to teach all children how to read not just those who respond to synthetic phonics (teacher applying for specialist teacher training, 2010).

TRAINING DIAGNOSTIC ASSESSORS

Formal diagnostic assessment differs from teaching. They have a similar knowledge base but two different skill sets. Both specialist teachers and qualified assessors of dyslexia need to understand the underlying cognitive differences that play a part in a specific learning difficulty (Backhouse and Morris, 2005; Boyle and Fisher, 2007). There is a distinction between the subjective tests which should be the battery of any specialist dyslexia teacher and the specialized psychometric tests required for a full dyslexia report.

In England, full diagnostic reports may be needed to pinpoint a learner's difficulties and to access and justify the provision of support. Skills for dyslexia assessors can be quite different: teachers are trained to help and enable learners, but assessors have to push students to the edge of their competence which can be uncomfortable for both tester and testee. A good teacher is concerned with helping a student achieve targets and become an independent learner in a safe, supportive environment where strengths are celebrated and weaknesses supported. However, administering dyslexia assessments not only requires a thorough understanding of psychological testing, both theory and practice (British Psychological Society, 2007), but involves deliberately placing learners in situations both challenging and difficult.

The psychometric tests required for full diagnostic assessments are standardized by testing large samples of the population in an identical way so that results can be compared. This presents a number of challenges for trainee assessors. For example, testers must adhere meticulously to scripts and procedures to ensure that all testees receive identical instructions. Many tests demand that testees perform to the limit of their abilities, possibly to the point of failure. For example, one reading test in England (WRAT4) requires a learner to make 10 single word spelling errors before it is stopped

(Wilkinson and Robertson, 2006). This can be as unpleasant and uncomfortable for the teacher as for the testee, and seemingly in direct conflict with the teacher's training, experience and indeed instincts to support and help a learner.

 Discussion Point

Many highly competent teachers sign on to courses covering specialist assessment and find it difficult not to offer help to children when they are carrying out formal standardized tests which require complete objectivity. Learners are pushed to the limit of their ability or attainment, which can be very uncomfortable for tester and testee. In what way are the contrasting skills of teaching and diagnostic assessment in conflict and how can trainers help participants to overcome the inherent contradictions in this change of roles?

Courses at this level develop trainees' clear understanding of statistical terms and their use and also their ability to interpret standardized tests. Diagnostic testing for dyslexia requires a blend of tests, depending on the level and needs of the student. Dyslexia diagnosis remains an art, not a science, and the diagnosis is made by the tester and not by the tests (Backhouse and Morris, 2005).

Trainees should understand and carefully consider the hopes and aspirations of the testee. Participants should anticipate that testees and sometimes their carers have an expectation of a result different from reality. Reporting and feeding back from tests require sensitivity and tact. Even when results meet expectations, the reaction may be hugely emotionally charged. For example, older learners may be delighted to find a reason why they have suffered throughout their schooling but this may also lead to feelings of anger and disappointment about lost opportunities in their past lives.

EVALUATION: A KEY SKILL AT ALL LEVELS

Trainees should be prepared carefully to measure and evaluate learner progress against measurable targets and to give equal attention to learner progress in 'soft' outcomes, not just measurable skills. Teachers and testers should be able to evaluate their own performance; self-evaluation is a key skill both in terms of evaluation of teaching and assessment. It is only by this process that specialist teachers will be able to map their methodology to individual learners' needs continually as teaching progresses.

Another facet of evaluation crucial to the professional development of teachers and testers is choosing and using published materials. There is a huge range of commercially produced materials available, many of which are excellent but many of which may well need adapting for use with particular learners (Brooks, 2007). Trainees learn to evaluate critically materials in order to choose carefully from an expanding and expensive market (McPhillips *et al.*, 2009). This is equally true for standardized tests.

It is also important that trainees learn to evaluate the wealth of research so that they can distinguish between reliable, evidence-based teaching programmes and tests and the 'snake oil' miracle treatments for dyslexia often marketed (Carter and Wheldale, 2008).

SUPPORTING THE TRAINEES

Training courses are demanding. Aimed at teachers and supporters already in full-time employment, there are conflicts between providing rigorous training and allowing trainees time to complete. SENCOs now have management roles in English schools with many conflicting demands on their time. But all SENCOs need to be trained in how to recognize and support individual difficulties within the dyslexic spectrum.

Dyslexia is not the only specific difficulty on the syllabus; the growing awareness of co-occurring difficulties such as dyspraxia, attention deficit, speech and communication problems and dyscalculia necessitates study of these areas so that teachers can learn to make referrals to other agencies if any of these conditions are suspected:

> This course was a 'must' for all SENCOs and extremely useful for all class teachers who want to improve the understanding and attainment of all children in their classroom (experienced SENCO, 2010).

Course providers can employ a variety of organizational training models to meet participants' needs, including twilight, whole days and using e-learning to supplement face-to-face tuition. Teachers undertaking the training may already be in full-time work with family commitments. Course providers must take care to support participants, many of whom may be returning to academic study after a break:

> I wasn't sure about studying again initially — it had been 20+ years since I last wrote an essay! But I needn't have worried. I thoroughly enjoyed every moment of Year 1 — in fact, it was great to study again. I wasn't as rusty as I thought I would be! (experienced SENCO, 2010).

Tutors can encourage peer support and ensure that these courses welcome and embrace the wide range of experience and achievement of trainees:

> During this course I have been made to feel not only welcome, but also part of a group of like-minded people (teaching assistant, 2010).

 Discussion Point

It is not unusual for teachers who themselves may have dyslexic tendencies to be attracted to specialist training. Many of these are excellent practical teachers but they may have difficulty in producing written assignments. While it is essential to make reasonable adjustments to enable teachers with dyslexia to complete specialist courses, it is also vital that they should be able to teach the necessary literacy skills at whatever level they are working. A course can be flexible to allow for providing plenty of time for such teachers to complete assignments. However, given this potential conflict, what other ways can support be provided to such teachers and to what extent should they be expected to manage their own challenges?

SUMMARY

Moving into the Future

This is an optimistic period for training dyslexia specialists. In the past ten years the profession has become more recognized. Through a series of national policies and protocols backed up by legislation, dyslexia is increasingly recognized in educational establishments and, to some extent, within the wider population. The professional competences of teachers and assessors are currently a subject of debate at national level which will result in an agreed raft of learning outcomes to inform course providers. However, the nature of good practice has not changed radically: with the exception of an increasingly expanding range of assistive technology on offer, the basics of good teaching and assessments remain the same. Training for specialist teachers is effective for teaching *all* students with literacy difficulties, not just those who have been diagnosed as dyslexic. Dyslexia is present across all levels of ability and language backgrounds, so it is vital that specialists are employed in all schools to help equip everyone with the skills needed to survive in a world increasingly driven by text. As we move into the future it is vital that economic constraints do not prevent us from training the teachers and assessors who can make such a difference to the lives of people with dyslexia at all levels.

ACKNOWLEDGEMENTS

With thanks to participants on courses for specialist teachers and assessors of learners with specific learning difficulties (dyslexia) at the Helen Arkell Centre, Farnham, and the School of Education, the University of Northampton, who generously shared their words for the quotations in this chapter.

Further Reading

Backhouse, G. and Morris, K. (eds) (2005) *Dyslexia Assessing and Reporting*. London: Hodder Murray. This book covers a range of knowledge and skills which would be a good basis for a course for specialist assessors dyslexia.

Carter, R. (2010) *Mapping the Mind* (2nd edn). London: Orion Publishing. This book relates current medical neurological research to learning in an accessible way.

Rose, J. (2009) *Identifying and Teaching Children and Young People with Dyslexia and Literacy Difficulties*. London: Department for Children, Schools and Families.

This report provides a clear overview of the training needs for specialist teachers and assessors.

References

Armstrong, D. and Humphrey, N. (2009) 'Reactions to a diagnosis of dyslexia among students entering further education: development of the "resistance–accommodation"', *British Journal of Special Education,* 36: 95–102.

Backhouse, G. and Morris, K. (eds) (2005) *Dyslexia Assessing and Reporting.* London: Hodder Murray.

Boyle, J. and Fisher, S. (2007) *Educational Testing: A Competence Based Approach.* Oxford: Blackwell.

British Psychological Society (2007) *Code of Good Practice for Psychological Testing.* Leicester: Psychological Testing Centre.

British Psychological Society (1999) *Dyslexia, Literacy and Psychological Assessment.* Leicester: BPS.

Brooks, G. (2007) *What Works for Pupils with Literacy Difficulties?* London: DCSF.

Burden, R. (2005) *Dyslexia and Self-concept: Seeking a Dyslexic Identity.* London: Whurr.

Carter, M. and Wheldale, K. (2008) 'Why can't a teacher be more like a scientist? Science, pseudo-science and the art of teaching', *Australian Journal of Special Education,* 32: 5–21.

Department for Children, Schools and Families (DCSF) (2009) *Sir Jim Rose Presents Findings of Review into Dyslexia, 22 June 2009. Press Notice 2009/0114.* London: DCSF.

Department for Education and Skills (DfES) (1995) *Disability Discrimination Act 1995.* London: HMSO.

Department for Education and Skills (DfES) (2001) *SEN Code of Practice on the Identification and Assessment of Pupils with Special Educational Needs.* London: DfES.

Doveston, M. and Cullingford-Agnew, S. (2006) *Becoming a Higher Level Teaching Assistant: Primary Special Educational Needs.* Exeter: Learning Matters.

Goodman, K. (1967) 'A linguistic study of cues and miscues', *Elementary English,* 42: 639–43.

Jamieson, C. and Morgan, E. (2008) *Managing Dyslexia at University.* Abingdon: Routledge.

Lamb, B. (2009) *Report to the Secretary of State on the Lamb Inquiry Review of SEN and Disability Information.* London: DCSF.

Lewis, A. and Norwich, B. (2001) 'Do pupils with learning difficulties need teaching strategies that are different from those used with other pupils?', *Topic,* 26: 1–4.

McPhillips, T., Bell, S. and Doveston, M. (2009) 'Identification and intervention for primary pupils with dyslexia in Ireland and England: finding a path through the maze', *REACH Journal of Special Needs Education in Ireland,* 22: 67–81.

Pennington, B.F. and Olson, R.K. (2005) 'Genetics of dyslexia', in M.J. Snowling and C. Hulme (eds). *The Science of Reading.* Oxford: Blackwell.

Rose, J. (2009) *Identifying and Teaching Children and Young People with Dyslexia and Literacy Difficulties.* London: Department for Children, Schools and Families.

Singleton, C. (2008) 'Visual factors in reading', *Educational and Child Psychology,* 25: 8–20.

Singleton, C. (1999) *Dyslexia in Higher Education: Policy, Provision and Practice (Report of the National Working Party on Dyslexia in Higher Education).* Hull: University of Hull.

Wilkinson, G.S. and Robertson, G.J. (2006) *Wide Range Achievement Test 4 Professional Manual (WRAT4).* Lutz, FL: Psychological Assessment Resources.

LITERACY

Margaret Crombie

Learning objectives

This chapter will help readers to:

- understand how literacy and literacy difficulties fit into the context of the twenty-first century;
- appreciate how literacy has come to be viewed as it is, and the impact this has had on those learning to become literate;
- recognize how early intervention can minimize and/or prevent failure in literacy development; and
- understand what can be done to assist learning and ensure accessibility to literacy for those who experience difficulties.

BACKGROUND

Literacy and literacy difficulties in the twenty-first century are the subjects of much debate. Everyone seems to have a view on how literacy should be dealt with, and how illiteracy should be eliminated. While we surely all agree that an end to illiteracy would be desirable, there is absolutely no agreement on how this might be done. Politically literacy is richly debated (Rose, 2006; Wyse and Styles, 2007; Scottish Parliament, 2010), practitioners and researchers discuss methodologies, governments invest large amounts of money in it, schools spend considerable time dealing with it, newspapers give much column space to it and, across the world, countless millions are spent researching it, yet the problems associated with low literacy levels remain!

Before considering what literacy (and therefore illiteracy) is, and looking at the reasons for the widespread disagreement on how to deal with literacy difficulties, it is worth emphasizing that there are many different literacies: financial literacy, emotional literacy, spiritual literacy, scientific literacy, health literacy, game literacy, media literacy, visual literacy, digital literacy, to name but a few. Defining literacy can, it seems, be problematic with all these areas to cover. The National Literacy Trust (Jama and Dugdale, 2010) views literacy as being more than reading and writing and includes listening and speaking. In their *State of the Nation* document, which gives a 'picture of literacy in the UK today', listening and speaking are given scant mention with the main part of the document given over to consideration of reading and writing with one in six people in the UK struggling with 'literacy' and having 'literacy levels below what would be expected of an eleven year old'.

The Scottish Curriculum for Excellence defines literacy as 'the set of skills which allows an individual to engage fully in society and in learning, through the different forms of language, and the range of texts, which society values and finds useful' (Learning and Teaching Scotland, 2008: 1). The intention of this definition is to make it general enough to be 'future proofed' and take account of the developments we may not yet have considered in the current digital age. In England, though the literacy curriculum has been founded on developing oracy skills alongside reading and writing, political planning is very clearly focused on decoding and encoding text through developing phonics as the route to becoming literate (Department for Education, 2010a).

Wells states that 'to be fully literate is to have the disposition to engage appropriately with texts of different types in order to empower action, feelings, and thinking in the context of purposeful social activity' (1990: 14). Engaging with texts suggests a form of literacy focusing on reading and writing or typing in a range of mediums. Soler (2010: 180) considers that 'from a socio-cultural perspective literacy learning can be viewed as embedded in culturally crafted, meaning making practices and discourses taking place within social groups.'

While acknowledging all the literacies that do exist and accepting that being literate in each case means being able to talk, listen, read and write in a reasonably competent fashion, in this chapter I focus on a discussion of the text-based literacies that allow us to access information, culture and knowledge through reading and writing – the literacies that everyone who went to school has been taught (for better or worse).

THE RANGE OF LITERACY

While speaking and listening seem to happen 'naturally' before children enter nursery or school, either because the skills are innate (as Chomsky suggests in proposing every child is born with a language acquisition device (LAD); Chomsky, 1965) or absorbed through the support and social experiences of growing up in a social community or family (as Bruner, 1983, proposes in his LASS (Language Acquisition Support System)), it is consequently reading and writing that are politically and educationally more controversial. Though the development of oracy and listening skills are undoubtedly important, politically speaking pedagogy appears a more important issue with regard to reading and writing (Department for Education, 2010a).

In terms of being able to extract and embed meaning in and from texts what, then, does it really mean to be literate in the twenty-first century, and for those who are not considered to be literate, what can be done? While acknowledging the inextricable links that there are between all four elements (speaking, listening, reading and writing), this chapter considers text-based literacies and what happens when the processes which normally develop these literacies break down, and children fail to learn to read and write adequately. In addition, the chapter looks at various perceptions of why literacy and illiteracy (lack of abilities in reading and writing) may be problematic and it also acknowledges the role now played by the various technologies in helping to circumvent and overcome literacy difficulties.

Over the years, literacy and academic writing on the subject tend to have fallen into distinct and different camps with those who consider the cognitive within-person factors, those who value the psycholinguistic traditions that have developed largely from the work of Chomsky, and those who see literacy as a socio-cultural activity, being in their own distinct camps! While there has been some individual movement between camps, in general these divisions have got us nowhere in terms of eradicating illiteracy and those at the centre, the 'illiterates' and 'semi-literates' for want of better words, gain very little. These are the people who are in danger, through their lack of literacy, of becoming demotivated, disengaged and if not wisely counselled, they can sink into a life of depression, crime or isolation.

Educators interested only in improving the lot of their charges, and politicians interested in their electorate, find it difficult to know which camp to join, so over the years we have seen policies swing widely between extremes with teachers drawn up in the mood of the moment. These swings from phonics to 'real' reading (without phonics) to an integration of the two, and again back to a domination of phonics are changes which come with scant consideration for the huge range of factors that influence each and every one of our students in the real world. Adams, in her book *Beginning to Read: Thinking and Learning about Print,* which reviews, evaluates and integrates a vast body of research and its implications for children learning to read, uses headings such as 'Words and Meanings: From an Age-old Problem to a Contemporary Crisis', 'Concerns and Conflicts' (1990: 1). Even the titles of the research, stretching far beyond the UK, tell us that all has not been unity and harmony in the field of reading research. Only when we agree to acknowledge the whole range of perspectives and take account of the views of those who adopt different views from ourselves, and look at the needs of developing learners will we gain greater harmony and the insights we need to improve literacy levels overall.

LITERACY DIFFICULTIES

Children can have difficulties in learning to read and write for a multitude of reasons, some of them within the child (e.g. cognitive functioning problems) and others external to the child (e.g. a lack of exposure to books at home). When discussing literacy and literacy difficulties, one cannot ignore dyslexia as it is claimed that somewhere between 2 and 15% of the population are dyslexic to some degree (Parliamentary Office of Science and Technology, 2004). The particular degree will of course depend on how you view dyslexia and how you define it. The 15% is likely to cover those who have mild difficulties and the 2% only those who have severe difficulties.

There is a multitude of views and debates on whether it is possible to distinguish dyslexia from other difficulties with literacy (Stanovich, 1988, 1996; Crombie, 2002, 2005;

Elliott, 2006). These arguments should inevitably centre on definitions of both literacy and dyslexia and whether through a definition of dyslexia we seek to look for discrepancies and differences as well as difficulties (Reid, 1996, 2009). For the purposes of this chapter, those debates will remain academic as if there is a difference as I believe there is, then there is undoubtedly a point on the continuum of literacy difficulties where it is almost impossible to be entirely sure whether we are dealing with dyslexia or not.

IDENTIFYING LITERACY DIFFICULTIES

Screening and subsequently assessment are important means of determining a child's strengths and weaknesses. Early identification of concerns can be beneficial in ensuring that everything that can be done to prevent and/or overcome any difficulties is done before the child begins to realize failure. However, appropriate intervention and support must follow from the identification of concerns. Knowing how to support children is therefore vital for their progress. Knowledge of the range of possible approaches and when to employ them can make the difference between success and failure in school learning. Goswami (2010: 103) emphasizes the importance of children's understanding of phonology in the early years and its relation to the later development of literacy: 'The brain develops phonological "representations" in response to spoken language exposure and learning to speak, and the quality of these phonological representations determines literacy acquisition' (p. 103). This makes it quite clear that the better the exposure to language, and the more the child is encouraged to participate in language activities such as rhyming, alliteration and generally listening to, and participating in all types of language 'games', the more likely success in later literacy will be (Muter *et al.*, 2004). Specific problems in the phonology sphere are likely to lead to difficulties in the acquisition of literacy.

For those children who do have literacy difficulties, how then is it possible to marry up the various approaches previously mentioned to benefit the children in our schools? If we consider first the psycholinguistic tradition, we think of the guessing games that Goodman (1967, 1992) describes, as children, seeking to understand the words they are reading on the page before them, consider the context and insert a meaningful word if they are unsure. If they can do this (e.g. saying pony for horse), they are considered to be using their knowledge of semantics appropriately. If, however, they insert a word that is phonically similar in appearance (e.g. starts with the same letter, or has a similar letter pattern), but is not meaningful in context, then they are said to be over-relying on graphophonic cues and not fully understanding what it is they are reading about. Syntactic errors (such as omission of 'can' in a phrase like 'I can read') would indicate an acceptable miscue as the meaning is largely maintained. Goodman termed the children's errors as miscues rather than mistakes perhaps to indicate that the child was at least partially correct in coming to terms with the complexities of reading. Competent readers make fewer mistakes that are semantically and syntactically acceptable than weak readers, and when they do make such miscues, they tend to self-correct using their phonic knowledge to confirm their correction.

So, from an analysis of the miscues that a child makes, we can determine where we need to focus attention. Does the child have the phonic knowledge to self-correct errors that don't make sense? Can the child recognize when something does not make sense, but can't use graphophonic knowledge to help increase accuracy and, thence, understanding? Does the child carry on regardless of omissions and substitutions if the sentence makes some kind of sense? If a word fits into the context of the story, will the child read on regardless? Though some aspects of miscue analysis have been criticized and discredited as not identifying skill needs in the area of word recognition and being too dependent on context (McKenna and Picard, 2006), there are aspects which teachers can use to help them understand the process the child is going through, and so gain 'a window into the mind' of the reader (Farrington, 2007). What kind of help will enable the learner to produce the desired reading accuracy to gain more precise meaning from the text? How can we help the child to adopt a more accurate approach to reading without affecting their confidence for reading? How can the children themselves be sure of what they are reading and have confidence in their own abilities to decode and understand as the author intended?

The notion of miscue analysis was developed to help understand the processes that children go through in their efforts to make sense of the world of reading and language, and as such can be a tool for educators to use to gauge how a child approaches reading, and to identify precise areas that may require attention and direct teaching support. Thus the psycholinguistic approach, with its emphasis on making meaning through being able to guess, and then self-correct when a wrong guess is made can be useful, but what if …?, what if a child simply does not know where to start, and doesn't get to the point of being able to insert meaningful words? What if the child misreads a word or two, and then guesses – what will happen to the context clues then? Here the psycholinguistic 'guessing game' can make the child the target of ridicule from classmates who simply don't understand why their peer isn't able to 'catch on', and can destroy confidence for a lengthy period of time.

Perhaps then for these children a cognitive approach might have more to offer. If the child can learn letter-sound combinations and has some mastery of phonics, then the possibilities of being able to get started on to the reading process are realizable. However, if they have failed to learn to read through psycholinguistic guessing, then time will be required to form automatic responses to visual symbolic language cues – initially that is letter(s)/sound combinations. These responses require to reach the point of automaticity before the child will be able to cope competently with decoding and understanding reading matter at the same time:

> Automaticity frees cognitive resources for the more difficult task of integration and comprehension. If attention and effort are devoted to low-level processes, like decoding the pronunciation of a letter string, there may be insufficient resources to execute processes needed for comprehension (Klein and McMullen, 1999: 3).

Reaching automaticity with phonics is vital as these children struggle to make connections between the symbols they see and the sounds they make.

INTERVENTION

The conditions that cause reading difficulties are undoubtedly complex with social factors clearly influencing the literacy learning of many poorer children. A child who grows up in a home where there are no books or magazines and where no value is given to being able to read and write is unlikely to have the same desire to learn to read as those from literate homes with an endless ready supply of meaningful literature. Although children growing up in depressed areas are less likely to be motivated to adopt positive images of literacy and learning, it is important to remember that there is much that can be done. We must not fall into the trap of assuming that poor social circumstance means that children are doomed to failure from the start: 'Poor performance does not automatically follow from low socio-economic status' (Clark and Akerman, 2006: 1). We must take care and consider the old adage that 'correlation does not necessarily imply causation'. Statistics tell us that children from poorer backgrounds have lower levels of literacy than those in better-off circumstances. Social circumstances can undoubtedly impact on children's prospects and motivation to learn. Helping disadvantaged students to overcome negative feelings about their environment can contribute greatly to literacy learning.

Engagement is critical, but how to engage children and young people can be a problem when reading skills are weak and in danger of preventing the young person's access to the curriculum and to literature more generally. Parents can be a huge source of support to children when learning: 'Attracting parents to participate actively in educational and school endeavours can serve to form social networks where parents get to know and help each other' (OECD, 2010: 157). Involving parents can also be a source not just of support to the school but also of support to individual children who may struggle to learn to read. Epstein (2001) emphasizes the importance of schools working with parents and not assuming that parents will automatically know how to help their own children.

SCHOOL/PARENT PARTNERSHIPS

'School, family, and community partnerships cannot simply produce successful students. Rather, partnership activities may be designed to engage, guide, energise, and motivate students to produce their own successes' (Epstein, 1995: 703). Where children struggle in specific areas such as literacy, home–school reading partnerships, paired reading with appropriately trained volunteers and other supportive practices can ensure that no child is left struggling without understanding and empathetic help for their difficulties (Topping, 1992; Wolfendale, 1992). Schools, however, do need to learn how to organize parental support sensitively so that no child becomes stigmatized through inappropriate comments or lack of consideration (Epstein, 2001). Teachers and managers may not be able to change children's environments as some would like, but can work within social boundaries to encourage parents to value their children's efforts and to ensure parents feel welcome in schools to discuss any problems and get involved in supporting not just their own children but the whole school, in whatever ways they are able (Department for Education, 2010b).

Kellett and Dar (2007) trained and employed 11-year-old children from two UK schools – one from an area of deprivation and the other from a socioeconomically advantaged area – as researchers. Findings common to both areas were that throughout the studies, 'themes of enjoyment, choice and ownership came through strongly as being effective ways for children to engage with literacy'. Consideration was given to how the schools could bridge gaps and compensate for their areas of difference relating to their varying socioeconomic statuses. It was felt that homework clubs, adult literacy classes and the teaching of lifelong learning skills, such as ICT, could help.

 Case Study

Carolann has experienced difficulties with literacy development since starting school. Carolann is now 14, and her school, in a deprived area of London, has recently started a parental involvement scheme whereby parents are welcomed into school, and can work with teachers and other volunteers on a paired reading scheme. Though Carolann is still not a fluent reader, she has started to enjoy books, and is increasing her skills. Teaching staff mentioned recently that Carolann can now access some information from the Internet which would previously have been unlikely. Though Carolann still struggles with written work, teaching staff are hopeful that the increase in reading skills will lead to an overall improvement in literacy more generally.

LITERACY ACCESS

In the twenty-first century it is becoming more and more important that students can access literacy not just through printed matter such as books and magazines but also through the vast knowledge basket that is the Internet. The skills of decoding and understanding are supplemented by skills of skimming and scanning to find information quickly. The need for students to be discriminating and critical in what they 'read' is vital if they are not to be lead astray by irrelevant and misleading information and extraneous matter! For those with low reading skills, the effort required can be enormous.

'Metacognition in reading refers to the awareness of and ability to use a variety of appropriate strategies when processing texts in a goal oriented manner' (OECD, 2010: 72). Metacognitive skills are necessary for all types of reading in this information age. Students need to learn to consciously question, identify the main ideas, monitor their own comprehension, check and clarify as they go. However, the good news on metacognition is that it 'can be taught' (OECD, 2010: 23). It seems, too, that the teaching of metacognition to students has a positive effect on their reading literacy.

Reading and writing are two sides of the same coin. The processes of decoding and encoding, though different, are therefore inextricably linked. For children who find decoding difficult, it is likely that encoding will be equally or more difficult, relying not just on recognition processes as are necessary for reading, but also on memory for shape for letter formation, linking letters, spacing words and so on. Inputting letters and words into digital technology may not represent quite such a large challenge as handwriting, but there are still issues of putting together letter combinations to form words rather than just being able to recognize the words as they appear on the page or screen. Students today have to deal not just with handwriting and book reading but also with screen reading and word processing – vital skills for the digital era in which we live.

For young people with reading difficulties, the need to read lengthy texts can be minimized through digital books and journals, and screenreaders. In Scotland the *Books for All* project (CALL Scotland, 2010) is working with publishers and teachers to ensure that textbooks are made available to anyone who finds difficulty in accessing books through reading. Material available on screen can be read through screenreading technology, or material can be copied and read aloud by a computer. Similarly the necessity to write has become less pressured through computer programs, such as *Dragon Naturally Speaking* speech-recognition software (Nuance, 2010). Technology, while it presents us with challenges, is constantly evolving new approaches and possible solutions.

Digital recording of homework simply presents the same material differently and can be assessed and commented on by teachers. Teachers can record notes in digital format for pupils to listen to at any time, thus easing the burden on the pupils in class, and enabling parents' awareness of what their children are studying. For children listening to MP3 players, there is no stigma attached to lack of reading ability as teachers make reading accessible to those who are having difficulties. For those who cannot overcome their early difficulties, their lives need not be impaired by a lack of reading and writing abilities. For Scottish pupils, the need to read and write exams is being overcome through the use of digital technology:

> Candidates can read the question paper 'on screen', using speech technology, where appropriate. Also, where the format of the question paper is a question/answer booklet, such candidates can also write/speak their responses 'on screen' (Scottish Qualifications Authority, 2010)

thus relieving the load of reading and writing for pupils who have significant literacy difficulties.

Though reading and writing problems can often be circumvented or overcome by the use of technology, it is still desirable for learners to read and write to the best of their abilities. Linking literacy teaching to the needs of individual learners with difficulties is no easy matter. The famous quotation by Huey (1908) that

> to completely analyse what we do when we read would almost be the acme of a psychologist's achievements, for it would be to describe very many of the most intricate workings of the human mind, as well as to unravel the story of the most remarkable specific performance that civilization has learned in all its history

is no less important today than it was over a century ago. An understanding of reading in the context of literacy development across the curriculum is absolutely vital for all teachers in the twenty-first century to ensure that students are prepared for the breadth of literacy they will meet now and in the future. It would seem that we still have a considerable way to go before we can claim to be able 'to completely analyse what we do when we read'. Moreover, we still have a considerable way to go before we can claim to be able to completely analyse what happens when those who fail to learn to read appear in our classrooms. Neuroscience and research still have a way to go before we reach the point of 'unravelling' the whole 'story' with regard to reading and literacy.

However, the reason we have not 'unravelled' this story from the educators' perspective may be that we are searching for something that isn't there, like an 'invisible unicorn'. The unicorn is something that we can all imagine – we've seen it in pictures – but the invisible unicorn goes beyond this, and though it doesn't exist in the first place, its invisibility means that we are in fact searching for something we will never find. In the case of reading, we are seeking to find the way in which children learn to read, and hence how we can help them. This is not to say that we can't help them, but to find one way is not going to be the solution. If it had been we'd already have discovered our 'unicorn'. One size most definitely doesn't fit all! We must consider the individuality of every reader, in particular, every failed reader or every reader we have failed, and ask ourselves:

- Is there anything we can do in our classrooms to help ensure access to the curriculum for all our students with literacy difficulties?

We can further break down these questions:

- Do we have the attention of each and every student?
- Do we use language that every learner can understand?
- Can each and every learner follow what we are saying at the pace we are saying it?
- Do we direct each student appropriately, or do we assume that, because most students learn from us, that is the way we should teach?
- Do we know how each of our students learns best?
- Is our manner in approaching each student conducive to the learning of that student?
- Do some students seem to have cognitive processing factors that seem to be blocking out specific types of learning?
- Does this child want to learn?
- Are there emotional factors that are influencing learning?
- What can we do in one period of 50 minutes that will help (if that is all the time we have in one session)?
- Can we organize our pupils so that each student with specific learning needs can receive the help they need (either independently, through the use of aids and minimal guidance, or with help – peers, teacher, teaching assistant) or simply by an increase in our understanding and empathy of what works well for these particular students?

There are also some quite basic factors that might be influencing learning too:

- Has this child had breakfast this morning? Did they go to bed last night?
- Do we know if this child is a carer who has to look after someone at home before coming to school?
- Is there a space at home where the student can work?

Some of these questions may sound basic, and we may feel we are powerless to influence home and cognitive processing factors, but, as a result of answering these questions, can we improve matters for all our students? Can we adapt to the changing needs of our students (what works today will not always work tomorrow)? Can we perhaps through influencing whole-school policy, improve learning and literacy?

MANAGING LITERACY IN THE CLASSROOM

No one can overestimate how hard it is to manage a classroom, let alone a whole school of totally different individuals, all of whom have their own learning needs. However, just as teachers differ, the learning process is sufficiently different for each and every child that if a child does not learn to read, pushing in one direction by one approach is not likely to be the answer. We have research that tells us that phonics works (Ehri, 1998; Johnston and Watson, 2005; Rose, 2006, 2009), that 'real reading' works (Waterland, 1988), that specific programmes are the answer … but for whom, and to what extent? It is for literacy teachers, and therefore every teacher, to evaluate the research that does exist, not just on the teaching of literacy, but on teaching more generally. Each piece of research exists in a context, but each only gives us partial answers.

Literacy, and therefore teaching literacy too, are complex issues with many processes involved (Adams, 1990; Ehri, 1998; Rassool, 2009; Stuart *et al.*, 2009; OECD, 2010). If learners do not respond to one particular approach, then another should be tried in order that all can somehow be included in literacy practices (Crombie, 2002; Reid, 2009). It is important, then, for teachers to have a full range of approaches at their fingertips, to acknowledge that there is no one way that will work for all and to explore all the factors that are involved – classroom, teaching, support, cognitive within-child, social, emotional, interactional – and also to look at their own teaching needs and who can help with those.

 Discussion Points

- How can the wider definition of literacy to include new technologies benefit learners?
- Debates over teaching children to read, and the Reading Wars as they have become known, have not resolved the issues around how children should be taught. The relationship between writing and reading is a complex one. There are issues around 'code' and 'meaning' in learning to read and to write. Bearing in mind that every child is an individual, can these issues really be resolved?

SUMMARY

- Literacy teaching is complex but should involve every teacher and educator if young people are to be adequately prepared for life in the twenty-first century.
- There is a considerable body of research on all aspects of literacy and teaching literacy.
- No one approach has all the answers and some approaches raise further questions.
- Preparing children's literacy abilities for life in today's world of digital as well as traditional literacies presents opportunities and challenges for all.
- Technology poses new challenges, but also offers new solutions.
- Educators must have a range of evaluative skills to enable them to approach literacy teaching and learning in a solution-focused way.

Further Reading

Hall, K., Goswami, U., Harrison, C., Ellis, S. and Soler, J. (eds) *Interdisciplinary Perspectives on Learning to Read*. Abingdon: Routledge. Considers a range of perspectives relating to literacy and reading.

Larson, J. and Marsh, J. (2005) *Making Literacy Real: Theories and Practices for Learning and Teaching*. London: Sage. Relates literacy theory to practical aspects of teaching – grounded in social and cultural perspectives.

Palmer, S. and Corbett, P. (2001) *Literacy: What Works?* Cheltenham: Nelson Thornes. Practical information to assist the primary practitioner.

Useful Websites

BBC Literacy (for 4–11-year-olds) http://www.bbc.co.uk/schools/websites/4_11/site/literacy.shtml; (for older learners) http://www.bbc.co.uk/skillswise/

British Dyslexia Association http://www.bdadyslexia.org.uk/

National Literacy Trust http://www.literacytrust.org.uk

UK Literacy Association National Literacy Trust http://www.ukla.org/publications/literacy/

References

Adams, M.J. (1990) *Beginning to Read*. Oxford: Heinemann Educational.

Bruner, J.S. (1983) *Child's Talk: Learning to Use Language*. New York, NY: W.W. Norton & Co.

CALL Scotland (2010) *Books for All* (University of Edinburgh). Retrieved 3 July from http://www.books4all.org.uk/Home/.

Rassool, N. (2009) 'Literacy: in search of a paradigm', in J. Soler *et al.* (eds) *Understanding Difficulties in Literacy Development: Issues and Concepts*. London: Sage.

Chomsky, N. (1965) *Aspects of the Theory of Syntax*. Boston, MA: MIT Press.

Clark, C. and Akerman, R. (2006) *Social Inclusion and Reading: An Exploration*. London: National Literacy Trust.

Crombie, M. (2002) 'Dealing with diversity in the primary classroom – a challenge for the class teacher', in G. Reid and J. Wearmouth (eds) *Dyslexia and Literacy: Research and Practice*. London: Wiley.

Crombie, M. (2005) 'Dyslexia is all too real for sufferers', *The Times Educational Supplement Scotland*, Scottish Opinion, p. 21.

Department for Education (2010a) *The Importance of Teaching (The Schools White Paper 2010)*. London: HMSO.

Department for Education (2010b) *Parental Opinion Survey 2010*. London: HMSO.

Ehri, L.C. (1998) 'Grapheme–phoneme knowledge is essential for learning to read words in English', in J.L. Metsala and L.C. Ehri (eds) *Word Recognition in Beginning Literacy*. Mahwah, NJ: Erlbaum.

Elliott, J.G. (2006) 'Dyslexia: diagnoses, debates and diatribes', *Education Canada*, 46: 14–17.

Epstein, J.L. (1995) 'School/family/community partnerships: caring for the children we share' *Phi Delta Kappan*, 76: 703.

Epstein, J.L. (2001) *School, Family, and Community Partnerships: Preparing Education and Improving Schools*. Boulder, CO: Westview Press.

Farrington, P. (2007) 'A window into the mind: using miscue analysis', *Literacy Today*, 52: 10–11.

Goodman, K.S. (1967) 'A psycholinguistic guessing game', *Journal of the Reading Specialist*, 6: 126–35.

Goodman, K. (1992) 'Why whole language is today's agenda in education', *Language Arts*, 69: 354–63.

Goswami, U. (2010) 'Phonology, reading and reading difficulties', in K. Hall *et al*. (eds) *Interdisciplinary Perspectives on Learning to Read*. Abingdon: Routledge.

Green, B. and Kostogriz, A. (2002) 'Learning difficulties and the New Literacy Studies: a socially-critical perspective', in J. Wearmouth *et al*. (eds) *Contextualising Difficulties in Literacy Development: Exploring Politics, Culture, Ethnicity and Ethics*. London: RoutledgeFalmer.

Huey, E.B. (1908) *The Psychology and Pedagogy of Reading*. Cambridge, MA: MIT Press.

Jama, D. and Dugdale, G. (2010) *Literacy: State of the Nation: A Picture of Literacy in the UK Today*. London: National Literacy Trust.

Johnston, R.S. and Watson, J. (2005) *A Seven Year Study of the Effects of Synthetic Phonics Teaching on Reading and Spelling Attainment*. Edinburgh: Scottish Executive Education Department.

Kellett, M. and Dar, A. (2007) *Children: Researching Links between Poverty and Literacy*. York: Joseph Rowntree Foundation.

Klein, R.M. and McMullen, P. (eds) (1999) 'Introduction: the reading brain', in R.M. Klein and P. McMullen (eds) *Converging Methods for Understanding Reading and Dyslexia*. Cambridge, MA: MIT Press.

Learning and Teaching Scotland (2008) *Curriculum for Excellence: Literacy across Learning*: Principles and Practice. Dundee: LTS.

McKenna, M.C. and Picard, M.C. (2006) 'Revisiting the role of miscue analysis in effective teaching', *Reading Teacher*, 60: 378–80.

Muter, V. Hulme, C. Snowling, M.J. and Stevenson, J. (2004) 'Phonemes, rimes, vocabulary, and grammatical skills as foundations of early reading development: evidence from a longitudinal study', *Developmental Psychology*, 40: 665–81.

National Literacy Trust (2010). *Transforming lives*. Retrieved 28 May from http://www.literacy-trust.org.uk.

Nuance Communications (2010) *Dragon Naturally Speaking*, Burlington, MA: Nuance. Retrieved 27 July from http://www.nuance.com/naturallyspeaking/products/default.asp.

OECD (2002) *Reading for Change: Performance and Engagement across Countries*. Paris: Organisation for Economic Cooperation and Development.

OECD (2010) PISA 2009 *Assessment Framework: Key Competencies in Reading, Mathematics and Science*. Paris: Organisation for Economic Cooperation and Development.

Parliamentary Office of Science and Technology (2004) 'Dyslexia and dyscalculia', *Postnote*, 226: 1.

Rassool, N. (1999) *Literacy for Sustainable Development in the Age of Information*. Clevedon: Multilingual Matters.

Reid, G. (ed.) (1996) *Dimensions of Dyslexia: Assessment, Teaching and Curriculum*. Edinburgh: Moray House Publications.

Reid, G. (2009) *Dyslexia: A Practitioner's Handbook* (4th edn). Chichester: Wiley.

Rose, J. (2006) *Independent Review of the Teaching of Early Reading (Rose Review)*. Nottingham: Department for Education and Skills.

Rose, J. (2009) *Identifying and Teaching Children and Young People with Dyslexia and Literacy Difficulties: An Independent Report from Sir Jim Rose to the Secretary of State for Children, Schools and Families*. Nottingham: DCSF Publications.

Scottish Parliament (2010) *Literacy Action Plan*. Retrieved 4 December from http://www.they workforyou.com/sp/?id=2010-10-27.29589.0&s=speaker%3A13994.

Scottish Qualifications Authority (2010). *Assessment arrangements: Digital question papers*. Retrieved 3 July from http://www.sqa.org.uk/sqa/30030.1259.html.

Soler, J. (2010) 'Dyslexia lessons: the politics of dyslexia and reading problems', in K. Hall *et al.* (eds) *Interdisciplinary Perspectives on Learning to Read*. Abingdon: Routledge.

Stanovich, K.E. (1988) 'Explaining the difference between the dyslexic and the garden-variety poor reader: the phonological-core variable-difference model', *Journal of Learning Disabilities*, 21: 590–612.

Stanovich, K.E. (1996) 'Toward a more inclusive definition of dyslexia', *Dyslexia*, 2: 154–66.

Stuart, M., Stainthorp, R. and Snowling, M. (2009) 'Literacy as complex activity: deconstructing the simple view of reading', in J. Soler *et al.* (eds) *Understanding Difficulties in Literacy Development: Issues and Concepts*. London: Sage.

Topping, K.J. (1992) 'Short- and long-term follow-up of parental involvement in reading projects', *British Educational Research Journal*, 18: 369–79.

Waterland, L. (1988). *Read With Me: An Apprenticeship Approach to Reading*. Stroud: Thimble Press.

Wells, G. (1990) 'Talk about text: where literacy is learned and taught', *Curriculum Inquiry*, 20: 369–405.

Wolfendale, S. (1992) *Empowering Parents and Teachers: Working for Children*. London: Continuum International.

Wyse, D. and Styles, M. (2007) 'Synthetic phonics and the teaching of reading: the debate surrounding England's "Rose Report"', *Literacy*, 47: 35–42.

12 THE MORPHOLOGICAL APPROACH: FROM THEORY TO PRACTICE

E. Neville Brown and Daryl J. Brown

Learning objectives

This chapter will help readers to:

- understand the role of morphology in literacy acquisition;
- explore a viable, alternative mode of treatment for those who fail to respond to phonics-cum-multisensory approaches to literacy acquisition;
- to consider the impact of different approaches on school organization; and
- to challenge the theoretical assumptions underlying current practice.

INTRODUCTION

The morphological approach to literacy acquisition is presented not only as an alternative for those who have failed to acquire literacy adequately by what has been regarded since the 1970s as the conventional phonics-cum-multisensory approach to literacy acquisition but also as a challenge to the underlying assumptions of current pedagogy. The morphological approach is described as practised at the Maple Hayes Dyslexia School and Research Centre (in Lichfield, Staffordshire) over the past 30 years and entails a reappraisal of the nature of attention in the initial learning act; a more detailed description of the theory underpinning the work there is to be found in Brown and Brown (2009). We argue for a value-free, information-processing approach to the study of literacy acquisition and expression instead of reliance on a deficit hypothesis as is currently the case (see the 'Effective Interventions' recommended by the Rose Report, 2009). We also argue for greater transparency in the revelation of outcomes of the various models of provision and in particular the use of a revised and acceptably validated value added (VA) calculation of educational progress in this respect. Leckie and Goldstein (2009) are adversely critical of the current calculation of VA, particularly the unreliability of the mathematical formulæ used to predict the results expected at GCSE. We agree with Nick Seaton's (of the Campaign for Real Education) comment on the Internet following the Leckie and Goldstein report that 'it is not tables of raw test and examination results that are at fault. It is the way raw results are manipulated by the CVA [calculation of value added] process, then presented to suggest that an underperforming school is better than it is'. We do not agree with him that CVA measures should be scrapped; they should be reformed to reflect the progress made by pupils in their respective schools irrespective of gender, eligibility for free school meals, ethnicity and low income. Ignoring such variables would enable comparison of state schools with independent and mainstream with special.

THE CONTEXT

The seriousness of the current state of literacy achievement, not only in Britain and English-speaking countries but perhaps also more widely where Indo-European alphabetic languages are used, is arguably parlous (e.g. OECD, 2009). In Britain, it is widely accepted that about 20% of children moving from Key Stage 2 to 3 are functionally illiterate, and about the same percentage leave school without any worthwhile accreditation. Not surprisingly, about 80% of the young offenders in prisons are likewise reported to be functionally illiterate. Initiatives and measures promoted, often imposed, by the government have been observably unsuccessful in changing the position in the longer term, despite initial promise and an unprecedented level of funding.

We would argue that research into the outcomes of special provision has tended to be specious, and often to the extent of being a political agenda. Thomas (1996) of the Centre for Studies on Inclusive Education, compared examination results for all kinds of special schools with those of non-special educational needs (SEN) pupils in state secondary schools, reaching the conclusion that special schools failed their pupils, noting that 'Only 4 per cent of children in Year 11 of special schools achieved 5 or more grades A–G at GCSE, against 87 per cent in mainstream schools'. Among Thomas's data, the 5 A–G scores of the approved independent special schools for specific learning difficulties (SpLD) ranged from 39% to 100% (the 100% being for Maple Hayes) and for the only two LEA special schools for SpLD, 85% and 86%, all significantly above his average and all comparable with scores for mainstream schools. Similarly, the Rose Report (2009) does not mention 'morphology' despite the researchers being given clear evidence of the effectiveness of a morphological approach to the resolution of severe literacy underachievement. We argue that the use of a reformed VA measure and comparison of like to like would overcome the above difficulties.

In 1974, when the first author began research into unexpected literacy failure, the widespread assumption was, much as now, that phonological, more specifically phonemic awareness and discrimination were an absolutely essential prerequisite for learning to read and spell. We note a recent shift towards the view that the relationship between development of phonemic awareness and reading is more one of reciprocity than of prequisition (as noted in a survey of literature in Rispens and Parigger, 2010). Not surprisingly, in those early days, journal paper after paper came to the conclusion that those who had not developed these skills must need over-teaching by the prescribed remedial methods. Failure to progress was then, as often now, attributed to failure on the part of teachers to get across their message. There was, however, a logical lacuna between the premise and the conclusion; the conclusion could equally have been to abandon the phonics approach in favour of an alternative. 'There was also the arguably blinkered approach by some academics to research findings, sometimes from other areas of inquiry, which cut across the grain of their beliefs and prejudices. An example of this is the report by Saffran and Marin (1977), *Reading without Phonology*; another is Nishio's (1981) paper on the teaching a language-disabled child to read with Kanji; yet another is the report of Maria Carbonell de Grampone (1974) of children who can spell better than they can read. Although they did not have the benefit of insight into the morphology of the language, Chomsky and Halle (1968: 49) took the view that 'English orthography, despite its often cited inconsistencies, comes remarkably close to being an optimal orthographic system'. The problem then was that there was no alternative to phonics beyond Look-and-Say for reading and none at all for spelling, and Look-and-Say was only possible for the short words in the Years 1 and 2 build-up of sight-word vocabulary in reading and spelling. This is where morphology came in.

The problem was also, as presented by the philosopher, John Searle, in an Open University broadcast in 1975, that there was no theory of language to underpin all areas of inquiry. This is also where morphology potentially came in.

MORPHOLOGY

A morpheme is commonly agreed as the smallest semantic unit in the language, perceptible in longer words at sub-word level. In alphabetic written languages, morphemes are most easily recognized in the written language as letter strings which can occur in a range of longer words. In contrast, phonemes and their extension into syllables are not held to have intrinsic semantic meaning. One does not have to discriminate phonemes in order to learn the oral language and, it is argued, reading is not a natural act. When one has learnt the sound of a word, then one learns, quite separately, how a word is applied; this is done by association, as described by Pinker (2007: 237):

> All words have to be coined by a wordsmith at some point in the mists of history. The wordsmith had an idea to get across and needed a sound to express it. In principle, any sound would have done — a basic principle of linguistics is that the relation of a sound to a meaning is arbitrary — so the first coiner of a term for political affiliation, for instance, could have used *glorg* or *schmendrick* or *mcgillicuddy*. But people are poor at conjuring sounds out of the blue and they probably wanted to ease their listeners' understanding of the coinage rather than having to define it or illustrate it with examples. So they reached for a metaphor that reminded them of the idea and they hoped would evoke a similar idea in the kinds of the listeners, such as *band* or *bond* for a political affiliation. The metaphorical hint allowed the listeners to cotton onto the meaning more quickly than if they had had to rely on context alone, giving the word an advantage on the Darwinian competition among neologisms.

To Pinker, the affixes to roots of longer words are inexplicable except in terms of grammatical modifiers that would presumably be initially arbitrary and then agreed. The mind boggles not only at the sheer complexity of it all but that humans could ever remember the millions of arbitrary configurations of equally arbitrary sounds; each word and its referent would need to be learnt individually with no possible economy of effort.

Traditionally, at least since the 1970s, and in accordance with this theoretical position, the focus on illiteracy has been on deficits within the learner in respect of phonological awareness and phonic skills, with remediation by rote-phonics of one variety or another.

On the other hand, morphemes must, by definition, have meaning that is inherent and not associative. The morpheme *dog* is also a word, but a word that occurs in such disparate non-canine contexts such as carpentry, crab-fishing, lawn mowers and fire baskets (Brown and Brown 2009: 112). As a bound morpheme in the Greek strand of the English language, it also occurs in word like *dogma*, again carrying its inherent meaning with it. When we think morphologically, we have to consider why we can apply the morpheme in such disparate contexts and why it would not be appropriate to do so in other contexts.

Morphology is not simply a matter of knocking prefixes and suffixes off words so that what is left must be the root, as those not well versed in this aspect of linguistics suggest. With limited knowledge of morphology we can strip *unforgettable* down to *forget*, or *magician* down to *magic*; each of these 'roots' isn't actually one morpheme but two. An early compromise approach between phonics and morphology, Corrective Spelling Through Morphographs (Dixon and Engelman, 1979), had *ap-*, *at-* and *com-* as morphemes, which are adjustments to *ad-* and *con-* in prefix position rather than morphemes in their own right, in addition to being unnecessarily proliferative and confusing.

A further problem is that the construction and generation of words with morphemes behave differently across the various linguistic strands in English (notably the Germanic or Anglo-Saxon, Norman-French, Latinate and Greek, in the main); this is explained in Brown and Brown (2009) and the implications for the teaching and learning of literacy explored. A casualty of the prefix, root and suffix mode of thought is overgeneralizing and oversimplifying a rule; we can teach that all words ending in *-ian* refer to people and all ending in *-ion* refer to the formation of abstract nouns (not a truly morphological consideration, we argue), but what about *meridian* and *amphibian*? Knowledge of morphology would certainly explain what appear at first sight to be exceptions to a rule to be dismissed as of no great consequence or as aberrations or mistakes made by the original coiners of the words. We leave the reader to puzzle out the morphological reasons for these apparent anomalies, perhaps in readiness for a challenge from a sharp-witted student for an explanation.

Essential to our understanding of morphology is that a morpheme is a morpheme irrespective of its position in a word, irrespective of its assumed grammatical function and irrespective of the variation in sounding across the words in which it occurs. Although in long words a particular morpheme may assume a dominant rank among others in the hierarchy of importance or force, this will vary across the words in which it occurs. Thus *re* in *real* is a morpheme in root or dominant position while it is in prefix position in *reproduction* and in suffix position in *metre*.

A significant finding of Brown (1978a) was that the syllable division of longer words was not always coincident with the morphemic division; he called these incongruencies 'baulk' words as they tended to present more difficulty (as measured by reaction time) for apprentice readers to process than congruent words of similar length. The syllabic division of conductor, *con-duc-tor*, does not follow the morphemic division, *con-duct-or*. *Sign* is a morpheme and in the word *sign* it is also a syllable but it is not a syllable in the word *signature (sig-na-ture)*, or *resignation (res-ig-na-tion)*. Brown (1999), (cited in Brown and Brown, 2009) related this phenomenon to the availability of dual- and possibly multiple-processing channels available to be used by the successful learner. We attribute unexpected literacy failure to attentional difficulties induced by inappropriate pedagogic set, albeit in those with a certain tendency, trait or predisposition. Both regard the dyslexic in the educational context as one who had failed to develop the strategies developed by the successful learners (subject to the same classroom environment), strategies that are not actually taught and may be in apposition to those explicitly taught. Because a child is taught in a particular and specific way does not mean that they must have learnt that way.

In the Maple Hayes school, much as in the original research programme, each morpheme is taught by semantic association with an 'icon' or rudimentary drawing which encapsulates its meaning, which is demonstrated first by actions and gesture, *and also serves to divert attention from the phonology*, especially in consideration of the often huge variations in pronunciation of a short letter string across all the words in which it appears. Thus the act of reading in this way, from the visual stimulus to meaning, can be understood as uni-sensory as opposed to multi-sensory, thus being compatible with theory and research into selective attention (e.g. Treisman and Geffen, 1967; Treisman and Riley, 1969; Treisman and Gelade, 1980) and divided attention (e.g. Hampson, 1989; Eysenck and Keane, 1990), because (in either scenario) any interference between processes will prevent them being dealt with relative to the extent of the interference. The analysis and synthesis of words using morphemes (which very rarely exceed five letters in length) enables the teaching of meaningful 'chunks', taking account of Miller's (1956) limits of memory capacity. Surely, the division of words into syllables cannot be held to be 'chunking' in Miller's sense?

While the principle of teaching morphology is clearly applicable to education in general, not only for literacy but also for the development of thinking and language skills, at Maple Hayes it is specifically applied to those children who have fallen significantly behind their peers in literacy and general achievement and are thus the most disadvantaged and vulnerable to low self-esteem and disaffection. A fairly typical profile of a dyslexic candidate for Maple Hayes would be as shown in Table 12.1.

Table 12.1   Results of psychometric testing (G, male, aged 10.2 years, mid Year 6)

Wechsler Intelligence Test for Children (WISC-IV)	Standard score	%ile	
Verbal Comprehension 2009	112	79	
Perceptual Reasoning 2009	98	45	
Auditory Working Memory 2009	97	42	
Processing Speed 2009	88	21	
Wechsler Individual Achievement Test (WIAT-II)	Standard score	%ile	'Age'
Word Reading 2007	59	0.3	6:00
Word Reading 2009	68	2.0	6:08
Reading Comprehension 2007	49	<0.1	below scale
Reading Comprehension 2009	64	1.0	6:00
Pseudoword Decoding 2007	69	2.0	<5:00
Pseudoword Decoding 2009	71	3.0	5:08
Spelling 2007	57	0.2	5:04
Spelling 2009	70	2.0	6:08
Written Expression 2007	no score		below scale
Written Expression 2009	67	1.0	6:00
Numerical Operations 2007	78	7.0	6:04
Numerical Operations 2009	82	12.0	8:04

   Case Study

G attended his local SpLD centre for one session a week (10% of his school time) for two years, recorded as having these resources: 'Beat Dyslexia, The Handwriting File, Stile activities, Various computer programmes e.g. Lexia, Wordshark etc., Multisensory writing materials: sand-trays, smart-board, mnemonics etc.' He also had one hour a week private tuition from a teacher specializing in phonics and multi-sensory teaching. G's score on the Pseudoword Decoding test of Phonic skills in reading is indicative of his lack of progress with specific phonics teaching: for example, *cind* was rendered as *chang* and *flid* as *fild*, despite G sounding out letter by letter laboriously before attempting to blend into each word.

G's spelling test not only revealed poor discrimination of sounds but also exceptionally poor recognition of rudimentary morphological structures such as *-ed*, *-less* and *de-* for a Year 6 pupil of adequate verbal ability about to go to secondary school. G's performance on the Written Expression component of the WIAT-II was also very poor: he could not join two pieces of information together reliably, even with the words before him to copy. His extended writing was inchoate (see Figure 12.1).

(Continued)

(Continued)

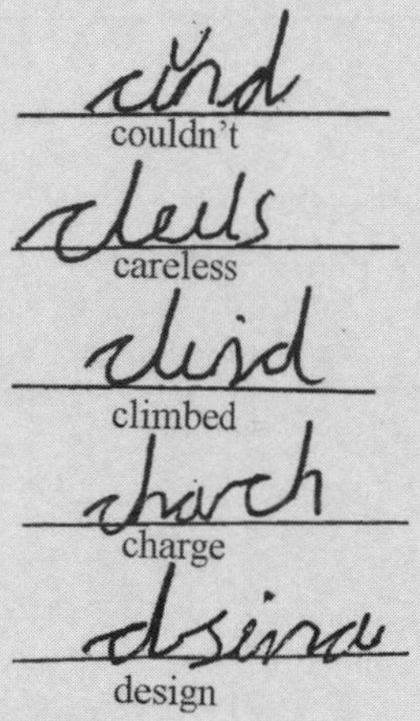

Figure 12.1 G's WIAT spelling

   Despite G's extremely poor phonic skills after considerable extra tuition directed specifically to their development, his eventual Statement of Special Educational Needs after some
two years' pressure on the LEA by his parents prescribes 'the use of multisensory techniques
and resources to support his access to the curriculum'. In recognition of the failure to make
progress with these methods, alternative (in our opinion defeatist) strategies are prescribed
to avoid literacy altogether: 'encouragement and opportunities to use alternative methods
of recording his work such as Mind Maps, pictures and the use of a Dictaphone, ICT equipment or scribe as appropriate.'

   G's case highlights the problem of the youngster who has fallen so far behind that he
can only be kept in a mainstream school by what is now recognized as 'internal exclusion'
from the means of accessing the curriculum normally and thereby from an understanding
of the concepts of the subjects of the curriculum. In education, the problem of dyslexia,
specific literacy difficulty or whatever is inextricably bound up with the wider problems of
underachievement, disadvantage and disaffection.

   At interview, every prospective pupil for the school is given a criterion-referenced assessment of learning to spell, read and write morphologically words that they could not spell
by the methods acquired during mainstream schooling. G's rendering of *construction* was
indecipherable, as one would expect from the example in Figure 12.1. To assess G's potential for learning by a morphological approach, we suppressed phonics by the use of 'icons',
graphic embodiments of the meanings of morphemes, in order to establish more direct
links between morphemes (strictly, morphographs) and meaning, however the morphemes
are pronounced in the words in which they occur (Brown, 1978b).

   Using the icons for *con*, *struct* and *ion* successively, G was able to hold one, then two,
then three morphemes in short-term visual memory and then write the word construction
correctly. Connection with the sound of the word was delayed until the spelling and meaning of the word had been learnt. He was then taught *de-* and was able to apply the concept

of *de-struct-ion* correctly in context with correct spelling. Further still, he was then able to form the word *reconstruction* in a similar manner. Descriptions of the development of the semantics of the icons were given mostly by 'translation' to the Germanic strand of the English language running alongside practical demonstrations by gesture and graphics of the applications of the morphemes. Success in learning each morpheme is demonstrated by correct writing three times without any copying permitted, similarly for each word constructed, followed by correct writing on delayed recall (a description of how to teach a deaf person by the same method is given in Brown and Brown, 2009: chap. 5).

MAPLE HAYES SCHOOL

Questions of preferred learning style are not considered because the approach used is not a deficit one but an information-processing approach which focuses on getting from A to B, in this case from print to meaning, and from B to C, from meaning to writing, by the most direct and therefore, we argue, the most efficient routes.

Performing in a one-to-one situation is not schooling, however, but therapy and, of course, there has to be consideration of cost or 'the efficient use of resources' (as dictated by the Education Act 1996). Following successful individual criterion-referenced assessment, a week's placement in a suitable class is offered, with a review at the end of the week in which the pupil participates. Coping with the morphological programme and competing with the rest of the class on tests on the week's work enable school, parents and, most importantly, the pupil to ensure that the offer of a place is appropriate and has a high probability of success.

In the school, then, the principles described above are followed but in the context of a small class of pupils of similar age and achievement levels. Three 'driver' lessons are given each week, two taught as described above and one on computer (with bespoke software). All tuition is on a class basis without any individual withdrawal. As with G above, we are able to teach the longer words required by an age- and ability-appropriate curriculum, though a Key Stage 3 pupil may continue to make some errors on Key Stage 1 vocabulary; these will be attended to gradually and piecemeal.

The material from the 'driver' lessons features in a workbook, specially printed in colour for each class every week, which is used in the literacy lessons, first of the day, to rehearse the morphemes, the building into words and the correct usage in sentences according to context. As the booklet is produced in-house, it is capable of adjustment according to the pace of delivery of the programme, the issues raised in the driver lessons and according to the vocabulary demands of the developing mainstream curriculum which runs alongside the programme. Extension work is included in the workbook to accommodate different rates of execution of the work. End-of-week tests are only on the week's work so that those who joined the class belatedly are not handicapped. A test of longer-term recall is administered at the end of each term. Rewards and celebrations of success, although not confined to performance on these tests, are similarly given on both a weekly and termly basis through a well wrought merit award system. The enhancement of self-esteem is thus regarded as matter not of a special, add-on programme, as we find is often prescribed in statements of SEN, but results from success in competing with others at what the pupil now perceives as age- and intellect-appropriate outcomes.

A pupil of 11 or 12 with a 6-year literacy level such as G can be taught quite easily the component morphemes of *conductor* (see above) drawing attention to *duct* and then to the process of *conduction* of heat or electricity or the *induction* of electrical current in physics, the importance of having a lightning *conductor* on a house or the *reducing* of oxygen from a chemical compound by *reduction*. A bus *conductor*, albeit still in the memory of those of mature years, is of course now relegated to social history! At the same time, as the morphological approach does not assume a developmental progression from simple to complex, a pupil such as G (see his spelling) would clearly also need to learn the force of *-ed*, however pronounced, and other high-frequency morphemes which are expected in others to have been absorbed by Year 2. It is noteworthy that others (e.g. Bourrassa and Treiman, 2008) have found that dyslexic children are as capable as non-dyslexics of adhering to the principle of morphological constancy in the spelling of morphological complex words; the difference, we maintain, is that the pedagogic set of learning phonics actually inhibits this in the dyslexics. Given the boost to self-esteem from learning the meaning, reading and spelling of complex vocabulary perceived to be at or above age-appropriate levels, the ignominy of having to learn what would in other contexts be regarded as insultingly infantile is offset.

Outside the structured, precision teaching of the morphological programme, the pupils enjoy a normal, age-appropriate, demanding subject curriculum usually, but not always, with the exception of an MFL (modern foreign language). A 40-minute homework session, taken by the class literacy tutor, rounds off the school day which finishes at 4.40 p.m. The class therefore starts and ends the day with the literacy tutor, who will also be a specialist science, art or technology teacher, etc.

Because the subject teachers at the school are also literacy tutors, they have to be trained in the delivery of the literacy programmes. In addition to initial training for a new teacher, three weeks in the year are reserved for continuing professional development and each class literacy tutor attends one of the driver lessons for their class each week. This raises another issue: the specific accreditation of teachers for dyslexia by relevant bodies entails adherence to the phonics-cum-multisensory belief system. Although impartial courses for higher degrees are available at some universities (e.g. the MEd 'Psychology of SEN' course at Nottingham University) and other institutions, they cannot be held to promote rational consideration of such antithetic approaches to literacy acquisition as the morphological and phonics-cum-multisensory. The 'Reading Diploma' of the Open University (on which the first author was a tutor) offered this value-free approach but was discontinued in the 1980s.

CO-MORBIDITY

As has pointed out elsewhere (e.g. Price and Humphreys, 1993), there are deficits that frequently co-occur with the dyslexic problems. From our perspective, we consider these to be variants of cerebral organization and treatable by different methods from the conventional approaches that would be applied under the deficit hypothesis.

Visual Dysgraphia

Among those who present for assessment and/or for consideration of placement, there is a high correlation (of 0.4 or so) between phonological dyslexia (with its working definition as failure to make adequate or expected progress with phonic methods) and *visual dysgraphia* (VDG). In treatment terms we prefer to think of VDG as a difference from the typical in cerebral organization rather than a deficit, otherwise we would be in the mindset of correcting the deficit by the very measures that have been applied previously and have failed. As with the dyslexia, we take the view that the problem – or at least the severity of the problem – is exacerbated by pedagogic set; in this case how writing is taught. A VDG child will have difficulty with the formation of letters, reversing *b*s and *d*s the most usual, and with the order of letter in words. Like Eric Morecambe's piano playing, even where, on the rare occasion, the VDG child gets the right letters they may not be in the right order. B and C are typical VDG as could be predicted from their processing speed ratings on the WISC-IV as well as from their handwriting on the WIAT spelling test (see Figures 12.2 and 12.3).

In over a thousand cases over the years, we have found a very high negative correlation between the incidence of visual dysgraphia and scaled scores on the Coding subtest of the WISC-III and WISC-IV. This used to be held as an indicator of dyslexia in the ACID profile but we take the view, on the basis of difference in treatment, that VDG is a condition quite distinct from dyslexia. We have also found that the correlation between VDG and more general dyspraxia is not perfect; we have met youngsters accomplished, in terms of eye–limb co-ordination, in sporting activities who are nevertheless dysgraphic when it comes to handwriting.

Given that our approach to phonological dyslexia is to eschew phonology/phonics in the learning act, engaging sound at the last or at least a late stage, our approach to the

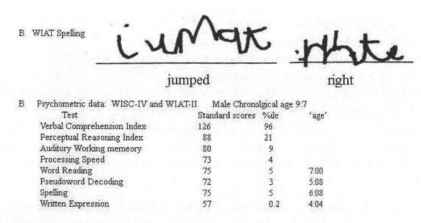

B   WIAT Spelling

jumped   right

B   Psychometric data: WISC-IV and WIAT-II   Male Chronolgical age 9:7

Test	Standard scores	%ile	'age'
Verbal Comprehension Index	126	96	
Perceptual Reasoning Index	88	21	
Auditory Working memeory	80	9	
Processing Speed	73	4	
Word Reading	75	5	7:00
Pseudoword Decoding	72	3	5:08
Spelling	75	5	6:08
Written Expression	57	0.2	4:04

Figure 12.2   VDG (child B)

C WIAT Spelling

right   jumped (note correction)   charge   know

C Psychometric data: WISC-IV and WIAT-II   Male Chronolgical age 7:8

Test	Standard scores	%ile	'age'
Verbal Comprehension Index	112	79	
Perceptual Reasoning Index	94	34	
Auditory Working memeory	62	1	
Processing Speed	62	1	
Word Reading	81	10	6:04
Pseudoword Decoding	80	9	6:00
Spelling	81	10	6:08
Written Expression	76	5	5:04

Figure 12.3 VDG (child C)

treatment of severe VDG would also be construed as unisensory because we attribute the problem to an opposition between sight and kinæsthetic or hand-movement memory, a matter of cerebral organization. The morphemes for *conductor* (see above) would need to be input separately to kinæsthetic memory in the absence of visual control. This in turn would require fully cursive writing to establish the memory trace but in case of severe VDG, as reported in Brown (1990), it would be necessary to 'switch off' or disable visual as well as auditory control to enable learning; the measure of success would be the achievement of automaticity in output under semantic control.

Language and Communication Difficulties

As with VDG, we have found a correlation of about 0.4 between the incidence of phonological dyslexia and language difficulties such as might come under the label of semantic-pragmatic difficulty. We have also found a high correlation of above 0.8 between VDG and 'sem-prag' difficulties. Permutation could be made from the following list:

- Difficulties in understanding instructions.
- Misunderstanding of social situations.
- Difficulties in remembering sequences of instructions.
- 'Half-baked' grasp of concepts in the sciences, etc.
- Specific word-finding difficulties, often found as relatively very low scores on the Expressive Vocabulary component of the WIAT-II Listening Comprehension test.
- Very poor sentence composition in writing, often despite an adequate, sometimes excellent, score on the Sentence Comprehension component of the WIAT-II Listening Comprehension test.
- Printed handwriting with poor letter formation, problems already noted as highly correlated with autistic tendencies.

Although the children with such language, communication and mild autistic difficulties who present to us at Maple Hayes are referred primarily because of their literacy difficulties, we find that precision teaching not only of morphology but also of written language and handwriting with checks on learning and the avoidance of the use of teaching assistants in favour of informed, trained, expert teachers, ameliorates the difficulties of these children too and enables their inclusion in a normal educational programme. The likely impact on self-esteem, examination results, life chances and employment prospects is obvious.

THE IMPACT OF THE MORPHOLOGICAL APPROACH ON SCHOOL ORGANIZATION

As we have already stated, an inviolable principle at the school is that pupils should be taught in small classes, without any 'internal exclusion' or withdrawal for individual remedial tuition and/or therapy. This enables our provision to be more accurately, consistently and competitively costed. From information obtained under the Freedom of Information Act and from our considerable experience of what would usually be directed by a special needs tribunal to be put in a statement of SEN for a pupil like G who has fallen so far behind his peers, we are able to draw up a table to compare the provision that would be required to support such a pupil in a mainstream secondary school according to the two models of delivery (see Table 12.2).

Table 12.2   Provision to support a child with a statement of SEN

Maple Hayes specialist school	Mainstream secondary school with statement of SEN
Mainstream curriculum, usually except MFL	Withdrawal from mainstream curriculum for 5 hours per week literacy tuition and 1½ hours a week 1:1 numeracy individual teaching or therapy
Literacy programme integrated with the subject curriculum	
Provision for visual dysgraphia and sometimes for language/communication difficulties normally integral with the literacy programme and subject curriculum	15 hours per week in-class support from teaching assistant
	Withdrawal from normal curriculum for SALT* and/or OT*
Costs per pupil per annum (2010–11 fee structure):	Costs, per pupil per annum, including oncost, as obtained from an LEA school for a 2010 tribunal:
Up to 13 years £12,480	6½ hours specialist teacher @ £2,512 per hour = £16,328
13 years and over £16,980	15 hours TA @ £750 per hour = £11,250
Add costs of transport, dependent upon distance, reduced if pupils share	Age weighted pupil unit (AWPU) = £2,800
	Total = £30,378
	Add costs of SALT* and/or OT* at £2,512 per hour per week per year, plus travelling time at same rate
	Add costs of annual reviews and aids set out in statement

Note

*SALT = speech and language therapy; OT = occupational therapy.

Of course, the comparison is not for like-for-like provision. There are not only differences in provision between the models quantitatively but also in qualitative terms. From this one would expect there to be differences in outcomes as well as in costs to support judgements of effectiveness and comparisons of value where appraisal and comparisons are made of provision for children with statements of SEN for SpLD. Where uniformly derived VA data have been available, as in 2005, Maple Hayes has emerged on at least one occasion as the top school of any kind in the country for improvement of its pupils from Key Stage 2 to Key Stage 4.

Not only to evaluate initiatives such as that at Maple Hayes but also to accord recognition – and possibly tangible rewards – on all schools for the value they bestow on all their pupils, we strongly advocate the switch of emphasis from GCSE results to unmanipulated and better validated VA comparative data. Concomitant with this would be reform, but certainly not abolition, of the Key Stage 1 and 2 SATs to remove teacher assessments in favour of a reliance on externally marked *and supervised* examinations, which should be of short duration and managed to avoid stress but, above all, realistically informative. This, we argue, is preferable to the subjectivity of 'research' that too often consists of surveys of opinions as a basis for official policies at national and local levels.

SUMMARY

In conclusion, we argue that the morphological approach to literacy acquisition is not only more intellectually satisfying in its underpinning theory but also to its dyslexic recipients who can overcome formidable disadvantage to obtain GCSE and higher forms of accreditation towards fulfilling their intellectual potential and career aspirations. As a model for delivery of an inspiring curriculum generally for all children it is certainly of high attraction but would require considerable adjustment of existing models of school organization, admittedly much more so in secondary school than in primary. As a recent academic visitor to the Maple Hayes school observed, 'I believe that it will take 50 years and a paradigm shift in formal education, and in the underpinning academic understanding of language before these ideas and their application start to get the wider attention they deserve', the implication of which is that we should be searching scientifically and systematically for a literacy pedagogy for the twenty-first century that will avert underachievement and the need for palliative, 'catch-up' provision.

Further Reading

Pumfrey, P.D. and Elliott, C.D. (eds) (1990) *Children's Reading, Spelling and Writing Difficulties.* Lewes: Falmer Press.

Saffran, E.M. and Marin, O.S.M. (1977) 'Reading without phonology: evidence from aphasia' *Quarterly Journal of Experimental Psychology,* 29: 515–25.

Note

The government-commissioned Tickell Review of early years foundation stage (EYFS) reports concerns about the neglect or omission of teaching other than phonic (through unspecified literacy-learning strategies in the EYFS (see Ward (2011)).

References

Bourrassa, D.C. and Treiman, R. (2008) 'Morphological constancy in spelling: a comparison of children with dyslexia and typically developing children', *Dyslexia: An International Journal of Research and Practice*, 14: 155–69.

Brown, E.N. (1978a) 'Attentional style, linguistic complexity and the treatment of reading difficulty.' Unpublished PhD Thesis, University of Aston in Birmingham.

Brown, E.N. (1978b) 'Attentional style, linguistic complexity and the treatment of reading difficulty', in M. Knights and D. Bakker (eds) *Treatment of Hyperactivity and Learning Disordered Children*. Ottawa: Park Press, NATO Publications.

Brown, E.N. (1980) 'Coding strategies and reading comprehension', in M. Friedman *et al.* (eds) *Intelligence and Learning*. New York, NY: Plenum Press, NATO Publications.

Brown, E.N. (1990) 'Children with spelling and writing difficulties, an alternative approach', in P. Pumfrey and C.D. Elliott (eds) *Children's Difficulties in Reading, Spelling and Writing*. Brighton: Falmer Press.

Brown, E.N. and Brown, D.J. (2009) *Meaning, Morphemes and Literacy*. Brighton: The Book Guild.

Carbonell de Grampone, M. (1974) 'Children who can spell better than they can read', *Academic Therapy*, 9: 281–8.

Chomsky, N. and Halle, M. (1968) *The Sound Pattern of English*. New York, NY: Harper & Row.

Dixon, R. and Engelman, S. (1979) *Corrective Spelling through Morphographs*. Toronto: Science Research Associates.

Eysenck, M.W. and Keane, M.T. (1990) *Cognitive Psychology*. Hove: Lawrence Erlbaum Associates.

Hampson, P.J. (1989) 'Aspects of attention and cognitive science', *Irish Journal of Psychology*, 10: 261–75.

Leckie, G. and Goldstein, H. (2009) 'The limitations of using school league tables to inform school choice', *Journal of the Royal Statistical Society: Series A (Statistics in Society)*, 172: 835–51.

Nishio, M.R. (1981) 'Kanji reading by a prekindergarten language-disabled child: a pilot study', *Brain and Language*, 13: 259–89.

OECD (2009) *PISA Survey of Education Performance* (www.oecd.org/edu/pisa/2009).

Pinker, S. (2007) *The Stuff of Thought*. New York, NY: Allen Lane.

Price, C.J. and Humphreys, G.W. (1993) 'Attentional dyslexia: the effects of co-occurring deficits?', *Cognitive Neuropsychology*, 10: 569–92.

Rack, R. and Rooms, M. (1997) 'Hackney morning revisited (the Dyslexia Institute's project with Hackney LEA)', *Special Children*, 98: 16–19.

Rispens, J. and Parigger, E. (2010) 'Non-word repetition in Dutch-speaking children with specific language impairment with and without reading problems', *British Journal of Developmental Psychology*, 28: 177–188.

Rose, J. (2009) *Identifying and Teaching Children and Young People with Dyslexia and Literacy Difficulties*. Nottingham: DCSF Publications.

Saffran, E.M. and Marin, O.S.M. (1977) 'Reading without phonology: evidence from aphasia' *Quarterly Journal of Experimental Psychology*, 29: 515–25.

Solomon, R.L. (1949) 'An extension of control group design', *Psychological Bulletin*, 54: 52–68.

Thomas, G. (1996) *Exam Performance in Special Schools*. Bristol: Centre for Studies in Inclusive Education.

Treisman, A.M. and Geffen, G. (1967) 'Selective attention: perception or response?', *Quarterly Journal of Experimental Psychology*, 19: 1–17.

Treisman, A.M. and Gelade, G. (1980) 'A feature integration theory of selection', *Cognitive Psychology*, 12: 97–136.

Treisman, A.M. and Riley, J.G.A. (1969) 'Is selective attention selective perception or selective response: a further test', *Journal of Experimental Psychology*, 79: 27–34.

Ward, H. (2011) 'Phonics Knocked off perch by official review. Findings contradict ministers' policy', *Times Educational Supplement*, 1.4.2011.

13 MATHEMATICS LEARNING DIFFICULTIES AND DYSCALCULIA

Steve Chinn

Learning objectives

This chapter will help readers to:

- relate research into effective learning to the learning difficulties of dyscalculia;
- understand how the key research findings apply to the teaching of students with dyscaculia and mathematics learning difficulties; and
- appreciate the role of strategies in supporting problems with memory and learning.

INTRODUCTION

This chapter looks at mathematics learning difficulties and dyscalculia. It relates these specific difficulties to the key principles of learning as identified by research. Identification and intervention are discussed:

> To put the matter another way, if there is bad practice it seems likely that intelligent non-dyslexics may in many cases survive it without any major disaster, whereas its effect, even on the most intelligent dyslexics is likely to be catastrophic (Miles and Miles, 1992).

Specific learning difficulties could be viewed as a consequence of Howard Gardner's (1999) theory of multiple intelligences. A deficiency in logico-mathematical intelligence could be sufficiently severe as to be described as a mathematics learning difficulty or possibly dyscalculia. A learning difficulty could also be considered as a consequence of many interacting factors within the individual (for example, working memory and anxiety) or factors outside the individual (for example, an inappropriate curriculum or the culture of quick answers). It could also be due to a mismatch between the way the student learns and the way they are taught.

The research (Hattie, 2009) shows that any intervention will improve learning. My own experience of 24 years of teaching students with specific learning difficulties, coupled with the essential optimism of a teacher, suggests that appropriate teaching can make a positive difference. The objective is not to just make an improvement but to maximize learning. To do this it is helpful to consider three major factors:

- The learner's characteristics.
- The research into truly effective pedagogy and teaching.
- A teaching programme that meets the needs of the learner.

DYSCALCULIA: DEFINITION AND SOME IMPLICATIONS

After years of neglect, dyscalculia is beginning to attract more research. Definitions are evolving as knowledge increases. If we take a parallel with dyslexia, a specific learning difficulty in that other key intelligence, language, then the structure of that definition becomes almost inevitable:

> Dyscalculia is a condition that affects the ability to acquire mathematical skills. Dyscalculic learners may have a difficulty understanding simple number concepts, lack an intuitive grasp of numbers, and have problems learning number facts and procedures. Even if they produce a correct answer or use a correct method, they may do so mechanically and without confidence (Department for Education and Skills, 2004).

This definition focuses on numbers. It does not look at higher levels of mathematics, such as algebra. This makes sense for several reasons. Mathematics is very developmental. Concepts build and develop as numeracy progresses – for example, addition is rooted in counting on; multiplication is rooted in repeated addition.

If learners do not understand numbers they are not likely to learn number facts. They are not likely to develop linking strategies that would support poor long-term memory for these facts. This combination of poor retrieval of facts and poor number sense, which inhibits the development of compensatory strategies, has a hugely negative influence on learning mathematics and depresses motivation.

At the start of my lectures for teachers I often ask them about lack of motivation from students in mathematics lessons and when this occurs in enough pupils for them to notice. The responses I get, and this is the same for many countries world wide, is at 6 and 7 years. The cognitive problems create affect problems such as anxiety, lower self-esteem and poor motivation. This vicious circle, which often leads to learned helplessness, starts far too soon in children's learning history.

So, the definition of dyscalculia focuses on early arithmetic. This has implications. It means that pupils who fall behind in the early years will be handicapped by the impact of dyscalculia and maths learning difficulties on learning the fundamental facts and concepts on future attempts to learn maths. It also means that intervention for older (and adult) learners will almost certainly have to go way back to basic concepts.

DYSCALCULIA, MATHEMATICS LEARNING DIFFICULTIES AND RESEARCH

A thorough review of the research into dyscalculia was provided by Ramaa and Gowramma in 2002. The key factors that contribute to dyscalculia are as follows:

- A deficiency in retrieval of number facts and the ability to solve story problems (Russell and Ginsberg, 1984).
- Perseveration of counting strategies and counting errors (Geary, 1990).
- Persistence of fact-retrieval deficits (Ostad, 1997).
- Fact-retrieval deficits due to speed of processing (Ackerman and Dykman, 1995).
- Continuing difficulties with story problems (Parmer *et al.*, 1996).
- A delay or difficulty with conservation, seriation and classification (Ramaa, 1990).
- Extra stress, anxiety and depression (Magne, 1991).

A further review of research identified the main contributors to dyscalculia and mathematics learning difficulties as:

- the perseveration of counting strategies;
- speed of working (including speed of retrieval of facts and procedures);
- the recall of basic facts;
- word problems and problem-solving; and
- working memory.

Perseveration of Counting Strategies

The first procedure in arithmetic is counting. Children learn to count, one at a time, probably using their fingers as tallies. Children are more likely to practise counting up than counting down. Counting on fingers restricts the number of tallies to ten. Tallying on paper enables the child to use as many tallies as they need. The ten fingers are the reason we have a base-ten system of number. (If we counted like the Babylonians, we would use our thumb as the pointer to count the segments of the remaining four digits, giving base twelve.) Counting up is adding one each time. Counting down is subtracting one each time. As the child's skills develop then they are able to count up and back in chunks (for example, twos or tens). This is the transition stage to addition and subtraction. Later the pupil will learn to add 'lots of' the same number, which is multiplication. An understanding of place value is essential for understanding these operations. If the child does not progress from counting in ones then they will not develop arithmetical skills, nor will they understand algebra.

Speed of Working (Including Speed of Retrieval of Facts and Procedures)

From the perspective of knowing and understanding what children need to learn arithmetic and mathematics, it is clear that a deficiency in any of these factors will create learning problems. The extent of the impact is dependent on the interactions of several influences. For example, the culture of mental arithmetic is that the computation should be done accurately and quickly. The same culture applies to the retrieval of basic facts. They have to be retrieved accurately and quickly. Many learners with special needs in the cognitive domain, whatever those needs may be, are slower than average to process information. If success and positive feedback are dependent on accuracy and speed, then many pupils (and adults) with learning difficulties will fail. The role of anxiety cannot be overlooked. Anxiety often has a debilitating effect on performance. The demand to do things quickly, especially things a pupil finds difficult, is likely to create anxiety. Anxiety can have a negative effect on working memory (Ashcraft *et al.*, 1998).

Recall of Basic Facts

One of the key findings from the NRC's book, *How People Learn* (Bransford *et al.*, 2000), is that learners 'must have a deep foundation of factual knowledge'. What we may have never discussed for mathematics is just what constitutes essential knowledge. In terms of basic facts, it seems that the understanding of what constitutes 'a deep foundation ' is based on convention and mathematics culture, rather than a clinically scientific investigation. For example, prior to decimalization, knowing the 12 times facts was considered as essential. I recently met a 66-year-old German man who said that he had had to learn up to the 21x facts as a child. We have to ask, from the point of view of a mathematical necessity, 'What facts are essential?' Then we have to ask, 'What facts do many people find difficult to retrieve from memory?' Well, the answer lies in what people find memorable. Again, my experience working in the UK and abroad, asking teachers what they have found children and adults remember, is that it is the 10x, 5x, 2x and 1x. Just how much the inability to learn all the expected basic facts contributes to a learning difficulty depends on the specific demands of the maths curriculum and the way it is taught. This particular issue is a good test of attitude and understanding in teachers and tutors. If they believe that practice will eventually triumph, then they will be disappointed and may well cause significant stress and lower self-esteem in many learners … of all ages.

Word Problems and Problem-solving

Bryant *et al.* (2000) surveyed 391 teachers in the USA, asking them what they considered to be the most significant weaknesses for students learning mathematics. The first three items, out of 33, were difficulty with:

- word problems;
- multi-step problems; and
- the language of mathematics.

Word problems should test the learner's understanding of numbers and mathematics concepts. Unfortunately as Boaler (2009) observes of maths problems in the UK: 'Students come to know that they are entering a realm in which common-sense and real world knowledge are not needed.'

The objective of testing understanding by using word problems may not be achieved if the learner's involvement is not engaged. It could be said that many word problems are written to confuse the student or, to judge the writers more kindly, to catch them out if they are tempted to use simple, formulaic strategies. For example, the problem:

> Mark has 2 more pens than James. Mark has 8 pens. How many pens does James have?

Has only two numbers and thus no distracting number or extra numbers that identify the probability of a two-step problem. The numbers are simple. A pupil may seek out the 'operation word', in this case 'more', and then add without any deeper analysis. The question requires a subtraction, $8-2 = 6$. It's not the vocabulary. The reading level is quite low. It's the comprehension. It's spotting the trap. It's about being bothered about who has how many pens. Multi-step problems are not open to simple, expedient strategies.

The vocabulary of maths creates at least two problems. First there is the problem that everyday words, for example 'and', take on a new meaning in mathematics, so learners have to abandon their interpretation and transfer to the new language. They have to translate English into mathematics. Imprecise words take on precise meanings.

Secondly, there are some inconsistencies. We all seek consistency (Cialdini, 2007) because consistency helps us to focus on the important issues. Insecure learners seem to have a particular need for consistency. For example, in mathematics the vocabulary for the first two-digit numbers is inconsistent, first with 'eleven' and 'twelve' which are exceptions and then with the teen numbers which feature the unit digit before the ten as in sixteen (six-ten). In English we also have a range of words that can mean add, a range for subtract and choices for multiply and divide. Insecure learners would be better suited if there were only one word so that they could focus on the computation. Both these examples feature in children's early experiences of mathematics. As they seek to make sense of information and find patterns, the language and vocabulary confound them.

So, a weaker skill with vocabulary and language and a weaker facility with symbols will complicate and frustrate learning.

Working Memory

There is little doubt that a good working memory is an essential prerequisite for many areas of mathematics, most notably, mental arithmetic.

THE PREVALENCE OF DYSCALCULIA

It is difficult to make a precise judgement for the prevalence of dyscalculia since there is not an 'absolute' definition as yet. However, the research shows a range of values, varying, in part, because of the loose definitions currently available. The consensus of these research papers is that prevalence is around 5%. One of the earliest studies by Lewis *et al.* (1994) in the UK suggested that prevalence was around 3.3%. Gross-Tsur *et al.* (1996) in Israel found that 4.6% of their population were dyscalculic and Hein *et al.* (2000) in Germany found a prevalence of 6.6%. Ramaa and Gowramma (2002) in India carried out two studies using different criteria and found 5.5–6.0% of their subjects were dyscalculic. In all these studies the percentage of girls presenting with dyscalculia was approximately equal to the percentage of boys. This is not usually the case with other learning difficulties and special needs. In the USA, the term, 'mathematics learning difficulties (MLD)' is used to describe the bottom quartile of achievers.

BEING GOOD AT MATHEMATICS

It is useful to consider what skills and knowledge are considered necessary for success in mathematics. Krutetskii (1976) listed the Components of Mathematical Ability:

- An ability to formalize maths material (to abstract oneself from concrete numerical relationships).
- An ability to generalize and abstract oneself from the irrelevant.
- An ability to operate with numbers and other symbols.
- An ability for sequential, segmented, logical reasoning.
- An ability to shorten the reasoning process.
- An ability to reverse a mental process.
- Flexibility of thought.
- A mathematical memory.
- An ability for spatial concepts.

These skills are often weak in children with specific learning difficulties. As with other comments of this nature in this chapter, this is not meant to infer that nothing can be done to alleviate or circumvent problems. What students with learning difficulties need are teaching methods that do not assume that everyone is a perfect learning machine. They need methods that are relevant and appropriate to their learning profile.

Government-funded research in England (Rashid and Brooks, 2010) into the levels of attainment in literacy and numeracy of 13–19-year-olds, 1948–2009, shows that 22% of 16–19-year-olds are functionally innumerate and that this has remained at the same level for at least 20 years. It seems that England has not been able to address the problem of mathematics learning difficulties.

DIAGNOSIS

Diagnosis is another circular concept. Diagnosis will depend on the definition and the proposed concept of dyscalculia. For example, Butterworth (1999) considers 'numerosity' to be the underlying factor that causes dyscalculia. The Dyscalculia Screener (Butterworth, 2003), a computer-based tool, has test items that assess subitizing (dot enumeration) and number comparison (numerical stroop) as prerequisite skills that underlie ability with numbers.

Diagnosis in education may differ from diagnosis in health in that the medical diagnosis is usually followed by an intervention related to the diagnosis. A diagnosis for dyscalculia and mathematics learning difficulties can be based on the factors which handicap learning combined with an analysis of the conceptual gaps in mathematical learning.

A diagnosis should be predominantly clinical and should be a mix of formal activities and informal questions. If we want to know how a learner thinks and addresses maths, it makes sense to ask them rather than guess. The diagnosis should also guide intervention. Diagnosis is something you do *with* the student. Assessment is what you do *to* the student.

INTERVENTION AND PROGRAMMES FOR LEARNING

Intervention and indeed all teaching, since there will inevitably be students with learning difficulties in every class (and there will not be many perfect learners), should take into account their learning profile. If the programme does not cater for poor working memory, a limited long-term mathematical memory and speed of working then many students with learning difficulties will fail. The most efficacious way of addressing these factors is to teach for understanding and interlinking facts and procedures. Understanding and interlinking will support memory difficulties. They will also help learners to progress mathematically and develop their conceptual grasp of the subject.

If we can make general learning more efficacious for more students then we can reduce the number of students who need one-on-one tuition. Intervention will have to start at the point where learning is secure. The programme will have to be based on a clear understanding of the structure of arithmetic/numeracy which has to be delivered with the learning profiles of the students clearly in mind. A teacher at one of my courses explained that she had tried division by 'chunking' but it didn't work because her students could not subtract. Subtraction is an unavoidable component of the division process (not entirely true as it could be done as multiplication, the inverse operation). Progression has to follow a full pathway of topics.

There is another problem in England. School students have to take a national examination at 16 years of age. If they enter secondary school at an age of 11 years with a mathematics age of, say, 8 years, the implication is that they have made approximately six months progress per school year. If the intervention increases the progress rate to 12 months per school year, they will still be three years behind as they approach the examination. Catch-up is a challenging undertaking. The figures above make it clear that precision teaching cannot be the main answer. It is just too slow for catch-up.

The teaching programme will have to consider a number of key issues. The research found in two sources is extensive and compulsive. *How People Learn* (Brandsford *et al.*, 2000) provides the findings of a two-year study conducted by the Committee on

Developments in the Science of Learning of the National Research Council (NRC) of the USA. The three key findings are as follow:

1   Students come to the classroom with preconceptions about how the world works. If their initial understanding is not engaged they may fail to grasp the new concepts and information that are taught, or they may learn them for the purposes of a test but revert to their preconceptions outside the classroom.

This finding reflects the conclusions of Buswell and Judd (1925) that the first learning experience of a new topic provides strong input. If the first learning is wrong, it is hard to correct.

2   To develop competence in an area of inquiry, students must: a) have a deep foundation of factual knowledge; b) understand facts and ideas in the context of a conceptual framework; and c) organize knowledge in ways that facilitate retrieval and application.
3   A 'metacognitive' approach to instruction can help students learn to take control of their own learning by defining learning goals and monitoring their progress in achieving them.

John Hattie (2009) carried out a major meta-analysis of thousands of research papers on what made for effective education. He found that the highest effects accrued when teachers provided feedback data or recommendations to the students and that the programmes with the greatest effects used strategy-based methods. Although these findings are aimed at the whole learning spectrum, they have particular relevance for students with special needs.

The first finding of the NRC concerns preconceptions. Learners try to make sense of what they are trying to learn. Often this involves looking for patterns and relating the new information to something they already know. Unguided learning can result in misconceptions. I started teaching in the 1960s when learning by discovery was the big thing. Dangerous times in education, especially when you ignore the law of unintended consequences. If the child learns incorrectly, the Buswell and Judd findings become very pertinent.

As an example of lack of pattern in number, consider the child's first experience of two-digit numbers. Two-digit numbers are the first experience of place value, a sophisticated and vital concept. The symbols, 11, 12, 13 and so on, have logic symbolically, but not linguistically in the English language. Cantonese is regular.

With fractions the problem is reversed. It is the symbols that create the problem. The language of 'One fifth plus two fifths' suggests an answer of 'Three fifths'. The symbols, 1/5 + 2/5 suggest an answer of 3/10. There is a danger that children will simply rely on memory and a philosophy of 'if you say so'. It is not safe to assume that children will learn patterns and overlook the inconsistencies without guidance. If they do, it will be down to having a powerful memory.

The second finding from the NRC talks about knowledge in a (not surprisingly) highly realistic way. The first part of the finding is about having 'a deep foundation of factual knowledge'. This is so very pertinent for learners with specific learning difficulties

(SpLD). They are less able to learn large numbers of facts and procedures (the use of 'less' infers that this is not a problem that is exclusive to learners with SpLD). What we need to know is, what constitutes a 'deep foundation'? For example, if learning maths is made conditional on retrieval from memory all the multiplication facts from 1x to 12x, then many learners will fail. If learning maths is made conditional on retrieving formulas and algorithms from memory, even more will fail, and for many who do succeed at school, their retention of such information is likely to disappear when they leave school and no longer top up memory by frequent practice. Such methods contribute to a situation where innumeracy affects too high a percentage of adults.

The second and third parts of this finding are: b) understand facts and ideas in the context of a conceptual framework; and c) organize knowledge in ways that facilitate retrieval and application. These give guidance on how to address the problems on acquiring a 'deep foundation of factual knowledge'. The two parts can be interpreted together in relation to learners with learning difficulties in the sense that they could be considered to be mutually dependent. Understanding and linking facts and procedures can support recall of facts and procedures. For example, multiplication is defined as 'repeated addition' and children will sometimes say the words even if they have no idea what they mean. There is much to be gained in teaching multiplication facts in a developmental way, rather than by rote. The phrase, 'What else are you teaching?' should play a key role in any lesson planning.

One of the underlying and key developments in maths is the move away from counting in ones. However, that counting in ones is the base, and a number of concepts are beginning to be formed, including a sense of number values, what is bigger and smaller, what happens to make numbers bigger and smaller, a sense that counting on is adding and counting back is taking away, the role of direction and sequences and place value.

Adding and subtracting procedures should involve a progression from counting on and back in ones – for example, adding ten or twenty. Linking basic addition facts to place value suggests that the addition number bonds for 10 are a collection of key facts. It is not necessarily an automatic outcome that children will learn these facts, just because they are perceived as key facts. The pattern and links between the facts need to be taught, using visual images or manipulative materials, linked to the symbols, which should help to develop the concepts around this collection of facts, including the commutative property.

Manipulative materials are often advocated as a way of helping learners with learning difficulties. The connection between materials and learning is far from straightforward. Hattie's research survey found that the use of manipulatives had a medium impact on learning. Manipulatives have different characteristics and often work well for illustrating some concepts and not others. Also, not every learner 'sees' what the manipulatives are meant to show. A skilled teacher selects the appropriate manipulative, links it to the symbols and makes it a stage in the learning process. The Singapore Model method created significant gains when first introduced, but children became dependent on the models and more reluctant to move to the exclusive use of symbols. It is the skill of the teacher and their empathy with the learners that make manipulatives work. They should help learners develop concepts and not keep them at the concrete stage of learning.

Hattie found that the maths programmes with the greatest effect were strategy-based methods. Yet research from Gray and Tall (1994) cited in Boaler (2009) found that the lowest-achieving maths students did not use strategies, whereas the high-achieving students did.

Linking facts can help retrieval, but can also help understanding. For example, computing 12×8 as $10 \times 8 = 80$, plus $2 \times 8 = 16$, giving 96 as the answer, has benefits. It uses key (and easily remembered) facts to access another fact, by a method that is applicable to many other facts. It rehearses the key facts, topping up memory. It introduces the concept of partial products for multiplication. There seems to be no reason why the $12 \times$ facts should be retrieved from memory rather than computed using a strategy that introduces a mathematical concept.

Linking procedures can also help retrieval and understanding – for example, knowing that 10×8 is a development from $8 + 8 + 8 + 8 + 8 + 8 + 8 + 8 + 8 + 8$. Using 10×8 replaces 9 additions with one multiplication. A large part of the early maths curriculum is about computing numbers in an efficient way.

It is possible to look at the logical and interdependent progress of mathematics and thus find where a learner is failing as well as where gaps in learning occur, but it is those gaps that are lowest in the structure that are likely to have the greatest impact. Knowing the structure is a key element in making the teaching of mathematics diagnostic, which reflects Hattie's observation (paraphrased) that teachers need to listen to learners, either directly or through the use of diagnostic worksheets. For learners with specific learning difficulties, this will work even better if the teacher understands the profile of each learner. It makes communication, teaching and learning more empathetic and efficacious.

SUMMARY

- Dyscalculia is a specific learning difficulty.
- It is at the extreme end of mathematics learning difficulties.
- Both conditions require teaching that actively acknowledges the cognitive and affective profiles of the learners. More of the same, whether it be the procedures or the reliance on rote, will not work.
- Motivation will depend heavily on success, so the pedagogy has to be structured for success and structured to address failures in a way that does not destroy resilience in the learner.

Further Reading

Ashcraft, M.H. Kirk, E.P. and Hopko, D. (1998) 'On the consequences of mathematics anxiety', in C. Donlan (ed.) *The Development of Mathematical Skills*. Hove: Psychology Press. This chapter explains the detrimental effect of working memory on maths anxiety.

Boaler, J. (2009) *The Elephant in the Classroom*. London: Souvenir Press. A book full of experience and wisdom about the teaching of mathematics.

Bransford J. D. *et al.* (2000) *How People Learn*. Washington, DC: National Academy Press. A report on a major study carried out by the National Research Council of the USA. This includes three key findings on how people learn.

Bryant, D.P., Bryant, B.R. and Hammill, D.D. (2000) 'Characteristic behaviors of students with LD who have teacher-identified math weaknesses', Journal of Learning Disabilities, 33: 168–73. A survey of teachers in the USA as to what characteristics cause them concern about children learning mathematics.

Cialdini, R. (2007) *Influence: The Psychology of Persuasion*. New York, NY: Collins. This is included in this list because of its content on the role of consistency in our lives.

Hattie, J. (2009) *Visible Learning: A Synthesis of over 800 Meta-analyses Relating to Achievement*. Abingdon: Routledge. A huge study of research into what is effective in education.

Ramaa, S. and Gowramma, I.P. (2002) 'Dyscalculia among primary school children in India', Dyslexia, 8: 67–85. A comprehensive literature survey into dyscalculia and two thorough research studies.

Additional Further Reading

Ashlock, R. (2010) *Error Patterns in Computation* (10th edn). London: Allyn & Bacon.

Chinn, S. (2007) *Dealing with Dyscalculia: Sum Hope*. London: Souvenir Press.

Chinn, S. (2009) *What To Do When You Can't …* (series of basic maths books). Wakefield: Egon Press.

Chinn, S. (2011) *The Trouble with Maths* (2nd edn). London: Routledge.

Chinn, S. and Ashcroft, R. (2007) *Mathematics for Dyslexics* (3rd edn). Chichester: Wiley.

Clausen-May,T. (2005) *Teaching Maths to Pupils with Different Learning Styles*. London: Paul Chapman.

Dowker, A. (2005) *Individual Differences in Arithmetic*. Hove: Psychology Press.

Miles, T.R. and Miles, E. (eds) (2004) *Dyslexia and Mathematics* (2nd edn). London: RoutledgeFalmer.

Yeo, D. (2003) Dyslexia, *Dyspraxia and Mathematics*. Chichester: Wiley.

References

Ackerman, P.T. and Dykman, R.A. (1995) 'Reading-disabled students with and without comorbid arithmetic disability', *Developmental Neuropsychology*, 11: 351–71.

Ashcraft, M.H. Kirk, E.P. and Hopko, D.(1998) 'On the consequences of mathematics anxiety', in C. Donlan (ed.) *The Development of Mathematical Skills*. Hove: Psychology Press.

Boaler, J. (2009) *The Elephant in the Classroom*. London: Souvenir Press.

Bransford, J.D. *et al.* (2000) *How People Learn*. Washington, DC: National Academy Press.

Bryant, D.P., Bryant, B.R. and Hammill, D.D. (2000) 'Characteristic behaviors of students with LD who have teacher-identified math weaknesses', *Journal of Learning Disabilities*, 33: 168–73.

Buswell, G.T. and Judd, C.H. (1925) *Summary of Educational Investigations relating to Arithmetic*. Chicago, IL: University of Chicago Press.

Butterworth, B. (1999) *The Mathematical Brain*. London: Macmillan.

Butterworth, B. (2003) *The Dyscalculia Screener*. London: GL Assessment.

Cialdini, R. (2007) *Influence: The Psychology of Persuasion*. New York, NY: Collins.

Department for Education and Skills (2004) 'What do we know about dyscalculia?' (www.dfes. gov.uk/readwriteplus/understandingdyslexia).

Gardner, H. (1999) *Intelligence Reframed*. New York, NY: Basic Books.

Geary, D.C. (1990) 'A componential analysis of an early deficit in mathematics', *Journal of Experimental Child Psychology*, 49: 363–83.

Gross-Tsur, V. Manor, O. and Shalev, R. (1996) 'Developmental dyscalculia: prevalence and demographic features', *Developmental Medicine and Child Neurology*, 38: 25–33.

Hattie, J. (2009) *Visible Learning: A Synthesis of over 800 Meta-analyses Relating to Achievement*. Abingdon: Routledge.

Hein, J. Bzufka, M.W. and Neumaerker, K.J. (2000) 'The specific disorders of arithmetic skills. Prevalence studies in a rural and urban population sample and their clinico-neuropsychological validation', *European Child and Adolescent Psychiatry*, 9: 87–101.

Krutetskii, V.A. (1976) *The Physiology Mathematical Abilities in School children* J. Kilpatric and I. Wirszup (eds.) Chicago, IL: University of Chicago Press.

Lewis, C. Hitch, J.G. and Walker, P. (1994) 'The prevalence of specific arithmetic difficulties and specific reading difficulties in 9 to 10 year old boys and girls', *Journal of Child Psychology and Psychiatry*. 35: 283–92.

Magne, O. (1991) *Dysmathematics-Facts and Theories Concerning Mathematics Learning for Handicapped Pupils*. Lund: Department of Educational and Psychologic Research, Lund University, Sweden.

Miles, T.R. and Miles, E. (eds) (2004) *Dyslexia and Mathematics* (2nd edn). London: RoutledgeFalmer.

Ostad, S.A. (1997) 'Developmental differences in addition strategies. A comparison of mathematicaly disabled and mathematicaly normal children', *British Journal of Educational Psychology*, 67: 345–57.

Parmer, R.S. Cawley J.R. and Frazita, R.R. (1996) 'Word problem solving by students with and without mild disabilities', *Exceptional Children*, 62: 415–29.

Ramaa, S. (1990) *Study of Neuropsychological Processes and Logico-mathematical Structure among Dyscalculics. NCERT Project Report*. Mysore, India: Regional College of Education, NCERT.

Ramaa, S. and Gowramma, I.P. (2002) 'Dyscalculia among primary school children in India', Dyslexia, 8: 67–85.

Rashid, S. and Brooks, G. (2010) *The Levels of Attainment in Literacy and Numeracy of 13- to 19-year-olds in England, 1948–2009*. London: National Research and Development Centre for Adult Literacy and Numeracy.

Russell, R.L. and Ginsberg, H.P. (1984) 'Cognitive analysis of children's mathematics difficulties', *Cognition and Instruction*, 1: 217–44.

Part III

SYNDROMES AND BARRIERS

14 ATTENTION DEFICIT HYPERACTIVITY DISORDER (OR HYPERKINETIC DISORDER)

Richard Soppitt

Learning objectives

This chapter will help readers to:

- understand the characteristics of attention deficit hyperactivity disorder (ADHD) and its relationship with other common developmental and mental disorders;
- appreciate that ADHD is caused by a complex interaction between genes and social and environmental factors;
- understand treatment interventions, including educational, parenting, cognitive behavioural therapy and pharmacological; and
- appreciate that ADHD remains a highly pernicious chronic condition and that effective interventions can help prevent associated social and educational exclusion.

DISORDERS, DIFFICULTIES AND DIFFERENCES

Mental-health difficulties in childhood and early adolescence are best understood as emotions or behaviour outside the normal range for age, sex and cognitive ability, linked with an impairment of development and where the child suffers as a result. It is usually not the child who complains about the problem but rather one of the many adults involved in that child's life.

In contrast to most adult mental health disorders, ADHD is a neurodevelopmental disorder and represents a quantitative shift from normality within a developmental framework. It describes the most severe 1–3% of the childhood population in terms of hyperactivity, inattention and impulsiveness in more than one setting which is usually assessed within community paediatrics and Child and Adolescent Mental Health Services (CAMHS) teams for pharmacotherapy.

Applying a life-course perspective to ADHD, we know that present diagnostic criteria require symptoms of ADHD be present before the age of 7. However, evidence shows that ADHD can be diagnosed competently in pre-schoolers and the correlates of pre-school ADHD are similar to those found in school-age samples and include deficits in executive functioning and delay aversion regarded as essential features of core ADHD.

The key clinical features of ADHD can be summarized into a triad from early childhood of severe restlessness, inattention and impulsiveness. Brown (2000) produced a helpful model of executive function seen in ADHD focusing on six areas, alongside which he listed the expected impairments:

1 Prioritizing and organization.
2 Attention focus and control.
3 Alertness regulation and speed of processing.
4 Frustration and emotional management.
5 Memory recall and working memory.
6 Monitoring and regulation of actions.

MEDIA MYTHS AND CONTROVERSY

Media myths abound and the tabloid press is full of headlines such as 'ADHD an excuse for bad parenting'. Undoubtedly a controversial diagnosis, the issue of reliance on medication without addressing social, educational or family issues can lead to justified criticism. On the other hand, the consensus of evidence to date supports medication using stimulants (e.g. methylphenidate or ritalin) or non-stimulants (atomoxetine) as being the most effective intervention (Molina *et al.*, 2009). Without medication, many of the other sensible angles in treatment (such as specialist education) cannot be easily accessed by the pupil. However, with appropriately specialized teaching within small classes and high adult-to-pupil ratios, a child with ADHD may not require medication or at least need a lower dose.

EPIDEMIOLOGY OF ADHD

Multiple coexisting psychiatric conditions have been reported with childhood ADHD. Indeed, it is uncommon to have a child with merely ADHD alone. In a Swedish population sample with ADHD, the prevalence rate for another condition was 87%, while the prevalence rate for two or more comorbidities was 67%. The most common comorbid conditions reported have been antisocial disorders, especially conduct disorder (CD) in up to 25% and oppositional defiant disorder (ODD) in up to 50%. The presence of comorbid antisocial disorders could often be linked to mothers' psychiatric disorders or to negative parenting practices. A wide spectrum of developmental and learning disorders has been found to be associated with children with ADHD. These include specific learning difficulties, such as dyslexia, dysgraphia, dyscalculia and dyspraxia; Tourette's syndrome; and tic disorders. Until recently the presence of pervasive developmental disorder (i.e. autistic spectrum disorders) was thought to rule out a diagnosis of ADHD. However, research and practice have demonstrated that the two can be diagnosed as separate conditions in the same individual. It has been shown that other syndromes on the autistic spectrum, such as Asperger's syndrome, can co-occur with ADHD. ADHD is associated with a five-fold increase in mental disorders such as depression.

ASSESSMENT AND DETECTION OF ADHD

 Case Study

Kieran was on the go all the time from his first steps at the age of 15 months. He was into everything and did not sleep properly through the night until he was nearly 5. His parents were exhausted and found that their extended family were not keen to look after him. By the start of primary school, Kieran had fractured his clavicle and elbow from jumping off trees and heights.

During infant school, Kieran struggled to sit still at circle time and was not popular with his peers. The school special educational needs co-ordinator (SENCO) discussed the class teacher's concerns with the parents. He was referred by the GP to the local community paediatrics team who recommended parent training around positive reinforcement and giving him some additional support to remain on task in school at School Action Plus of the code of practice. His parents felt blamed as bad parents by their friends but had two other older boys with no difficulties at all.

After a six months' trial of positive behavioural management and parenting classes, the parents were less punitive and found that there had been a short-term response to praise and clear targets. However, the progress did not last and he continued to 'be all over the place' and not able to sit and watch a film all the way through without getting up and making a nuisance of himself. He had no friends at school. His morale was low and he was struggling to read.

The community paediatrician discussed medication options with the parents who initially were sceptical as they were worried about side-effects and using medication in such a young child now aged 7. After careful reassurance, they decided that something was needed to improve Kieran because he was being excluded for disruptive behaviour and hitting his peers. He seemed to be gravitating towards all the 'problem children' at the school.

After a few months he was being invited to parties again for the very first time and his parents were in tears as they had been so worried about his social isolation.

The primary school took advice from the behaviour support specialist teacher service and instigated individualized approaches with as much one-to-one time with his teaching assistant as possible; increased computer-based learning helped his focus; and egg timers were employed to help with time management and awareness. Kieran was provided with a 'tangle' which is a plastic spiral that allowed him to fiddle with his hands under the table and not distract other children near him. He sat on a table close to the teacher so that he did not have the additional distraction of people in front of him. The tactical ignoring of attention-seeking behaviour and the use of visual cards to prompt him to remain on task were found to work. Target charts were used between home and school to reward him for clear goals and immediate rewards were given wherever possible. Kieran was placed with good role models to help him with learning appropriate behaviour. Nuisance items, such as rubber bands and rulers, were strategically removed, while activity reinforcement was employed using the less desirable task before the more desirable reward task. The parents were included as partners in Kieran's success. Close home-school liaison was maintained with email and diaries with the focus on the positives and reinforcing targets.

(Continued)

(Continued)

Exercise was found to promote Kieran's focus. He enjoyed football and could concentrate better in a team now although he would need prompting when group instructions were given. His parent joined ADDIS UK and the local ADHD support network for parents.

Careful planning for the transition to secondary school was undertaken involving both the SENCO and the community paediatrician. His parents found a school which also provided nurturing for the Year 7 transition and had good links with the local community paediatrics and CAMHS team.

Kieran's medication needed to be changed to a preparation which covered the early evenings as well as during the school day and a suitable longer-acting preparation of methylphenidate was started. Kieran's sleep pattern needed help with melatonin to assist him at night.

AETIOLOGY AND UNDERLYING THEORETICAL MODELS

Biological Factors

The diagnosis of ADHD does not imply a particular underlying cause. The presence of psychosocial adversity or risk factors should not exclude the diagnosis of ADHD, which involves the relationship between multiple genes and environmental factors. ADHD is viewed as a disorder with many different subtypes resulting from the interplay of different risk issues.

Genetic Influences

ADHD symptoms show powerful genetic influences. Twin studies suggest that genes explain around 75% of the heritability of ADHD symptoms in the population (heritability estimate of 0.7 to 0.8). The genes affect the distribution of key ADHD symptoms across the wider population. No single gene has been identified in ADHD.

Environmental Influences

A range of biological factors can negatively affect brain development during the perinatal period and early childhood is associated with an increase in the risk of ADHD or attention deficit disorder (ADD). Such risk factors include maternal substance misuse during pregnancy, foetal hypoxia and very low birth weight; also brain injury, and exposure to toxins such as lead and a deficiency of zinc.

Epidemiological research indicates a link between additives in the diet and levels of hyperactivity; and a small proportion of children with ADHD demonstrate individual reactions to some foods or artificial additives, and could be helped by an exclusion diet with appropriate dietetic or medical advice (Richardson, 2004).

Psychosocial Factors

ADHD has been associated with severe early psychosocial adversity – for instance, in children who have survived depriving institutional care (Roy *et al.*, 2000). The mechanisms are not known but may include a failure to acquire cognitive and emotional control and the impact of early emotional neglect on brain development as well the probability of disrupted parenting due to familial ADHD and substance misuse by parents.

Parental–child relationships can be improved in children where ADHD symptoms have been successfully treated with stimulants. Parents themselves may also have unrecognized and untreated ADHD, which can also undermine relationships.

Dysfunctional relationships are more common in the families of young people with ADHD. Stressful family relationships may be related to the problems of living with a child with ADHD as well as a risk for the disorder itself. In ADHD, a harsh and punitive parenting style is a risk factor for developing oppositional and conduct problems.

Focus groups of children with ADHD have expressed very clear desires for better public understanding of the condition. They asked for empathy for their situations and less stigma attached to ADHD diagnoses. Experiences of stigma, such as bullying, name-calling, negative assumptions and differential treatment, were distressing to children, and negatively affected their self-evaluations, self-esteem and self-confidence. Close friendships were an important protective factor against the initiation and/or continuation of fights that arose as a result of the child with ADHD being bullied. These friendships were mentioned at least as often as medication as factors that helped children to restrain their impulse to fight and/or to continue fighting (NICE, 2008).

TREATMENT INTERVENTIONS

Psychological Therapies and Parenting Interventions

Parent-effectiveness training is a behaviour therapy intervention supporting parents of children with ADHD to use behaviour therapy techniques with their child. Parent training originated in the 1960s based on behavioural learning theory and play therapy. This intervention has developed further addressing beliefs, emotions and wider social issues as well as targeting poor self-confidence, depression, social isolation and marital difficulties (Scott, 2002). The focus is primarily with the child or young person's main caregiver, although some programmes add a child-directed component based on the principles of social skills training.

NICE (2006) recommended that all parent-training/education programmes, whether group or individual based, should include elements of the following:

- Social learning theory to underpin the curriculum.
- Strategies to improve relationships.
- A reasonable number of sessions – eight to twelve are suggested.

- Empowering the parents to identify aims and targets.
- Role play and homework to support the generalization of skills.
- Therapeutic alliance achieved through appropriately trained and experienced operatives.
- Consistent implementation promoted through manualization and adherence to the manuals involved.

Examples of programmes that demonstrated the essential characteristics listed above included the Webster–Stratton Incredible Years Programme and the Triple P – Positive Parenting Programme. Parents who might have the greatest needs could find it difficult to engage in groups and a more home-based and tailored approach may be required.

Behaviour Therapy

The chief technique involves the use of rewards or positive reinforcers that are thought likely to encourage the young person to make helpful changes in motor, impulse or attentional control. This may involve concrete rewards, such as extra time for recreational and leisure activities or the means to obtain items that the young person values. 'Tokens' (such as stars, chips, marbles and so on) may work for younger children in their own right, whereas for older children tokens will need to be exchanged for items of value to them. Social approval, such as praise or achievement certificates and self-praise, is a useful adjunct in such programmes.

Rewards are specific to an individual and what is of value to one child is not necessarily of value to another. There are also practical, financial, cultural and moral issues that make some rewards more suitable for some parents or teachers than others. Parents often argue against the use of 'black mail' or 'bribery' when discussing similar techniques.

A further set of techniques involves punishments or negative reinforcers. This approach may have some value when a particular impulsive behaviour is offensive to others and needs to cease immediately. Verbal reprimands, which have the merit of being simple and effective, may be delivered by parents, carers and teachers. Response cost techniques involve the loss of a potential reinforcer. These can take the form of deductions either from rewards already earned or from an agreed set of rewards given in advance but from which deductions can be made for inappropriate behaviour.

The third most common technique is 'time out' from social reinforcement, and is helpful where it is felt that inappropriate behaviour is being reinforced by the attention of others.

There is no evidence yet that psychological interventions for children with ADHD have measurable positive effects on teacher ratings of either ADHD symptoms or conduct-related behaviours. The beneficial effects of psychological interventions for ADHD therefore do not appear at present to transfer to the classroom environment. However, psychological interventions for children with ADHD, taking into consideration their developmental level, have moderate helpful effects according to parent ratings of ADHD symptoms and conduct problems, both for children not on medication and as an adjunct to continued routine medication for ADHD. Combining medication with psychological interventions may be especially important in the management of older adolescents and adults with ADHD and comorbid antisocial behaviour, and these individuals benefit from interventions to develop prosocial skills, emotional control, problem-solving negotiation and conflict resolution.

EDUCATIONAL INTERVENTIONS

It is well established that children with ADHD fall behind their peers academically. It has been shown that this trend extends to children who are severely inattentive, hyperactive and impulsive in the classroom, even if they do not have a formal diagnosis of ADHD. The studies by Merrell and Tymms are based on a large sample of English school children aged between 5 and 7 years, and they found that inattention was particularly related to academic underachievement and that impairment was proportionate to the number of key symptoms (Merrell and Tymms, 2005). Moreover, children who had been identified by their teachers in the reception year of school as having severe ADHD symptoms were found to fall behind their peers academically until the end of primary schooling at the age of 11 years and beyond.

Situational variation with how ADHD presents is well established in schools. There are clear differences in behaviour across secondary schools using observation and self-report measures which have been replicated. Galloway et al. (1995) proposed that 'differences between teachers are substantially greater than differences between schools', and posited that the teacher was the dominant influence on behaviour in the classroom. Gray and Sime (1988) suggested that the majority of the variance in behaviour lay within schools themselves. In the Elton Report (HMSO, 1989) it is stated that 'a teacher's general competence has a strong influence on his or her pupils' behaviour'.

A study set in one LEA found that more than half the teachers had some experience of teaching a child with a diagnosis of ADHD (Sayal et al., 2006), and that a time-limited educational intervention for teachers had been found to raise awareness and improve recognition of children with possible ADHD (Sayal et al., 2006).

Teacher-led educational interventions consist of managing academic activities or adapting the physical environment. A description of a wide range of educational strategies for use with children with ADHD is given by Cooper and Ideus (1996), who suggest techniques such as the following:

- Awareness of potential distractions and manage those within the classroom by close proximity with the teacher.
- The child can use a stipulated quiet area.
- Appropriately interesting activities.
- Instructions need to be simple and unambiguous.
- Promotion of structure and predictability.
- Avoiding boredom through needless repetition.
- Simplification by dividing into manageable chunks.

- Promoting praise for positive results.
- Paired working as opposed to larger groups.
- Time out when misbehaving.
- Positive reinforcement using tangible tokens.
- Removal of tokens in response to inappropriate behaviour.

The provision of in-service training, peer observation and coaching by professionals can be effective, but the process takes time, and Adey *et al.* (2004) suggested that 30 hours of in-service provision are necessary to create sustained changes to teachers' classroom practice.

Teacher-led interventions, such as giving clear and effective commands, have large beneficial effects on the behavioural problems of children with ADHD. Teachers who have received training about ADHD and its management should provide behavioural interventions in the classroom to help children and young people with ADHD.

DIETARY RECOMMENDATIONS

Health professionals need to emphasize the importance of a balanced diet, good nutrition and regular exercise for those of any age with ADHD. Some have found the elimination of artificial colouring and additives from the diet to be helpful. Dietary fatty acid supplementation (e.g. omega 3) is not recommended by NICE.

PHARMACOLOGICAL TREATMENT

The Multimodal Treatment Study of Children with ADHD ((MTA) Jensen *et al.*, 2007) was a large (*n* 579), randomized trial with children assigned to one of the following groups: medication management, intensive behavioural treatment, combination treatment or community care (which included medication for approximately two thirds of the sample).

KEY FINDINGS

At 14 months (MTA Co-operative Group, 1999) the outcome strongly favoured careful medication (irrespective of the presence or absence of behaviour therapy); at that point the randomization ended, families were free to choose treatment or not, and the intensive interventions (medication monitoring and behavioural work) were discontinued. Later reports have provided details of follow-up of the groups at 24 (Jensen *et al.*, 2007) and 36 months after randomization. By the three-year mark, the outcome was similar for all four groups.

Molina *et al.* (2009), in their eight-year MTA follow-up study, found that the type or intensity of 14 months of treatment for ADHD in childhood does not predict functioning six to eight years later. Rather, the early ADHD symptom trajectory, regardless of treatment type, is prognostic. Innovative treatment approaches targeting specific areas of adolescent impairment are needed. Adverse events at the 24 and 36-month points after randomization included influences on growth in height and weight – an effect of 0.75 inches at the two-year mark, with no further loss at the three-year point and catch-up growth by the eight-year point, suggesting no growth suppression in that timescale.

SAFETY ISSUES

In 2006 the US Food and Drug Administration (FDA) conducted a review on reports of sudden death in patients treated with ADHD medications using data from the Adverse Event Reporting System (AERS) (http://www.fda.gov/ohrms/dockets/ac/06/briefing/2006-42106-07-01-safetyreview.pdf). The review concluded that the rate of sudden death with methylphenidate and atomoxetine was below background rates available. The Medicines and Healthcare products Regulatory Agency (MHRA) (UK) published a drug safety update in January 2010 and concluded:

> The benefits of methylphenidate continue to outweigh the risks when used to treat ADHD in children aged 6 years or older and adolescents. The longer-term safety of methylphenidate remains under close review, and the results of ongoing studies to characterise the known or potential risks of ADHD medicines will be evaluated when available (http://www.mhra.gov.uk/Publications/Safetyguidance/DrugSafetyUpdate/CON06829)

People with ADHD have a higher risk than the general population for running into problems with substance misuse. The risk appears to be linked with the presence of conduct disorder and social adversity. In UK clinical experience, however, the misuse of prescribed drugs by people with ADHD is very uncommon. The use of illicit drugs, such as cannabis and cocaine, is probably not increased by receiving stimulants, at least in the short term. It may even be reduced according to a meta-analysis by Wilens *et al.* (2003), which suggested that treatment with stimulants for ADHD was associated with a substantial reduction (approximately twofold) in drug misuse.

Observational follow-up of the MTA trial has found that medication does not contribute significantly to the risk for substance misuse in adolescence and behaviour therapy is associated with reduction of risk (Molina *et al.*, 2009). The reasons for a reduced risk of substance misuse with treatment are likely to impact upon impulsivity and conduct disorder symptoms with enhanced academic performance and family functioning.

It is important to note that use of alcohol or cannabis is not a contraindication to stimulant prescribing but rather should raise the possibility of drug diversion and should impact upon the choice of preparation in favour of the longer-acting medicines with very low abuse potential. Concomitant cannabis and stimulant use should be closely monitored because of the theoretical risks of increased dopamine in the genesis of psychosis in some studies.

Methylphenidate at a higher dose is more likely than placebo to cause the following short-term adverse effects: insomnia, anorexia, irritability, moodiness, thirst, itching, diarrhoea, palpitations, stuttering, reddened eyes, incoherent speech and decreased bodyweight. The long-term studies of methylphenidate indicate an increased risk of side-effects, including an increase in systolic blood pressure and heart rate increase. Methylphenidate is thought to increase intrasynaptic concentrations of the neurotransmitters dopamine and noradrenaline (norepinephrine) in the frontal cortex as well as subcortical brain regions associated with motivation and reward and thus it improves the saliency of academic tasks.

Atomoxetine is a non-stimulant drug relatively recently introduced into the UK, licensed for use in children of six years and over and young people for the treatment of ADHD, as well as having a continuation licence into adulthood. It is thought that it works by selectively inhibiting the presynaptic noradrenaline transporter, thus inhibiting noradrenaline reuptake. Atomoxetine has less potential for misuse and does not require the same strict prescribing and storage conditions as methylphenidate and dexamfetamine as it is not a controlled drug.

Methylphenidate and atomoxetine have a similar side-effects profile with respect to effects on appetite, growth, pulse and blood pressure, requiring similar monitoring. Rarer harm events associated with atomoxetine include initial increased risk of suicidal thoughts and (very rarely) hepatic damage.

Drug treatment is not indicated as the first-line treatment for all school-age children and young people with ADHD. It should, rather, be held back for those with severe symptoms, such as those with the more severe ICD 10-defined hyperkinetic disorder (1–2% of the child population) and impairment or for those who have refused non-drug interventions or have not responded sufficiently to parent-training/education programmes or group psychological treatment (http://www.who.int/classifications/icd/en/bluebook.pdf). However, NICE (2008) recommends that, following treatment with a parent-training/education programme, children and young people with ADHD and persisting significant impairment should be offered drug treatment. The use of medicines in the treatment for children and young people with ADHD should always form part of a comprehensive treatment plan that includes psychological, behavioural and educational advice and interventions.

It is mandatory that, before starting drug treatment, children and young people with ADHD should have a full pre-treatment assessment, which should include the following:

- A full mental-health and social assessment.
- A full history and physical examination, including:

  o assessment of history of exercise syncope, undue breathlessness and other cardiovascular symptoms;
  - heart rate and blood pressure (plotted on a centile chart);
  - height and weight (plotted on a growth chart); and
  - family history of cardiac disease and examination of the cardiovascular system.

- An electrocardiogram (ECG) if there is past medical or family history of serious cardiac disease, a history of sudden death in young family members or abnormal findings on cardiac examination.
- A risk assessment for substance misuse and drug diversion (where the drug is passed on to others for non-prescription use).

FUTURE DIRECTIONS FOR TRAINING AND MULTIAGENCY DEVELOPMENT

Multiagency working in relation to ADHD raises challenges. Different models of disability and how to respond to it are held by different agencies. Parents, young ADHD patients and carers also need to be able to be part of steering groups or have their views represented. A number of successful multi-professional teams for ADHD are emerging with protocols for multi-professional working, including the role of GPs in monitoring aspects of care, and the GP with a special interest model has proved helpful for ADHD transitional and adult clinics. There remain, however, difficulties regarding transitional arrangements between CAMHS and adult mental health services and a general lack of support for adults with ADHD because of the difficulties associated with getting a diagnosis and treatment.

SUMMARY

- Apart from the impact on the individual, ADHD has a pernicious impact on society in the following areas (Coghill, 2006):
  o There is a dramatic increase in healthcare attendance through bike accidents and a tripling of related vehicular accidents.
  o There are exclusions in nearly one half of cases and a one-third drop-out of education, with lower occupational aspirations.
  o There is a significant increase in parental divorce rates and a similar increase in sibling conflict.
  o Absenteeism and decreased productivity at work.
  o A doubling of the substance misuse rate and a risk of earlier involvement and complexity of treatment.
  o Quality-of-life research indicates that children with ADHD are in the bottom one twentieth on measures of quality of life.

- Research has shown (Brassett-Grundy and Butler, 2004) that men and women who had childhood ADHD were significantly more likely than those without ADHD to face negative outcomes in adulthood, affecting various degrees of social exclusion. ADHD is as much a female problem, as it is a male problem and the adult lives of those with childhood ADHD are typified by social deprivation and adversity.
- The recommendations for cutting down the public and personal cost of ADHD include:
  o better screening for ADHD, perhaps in primary care.
  o wider use of sensitively designed early interventions and individually tailored treatment plans.
  o ongoing treatment and support for those with ADHD through adolescence into adulthood; and
  o raised awareness of ADHD amongst parents, health professionals, social-care workers, educationalists and those in the criminal justice system.
- These measures will help to ease the negative impact that childhood ADHD has on the life-course, stopping young sufferers from becoming socially excluded and unproductive adults.

Further Reading 📖

Cooper, P. and Bilton, K. (2002) *ADHD: A Practical Guide for Teachers*. London: David Fulton. This is a user-friendly and concise resource.

O'Regan, F. (2007) *ADHD* (2nd edn). London: Continuum International. Fintan O'Regan was a headteacher of the only specialist school in the UK for teaching and managing ADHD (Centre Academy).

Phelan, T.W. (2003) *1–2–3 MAGIC: Effective Discipline for Children*. Glen Ellyn, IL: Barnes & Noble. Training your child to do what you want them to do. Written by the parent of an ADHD child, this book provides easy-to-follow steps for disciplining without yelling, arguing or smacking.

Spohrer, K.E. (2009) *Teaching Assistants' Guide to ADHD*. London: Continuum International. This book demonstrates the importance of recognizing and developing the abilities of all children with ADHD.

References

Adey, P. *et al.* (2004) *The Professional Development of Teachers: Practice and Theory*. London: Kluwer.

Brassett-Grundy, A. and Butler, N. (2004) *Attention-deficit/hyperactivity disorder: An Overview and Review of the Literature relating to the Correlates and Lifecourse Outcomes for Males and Females. Bedford Group for Lifecourse and Statistical Studies Occasional Paper 1*. London: Institute of Education, University of London.

Brown, T. (2000) *Attention Deficit Disorders and Comorbidities in Children, Adolescents and Adults*. Washington, DC: American Psychiatric Press.

Coghill, D. (2006) 'Making the most of scant resources: the development of an effective ADHD service', in *ACAMH Occasional Papers 24: The ADHD Spectrum*, 39–49.

Cooper, P. and Ideus, K. (1996) *Attention Deficit/Hyperactivity Disorder: A Practical Guide for Teachers*. London: David Fulton.

Egger, H.L. and Angold, A. (2006) 'Common emotional and behavioural disorders in preschool children: presentation, nosology and epidemiology', *Journal of Child Psychology and Psychiatry*, 47: 313–37.

Galloway, D. *et al.* (1995) 'Motivational styles in English and mathematics among children identified as having special educational needs', *British Journal of Educational Psychology*, 65: 477–87.

Gray, J. and Sime, N. (1988) 'A report for the Committee of Inquiry into Discipline in Schools. Part 1. Findings from the national survey of teachers in England and Wales', in *Enquiry into Discipline in Schools the Elton Report)* (1989). London: HMSO.

HMSO (1989) *The Elton Report: Enquiry into Discipline in Schools*. London: HMSO.

Jensen, P.S. *et al.* (2007) '3-year follow-up of the NIMH MTA study', *Journal of the American Academy of Child and Adolescent Psychiatry*, 46: 989–1002.

Merrell, C. and Tymms, P. (2005) 'A longitudinal study of the achievements, progress and attitudes of severely inattentive, hyperactive and impulsive young children.' Paper presented at the annual conference of the British Educational Research Association, University of Glamorgan, September.

Molina, B.S. *et al.* (2009) 'The MTA at 8 years: prospective follow-up of children treated for combined-type ADHD in a multisite study'. *Journal of the American Academy of Child and Adolescent Psychiatry*, 2009: 48(5): 484–500.

MTA Co-operative Group (1999) 'A 14-month randomized clinical trial of treatment strategies for attention deficit/hyperactivity disorder', *Archives of General Psychiatry*, 56: 1073–86.

NICE (2006) *Technology Appraisal Guidance 102: Parent-training/Education Programmes in the Management of Children with Conduct Disorders*. London: NICE.

NICE (2008) Guidance on ADHD. http://www.nice.org.uk/nicemedia/pdf/ADHDFullGuideline. pdf.

Richardson, A. (2004) 'Long-chain polyunsaturated fatty acids in childhood developmental and psychiatric disorders', *Biomedical and Life Sciences*, 39: 1215–22.

Roy, P., Rutter, M. and Pickles, A. (2000) 'Institutional care: risk from family background or pattern of rearing?', *Journal of Child Psychology and Psychiatry*, 41: 139–49.

Sayal, K. *et al.* (2006) 'Identification of children at risk of attention deficit/hyperactivity disorder: a school-based intervention', *Social Psychiatry and Psychiatric Epidemiology*, 41: 806–13.

Scott, S. (2002) 'Parent training programmes', in M. Rutter and E. Taylor (eds) *Child and Adolescent Psychiatry* (4th edn). Oxford: Blackwell.

Wilens, T.E. *et al.* (2003) 'Does stimulant therapy of attention-deficit/hyperactivity disorder beget later substance abuse? A metaanalytic review of the literature', *Pediatrics*, 111: 179–85.

Wolpert, M., Fuggle, P., Cottrell, D., Fonagy, P., Phillips, J., Pilling, S., Stein, S. and Target, M. (2006) *Drawing on the Evidence CAMHS publications* (2nd edn). London: CAMHS Evidence Based Practice Unit, University College, London (www.acamh.org.uk/site/upload/document/ Drawing_on_the_Evidence_-_text.pdf).

15 VISUAL IMPAIRMENT AND MAINSTREAM EDUCATION: BEYOND MERE AWARENESS RAISING

John Ravenscroft

Learning objectives

This chapter will help readers to:

- understand the national register of severely sight-impaired and sight-impaired people;
- appreciate the difference between clinical and functional visual assessments;
- explore current research on the profile and prevalence of children with visual impairment living in the UK;
- understand the roles of the qualified teacher of the visually impaired in empowering the mainstream teacher; and
- explore the balance between academic attainment and independent daily living skills.

BACKGROUND

The parents of a child with vision impairment often face the difficult task of deciding which school their child should attend. Parents, however, cannot fully participate in this decision process if they have not been provided with the information and knowledge that will allow them to make informed choices as an equal member of the team that is involved in the child's education. Often parents feel unsure about what is the best way forward for their child. They may want to know more about their rights as parents and about what types of educational placement would suit their child. Parents may want to know if any special preparations will be made for their child starting school and/or be concerned about how they will cope once there. Parents may desire more information about the school curriculum; the level of specialist vision impairment support provided; access at the school; and about extracurricular activities. Most of all, as we have seen from a variety of studies (see the Royal National Institute of the Blind's *Shaping the Future* (2000, 2001a, 2001b, 2001c) studies; Roe, 2008; Ravenscroft, 2009), children and parents may be worried about whether they (or their) child will 'fit in' and will have friends and enjoy school.

A theme that frequently emerges from the literature is the requirement for integrated services to meet the needs of children with visual impairment. It is essential that parents, educationalists and other professionals work closely together to determine the successful delivery of an appropriate, planned education that enables the child with vision impairment to thrive at school (Townsley *et al.*, 2004). The driving force of having an integrated approach is the belief that co-ordination of services will avoid duplication of effort and provide children and families with better outcomes. Atkinson *et al.* (2007) identified several positive outcomes for those who have adopted a multiagency approach. These outcomes include access to services not previously available to children and families, improved educational attainment for children within mainstream schools and a reduced need for more specialist services. Integrated service provision also leads to significant benefits for those staff and services that are part of a multiagency framework (Gray, 2008).

In order to plan and develop successful integrated services, well trained and competent professionals need to acquire an accurate demographic profile detailing numbers of visually impaired (VI) children who will require support. Yet in the UK there is no accurate record of how many children and young adults there are who have a significant visual impairment. This gives policy-makers and managers charged with the forward planning of integrated service provision the difficult task of delivering services based on information that may not describe the full scale or spectrum of children needing support. Perhaps a simple analogy would help to express the concerns being issued here. By not having accurate details on the numbers (and potential numbers) of users of services such as education, health and social work, is surely like an architect planning a large public building but not knowing how many people will go into it or, consequently, what the internal and external requirements should be.

CERTIFICATION AND REGISTRATION OF PEOPLE, INCLUDING CHILDREN WHO ARE VISUALLY IMPAIRED

In the UK the current certification system is when a consultant ophthalmologist can certify that a person who is either severely sight impaired (blind) or sight impaired (partially sighted) is eligible to be placed on a register, usually held by either a blind welfare society or local authority social work department. Only a consultant ophthalmologist can certify that a person is either blind or partially sighted; however, there are pathways of referrals from either the eye clinic or the optometrist directly to social services which alert them to the needs of people with vision impairments in advance of certification (Durnian *et al.*, 2010).

There are many problems with the current registration system, the main one being under-registration. There is a growing body of evidence which suggests that data from the register(s) are unreliable (Barry and Murray, 2005) and particularly so for children (Clunies-Ross and Franklin, 1997; King *et al.*, 2000; Ravenscroft *et al.*, 2008). Possible explanations for this under-representation of children may include a lack of awareness that children and parents have about the process of certification and registration and the people who may provide their support. It is also not compulsory and some children and adults may already be in receipt of any benefits they are entitled to. There could also exist a communication gap, perceived or real, between social, educational and health-care staff, for it has been claimed that there is a lack of awareness in staff in schools and local authority education/children and family departments about the process of certification and registration (Scottish Executive, 2001; Alexander, *et al.*, 2009). Despite the failings of the registration system, local authority services still refer to the register and use it as a guide to anticipate the expected number of VI children who may need support and to initiate funding and implement strategic processes.

CLINICAL ASSESSMENT OF PEOPLE WITH VISION IMPAIRMENTS

Before we examine the profile of children with visual impairments we need to ascertain what exactly we mean by vision impairment and how it is measured. We measure how well a person sees by measuring visual acuity. The term 'visual acuity' was introduced by Donders in 1862 to describe 'sharpness' of vision, although nowadays it is the ability to resolve fine detail and, specifically, to read small, high-contrast letters. Visual acuity is therefore the best direct vision that can be obtained, with appropriate spectacle correction if necessary, with each eye separately, or with both eyes (Thomson, 2005).

In a formal clinical setting the standard measure of visual acuity is usually assessed through the 'Snellen' notation. The 'Snellen acuity' uses letter recognition on a Snellen Vision Chart as shown in the left of the chart in Figure 15.1. If another test is used to measure acuity it will often have a Snellen equivalent since this is most easily interpreted vision-scoring method.

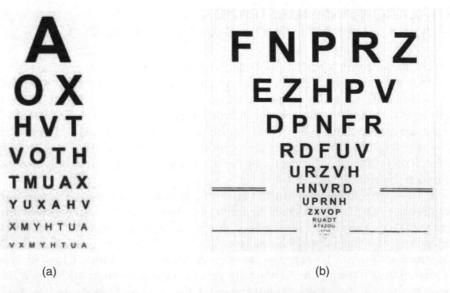

(a)   (b)

Figure 15.1   A comparison of the Snellen (a) and LogMAR (b) charts

Source: Image provided by National Vision Research Institute of Australia and is reproduced with permission.

A Snellen vision score is derived from the number of letters correctly identified on a Snellen vision chart from a recommended testing distance of 6 metres (6 metres in the UK or 20 feet in the USA). The Snellen score is found by recording the smallest size of letter that can be correctly identified and is recorded as a fraction. For example, if only the top letter of a standard Snellen chart is correctly identified the resultant Snellen score will be 6/60. The numerator (6) corresponds to the testing distance, while the denominator (60) equates to the size of the letter. The value 6/60 indicates that a person can correctly identify a letter at 6 metres, which a person with normal vision would be able to identify at distance of 60 metres. A 6/60 value indicates poor vision. In contrast, a score of 6/6 would denote a vision within normal/average range since the letter is correctly identified at 6 metres.

The Snellen chart, although universally accepted, does have its flaws (McGraw *et al.*, 1995). For example, the limited number of letters at the top of the chart does put people with very poor visual acuity at a disadvantage compared with those with better acuity. There is also the problem of the irregular progression of letter sizes within the Snellen chart. The jump in difference between the letters representing acuities of 6/5 – 6/6 is an increase of 120%, whereas the difference from 6/36 to 6/60 is 167%. As Thomson (2005: 57) states: 'this is analogous to a ruler which is marked with different length graduations.'

Bailey Lovie (1976) charts, which negated some of the disadvantages of the Snellen chart, are now being introduced. The Bailey Lovie charts (see Figure 15. 1) convert a geometric sequence of letter sizes to a linear scale, and give a LogMAR notation of vision loss. LogMAR vision testing offers a consistent and scientific method of recording vision scores. Although LogMAR is seen as the gold standard in measuring visual acuity it is still common parlance to use the Snellen notation, and to convert it using a similar table as found in Table 15.1. However, due to the reasons just explained, these conversions are only approximately and good practice dictates that comparisons between LogMAR and Snellen should not be made.

Table 15.1   LogMAR to Snellen conversion

LogMAR	Snellen equivalent
0.0	6/6
0.3	6/12
0.5	6/18
0.6	6/24
0.8	6/36
0.9	6/48
1.0	6/60
1.1	6/72
1.3	6/120
1.5	6/180
1.8	6/360

DEFINITION OF VISUAL IMPAIRMENT

We can now consider the term 'visual impairment and certification' as it relates particularly to children and young adults. In the UK it is the National Assistance Act 1948 that defines 'blindness' for certification. The act states that a person can be certified as severely sight impaired if they are 'so blind as to be as to be unable to perform any work for which eye sight is essential' (s. 64(1)). In this definition the language of certification and registration is closely related to the adult world and clearly has no relevance at all to children. Nowadays, the explanatory notes issued to consultant ophthalmologists and hospital eye-clinic staff from the UK's Royal College of Ophthalmologists (Levy, 2007) are used and define three distinct levels of certification for severely sight-impaired people. The first of these are for people who may be regarded as blind[1] who have an acuity score of less than 3/60 Snellen. The second group are those who have an acuity of 3/60 but are less than 6/60 Snellen.[2] The remaining severely sight-impaired people are those who have a visual acuity of 6/60 or better and who would not normally be regarded as being blind but are certified (blind) if the field of vision is considerably contracted, especially in the lower part of the visual field.

For those children and adults who are partially sighted there is no legal definition and so there are only guidelines which indicate that a person should be certified as sight impaired if they have a visual acuity of 3/60–6/60 Snellen and a full visual field – or up to 6/24 Snellen with a moderate contraction of the visual field, or even 6/18 Snellen if there is a gross visual field deficit. Generally, it is likely that a child will receive intervention from a qualified teacher of visual impairment (QTVI) in the UK if the child's visual acuity is less than 6/18, or if the child has very good acuity but has a significant reduction of visual field or if the child has cerebral visual impairment. The child's use of vision will be monitored by a multiagency team if the congenital eye condition is likely to deteriorate.

FUNCTION VISUAL ASSESSMENTS

It is important to recognize the distinction between measurements of visual acuity for a clinical measure which can be part of a diagnostic assessment or is enveloped within a treatment regime and measurements of visual acuity/function within a functional assessment. Clinical measures are measures of visual function which depend on the status of ocular, refractive and ocular-motor systems as well as the visual pathway (Hansen and Fulton, 2005). The purpose of functional assessments should be to obtain information which can be used to gain an understanding of the impact of visual impairment and the use of vision in everyday activities for the individual and to observe the ways in which the person's remaining vision is used or could be used in a variety of real-life environments.

Children do not develop and learn how to acquire skills and concepts in isolation – for example, we do not see play, socialization, language and cognition all developing in isolation from each other. What we do see is a complex interweaving of cognition, mobility and orientation, language, emotional and social integration skills, in which functional vision impacts. Deficit models of assessment, those that are commonly found within a medical context, tend not to unwrap this complex weave, nor do isolated tests within functional assessments achieve any better results. There is a requirement, therefore, to move from this deficit stance if we are to move towards more appropriate assessments for the child with visual impairments; assessment that is encapsulated within a strength-based paradigm, a paradigm that sees the child holistically, and one that emphasizes the capabilities or the positive aspects of the child's vision.

Functional visual assessments are therefore best achieved by through a multiagency approach, but the multiagency team must take into account their own constructions of the child they are assessing, for we can learn from those theorists (such as Woodhead and Faulkner, 2000) who see concepts of childhood as being created. In other words, we need to be careful that functional assessment teams, where the assessment tools are being guided by this construction, do not measure a child's functional vision within a preconceived framework of that child. The framework could contain issues of class, gender, race and even parental expectations. Teams need to examine the appropriateness of the functional assessment tools they use to assess a child's vision, for it is the assessment tools that will in part shape that child's life and determine future support and need.

THE PROFILE OF CHILDREN WITH VISUAL IMPAIRMENT

In the last two decades there have been various attempts at determining the numbers and profile of VI children living in the UK (see Evans, 1995; Rodgers, 1996; Foster and Gilbert, 1997; Rahi and Dezateaux, 1998; Keil and Clunies-Ross, 2003; Rahi and Cable, 2003; Bodeau-Livinec et al., 2007; Ravenscroft et al., 2008). In 2003, the Royal National Institute of Blind People (RNIB) estimated that there were 23,680 children and young people known to visual impairment services across England, Scotland and Wales (Keil and Clunies-Ross, 2003). This figure can be compared with the number of children who are officially registered blind or partially sighted in 2005 across England, Wales and Scotland. This number of 11,514 clearly shows the under-registration of children on local authorities' registers. Nevertheless, in 2007 the RNIB commissioned another study developed by Morris and Smith (2008) and found, by sending questionnaires to local authorities in England, Wales and Scotland, that 16,008 children were receiving support from their local authority due to their visual impairment. Morris and Smith claim their data only represent 66% of children with visual impairment educated in England, and 34% of children in Scotland and 80% of children educated in Wales. Consequently, Morris and Smith suggest the original figure of sixteen thousand (with some caveats) should extrapolated using data from the 2006 census to 25,305.

Two influential studies (Rahi and Cable, 2003; Bodeau-Livinec et al., 2007) that examined the rates of VI and blind children within the UK population reported very similar results. Children with a corrected visual acuity of 6/18–6/60 in the better eye were defined as having visual impairment and children with corrected visual acuity in the better eye of less than 6/60 or no useful vision are defined as having severe visual impairment or were blind. Bodeau-Livinec *et al.* (2007: 1101) suggest that 13 in every 10,000 children born in the UK will be diagnosed with a visual impairment by their 12th birthday, which amounts to around 950 new cases a year. They also found a cumulative incidence rate of 5.8 per 10,000 at 5 years of age for children who were severely VI or blind, which supports Rahi and Cable's (2003) finding of 5.3 per 10,000.

Ravenscroft *et al.* (2008), using data from the Visual Impairment Scotland (VIS) notification database, found the most single cause of childhood visual impairment was not due to damage of the eyes but due to damage to parts of the brain that are responsible for seeing. The study claims that in over half (51%) of the 850 children notified at time of analysis, visual impairment was due to some form of damage to the brain or visual pathways, exactly the same percentage as Bodeau-Livinec *et al.* (2007). There were a total of 75 different conditions named by eye-health professionals as the primary cause of visual impairment in the children listed on the VIS database. However on closer analysis of the children on the database, 18% of all children had cerebral visual impairment (CVI) as the most identified single primary diagnosis given by the child's ophthalmologist. Albinism (with 9%) was a distant second. Given that damage to the brain is a major factor responsible for a child's visual impairment, it is of no surprise that the study found the majority (71%) of children with visual impairment also had some additional disabilities (in addition to their visual impairment).

The majority of children on the VIS dataset, who were able to be examined either clinically or functionally, fell within the 6/18–6/60 visual acuity range. This highlights the fact that very severe loss of sight or blindness is of very low incidence in children, indicating the term 'blind' is in fact quite misleading for most children with visual impairment who have some vision. Again this comes back to the notion of the constructions we make about children. More often or not the 'blind' child can be a seeing child and it is important mainstream classroom teachers and QTVIs utilize what vision the child has and, for most cases (except those where the child has no light perception at all), to support the child as a 'seeing' child rather than as a 'blind' one.

Although in the VIS study there was an increase in the number of children who attended special schools, when the child reached secondary school age most children attended mainstream schools. This was true for both primary and secondary school age and the children were supported by the visiting/itinerant QTVI support service. The study also found that pre-school children were supported by the QTVI service visiting the children at home and at nursery, thus making the transition to school much easier for the child. This supports recent findings by Cebulla and Chanfreau, (2009) that the majority of blind and partially sighted pupils attend mainstream schools.

By examining the case study, issues and strategies for teaching and learning for Peter (a boy with oculocutaneous albinism,[3] with low vision and nystagmus[4]) can be explored.

Case Study

Peter is 9 years old and at a local mainstream primary school. As a result of his albinism he is photophobic and dislikes the bright light. He also doesn't like to go out into the playground and needs sun glasses and a hat, but he dislikes wearing his hat as it affects his field of vision. He has no additional disability over and above his visual impairment, and is fully ambulant. He has poor vision and his distance vision has been assessed at 0.9 LogMAR. Therefore he needs support in seeing things at a distance. His near vision has also been assessed at 0.6 LogMAR, which indicates he will also need help with close-up work. A QTVI has identified that he likes materials presented to him in front size 24 and particularly with sans-serif fonts, such as Verdana or Helvetica. Peter has a hand-held magnifier, which stays in his bag until he is reminded to bring it out by his class teacher, especially at times when the class are reading story books. Peter is an average reader for his age although, as a result of his nystagmus, he reads very slowly and needs extra time for assessments.

In the classroom specific adaptations have been made in order for Peter to feel comfortable within the learning space and to access the curriculum. These adaptations include a considered seating position, lighting, high-contrast materials, slope boards and a reduction on the glare on computer screens, as well as a reduction on the amount of clutter on worksheets.

He is a shy boy and, although he does claim to have some friends, his class teacher would dispute this. He finds it difficult to maintain eye contact due to his nystagmus and does not look at people when talking to them. Peter does not do any extracurricular activities for he sees himself as clumsy and, as a result, his confidence and self-esteem are low. He can on occasion get a little disorientated and does not go far beyond his own local area. Although he tries to be independent about the school environment he is lacking in some basic core mobility and daily living skills.

 Discussion Point

Before reading the research about how to respond to the case study, what immediate questions do you have? What approaches would you take and why?

RESPONSES TO THE CASE STUDY

Empowerment of the Mainstream Class Teacher

Peter is visually impaired. The policies that are in place within his local authority mean that he has been included in the early intervention strategies since he was a few months old. Peter has routinely been included in multiagency team assessments. A single shared report is given to himself, his parents and other professionals within the team and is used to constitute a significant part of the information necessary for completion of Peter's individual education plans, the personal learning plan, individual transition plans and other planning documents. However one of the most important issues to consider for Peter is that he is a full member of the classroom and, as such, he should be treated as any other member. Gale *et al.* (1998: 147) suggest quite correctly that Peter 'is more similar to, than different from his sighted peers'. They stress the importance of the classroom teacher providing a positive role model to encourage Peter's peers to accept him. The classroom teacher may require support to achieve this aim.

Support for the classroom teacher is available from many sources, but one of the most fundamental sources of support will be the QTVI. One of the main roles of the QTVI is to empower others, by collaborating and consulting with the classroom teacher and others (including Peter's peers) and to provide awareness raising that will inform them about the implications a visual impairment may have. Importantly, though, the concept of empowerment goes beyond mere awareness rising in order to change the behaviour and assumptions that surround the pupil with visual impairment. Clearly stated, awareness raising, although necessary, is simply not sufficient. Awareness raising for staff and pupils is a one-way process, placing little responsibility on the recipient for they are passive receptors of the information given to them by QTVIs. Mainstream teachers need to be empowered to change their practice. As Coburn (2001) and, more recently supported by Printy (2008), suggests, teachers change their practice dramatically as a result of interaction with individuals who are out with their own 'community of practice'. If this is the case the importance of the role of the QTVI in empowering the actions of the mainstream teacher cannot be underestimated.

The responsibility for changing behaviours must not lie only with the QTVI. Stein and Nelson (2003: 425) argue that 'teachers must believe that serious engagement in their own learning is part and parcel of what it means to be professional and they must expect to be held accountable for continuously improving instructional practice'. Empowerment in this context, then, is a two-way relationship between the QTVI and the mainstream teacher' in that the QTVI must set the right enabling conditions for empowerment to occur, through dialogue and consultation. However, the mainstream teacher themselves, through self-agency, must take hold of these conditions and deliver change themselves.

Research tells us that having a special health-care need is generally associated with being bullied (van Cleave and Davis, 2006). Sweeting and West (2001: 225) found increased bullying was more likely 'among children who were less physically attractive, overweight, had a disability such as a sight, hearing or speech problem'. We see in the case study a disconnect between the teacher's perception of friendship and Peter's. Pupils with visual impairment appear to use the concept of friendship to protect themselves against bullying (Buultjens *et al.* 2002), and professionals need to beware of the exact status and nature of friendship among pupils with visual impairment. Roe (2008), developing Buultjen *et al.*'s stance, defines the issue clearly in that professionals need to create a variety of social contexts to promote social inclusion and, in each of these contexts, the child should not been seen as one with difficulties but each of these created contexts should be examined to assess how it impacts on the child with visual impairment. Roe is almost right. However, in order to have a positive impact on learning, mainstream teachers need to feel empowered to be able to create the right contexts, and empowerment again comes in part from discourse with the QTVI and other professional colleagues.

Empowerment from Orientation and Mobility

Empowerment for Peter is essential; however he must develop his mobility skills so that he is able to move around confidently in his surrounding environment. Orientation and mobility skills should be delivered by qualified habilitation[5] instructors who are trained to work with children. It is not enough to have instructors who are trained to work with adults who suddenly find themselves working with children: this smacks of viewing the child as a 'little adult'. Nor are QTVIs qualified to plan and deliver these skills either. QTVIs do receive some training in sighted guide techniques, but this is not commensurate with fully qualified orientation and mobility instructors. Students who receive mobility and orientation instruction are more likely to be employable, have higher levels of independence and have the skills necessary to utilize a variety of transport options that are not limited to 'getting a taxi' (Carey, 2006). However conflict can arise within the school environment. There are issues of when the instruction is going to take place within the school timetable: is the pupil, for example, expected to miss classes of core subjects to receive mobility training? Importantly, instruction also needs to take place at home, and between home and school. The rhetoric of the 'community school' is entrenched within policy and ideology yet, when it comes to orientation and mobility training for the VI child, this rhetoric often gets ignored.

 Discussion Point

Peter's social competence, his confidence and independent skills are affecting his home and school life. However, he is obtaining average grades. If pushed Peter might be able to obtain even higher grades. As a mainstream teacher, to what degree would you focus on Peter obtaining good academic grades at the expense of his own social competence skills, or would you focus on ensuring that when Peter leaves school he can live a full and independent life which may mean limiting his academic achievements?

Relate this case study to your own area of practice and discuss how social competence is promoted.

INDEPENDENT LIVING SKILLS OR ATTAINMENT?

Related to core mobility issues is employment. One of the major problems facing professionals involved in the education of children and young people who are VI is the employment/further education rates of children leaving education services. Research shows that there is a high unemployment rate for people with visual impairment and especially those with additional support need(s) (see Douglas *et al.*, 2006; Meager and Carta, 2008; Douglas *et al.*, (2009). Meager and Carta (2008) report the overall employment rate for people with seeing difficulties as low, and even lower for people who are disabled by their sight problems. If they have additional disabilities or health problems the employment rate drops even lower. However, a low unemployment rate should not be automatically equated with levels of educational attainment. Cebulla and Chanfreau (2009) highlight a small education attainment gap for pupils with visual impairment if visual impairment is the pupil's only additional support need: 64% of children who had no special educational needs obtained 5 or more GCSE A*– C passes, whereas 54% of children who were usually impaired with no additional support needs obtained the same number of passes.

If pupils with visual impairment but with no other additional support needs are achieving only slightly less in attainment than their sighted peers but have a higher unemployment rate, what could be causing the disparity between the two? I would like to suggest that part of the problem is the delivery (or not) of the mobility and independence curriculum. If single disability VI children are achieving near standard attainment rates but are leaving school with very little independent living skills, then although their attainment levels may allow the student to be called for an interview with prospective employers, the employer soon recognizes the poor independence and social skills that are presented and subsequently the student is less likely to be successful in obtaining employment. It is important to point out in this scenario that it is not the visual impairment *per se* that causes the difficulty; it is the lack of mobility and independent living skills. The two are separate issues.

If VI pupils leave school but are unable to go shopping, wash their clothes or cook for themselves then I would suggest the academic attainment counts for very little. If VI people are to lead full and successful lives within a working, day-to-day environment they must be able to do so independently.

This is not an easy problem to solve: what could be a possible solution to ensure VI children are able to access a curriculum that includes independence and daily living skills within a mainstream school? Controversially, I suggest that for some pupils (especially those who should be accessing independent living skills lessons) it may be appropriate to ignore or, if this seems too strong, to focus less on academic attainment and concentrate mainly or even wholly on developing independence living skills. Academic attainment may be achieved later, as it does for many young sighted adults who attend further education colleges. If this suggestion is accepted in schools then the training of independent living skills must be supported by appropriately trained habilitation workers, employed by local education authorities, and then supported by social work habilitation workers during out-of-term time. This mixed model of delivery ensures that all aspects of daily living and mobility needs are catered for not only at school but within the community as well.

To be clear I am not advocating that VI children are taken out of mainstream classes to be instructed in their daily living skills. This may lead to segregation and greater feelings of isolation, but it may be possible within the mainstream classroom to increase the independent living skills of children through project-based learning. Take, for example, the new Scottish Curriculum for Excellence (Scottish Government, 2004) where it is stressed that every child and young person is entitled to develop skills for learning, skills for life and skills for work. Within the new curriculum there will be a shared responsibility within schools and partners to take a holistic approach to ensure that children and young people are fully engaged members of society. Thus we may find that adapting to such an approach is not in conflict with the mainstream curriculum, but is in fact wholly supported by it.

To conclude, if the trend is to include pupils who are VI within mainstream continues, then there is a need to think very strongly about the relationship between academic attainment and independent living skills. With the introduction of new curricula, the time may be right to readdress the balance, and to take a brave step forward and focus on ensuring that children who are blind or partially sighted can function independently, to the best of their ability, in a sighted world and not, as at present, have some children who attain excellent grades but cannot engage with the world around them.

SUMMARY

- There are a number of issues concerning the assessment, registration and education of children in mainstream schools.
- The main certificate of visual impairment register is inappropriately used as a tool for the future planning of services, including education, for children with visual impairment due to the under-representation of children on the register.
- It is important to develop a two-way relationship between the QTVI and the mainstream class teacher, and the chapter has focused particularly on the role of the QTVI in empowering the mainstream class teacher rather than simply providing guidance or informative awareness-raising sessions.
- There is an interaction between academic attainment and daily living skills, with an emphasis for some on concentrating on developing greater social competence within the child rather than trying to achieve some degree of academic success.

Notes

1 Note that some vision may still remain.
2 This group of people will also be classed as blind if their visual field is contracted. The visual field is the portion of the subject's surroundings that can be seen at any one time (Wilson, 2005).
3 Oculocutaneous albinism is a group of conditions that affect the pigmentation of the skin, hair and eyes, and it also reduces pigmentation of the iris and the retina.
4 Nystagmus is uncontrolled movements of the eyes. In most people who have nystagmus the eyes usually move from side to side, but in others the eyes can move so that they swing up and down or even in a circular motion.
5 Notice the term is habilitation instructors and not rehabilitation instructors. Children with visual impairment do not need to be rehabilitated in their orientation, mobility and daily living skills.

Further Reading

Corn, A.L. and Erin, J.N. (2010) *Foundations of Low Vision: Clinical and Functional Perspectives* (2nd edn). New York, NY: American Foundation for the Blind Press. An excellent second edition on how best to assess and support both children and adults with low vision and on how to plan programmes and services.

LaVenture, S. (ed.) (2007) *A Parent's Guide to Special Education for Children with Visual Impairments.* New York, NY: American Foundation for the Blind Press. For the parent and training practitioner this gives a comprehensive guide to understanding the process of educating a child with visual impairments.

Roman-Lantzy, C. (2007). *Cortical Visual Impairment: An Approach to Assessment and Intervention.* New York, NY: American Foundation for the Blind Press. An excellent book for the practitioner who is interested in cortical/cerebral visual impairment.

Salisbury, R. (ed.) (2007) *Teaching Pupils with Visual Impairment: A Guide to Making the School Curriculum Accessible.* London: Routledge. A book that has many practical ideas on making the curriculum asscessible. Many of the chapters are written by experienced teachers of pupils with visual impairment.

Useful Website

http://www.ltscotland.org.uk/curriculumforexcellence/index.asp   An all-encompassing website for the Curriculum for Excellence

References

Atkinson, M., Jones, M. and Lamont, E. (2007) *Multi-agency Working and its Implications for Practice: A Review of the Literature.* Reading: CfBT.

Alexander, P., Rahi, J.S. and Hingorani, M. (2009) 'Provision and cost of children's and young people's services in the UK: findings from a single primary care trust', *British Journal of Opthalmology,* 93: 645–9.

Bailey, I.L. and Lovie, J.E. (1976) 'New design principles for visual acuity letter charts', *American Journal of Optometry and Physiological Optics,* 53: 740–5.

Barry, R.J. and Murray, P.I. (2005) 'Unregistered visual impairment: is registration a failing system?', *British Journal of Ophthalmology,* 89: 995–8.

Bodeau-Livinec, F., Surman, G., Kaminski, M., Wilkinson, A.R., Ancel, P.Y. and Kurinczuk, J.J. (2007) 'Recent trends in visual impairment and blindness in the UK', *Archives of Disease in Childhood,* 92: 1099–104.

Buultjens, M., Stead, J. and Dallas, M. (2002) *Promoting Social Inclusion of Pupils with Visual Impairment in Mainstream Schools in Scotland.* Edinburgh: Scottish Sensory Centre.

Carey, K. (2006) 'Visual impairment in a time of change: self understanding as the basis for effective living.' Key note address: Institute for Blind and Visually Impaired Young People and Adults in Copenhagen and Vision Centre Refsnaes for Children. Retrieved 20 June from http://www.humanity.org.uk/articles/blindness-visual-impairment/self-understanding-effective-living.

Cebulla, A. and Chanfreau, J. (2009) Educational attainment of blind and partially sighted pupils. Retrieved 22 June from http://www.natcen.ac.uk/pzMedia/uploads/Downloadable/f4ef4271-f81d-41d8-b758-2ff39a3deb2b.pdf.

Clunies-Ross, L. and Franklin, A. (1997) 'Where have all the children gone? An analysis of new statistical data on visual impairment amongst children in England, Scotland and Wales', *British Journal of Visual Impairment*, 15: 19–20.

Coburn, C.E. (2001) 'Collective sensemaking about reading: how teachers mediate reading policy in their professional communities', *Educational Evaluation and Policy Analysis*, 23: 145–70.

Douglas, G., Corcoran, C. and Pavey, S. (2006) *Network 1000: Opinions and Circumstances of Visually Impaired People in Great Britain: Report based on over 1000 Interviews*. Birmingham: Visual Impairment Centre for Teaching and Research, University of Birmingham.

Douglas, G., Pavey, S., Clements, B. and Corcoran, C. (2009) *Network 1000: Access to Employment amongst Visually Impaired People*. Burmingham: Visual Impairment Centre for Teaching and Research, University of Birmingham.

Durnian, J.M., Cheeseman, R., Kumar, A., Raja, V., Newman, W. and Chandna, A. (2010) 'Childhood sight impairment: a 10-year picture', *Eye*, 24: 112–17.

Evans, J. (1995) *Causes of Blindness and Partial Sight in England and Wales, 1990–1991. Studies on Medical and Population Subjects* 57. London: HMSO.

Foster, A. and Gilbert, C. (1997) 'Epidemiology of visual impairment in children', in D. Taylor (ed.) *Paediatric Ophthalmology* (2nd edn). Oxford: Blackwell Science.

Gale, G., Kelley, P., d'Apice, P., Booty, J., Alsop, P., Bagot, N., Foreham, B., Williams, B., Pfisterer, U. and Sheik, K. (1998) 'Accessing the curriculum', in P. Kelly and G. Gale (eds) *Towards Excellence: Effective Education for Students with Vision Impairments*. London: Royal Institute for Deaf and Blind Students.

Gray, C. (2008) 'Support for children with a visual impairment in Northern Ireland: the role of the rehabilitation worker', *British Journal of Visual Impairment*, 26: 239–54.

Hansen, R.M. and Fulton, A.B. (2005) 'Development of the cone ERG in infants', *Investigative Ophthalmology and Visual Science*, 46: 3458–62.

Keil, S. and Clunies-Ross, L. (2003) *Survey of Educational Provision for Blind and Partially Sighted Children in England, Scotland and Wales in 2002*. London: RNIB.

King, A.J.W., Reddy, A., Thompson, J.R. and Rosenthal A.R. (2000) 'The rates of blindness and partial sight registration in glaucoma patients', *Eye*, 14: 613–19.

Levy, G. (2007) Certificate of visual impairment. Royal College of Ophthalmology. Retrieved 22 June from http://www.rcophth.ac.uk/standards/cvi.

McGraw, P., Winn, B. and Whitaker, D. (1995) 'Reliability of the Snellen chart', *British Medical Journal*, 310: 1481–2.

Meager, N. and Carta, E. (2008) *Labour Market Experiences of People with Seeing Difficulties: Secondary Analysis of LFS Data*. London: Institute for Employment Studies/RNIB.

Morris, M. and Smith, P. (2008) *Educational Provision for Blind and Partially Sighted Children and Young People in Wales*. London: NFER/RNIB.

Printy, S.M. (2008) 'Perspective leadership for teacher learning: a community of practice', *Educational Administration Quarterly*, 44: 187–226.

Rahi, J.S. and Cable, N. (2003) 'Severe visual impairment and blindness in children in the UK', *Lancet*, 362: 1359–65.

Rahi, J.S. and Dezateaux, C. (1998) 'Epidemiology of visual impairment in Britain', *Archives of Disease in Childhood*, 78: 381–6.

Ravenscroft, J. (2009) 'What parents of children with vision impairment ask their child's teachers?', *Journal of South Pacific Educators of Vision Impairment*, 4: 34–40.

Ravenscroft, J., Blaikie, A., Macewen, C., O'Hare, A., Creswell, L. and Dutton, G.N. (2008) 'A novel method of notification to profile childhood visual impairment in Scotland to meet the needs of children with visual impairment', *British Journal of Visual Impairment*, 26: 170–89.

Roe, J. (2008) 'Social inclusion: meeting the socio-emotional needs of children with vision needs', *British Journal of Visual Impairment*, 26: 147–58.

Rogers, M. (1996) 'Visual impairment in Liverpool: prevalence and morbidity', *Archives of Disease in Childhood*, 74: 299–303.

Royal College of Ophthalmology (2007) Certificate of blindness or defective vision. Retrieved 22 June from http://www.rcophth.ac.uk/docs/profstands/ScottishCVI.pdf.

Royal National Institute of the Blind (2000) Shaping the Future *(Summary Report)*. London: RNIB.

Royal National Institute of the Blind (2001a) *Shaping the Future: The Educational Experiences of 5 to 16 Year-old Blind and Partially Sighted Children and Young People*. London: RNIB.

Royal National Institute of the Blind (2001b) *Shaping the Future: The Social Life and Leisure Activities of Blind and Partially Sighted Children and Young People Aged 5 to 25*. London: RNIB.

Royal National Institute of the Blind (2001c) *Shaping the Future: The Health and Wellbeing of Blind and Partially Sighted Children and Young People Aged 5 to 25*. London: RNIB.

Scottish Executive, Social Work Services Inspectorate (2001) *Report of the Certification and Registration Working Group* (May). Edinburgh: Scottish Executive.

Scottish Government (2004) A curriculum for excellence – the Curriculum Review Group. Retrieved 19 June from http://www.scotland.gov.uk/Publications/2004/11/20178/45862.

Stein, M.K. and Nelson, B.S. (2003) 'Leadership content knowledge', *Educational Evaluation and Policy Analysis*, 25: 423–48.

Sweeting, H. and West, P. (2001) 'Being different: correlates of the experience of teasing and bullying at age 11', *Research Papers in Education*, 16: 225–46.

Thomson, D. (2005) 'VA testing in practice: the Snellen chart', *Optometry Today*, April: 57.

Townsley, R., Abbott, D. and Watson, D. (2004) *Making a Difference? Exploring the Impact of Multiagency Working on Disabled Children with Complex Health Care Needs, their Families and the Professionals who Support them*. Bristol: Policy Press.

Van Cleave, J. and Davis, M.M. (2006) 'Bullying and peer victimization among children with special health care needs', *Pediatrics*, 118: 1212–19.

Wilson, F.M. (2005) *Practical Ophthalmology* (5th edn). San Francisco, CA: American Academy of Ophthalmology.

Woodhead, M. and Faulkner, D. (2000) 'Subjects, objects or participants? Dilemmas of psychological research with children', in P. Christiansen and A. James (eds) *Research with Children: Perspectives and Practices*. London: Falmer Press.

16 STUDENTS WITH HEARING LOSS

Jill Duncan

Learning objectives

This chapter will help readers to:

- understand the central issues related to students with a hearing loss, including hearing technology, communication modality, literacy and cognition;
- appreciate the barriers to family–school engagement and the cultural diversity of families of children with hearing loss;
- learn practical strategies for supporting classroom teachers; and
- identify specialist practitioner teaching behaviours for students with a hearing loss.

Understanding children with hearing loss is a complicated endeavour because there is rarely one explanation that justifies a particular approach to the child's education. Important matters, such as communication modality and educational support, fall along a continuum. In addition, political and emotional undercurrents frequently burden the sector. However, controversial issues will not be addressed here. Instead, this chapter brings to light critical issues important for educating all students with hearing loss. Bear in mind that this is an introductory chapter and the reader is encouraged to investigate the selected readings at the end of the chapter for a detailed examination of pertinent issues.

The terms used in this chapter require an explanation. For our purposes, 'children with hearing loss' is inclusive of children who are culturally deaf, who use signed language, who are hearing impaired and who use an auditory-based spoken language to communicate. The term 'caregiver(s)' denotes the person(s) primarily responsible for the needs of the child. 'Specialist practitioner' refers to the teacher of the deaf, an auditory-verbal therapist/educator, a speech language pathologist or an audiologist – not the classroom teacher. 'Intervention' refers to any specialist practitioner support – either direct intervention to the child/family or indirect intervention via support to the classroom teacher.

POPULATION OVERVIEW

More than 665,000 babies with moderate, severe or profound hearing loss are born worldwide each year (Olusanya and Newton, 2007). Because hearing loss can be either present at birth or acquired after birth, the prevalence of childhood hearing loss increases with age and nearly doubles by 9 years of age (Fortnum *et al.*, 2001; Olusanya, 2005).

Children with hearing loss are reportedly at increased risk of medically and educationally diagnosed disorders (McClay *et al.*, 2008). They are heterogeneous in nature for a range of factors, including aetiology, the potential for a coexisting disability and family or environmental characteristics. This diversity is reflected in the range of communication abilities and literacy, cognitive and auditory skills of children with hearing loss (Duncan *et al.*, 2012). Children with hearing loss who have an additional disability have needs that are distinct from children with hearing loss as a single disability. When this occurs, specialist practitioners with expertise other than hearing impairment are required, making collaboration among interdisciplinary team members essential.

ASSISTIVE HEARING TECHNOLOGY

Assistive hearing technology includes digital programmable hearing aids, bone-anchored hearing aids, cochlear implants, hybrid cochlear implants and personal frequency modulation (FM) systems. The purpose of hearing technology is to make spoken language accessible (Seewald *et al.*, 2005; Duncan *et al.*, 2012). The choice of hearing technology is based on the severity of hearing. Most children with hearing loss in westernized countries use binaural amplification. In general, the earlier and more consistent the hearing aids and/or cochlear implant are used by the child, the better the outcome (Duncan *et al.*, 2012).

The care and maintenance of the hearing technology are transferred from the specialist practitioner to the caregiver through explicit instruction and practical experience. Eventually the child becomes responsible for the hearing technology and audiological management. The goal is to have the student assume full responsibility of the hearing technology and audiological management by the end of secondary school. Classroom teachers also require a knowledge of hearing technology – in particular the FM. This is because children with hearing loss may have difficulty listening in situations characterized by background noise or reverberation, such as classrooms (Zheng *et al.*, 2001).

COMMUNICATION MODALITY

Children with hearing loss may use signed language, spoken language or a combination of signed and spoken language. The communication modality of children with hearing loss falls along a continuum. At one end of the continuum is the exclusive use of visual (signed) language and, at the other end, is the exclusive use of an auditory-based spoken language. Upon diagnosis and after unbiased information has been provided to the family, caregivers choose the communication modality that best suits the culture of the family. Occasionally aetiology may dictate a communication modality. (Duncan *et al.*, 2012)

It is essential that the child and caregivers are fluent in the same communication modality –whether it is signed language or an auditory-based spoken language. It is also critical that caregiver–child interaction is abundant and consistent throughout the child's life so that, among other things, communication development is maximized.

LITERACY

A strong spoken language foundation facilitates reading development (Duncan *et al.*, 2012). A child who has atypical early exposure to spoken language may be at a disadvantage for developing adequate phonological representations (Dillon and Pisoni, 2006). If a spoken language gap existed in early childhood and persists, students with hearing loss may encounter barriers to developing fluent literacy skills. Students who use signed language can become literate adults. However, for this to occur requires vigilant family and specialist practitioner assistance in developing key skills, such as phonological awareness, decoding, fluency, comprehension and vocabulary.

Literacy demands increase in complexity as the difficulty of vocabulary and syntax increases. Students with hearing loss require the capability to talk about words, word structure and word meaning in a specific, decontextualized manner that demonstrates a conscious understanding of metalinguistics, including phonological and morphological awareness (Duncan *et al.*, 2012). High-level literacy skills are required in order to participate in sophisticated problem-solving and communication skills in academic and work environments.

Each reader's overall life experiences, or world knowledge, will influence the interpretation of the text. In literacy, the reader and writer do not share the same experience of time and physical environment. Ambiguity and the interpretation of the text are not as open for clarification as in face-to-face communication (Duncan *et al.*, 2012). It is important for the specialist practitioner and classroom teacher to consider the contribution of the different components of language to reading outcomes, given the interaction of associated top-down and bottom-up processes. Early and appropriate evidence-based literacy instruction is critical for successful literacy development and, if necessary, remediation (Mody, 2007).

 Discussion Point

In order to maximize the literacy development of students with profound hearing loss who use an auditory-based spoken language to communicate, the school principal, specialist practitioner, classroom teacher and parents might consider these options. The principal might facilitate the classroom teacher's attendance at hearing loss-related seminars. Upon consultation with the classroom teacher, the specialist practitioner might integrate phonological awareness into direct intervention with the student while using key subject vocabulary. The classroom teacher might integrate literacy-based activities into all academic subjects. The parents might provide an abundant supply of highly motivating reading materials and the opportunity for the student to practise oral reading regularly.

COGNITION

Historically, children with hearing loss generally fall behind their hearing peers in academic subjects, including literacy and mathematics (Marschark, 2003). This is due to a number of reasons, including age of diagnosis, aetiology, language and instructional practices. Marschark (2003), in reference to children who used signed language, surmises that it is reasonably possible that children with hearing loss have different knowledge bases, cognitive strategies and experiences that influence literacy and academic skills.

Executive function makes up the higher-order cognitive processing responsible for metacognition and behaviour regulation and is influenced by many factors. Children with hearing loss follow the expected milestones for executive function, although its development is closely related to family and school environments and practitioner instruction (Hauser *et al.*, 2008). Executive skills are essential skills that should be explicitly monitored and, if necessary, taught by the specialist practitioner and classroom teacher (Duncan *et al.*, 2012). Executive skills include:

- response inhibition
- working memory
- emotional control
- sustained attention
- task initiation
- planning/prioritizing
- organization
- flexibility (Dawson and Guare, 2010).

It is important for the specialist practitioner and classroom teacher to maintain vigilant surveillance of the executive function development of children with hearing loss because of its relationship to overall academic achievement.

FAMILIES

As children grow, their developmental capacities increase in both level and range, which in turn influences their relationship with caregivers and other significant people in their lives (Bronfenbrenner and Morris, 2006; Duncan, 2010). Caregivers remain the primary agents of change throughout childhood, which is why it is important to consider the family ecology (Dishion and Kavanagh, 2003; Duncan, 2010). However as the child develops, persons outside their immediate environment, such as peers and school personnel, become increasingly important (Bronfenbrenner and Morris, 2006). It then becomes essential for the specialist practitioner to review the influence of these individuals on the developing child (Duncan, 2010).

The family is a social system and so intervention with the child with hearing loss will influence the entire family (Markward and Bride, 2001). Therefore, it is impracticable to implement intervention with children without family involvement. Care should be taken to avoid isolated focus on the student with hearing loss and the specialist practitioner is encouraged to maintain a family systems approach (Duncan *et al.*, 2010).

A positive caregiver–child relationship is one in which the caregiver balances the needs of the child with the overall needs of the family (Dishion and Kavanagh, 2003). Family equilibrium can be difficult when a child has a disability. Caregivers may inadvertently allocate a disproportionate amount of time and resources to support the child with hearing loss.

A positive caregiver–child behaviour monitoring system is one in which the caregivers have continual developmentally appropriate surveillance of the child's behaviour (Dishion and Kavanagh, 2003). Developmentally appropriate surveillance is the suitable degree of supervision for the child's age and stage. The caregiver, specialist practitioner and classroom teacher should take care to relinquish control to the child as the child develops into a young adult.

A positive caregiver–school association is one in which the caregiver, school community, and specialist practitioner regularly communicate in a proactive and productive manner. The classroom teacher and specialist practitioner offer a menu of communication options depending on the age of the child and family needs, including email, a family communication journal, telephone meetings, an electronic bulletin board, a web-based portfolio and face-to-face meetings (Carlisle *et al.*, 2005; Thompson *et al.*, 2007; Knopf and Swick, 2008). Ongoing consistent communication assists in maintaining transparent and congruent child expectations.

SCHOOL AND CLASSROOM PLACEMENT

There is a continuum of educational placement options for students with hearing loss, depending on support requirements. At one end of the continuum is special school placement with no or little integration with hearing peers. This placement is for those students who have the highest specialist support needs. The further along the educational placement continuum, the more the child with hearing loss is integrated into the regular school. This is not to say that fully integrated children need no specialist support. Regardless of school and classroom placement, students with hearing loss require special provisions, including such things as a specialist practitioner, hearing technology, access to the curriculum in their first language – whether it be signed language or an auditory-based spoken language – and access to peers and/or mentors with hearing loss. It is critical that consistent access to learning opportunities occur in all classroom placements (Duncan *et al.*, 2012).

Attendance in a mainstream school does not automatically equal social inclusion (Angelides and Aravi, 2006/2007). Integration can cause children with hearing loss to feel isolated and it can influence identity and self-esteem. The essential elements for success are opportunities for peer and adult communication, which lead to developing healthy interpersonal skills.

Change in either classroom or school placement is inevitable and occurs for many reasons, including family relocation, academic concerns and incongruent school–family expectations. A change in schooling can be a time of increased family stress. Caregivers and the student undergo a process that requires them to weigh the benefits and disadvantages of placement options (Duncan, 2009). There may not be a perfect option and families may feel they are required to settle for second best. Paramount to facilitating a positive change for the student and family is unbiased access to information and a transparent knowledge of specialist service provision options.

FAMILY–SCHOOL ENGAGEMENT

The family-school relationship influences the student's self-educational expectations (Falbo *et al.*, 2001). Caregivers are encouraged to monitor the student's educational and social life so that school routines, teachers, friends and extracurricular activities are familiar to the whole family. This facilitates open and continuous family communication. Caregivers should endeavour to consider student academic information so that progress is transparent and the student receives adequate support. Caregivers are also encouraged to facilitate a positive peer network in which the student feels comfortable. Finally, caregivers make an effort to maximize direct school participation.

Family–school participation can occur in many formats, including communicating with the teacher or school personnel, attending school functions, volunteering in the classroom or the school, caregiver–teacher conferences, caregiver organizations and school governance roles (Harvard Family Research Project, 2007). These activities are important in several ways. School involvement assists the caregiver in understanding the school community and monitoring their child's participation in it. In addition, family–school participation conveys to the student the importance of the school.

When caregivers are involved in schools, they are more likely to obtain support from schools when assistance is needed (Anderson-Butcher and Ashton, 2004). There are many by-products of family–school collaboration. These include the fact that students and their families are supported, appreciated and valued, families feel empowered, caregivers gain parenting skills, school personnel and family working alliances are formed, and knowledge between parties is shared more easily (Anderson-Butcher and Ashton, 2004).

Establishing effective family–school–specialist practitioner partnerships is a process requiring honest, transparent intentions over time (Thompson *et al.*, 2007). No isolated intervention assures positive family–school relationships (Thompson *et al.*, 2007). Mismatches may occur when the home culture and values are at odds with the school or specialist practitioner.

CULTURAL DIVERSITY

Although the population of students in today's school is increasingly diverse, the population of teachers is not (Carlisle *et al.*, 2005; Duncan *et al.*, 2012). It is a fact that teachers most often come from the majority culture (Al-Hassan and Gardner, 2002). Carlisle *et al.* (2005) suggests that, when the family and specialist practitioner culture differs, caregivers may not feel their family's culture is understood or appreciated.

Further, some cultures may feel it is disrespectful to communicate with schools or specialist practitioners, making family participation more challenging (Carlisle *et al.*, 2005).

Specialist practitioners need to be aware that effective caregiving takes on various roles, depending on the culture of the family (Dishion and Kavanagh, 2003). The family's level of acculturation involves the extent to which caregivers have attained a social status and education level comparable with the dominant culture (Harry, 2008). Working with families requires a knowledge of cultural norms, regardless of whether the family is part of the minority or majority culture.

Potential barriers to participation by families with diverse needs include the following:

- A limited language proficiency.
- A lack of written information in the family's language.
- The specialist practitioner's unfamiliarity with the family's culture.
- Unfamiliarity with common practices and legislative rights.
- Differing views of the importance of family educational involvement (Al-Hassan and Gardner, 2002).

An increasing number of ethnically diverse families requires specialist practitioner and school personnel to have expertise in the influence of hearing loss in a variety of cultures. Specialist practitioners must recognize that identified strengths may vary from culture to culture (Duncan, 2007).

PEDAGOGY AND PRACTICE

A fundamental belief in deaf education is that learning occurs within a social learning paradigm, which views the specialist practitioner as a facilitator and the students as significant decision-makers as they learn from each other (Duncan *et al.*, 2012). Instruction is expected to be purposeful, and match students' interests and experiences. In order to maximize learning, the regular assessment of students with hearing loss is based on authentic, real-life procedures with direct and immediate carry-over into life. The specialist practitioner embraces the premise that learners construct knowledge based on their own experience and previous beliefs. Learning cannot be decontextualized: it does not occur in isolation from the circumstance in which it occurs. The specialist practitioner encourages opportunities for meaningful and genuine exploration, engagement in activities, interactive group work and student ownership of the learning process (Snider and Roehl, 2007). The responsibilities continuum views the classroom teacher as responsible for academic learning (e.g. the arts, maths and science) and the practitioner responsible for those aspects of the child's development, that will facilitate cognitive linguistic growth.

Underpinning all teaching strategies is the belief that no pedagogical domain is compartmentalized or can be considered in isolation but, rather, integrated (Duncan, 2006). Thus, specialist practitioners incorporate a range of suitable linguistic, auditory, cognitive, socio-emotional and speech objectives into all interactions. For example, the specialist practitioner targeting the goal of understanding non-literal language will also apply auditory and cognitive goals and, if appropriate, socio-emotional and speech goals. Regardless of the objectives, specialist practitioners create enjoyable and motivating environments while maintaining high but realistic shared expectations (Duncan *et al.*, 2012).

Within a mainstream school context, there are two primary models of specialist practitioner intervention for children with hearing loss – push in and pull out. In the 'push-in model', the specialist practitioner works within the classroom performing a variety of roles. These include team teaching with the classroom teacher, small-group discussion with the child with hearing loss and hearing peers, and one-on-one intervention in a quiet area of the classroom. There are three primary benefits of this model. First, the student does not leave the classroom, implying continuous membership. Secondly, the student avoids stigmatization as being different and needing to be taken out of the classroom for remediation. Thirdly, the specialist practitioner has a readily available model of hearing peers that assists in benchmarking the age and stage development of the student with hearing loss. The fundamental disadvantage of the push-in model is that the classroom is a noisy, busy environment, making specialist speech, language and auditory cognitive intervention difficult.

STRATEGIES FOR SUPPORTING SCHOOL PERSONNEL

There are many opportunities for school principals and specialist practitioners to support school personnel, especially the classroom teacher, in their endeavour to maximize student learning. There are four simple strategies:

- Allow classroom teachers to gain an authentic understanding of family perspectives.
- Provide hearing-related pre-service and in-service opportunities to classroom teachers.
- Ensure teachers have appropriate planning time to communicate with the specialist practitioner.
- Provide a meeting place, either virtual or face-to-face, for classroom teachers to communicate and support each other.

 Discussion Point

In an effort to support classroom teachers who have academic responsibility for students with profound hearing loss who use signed language to communicate, the school principal might organize access to three key activities:

- Signed language instruction for all school-based personnel.
- In-service training related to deafness.
- A face-to-face or online support group for classroom teachers.

The specialist practitioner might provide the classroom teacher with fortnightly sessions to review student progress and re-evaluate long and short-term goals.

GUIDING PRINCIPLES OF INSTRUCTION

Working with students with hearing loss is complex. It requires the continual surveillance of many learning domains concurrently. Duncan *et al.* (2012) generated a set of guiding principles that assist novice specialist practitioners (as well as classroom teachers) to focus on pedagogy and practice for students with hearing loss. These guiding principles are conceptually important to educational practice in general:

1 Use ongoing, consistent, formal and informal assessment as a foundation for setting goals and objectives.
2 Use predictable developmental hierarchies in all planning.
3 Prioritize essential knowledge and skills with the student and their caregivers.
4 Use a process-focused approach so that 'how to learn' is prioritized over 'learning what to learn'.
5 Use metacognitive strategic process knowledge with domain-specific knowledge in an effort to get the student to think about their own thinking.
6 Use a fluid, dynamic process approach, continuously scaffolding learning.
7 Use a responsive and needs-based approach to working with the student, family and school personnel.
8 Use challenging material that is meaningful to the student.
9 Recognize and promote student abilities.
10 Integrate learning so that no one domain (linguistic, auditory, cognitive, speech and social skills) occurs in isolation (Duncan, 2006; Duncan *et al.*, 2012).

ACCESS TO THE CURRICULUM

The fundamental responsibility of equal access to the curriculum resides with the school personnel. The specialist practitioner and family share a supporting role in the overall process of educating students with hearing loss. Accessing the curriculum is dynamic and dependent on many factors, including school and teacher ethos. The following case study illustrates one family's struggle to secure a learning environment that genuinely facilitated full access to the curriculum.

 Case Study

Adam became profoundly deaf because of meningitis at the age of 15 months and received a cochlear implant at 18 months. Adam uses an auditory-based spoken language to communicate. He is in Year 12 and has been fully mainstreamed throughout formal schooling. He received support from an itinerant teacher of the deaf, which decreased as Adam progressed in schooling. Adam has never required curriculum support but did receive some assistance from special education teachers at various times in his schooling.

(Continued)

(Continued)

The pre-school to school transition was difficult for Adam because he struggled with social skills expectations. The itinerant teacher of the deaf assisted in developing Adam's social skills and worked closely with his family, peers and school personnel.

Adam always uses an FM and has been consistently required to be responsible for it. This forced Adam to develop self-advocacy skills. No accommodations were offered to Adam without his parent's prior consent and without evidence of need. Adam's parents expected him to achieve at a level commensurate with his peers.

At times, the choice of school was difficult because schools were reluctant to commit to specific support prior to enrolment. In addition and at times, Adam's family struggled with understanding school culture. For example, in Year 5, Adam was bullied. When Adam self-reported the bullying, it annoyed the bullies and did not stop the behaviour, so Adam stopped self-reporting. The school was unhelpful. Adam changed schools before Year 7 and has not been bullied since. Adam has a close group of friends – hearing friends from school and some friends with hearing loss from a peer support group.

The factors that contribute to Adam's maximum access to the school curriculum include the following:

- The readiness of staff to use Adam's FM.
- The willingness of staff to make themselves available to Adam outside classroom hours, including via email.
- School-based special education staff consistently provide classroom teaching staff with information, strategies and support to meet Adam's needs.
- Ongoing encouragement of Adam to build self-esteem and self-advocacy skills.
- The refusal of teaching staff to 'helicopter' over Adam.
- Flexibility regarding due dates for language-intense assessments and when Adam has multiple assessments due within a short time.
- The staff's explicit effort to build rapport with Adam.

SPECIALIST PRACTITIONER TEACHING BEHAVIOURS

Despite early diagnosis, early intervention, the presence of residual hearing and the use of hearing technology, the process of learning may not be spontaneous for children with a hearing loss (Duncan, 2006; Geers *et al.*, 2008). Irrespective of the communication system used, children with hearing loss have a variety of learning styles, coping strategies and attitudes towards academic situations (Duncan *et al.*, 2012). It may therefore be necessary to structure specific learning conditions to encourage and facilitate the learning process (Duncan, 2007).

Specialist practitioners are encouraged to use a holistic, developmental approach whereby the development of cognitive and linguistic functioning is achieved through social interaction. Emphasis is placed on the development of communication through natural social discourse, including play, rhymes, songs and daily routines, as well as structured activities within and outside a formal learning context (Duncan *et al.*, 2012).

There are conventional teaching behaviours that facilitate learning for children with hearing loss. Duncan *et al.* (2010) identified such teaching behaviours thought to be facilitative of the learning process for children with hearing loss. These behaviours can be used by the specialist practitioner during intervention with young children and their caregivers or with school-age children without the caregiver present. These teaching behaviours assist novice practitioners to focus on key pedagogical practices. They are an elucidation of good teaching practice and are not to be used in isolation but concurrently.

Cognitive/linguistic

Where appropriate, the specialist practitioner will endeavour to:

- plan and implement a range of integrated cognitive, linguistic, auditory, social and speech objectives based on the stages of typical development;
- converse with the child/student slightly above their cognitive/linguistic level;
- communicate with the child/student and caregivers in a manner that facilitates natural social discourse;
- use expectant pauses/wait times to encourage turn-taking and auditory/cognitive processing;
- facilitate the transfer of the target language to informal social discourse; and
- employ strategies to stimulate creative and independent thinking.

Auditory

Where appropriate, the specialist practitioner will endeavour to:

- monitor hearing device function, use the hearing device properly and transfer responsibility of the hearing device to the caregiver/student;
- provide specific input through audition first and last;
- vary auditory stimuli length using word and/or sentence and/or discourse activities;
- maximize audition in both a formal and incidental context;
- use acoustic highlighting appropriately by proceeding from more to less;
- maximize audition by positioning the child/student/caregiver appropriately to encourage a listening attitude/posture; and
- develop and use an auditory feedback system to facilitate the child/student's self-monitoring of speech and spoken language production.

Speech

Where appropriate, the specialist practitioner will endeavour to:

- model and facilitate speech and spoken language with a natural rate, rhythm and prosody;
- accept or facilitate the child/student's intelligible speech production, including effectively implementing appropriate strategies for development/remediation; and
- facilitate the transfer of appropriate speech production into natural social discourse.

Caregiver/Student Guidance

Where appropriate, the specialist practitioner will endeavour to:

- provide opportunities for the caregiver/student to reflect and share relevant experiences;
- describe learning objectives to the caregiver/student before the beginning of each activity;
- model (demonstrate) and explain strategies and techniques clearly to the caregiver/student;
- discuss with the caregiver/student the outcome of each activity throughout the session or at the conclusion;
- identify with the caregiver/student the goals for future planning and carry-over;
- maintain rapport with the caregiver/student through active and constructive listening techniques;
- maintain active involvement/participation/practice of the caregiver/student through coaching in a constructive and supportive manner while creating an environment that is enjoyable and motivating.

Instructional Presentation and Planning

Where appropriate, the specialist practitioner will endeavour to:

- seize 'learnable' moments through informal and incidental opportunities;
- evaluate and review previous targets and set new targets as required, incorporating caregiver/student feedback and suggestions;
- use diagnostic teaching techniques by incorporating ongoing informal appraisal of student performance and share the results with the caregiver/students;
- use scaffolded teaching strategies, such as modelling, recasting, explaining and questioning;
- provide encouraging and appropriate feedback to the caregiver/student;
- maintain appropriate pacing that enables the caregiver/child/student to learn;
- provide a balance between child-led and adult-led activities, appropriate for the child's age and stage of development;
- select and implement a variety of instructional materials, activities and/or strategies to accommodate the needs, capabilities and learning styles of the caregiver/student;
- integrate appropriate pre-literacy/literacy activities linked to objectives;
- employ positive behaviour management techniques and transfer skills to the caregiver/student; and
- maintain adequate documentation record-keeping that ensures appropriate monitoring of the child/student's development (Duncan *et al.*, 2010).

SUMMARY

- Students with hearing loss have diverse learning needs.
- They, along with their families and classroom teachers, require specialist practitioner support in order to maximize learning potential.

- The appropriate choice and consistent use of hearing technology and communication modality is essential.
- Clearly delineated principles of instruction and specialist practitioner teaching behaviours contribute to maximizing the learning outcomes of students with hearing loss.

Further Reading

Duncan, J., Rhoades, E.A. and Fitzpatrick, E. (in press, 2012) *Adolescents with Hearing Loss: Auditory (Re)habilitation*. New York, NY: Oxford University Press. This recent book is progressive in its investigation of students with hearing loss aged 11–adulthood. Explanations include audiological management, psychosocial development and pedagogical foundations.

Marschark, M. and Spencer, P. (eds) (2010) *Oxford Handbook of Deaf Studies, Language and Education. Vol. 2*. New York, NY: Oxford University Press.

Marschark, M. and Spencer, P. (eds) (2011) *Oxford Handbook of Deaf Studies, Language and Education. Vol. 1*. New York, NY: Oxford University Press. In this two-volume set, Marschark and Spencer draw together top experts in deaf education to explore important issues. The study of its contents is essential for any specialist practitioner serving children with hearing loss and their families.

Rhoades, E.A. and Duncan, J. (eds) (2010) *Auditory-verbal Practice: Toward a Family-centered Practice*. Springfield, IL: Charles C. Thomas. This comprehensive book explains aspects of oral deaf education and its history and the role of families in maximizing the learning outcomes of their children. Chapter authors include family therapists, auditory-verbal practitioners and academics.

References

Al-Hassan, S. and Gardner, R. (2002) 'Involving immigrant parents of students with disabilities in the educational process', *Teaching Exceptional Children*, 34: 52–8.

Anderson-Butcher, D. and Ashton, D. (2004) 'Innovative models of collaboration to serve children, youths, families, and communities', *Children and Schools*, 26: 30–53.

Angelides, P. and Aravi, C. (2006/2007) 'A comparative perspective on the experiences of deaf and hard of hearing individuals as students at mainstream and special schools', *American Annals of the Deaf*, 151: 476–87.

Bronfenbrenner, U. and Morris, P.A. (2006) 'The bioecological model of human development', in W.W. Daman and R.M. Lerner (eds) *Handbook of Child Psychology. Vol. 1. Theoretical Models of Human Development*. New York, NY: Wiley.

Carlisle, E., Stanley, L. and Kemple, K. (2005) 'Opening doors: understanding school and family influences on family involvement', *Early Childhood Education Journal*, 33: 155–62.

Dawson, P. and Guare, R. (2010) *Executive Skills in Children and Adolescents: A Practical Guide to Assessment and Intervention* (2nd edn). New York, NY: Guilford Press.

Dillon, C. and Pisoni, D. (2006) 'Nonword repetition and reading skills in children who are deaf and have cochlear implants', *The Volta Review*, 106: 121–45.

Dishion, T. and Kavanagh, K. (2003) *Intervening in Adolescent Problem Behaviors: A Family-centered Approach*. New York, NY: Guilford Press.

Duncan, J. (2006) 'Application of the auditory-verbal methodology and pedagogy to school age children', *Journal of Educational Audiology*, 13: 39–49.

Duncan, J. (2007) 'Family-centred practice: concerns, barriers, controversies and challenges', *Deafness Forum Australia Newsletter*, 54: 3–4.

Duncan, J. (2009) 'Parental readiness for cochlear implant decision-making', *Cochlear Implants International*, 10(S1): 38–42.

Duncan, J. (2010) 'Circles of influence', in E.A. Rhoades and J. Duncan (eds) *Auditory-verbal Practice: Toward a Family Centered Approach*. Springfield, IL: Charles C. Thomas.

Duncan, J., Kendrick, A., McGinnis, M. and Perigoe, C. (2010) 'Auditory (re)habilitation teaching behavior rating scale', *Journal of the Academy of Rehabilitative Audiology*, XLII, 65–86.

Duncan, J., Rhoades, E.A. and Fitzpatrick, E. (in press 2012) *Adolescents with Hearing Loss: Auditory Rehabilitation*. New York, NY: Oxford University Press.

Falbo, T., Lein, L. and Amador, N. (2001) 'Parental involvement during transition to high school', *Journal of Adolescent Research*, 16: 511–29.

Fortnum, H.M., Summerfield, A.Q., Marshall, D.H., Davis, A.C. and Bamford, J.M. (2001) 'Prevalence of permanent childhood hearing impairment in the United Kingdom and implications for universal neonatal hearing screening: questionnaire based ascertainment study', *British Medical Journal*, 323: 536–40.

Geers, A., Tobey, E., Moog, J. and Brenner, C. (2008) 'Long-term outcomes of cochlear implantation in the preschool years: from elementary grades to high school', *International Journal of Audiology*, 47(Suppl 2): S21–S300.

Harry, B. (2008) 'Collaboration with culturally and linguistically diverse families: ideal versus reality', *Council for exceptional Children*, 74: 372–88.

Harvard Family Research Project (2007) 'Family involvement in middle and high school students' education', *Harvard Family Project*, 3: 1–12.

Hauser, P., Lukomski, J. and Hillman, T. (2008) 'Development of deaf and hard-of-hearing students' executive function', in M. Marschark and P. Hauser (eds) *Deaf Cognition*. New York, NY: Oxford University Press.

Knopf, H. and Swick, K. (2008) 'Using our understanding of families to strengthen family involvement', *Early Childhood Education*, 35: 419–27.

Markward, M.J. and Bride, B. (2001) 'Oppositional defiant disorder and the need for family-centered practice in schools', *Children and Schools*, 23: 73–83.

Marschark, M. (2003) 'Interactions of language and cognition in deaf learners: from research to practice', *International Journal of Audiology*, 42: S41–S48.

McClay, J.E., Booth, T.N., Parry, D.A., Johnson, R. and Roland, P. (2008) 'Evaluation of pediatric sensorineural hearing loss with magnetic resonance imaging', *Archives of Otolaryngology: Head and Neck Surgery*, 134: 945–52.

Mody, M. (2007) 'Neurobiological correlates of the language–literacy connection in normal and atypical development.' Paper presented at the 'Lifetime conference: research and application in neurodevelopmental research'. Washington, DC: Alexander Graham Bell Association for the Deaf and Hard of Hearing.

Olusanya, B.O. (2005) 'Can the world's infants with hearing loss wait?', *International Journal of Pediatric Otorhinolaryngology*, 69: 735–8.

Olusanya, B.O. and Newton, V.E. (2007) 'Global burden of childhood hearing impairment and disease control priorities for developing countries', *Lancet*, 369: 1314–17.

Seewald, R., Moodie, S., Scollie, S. and Bagatto, M. (2005) 'The DSL method for pediatric hearing instrument fitting: historical perspective and current issues', *Trends in Amplification*, 9: 145–57.

Snider, V. and Roehl, R. (2007) 'Teachers' beliefs about pedagogy and related issues', *Psychology in Schools*, 44: 873–86.

Thompson, J., Meadan, H., Fransler, K.W., Albert, S. and Balogh, P. (2007) 'Family assessment portfolios: a new way to jumpstart family/school collaboration', *Teaching Exceptional Children*, 39: 19–25.

Zheng, Y., Caissie, R. and Comeau, M. (2001) 'Perception of hearing difficulties by adolescents who are deaf or hard of hearing and their parents, teachers, and peers with normal hearing', *The Volta Review*, 103: 185–202.

17 AUTISTIC SPECTRUM DISORDER: CHALLENGES, ISSUES AND RESPONSES

Gavin Reid and Sionah Lannen

Learning objectives

This chapter will help readers to:

- understand autistic spectrum disorders;
- explore the criteria for identification and assessment;
- gain some insights into the branches of research and proposed changes to the *Diagnostic and Statistical Manual of Mental Disorders* (DSM) V; and
- understand intervention strategies.

BACKGROUND AND HISTORY OF AUTISTIC SPECTRUM DISORDER (ASD)

The last twenty years has witnessed a significant rise in the number of children diagnosed with autism. Of that there is absolutely no doubt. It has been suggested that ten years ago 1 in 500 children were diagnosed with autism; today the figure is 1 in 110 (Pinto *et al.*, 2010). Similarly in the USA the Center for Disease Control (CDC) found in studies conducted in 2007 that the incidence rate of ASD is higher than the rates found from studies conducted in the USA during the 1980s and early 1990s. The CDC survey (http://www.cdc.gov/mmwr/preview/mmwrhtml/ss5601a2.htm) assigned a diagnosis of ASD based on health and school records of 8-year-olds in 14 communities throughout the USA. The CDC estimates that 2–6 per 1,000 (from 1 in 500 to 1 in 150) children have an ASD. The risk is three to four times higher in males than females. Today the proportion of boys diagnosed with autism is around 60% of new cases, and this is more or less in line with that of 10–20 years ago.

In the UK estimates also indicate that the prevalence of autism is high. The figures suggest almost 40 in every 10,000 are autistic and 116 per 10,000 for the entire autistic spectrum (Baird *et al.*, 2006). There is some debate on whether this increase represents a true increase in the prevalence of autism or whether it reflects changes in the criteria used to diagnose autism, along with an increased recognition of the disorder by professionals. Many questions, hypothesis and accompanying explanations have been put forward for this dramatic rise in autism. These range from environmental factors to better and more accurate detection and neurobiological, chemical and emotional influences, or even misdiagnosis. Whatever the cause of this increase there is a need for teachers, parents and professionals to collaborate and work towards effective and lifelong intervention. This chapter looks at these issues and challenges and suggests some responses to them.

HISTORICAL ASPECTS

The term 'Kanner's syndrome' was first assigned to autism following the work of Dr Leo Kanner in 1943 of the Johns Hopkins Hospital in the USA. He studied a group of 11 children and introduced the label *early infantile* autism into the English language. At the same time a German scientist, Dr Hans Asperger, described a milder form of the disorder that became known as Asperger syndrome (Asperger, 1991). This latter group was characterized by Asperger by their social and communication deficits, their obsessions and dependence on rituals and routines. Kanner's syndrome was characterized by abnormal communication, abnormal social communication, ritualistic and stereotyped behaviour and resistance to change (Howlin, 2002). This is shown in detail in the *International Classification of Diseases and Related Health Problems* (ICD-10) (WHO, 1992) which stated, for example, that 'abnormal or impaired development' needs to be in one of the areas of receptive and expressive language, social attachment and reciprocal social interaction, and functional or symbolic play, and should be evident before the age of 3. ICD-10 also goes on to show specific symptoms in each of these categories (for example, in social interaction, a failure to make eye contact and inappropriate facial expression (body posture and use of gesticulation). In communication, for example this would be a delay in spoken language and a failure to sustain conversational exchange and, in play, a preoccupation with non-functional elements of play.

Thus these two disorders are also described in DSM IV TR (fourth edition, text revision) (APA, 1994) as two of the five pervasive developmental disorders (PDD), more often referred to today as ASD. All these disorders are characterized by varying degrees of impairment in communication skills and social interactions, and restricted, repetitive and stereotyped patterns of behaviour. The three PDDs that relate to autism are:

- autistic disorder (also called autism, classic autism and AD);
- PDD-NOS (pervasive developmental disorder – not otherwise specified); and
- Asperger's disorder (also called AS, Asperger's syndrome and Asperger syndrome).

DSM V (IMPLEMENTATION IN 2013)

A number of issues rise from these three differing PDDs, and these issues will gain more attention when DSM IV is replaced with DSM V in 2013. For example, DSM IV categorizes autism as a mental health disorder, but there is some debate about whether this classification is appropriate as some may classify it as a language disorder. Additionally there still remains some confusion on whether autism and Asperger's syndrome represent different conditions.

The draft for ASD is as follows:

Must meet criteria 1, 2, and 3:

1 Clinically significant, persistent deficits in social communication and interactions, as manifest by all of the following:

   a. Marked deficits in nonverbal and verbal communication used for social interaction
   b. Lack of social reciprocity
   c. Failure to develop and maintain peer relationships appropriate to developmental level

2 Restricted, repetitive patterns of behavior, interests, and activities, as manifested by at least TWO of the following:

   a. Stereotyped motor or verbal behaviors, or unusual sensory behaviors
   b. Excessive adherence to routines and ritualized patterns of behavior
   c. Restricted, fixated interests

3 Symptoms must be present in early childhood (but may not become fully manifest until social demands exceed limited capacities) (http://www.dsm5.org/ProposedRevisions/Pages/propose-drevision.aspx?rid=94)

Significantly, the draft version of DSM V indicates that one of the issues mentioned earlier will be addressed, as one of the changes in the draft DSM V is the loss of the Asperger's label, which has always been recognized as part of the autistic spectrum. Additionally the draft version indicates that the category PDD-NOS will no longer exist as a separate category and will be subsumed into the ASD label in the same way as Asperger's.

Yet Howlin (2002) suggests there are a number of factors that differentiate between autism and Asperger's syndrome. She suggests the prevalence rates may be higher for Asperger than for autism. She also suggests that the research indicates that there is often a significant difference in ages when children from the two groups are first diagnosed. In the autism group she suggests that the average age of diagnosis was 5.5 years, while in the Asperger group it was 11.3 years, and almost all (88%) of the children in the study with autism had been diagnosed before 10 years of age compared with only 45% of the Asperger group. At the same time it can be argued that the obvious similarities between the two syndromes suggest that they lie in the same continuum or spectrum. Asperger's syndrome is often considered to be a type of 'high-functioning' autism but there is some clinical controversy about whether it is a milder form of autistic disorder or a distinct disorder. Additionally, the term 'high-functioning' can be misleading as it does not necessarily translate to lower needs. This can have considerable implications for intervention and the allocation of resources.

CHARACTERISTICS OF ASDS

There are a number of key characteristics of ASD. The most prevalent are as follows:

Verbal and non-verbal communication:

- *Speech and language skills*: these may begin to develop but then lost, or they may develop very slowly or they may never develop. It has been estimated that around 40% of children with ASDs may not talk at all unless intensive early intervention is in place.
- *Communication*: gestures may be used or outstretching of the arm instead of attempting to use language. It may be difficult or impossible to imitate sounds and words.
- *Echolalia*: this is repeating something heard. For example, if you ask, 'Are you ready?' the response may be, 'Are you ready?' instead of answering the question. The repeated words might be said right away or much later and may be repeated over and over.
- *Non-verbal communication*: they may have difficulty in using gestures, such as waving goodbye, or using facial expressions to convey meaning.
- *Speech*: there is often an unusual pitch and rhythm in speech.

Social interaction:

- *Attention*: some people with ASDs may prefer to be left alone, showing no interest in people at all. They may not notice when people are talking to them.
- *Fitting in*: some people with ASD might be very interested in becoming part of a group, but do not know how to conduct themselves and relate to others. Difficulty 'joining in' is common in ASDs because they find it hard to 'read' or understand other people.
- *Peer group*: children with ASD may not relate to their own age group and prefer the company of adults or older children.
- *Eye contact*: some people with ASD make no eye contact or are less responsive to eye contact. Some may use peripheral vision rather than looking directly at others.
- *Facial expressions*: children with ASD may have difficulty in responding to or understanding facial gestures.
- *Tactile sensitivity*: children with ASD might not like to be held or cuddled, or might cuddle only on their terms. They can be sensitive in terms of touch.
- *Self-control*: they may have difficulty in controlling emotion and excitement

Repeated and unusual behaviours, interests and routines:

- *Ritualistic behaviours*: people with autism may have ritualistic actions that they repeat over and over again, such as spinning, rocking, staring, finger flapping and, in some cases, hitting themselves.
- *High anxiety state*: they can show intense anxiety or an unusual lack of anxiety. Anxiety, fear and confusion may result from being unable to 'make sense' of the world in the usual way.
- *Gait*: they can display unusual postures, walking or movement patterns.
- *Routines*: they might fiercely depend on routines and want things always to stay the same, and minor changes in the environment or in daily routines might trigger acute distress or fear.

Responses to sensations:

- *Stimulation processing*: they may have difficulty in making sense of environmental stimulation. People with ASD may have both auditory and visual processing problems, and sensory input may be scrambled and/or overwhelming to them. Sensory sensitivities vary in autism from mild to severe hyper and hypo-sensitivities.
- *Sensory stimulation*: they may have unusual sensitivities to sounds, sights, touch, tastes and smells.

RESEARCH

There is now considerable activity in the research field concerning explanations for autism and ASD and there is certainly too much to be discussed in any detail in this chapter. This chapter, however is more concerned with the issues and the challenges rather than recounting the details of research findings although, as we note, some of these issues will stem directly and indirectly from these. What is particularly staggering is the number of local initiatives taking place as well as major national and international projects. This can be noted when looking at the policy documentation of different areas of the country. For example, in Ireland, the report of the Task Force on Autism (2001), which was one of the earliest policy initiatives in the field, laid the groundwork for local research run by teachers, psychologists and parents. It recommended that, as a matter of urgency, research be conducted into the national prevalence of autistic and asperger disorder (p. 7). The report also suggested that formalized Department of Education and Science–university partnerships should be established to develop appropriate programmes for people with ASDs and that research should be carried out on methodologies and approaches, on the benefits of various clinical interventions and on the specific components of teacher and classroom assistant training, as well as on curricular interventions and strategies. The report suggested there needs to be a systematic evaluation of all pilot projects.

It is this connection between international and national initiatives and local pilot studies or policy studies that needs to be synchronized. If there are no local initiatives or clear policies to guide parents (and teachers), they may grasp at some sensational newspaper headline story offering new treatments and cures for autism and may select these, even though they may not be scientifically validated. It was interesting that the Republic of Ireland in their task-force report made considerable efforts to include parents at all stages of assessment and provision. For example, one of the recommendations was the introduction of Statutory Child and Adult Family Support Plans for those with an ASD. This multiagency co-ordination was also profiled in the Additional Support Needs Act 2004 in Scotland in terms of the development of co-ordinated support plans. While the Act does make it clear that a child does not necessarily need to have a diagnosis or disability to be considered as having additional support needs, it is also quite clear that people with an ASD will be considered as having a disability. This means that the parents of children who have been diagnosed with an ASD will need to ensure that their child receives the additional support necessary. The implication of this is that labels in themselves, although they can be helpful, will not necessarily guarantee addition support.

In England and Wales the Special Educational Needs Disability Act 2001 (SENDA) highlights the need for schools to make reasonable adjustments and that failure to make reasonable adjustments so that students have equal access to admission arrangements and to education services is unlawful. The reasonable adjustments duty requires schools to anticipate the barriers that disabled students, such as those with autism, may face. The National Autistic Society in the UK has provided an example of this where a boy with autism became anxious when the fire alarm sounded. There may have been reasonable adjustments the school could have made to prevent this. For example, staff at the school could have been trained about autism, about strategies to avoid difficulties and about how to overcome difficulties if they did arise. The pupil could have been given training for social situations and strategies for coping when the fire alarm is raised (http://www.nas.org.uk/nas/jsp/polopoly.jsp?d=1760&a=13883). It is clear, therefore, that legislation, policy and training all have a major role to play in ensuring that the needs of students with ASD are met.

THEORETICAL PERSPECTIVES

According to Pellicano (2007), the three main theories that relate to ASD are the theory of the mind (the ability to recognize one's mental states and that of others), the theory that relates to executive functioning (which involves independent and responsible thinking and dealing with new situations) and the theory of information processing (particularly relating to coherent and organized thought processes). But Pellicano also suggests that these accounts fall short of providing a full picture of ASD.

EARLY DETECTION AND GENETIC EXPLANATIONS

It is interesting to review data on the early detection of autism and particularly theories on causes. Roberts (2010) suggests that one of the recent achievements in this field is the possibility of identifying the neurobiological manifestations of autism as early as 9 months. She suggests that between 9 and 15 months infants with autism begin to withdraw and, with training and precise indicators, we could be looking at detection around that age range. This will clearly have a profound effect on the child's developing competencies. As Roberts suggests at this age one is more likely to be able to modify the association pathways of the developing brain before they are too firmly established. Despite the clear biological case for ASD, according to Gillberg and Coleman (2001: 111), 'there are as yet no reliable and valid biological markers for autism'.

There is, however, vigorous activity in the field of genetics in relation to ASD. The Autism Genome Project (which includes 50 academic institutions from 15 countries collecting data from 8,000 people and 1,600 families) represents a significant breakthrough in this area. The result is, as Szatmari (2010) claims, that more progress has been made in the last five years than in the fifty years previously (see also Pinto *et al.*, 2010). He suggests that 90% of autism arises from a result of genetic differences. The researchers in the project have located a considerable number of target genes which appear to play a role in how nerve cells communicate with each other. This is a current area of focus in early detection and may lead eventually to intervention and preventative work.

IDENTIFYING ASD

There are a great many issues and a great deal of controversy in the diagnosis of autism. These issues include either (or both) late diagnosis or misdiagnosis. There are examples of autism being misdiagnosed for attention deficit hyperactivity disorder (ADHD), auditory processing disorder, Rhett's syndrome, hearing difficulty, language disorders, speech delay, developmental delay and selective mutism. It is important therefore that a diagnosis should not rest on one test, or even one professional, but should be a multidisciplinary team approach using a range of assessment methods. A good example of this is in British Columbia where the Sunny Hill Health Center has a multidisciplinary team located at the Autism Spectrum Disorder Clinic. This team undertakes assessments for autism for children of all ages that are designed to meet individual needs, and it undertakes school planning and medical and/or behavioural management and links with the British Columbia Autism Assessment Network.

ASSESSMENTS PROCEDURES

The procedures for identifying autism should be clear to parents and they, themselves, should have an important role in this process. Ideally the process should include the following:

- An examination and evaluation of the child's sensory status (hearing, vision (including visual skills such as tracking), depth perception and auditory skills (such as source matching and auditory discrimination)).
- Interviews with parents, teacher and, where appropriate, the child.
- Direct behavioural observation in multiple settings.
- Completion of checklists by or with parents or caregivers.
- Formal psychometric evaluation of the child's cognitive, social, emotional, behavioural and adaptive functioning.
- An evaluation of literacy and numeracy readiness or attainment.
- An evaluation of the skills involved in the activities of daily living.
- A functional analysis of targeted behaviours (in cases where behavioural difficulties have been identified).
- An evaluation of learning style (e.g. preference for verbal or visual).
- An observation and evaluation of instruction (for example, how the child best scans and focuses to receive visual information, attention and concentration on tasks).
- An analyses of their problem-solving approaches.
- An examination and evaluation of the child's gross and fine motor skills, of sensory integrative functioning and lateral dominance.

- An evaluation of mental-health status and possible affective disorder.
- An assessment of the child's social status with peers.

It is important to note that the characteristics of children with ASD will vary greatly in severity from individual to individual. According to the National Institute of Mental Health (NIMH) in the USA, following an assessment using observations and test results, the specialist should only make a diagnosis of autism if there is clear evidence of poor or limited social relationships; underdeveloped communication skills; and repetitive behaviours, interests and activities. People with autism will normally have some impairment within each of these categories, although the severity of each symptom may vary. The NIMH diagnostic criteria also require that these symptoms appear by the age of 3.

TESTS AND STRATEGIES

In an interesting and forward-thinking discussion paper on autism in 1997 for Lancashire County Council in the UK, Connelly asserted that keeping the diagnosis of autism as a medical one may be helpful but it can cause confusion and 'can cause immense problems in terms of local people prepared to take on this role. 'I think [one] should accept that in local circumstances … local arrangements should be made to accept diagnosis by such groups as our own' (p. 13). This statement does capture the potential for conflict between the medical professionals and educational and psychological assessors. As the report goes on to say, however, 'with good liaison between various agencies … it is not important who makes the diagnosis'. It appears that the emerging consensus and best examples of practice in different countries are in fact those areas that have specially trained psychologists in the field of autism working collaboratively as part of a diagnostic team with other professionals and medical personnel. A number of medical authorities have taken initiatives for diagnosing autism. For example, in Scotland the National Health Service have convened a Scottish Intercollegiate Guidelines Network (SIGN) (2007). In their report of July 2007 (http://www.sign.ac.uk/pdf/sign98.pdf) they advocate the benefits of the diagnostic criteria of ICD-10 and DSM IV (see earlier in this chapter) and they quote three studies (e.g. Klin *et al.*, 2000) that agree that using DSM IV or ICD-10 will make the diagnostic procedure more reliable. They also suggest that the aim of specialist assessment is to formulate a multiagency management plan 'leading to an appropriate programme of supportive intervention'.

Although there are commonly used tests for autism, it is important to reiterate that a test alone will not be sufficient to diagnose autism accurately. It is also important to contextualize the assessment for practice and that interventions should result from the assessment as well as a diagnosis – if appropriate.

INTERVENTION

Just as in the area of assessment the often marked difference in perspectives between the medical and educational professions can be noted in intervention. This is an ongoing issue but with increasing legislation and a task group looking at the area of autism, there now appear to be more concerted and collaborative efforts by the range of professionals who are involved in ASD. We are aware that there is no known and unequivocally accepted cure for ASD. There are, however, a vast number of therapies and are interventions designed to remedy or modify specific symptoms, and these can bring about substantial improvement in many cases. Ideally the most effective intervention is one that coordinates 'therapies' and 'interventions' that meet the specific needs of individual children. Most educational and healthcare professionals agree that the earlier the intervention, the more likely a desirable outcome will result.

IMPACT ON LEARNING

The characteristics of ASD noted earlier in this chapter do mean that children in the ASD spectrum will have considerable challenges in learning. As a result they will need specific teaching methods in a sensitive and carefully planned environment. For example, in the educational setting they may show the following:

- An inability to imitate sounds, gestures and gross or fine motor movements that are all necessary for learning, particularly in the early years.
- An inability to focus on the task at hand. Some children will have a very short attention span or concentrate only on one thing obsessively.
- Difficulty working collaboratively with others in the class.
- Difficulty with abstract ideas, such as in using items or toys to represent real objects (make-belief play and role play).
- Difficulty grasping the concept of time and the order of events.

There are in fact numerous learning challenges that can be experienced by children in the ASD spectrum. Howlin (2002) notes the vast range and diversity of approaches that are used with children with ASD. These include auditory integration training; a range of different types of behavioural approaches; cranial osteopathy; dietary and vitamin treatments; facilitated communication; and Gentle Teaching (McGee, 1985; Jones and McCaughey, 1992) – a non-aversive method of reducing challenging behaviour that aims to teach bonding and independence through gentleness and respect. Other well-known methods include Holding Therapy – the aim of which is to provoke a state of distress until the child will feel a need for comfort though holding (Howlin, 2002).

Music therapy has become accepted as a useful intervention for people with autism since it was introduced to the UK in the 1950s and 1960s by such practitioners as Juliette Alvin, Paul Nordoff and Clive Robbins. Nordoff and Robbins describe significant changes in the communicative and social behaviour of individuals with autism who took part in music therapy (http://www.nordoff-robbins.org.uk/http://www.nordoff-robbins.org.uk/). In November 2005 the Nordoff–Robbins Research Department hosted a research symposium entitled 'Evidence-based practice and music therapy: a further perspective', with a keynote presentation by the sociologist,

Tia DeNora, on the role of music therapy. One of the many resulting publications offered stringent advice and procedures for empirical evaluations and randomized control trials of music therapy (Nordoff and Robbins, 2009). This publication has been internationally helpful in offering snapshots of current research supporting the use of music therapy.

Woodword (2004) found that music therapy can play an important role for the parents of children with autism by fostering relationships and developing positive interactions, and Gold *et al.*, (2006) found that music therapy may help children with ASD to improve their communicative skills. This theme is advanced by DeNora (2006) from health and sociological perspectives. Other therapies that have been noted include pet therapies; physical exercise; psychotherapy and sensory integration therapies. Some of the key points on intervention are commented on below.

EDUCATIONAL/BEHAVIOURAL INTERVENTIONS

There has been a recent increase in interest in verbal behaviour therapy in particular (Barbera, 2007). This type of therapy can be controversial because it is based on a philosophy – applied behaviour analysis (ABA) – which is an intensive, one-on-one, highly structured behaviourist programme. It is usually utilized by trained therapists employing intensive skills-oriented training sessions to help children with ASD develop social and language skills. ABA is based on the work of Ivor Lovaas, and studies such as McEachin *et al.* (1993) provide supportive evidence for its use. It is an intervention that is costly in terms of time as it can take around 40 hours a week of one-to-one intervention and it is unlikely to fit into the normal pattern of the inclusive school unless special arrangements are made. Barbera (2007: 162) however suggests it has considerable benefits for all children with ASD and remarks:

> some may ... try to convince you that your child is too high functioning or low functioning to benefit from ABA ... My experience tells me differently. It does not matter where your child falls on the spectrum – ABA ... can help.

FACTORS TO CONSIDER

When selecting therapies/intervention for autism, the following factors need to be considered:

Educational:

- Provision – extent of inclusion/specialist provision.
- Curriculum issues – is full curriculum offered/extent of differentiation?
- Is the individual education plan (IEP) appropriate and the classroom management strategies that are in place?
- Interventions and specialist therapies – the availability of verbal/behaviour approaches and other specialist programmes.

Home:

- Challenges and issues at home.
- Support available for parents and siblings.
- Links with school.

Social:

- Social models of disability – community support.
- Concept of neurodiversity – the role of individual differences – spectrum of differences rather than disabilities.

Post-school:

- Support available.
- Needs of young person – further education and the workplace.
- Issues for the family.

The above points raise some of the issues that can become a challenge for the young person and their school and family in relation to ASD. To discuss these here would be beyond the scope of this chapter but we have included at the end of this chapter a list of useful websites of relevant organizations that discuss and advise on these issues. Some have been referred to throughout this chapter and their work is both current and impressive. It is this sort of endeavour and supportive advice based on sound professional principles that can provide both hope and inspiration to all involved in this field.

In view of the number of behaviours, the spectrum from mild to severe and the proposed changes to DSM IV, which indicate that the category of Asperger's should not be used, it has been decided not to include a case study in this chapter because this may be misleading. But it is important to keep in mind the insightful and penetrating comment made by Rita Jordan (2010) when discussing intervention for children with ASD: 'treating them equally does not mean treating them the same, but treating them differently to ensure equal access.'

SUMMARY

- The prevalence of autism has increased in recent years, but the cause of this increase is subject to debate.
- The criteria for the identification and assessment of autism are due to change as a result of the redrafting of DSM IV. DSM V is due to be implemented in 2013.
- Autism and Asperger's syndrome are different disorders that lie somewhere on the same continuum.
- There are a range of specialized approaches that can be used for assessment, testing and intervention.

Further Reading

Baron-Cohen, S. *et al*. (2001) 'The autism spectrum quotient', *Journal of Autism and Developmental Disorders*, 31: 5–17.

Baron-Cohen, S. *et al*. (2006) *The Adult Asperger Assessment (AAA): A Diagnostic Method* (http://www.autismresearchcentre.com/tests/aaa_test.asp).

Gilliam, J.E. (2006) *Gilliam Autism Rating Scale* (2nd edn) (GARS-2). Upper Saddle River, NJ: Pearson Education. GARS-2 assists teachers, parents and clinicians in identifying and diagnosing autism in individuals aged 3–22. It also helps estimate the severity of the child's disorder. The items on the GARS-2 are based on the definitions of autism adopted by the Autism Society of America and DSM IV TR. See http://www.autism-world.com/index.php/2007/03/27/childhood-autism-rating-scalecars/ for a list of rating scales used in different countries.

Jordan, R. (1999) *Autistic Spectrum Disorders: An Introductory Guide for Practitioners*. London: David Fulton. This book has been reprinted a number of times and is an excellent resource. It is written for practitioners working in the field of autism and related disorders (including Asperger's syndrome) and it offers an overview of understandings of these disorders from a behavioural, biological and psychological perspective.

Le Couteur, A. (2003) *Autism Diagnostic Interview-Revised (ADI-R)*. San Francisco, CA: Western Psychological Services. The Autism Diagnostic Interview-Revised, better known as the ADI-R, is a set of interview questions that are administered to the parents of young children with possible symptoms of autism or an ASD (http://autism.about.com/od/diagnosingautism/f/ADI-R.htm).

Sara, S. *et al*. (2005) *Vineland Adaptive Behavior Scales* (2nd edn) (Vineland-II; Pearson's assessment). Forms: birth–90-years-old: Survey Interview Form, Expanded Interview Form and Parent/Caregiver Rating Form; 3:0–21:11: Teacher Rating Form (http://education.pearsonassessments.com/).

University of North Carolina School of Medicine (n.d.) *Treatment and Education of Autistic and Related Communication Handicapped Children (TEACCH)* (Appendix 2). Chapel Hill, NC: University of North Carolina, School of Medicine. Assessment criteria, checklists and tests.

Useful Websites

Autism Society, USA   http://www.autism-society.org/site/

Autistic Society, Canada   www.autismsocietycanada.ca

Checklist for Autism in Toddlers (CHAT)   http://www.autismresearchcentre.com/tests/chat_test.asp Kuwait Centre for Autism http://www.q8autism.com/

Mind Blind   www.mindblind.co.uk

National Autism Association, USA   http://www.nationalautismassociation.org/

National Autistic Society, UK www.nas.org.uk/

National Institute of Mental Health, USA   http://www.nimh.nih.gov/health/publications/autism/complete-index.shtml

Nordoff–Robbins Music Therapy   http://www.nordoff-robbins.org.uk/musicTherapy/research/index.html

Scottish Society for Autism   http://www.autism-in-scotland.org.uk/

TEACCH   http://www.teacch.com/

The US Department of Health and Human Services has a federal Interagency Autism Co-ordinating Committee. One of the committee's key functions is developing a strategic plan for spectrum disorder research http://sacramento.bizjournals.com/sacramento/stories/2010/04/26/daily69.html

World Autism Organisation http://www.worldautismorganisation.org/en/projects.html

References

APA (1994) *Diagnostic and Statistical Manual of Mental Disorders (DSM IV)* (4th edn). Washington, DC: American Psychiatric Association.

Asperger, H. (1991) '"Autistic psychopathy" in childhood' (translated and annotated by U. Frith), in U. Frith (ed.) *Autism and Asperger Syndrome*. New York, NY: Cambridge University Press (originally published in 1944).

Baird, G. *et al.* (2006) 'Prevalence of the disorders of the autistic spectrum in a population cohort of children in South Thames', *The Lancet*, 368: 210–15.

Barbera, M.L. with Rasmussen, T. (2007) *The Verbal Behaviour Approach: How to Teach Children with Autism and Related Disorders*. London: Jessica Kingsley.

Connelly, M. (1997) *Assessment and Diagnosis in Children with an Autistic Spectrum Disorder: A Discussion Paper*. Lancashire County Council.

DeNora, T. (2006) 'Evidence and effectiveness in music therapy: problems, powers, possibilities and performances in health contexts (a discussion paper)', *British Journal of Music Therapy*, 20: 81–99.

Gillberg, C. and Coleman, M. (2001) *The Biology of the Autistic Syndromes* (2nd edn). Cambridge: Cambridge University Press.

Gold, C., Wigram, T. and Elefant, C. (2006) 'Music therapy for autistic spectrum disorder', *Cochrane Database of Systematic Reviews*, issue 2, art. no. CD004381; DOI 10.1002/14651858. CD004381.pub2.

Howlin, P. (2002) *Children with Autism and Asperger Syndrome: A Guide for Practitioners and Carers*. Chichester: Wiley.

Jones, R.S.P. and McCaughey, R.E. (1992) 'Gentle teaching and applied behaviour analysis. a critical review', *Journal of Applied Behavioural Analysis*, 25: 853–67.

Jordan, R. (2005) 'Autistic spectrum disorders', in A. Lewis and B. Norwich (eds) *Special Teaching for Special Children: Pedagogies for Inclusion*. Milton Keynes: Open University Press.

Jordan, R. (2010) 'SpLD in the context of autism.' Paper presented at the Dyslexia Association of Singapore (DAS) seminar week, Perspectives on Specific Learning Difficulties, 25 November, Singapore.

Kanner, L. (1943) 'Autistic disturbances of affective contact', *Nervous Child*, 2: 217–50.

Klin, A., Lang, J., Cicchetti, D.V. and Volkmar, F.R. (2000) 'Brief report: interrater reliability of clinical diagnosis and DSM IV criteria for autistic disorder: results of the DSM IV autism field trial', *Journal of Autism Developmental Disorders*, 30: 163–7.

McEachin, J.J., Smith, T. and Lovaas, O.I. (1993) 'Long-term outcome for children with autism who received early intensive behavioral treatment', *American Journal of Mental Retardation*, 97: 373–91.

McGee, J.J. (1995) 'Gentle teaching', *Mental Handicap in New Zealand*, 9: 13–24.

Nordoff, P. and Robbins, C. (2009) *Presenting the Evidence: A Guide for Music Therapists Responding to the Demands of Clinical Effectiveness and Evidence-based Practice* http://www.web37859.clara-host.co.uk/musicTherapy/research/documents/PresentingTheEvidenceSecondEdition_002.pdf.

Pellicano, L. (2007) 'Autism as a developmental disorder: tracking changes across time', *The Psychologist*, 20: 216–19.

Pinto, D. *et al.* (2010) 'Functional impact of global rare copy number variation in autism spectrum disorders', *Nature*, 466: 368–72.

Roberts, W. (2010) 'Research: treatments and interventions "babies start to withdraw as early as nine months"', *The Globe and Mail*, 1 April.

Szatmari, P. (2010) 'Genome project identifies anomaly in DNA that may enable earlier diagnosis and treatment', *The Globe and Mail*, 1 April.

Task Force on Autism (2001) *The Report*. Dublin: Stationery Office.

WHO (1992) *International Classification of Diseases (ICD-10)* (10th edn). *Diagnostic Criteria for Research*. Geneva: World Health Organization.

Woodward, A. (2004) 'Music therapy for autistic children and their families: a creative spectrum', *British Journal of Music Therapy*, 18: 8–14.

Zwaigenbaum, L. (2010) 'Advances in the early detection of autism' *Neurology*, 23: 97–102.

18

UNDERSTANDING TOURETTE SYNDROME

Judy Barrow and John Davidson

Learning objectives

This chapter will help readers to:

- understand the traits and make-up of Tourette syndrome (TS);
- appreciate how TS impacts on the lives of children with the condition, particularly while at school;
- understand how gaining a sound knowledge of the condition can lead to effective management;
- appreciate how, by working together, practitioners can use techniques to overcome barriers to learning; and
- explore suggestions for overcoming situations that arise from the condition to alleviate exclusion or low attainment.

WHAT IS TS?

TS is a tic condition that is present from birth, that usually becomes evident in early childhood and that continues for life. The prime symptom is to have repeated tics, which are motor (bodily movement) and/or vocal in nature and have been present for more than a year. A tic is a repetitive, sudden movement or sound that has no purpose and, in general, you cannot help doing – for example, blinking, throat clearing, head nodding and making involuntary sounds. These can wax and wane and can vary from minor to severe, such as from just eye blinking to complex movements of the whole body.

The syndrome is a neurological, not a mental health, condition. Minor anomalies are known to occur in the structure and working of the brain in children and adults with TS. There is known to be an anomaly with a number of the brain chemicals, such as dopamine, serotonin and noradrenalin.

TS is frequently linked to other behaviours, such as obsessive-compulsive disorder (OCD) and attention deficit hyperactive disorders (ADHD). It is sometimes associated with high-functioning autism, such as Asperger's syndrome (AS), as many families presenting with a TS member also feature a member with AS. Therefore, a child who has TS is also likely to have one or more related conditions. The most common conditions seen with TS are as follows:

- Learning difficulties due to poor concentration on classwork (as the children are absorbed in suppressing the tics) – although the child may be of good intelligence.
- Mood disorders, such as depression or anxiety.
- Conduct disorders.
- Autistic spectrum disorders (ASD).
- Self-harming behaviours, such as head banging.
- OCD or obsessive-compulsive behaviour (OCB).
- ADHD.
- Central auditory processing disorder (CAPD).
- Sensory modulation difficulties (SMD).

What the above conditions have in common is that the children can't always process information in the same way as others because their ears, eyes and brain don't fully co-ordinate while they are dealing with the tics. With CAPD, something adversely affects the way the brain recognizes and interprets sounds, most notably the sounds composing speech; and the same is true for those who also have difficulty with the recognition of shapes or letters. Add to this, the pure concentration required to suppress a tic or simply to deal with the impacts of ticing while in the classroom and it is evident that the child can have a very negative educational experience.

However, children with TS can have many types of tics, or sudden movements and noises, and the tics can be prevalent throughout their life, although they do wax and wane. Tics may change in frequency and severity over periods of time, and new tics can manifest themselves without warning. TS is very 'suggestible'. Therefore the child or young person may develop a new tic within the classroom within the space of an afternoon.

Some 1 in 100 children and young people in the UK are thought to have TS, although the figure is thought to be higher due to misdiagnosis in the early part of the person's life. For example, it is recognized that some children have been thought to have had epilepsy before a later diagnosis of TS is made. Diagnosis is based on such factors as having chronic tics for more than a year, having them at night and TS being present within the family.

Much is misunderstood about TS and prejudice is widespread. Most commonly in the educational setting, a child will be scolded for being naughty or disruptive, particularly in primary education. It is crucial, therefore, that these pupils are supported and given the chance to explain their syndrome, through the teacher, peer pupils and their parents. In the early stages, if the TS is treated as a nuisance or ignored, then the child will go through their early life stigmatized and isolated.

PROFILE OF CHILDREN AND YOUNG PEOPLE WITH TS

The most notable features of TS, especially in children and young people, are multiple tics that can change and also wax and wane over time The presence of such tics can be identified as early as the age of 5. Most tics become very evident by the age of 8, and by this time the child has developed a range of either motor (bodily movement) and/or vocal tics. These can be further classified as simple or complex:

- *Motor tics* include things such as blinking, head turning, head nodding, kicking, facial grimacing, touching, licking or smelling objects. Complex movements are manifested as a series of movements at one time, from head to toe.
- *Vocal tics* include things such as throat clearing, coughing, sniffing, yelling or making animal sounds, mimicking and repeating whole sentences.

Tics in all forms come and go – the child may change the nature of a tic simply because another tic has suggested itself and thus becomes another part of their repertoire. There are several other symptoms that occur:

- *Coprolalia*: the involuntary use of obscenities and swear words. (This only occurs in about 1 in 10 people with TS. If this occurs, it should be noted that the child cannot help swearing, and it is not a reflection on their moral character or upbringing.)
- *Echolalia*: copying what others say, repeating their speech and phrases.
- *Palilalia*: repeating your own last word or syllable after the end of a sentence.
- *Non-obscene socially inappropriate (NOSI) behaviours*: such as saying inappropriate or rude personal comments.
- *Echopraxia*: imitation of other people's actions; copying of body movements.

These children can also experience sleeplessness as part of the syndrome, as they will be ticcing at night, even during deep sleep. Ongoing research has found that sleep was significantly disturbed in people with TS as against a comparison trial of those without TS. TS tics, particularly movements, were still clearly evident during sleep and led to repeated awakenings during the night. The severity of TS during the day correlated with the number of awakenings and with the percentage of sleep deficiency. In schoolchildren this has a detrimental affect on their being able to concentrate, remain alert or relax during the school day:

> he couldn't settle to sleep at night due to constant 'ticcing', that is, having loads of involuntary tics all through the night/and going through his OCD rituals during the night. It was a nightmare, he would be crying, or wandering around the house in the small hours ...he is just tired from not sleeping, he can't turn off at night, brain wasn't shutting down ...he finds it hard to totally unwind enough to get to sleep at night, or stop whatever he is compulsively doing at the normal bedtime ... TS keeps the stress levels at a high, in the past making it impossible to even be tired ... I feel like a Vampire... I can't sleep at night and then have to sleep the following day ... I feel like a recluse.

Therefore, lack of sleep is common due to the need to tic, hyperactivity and, sometimes, OCD. Some had night terrors and sleepwalking. This often leads to trouble waking up once asleep, through sheer tiredness; many said that the tics are very severe when waking up. This, in turn, leads to a lack of performance at school or in being able to attend school. At this point, parents and carers will be advised to find a method of inducing sleep, which could include mild medication or relaxation techniques.

In addition to this, research has shown that children with TS have a need to move about continually, to 'fidget' – whether pacing, twisting around or fiddling – and, as such, appear to be restless. This can mean that they lose calories while in the throes of the movement. It is acknowledged that children with TS have repetitive movements and generally move about more than others, as they are genetically inclined to do so – TS has involuntary movement in its portfolio of traits. These actions are called 'non-exercise activity thermo genesis', or NEAT. All this may be useful to know and bear in mind with regard to children who fidget in class.

UNIQUE FEATURES OF CHILDREN AND YOUNG PEOPLE WITH TS

The tics change in nature as the young child becomes a teenager, peaking at puberty, but certain social situations, such as the supermarket, can make them worse. Between the ages of 10 and 16 years this is particularly acute and often proves a difficult time for the young person. While their behaviour might be disruptive, it is very important to recognize that these behaviours are involuntary and driven by compulsion. This is particularly true of OCD-style behaviours and rituals, which make up the whole:

> When Paul has to put his things away in the same place everyday, the kids in class say that it's because he is too stupid to look for his stuff. When he walks in exactly the same places all the time, they laugh (parent of a TS child).

Because the tics are not consistent, it may be thought that the child is either 'putting it on' or doesn't have TS – that they are just being disruptive. This makes it more difficult for a mutual understanding to be reached, as the child will then try to suppress their tics or become unable to express themselves as having TS. Denial of having TS is common.

Unpredictability is the most predictable feature of TS. An adaptation in the classroom may work well one week and then not the next. Well thought-out plans may need to change, sometimes frequently. Recognizing this will reduce stress both for the teacher and the child, and reduce frustration when things do not appear to be going well.

Another parent says:

> The teacher didn't see anything that they recognized as Tourette Syndrome, so our son wasn't being identified as having the condition. Our son was coming home from school distressed, very tired, angry or touchy, and his tics were obvious to us. He was also often refusing to go to school because he was worrying about his tics in class. This manifested itself in tummy aches and headaches (mother of an 11-year-old TS boy).

It is often a feature of TS that the child feels particularly stressed, anxious and insecure, leading to absences while at school and in not attending school through a fear of being seen to tic.

UNDERPINNING RESEARCH

More health and educational practitioners are introducing 'evidence-based practice' with respect to TS. This means that individuals and their families, when wishing to gain effective support of their child's education, can seek out an expert who is familiar with the condition and who can liaise with the families and educators in a 'user-friendly' way. They can work together to demonstrate workable, proven interventions using models from evidence gained elsewhere. In this way, the families, student and educators can add to the evidence base.

Most research adheres to the theory that the condition is inherited. It is generally believed that a factor in genes is responsible for most cases of TS. Genes are passed on to a child from each parent; a child is more likely to develop TS if they have a father, mother, brother or sister with the condition or related conditions. It has been said that environmental factors can exacerbate the development of the condition, but this has not been proven. In many cases, the diagnosis of the child leads to a diagnosis for older members of the family, as diagnostic methods have improved over the past decade. However, it is clear that the presence of certain factors does have an effect on the child or young person with TS. Noise, whether sudden or in the background, smells or a change in usual settings have the effect of triggering a range of tics, through an anxiety response. It is crucial to understand the compulsive side of TS – that the urges are involuntary and necessary to the child and that the syndrome is a mix of compulsions and behaviours.

In terms of SMD, this is a part of the syndrome 'mix', and teachers can play an invaluable part in understanding the child's particular sensory issues. However, there is nothing like teacher–parent collaboration to assist in identifying and supporting the child's needs – for example, significant food preferences due to hypersensitivities to taste and touch in the mouth may limit opportunities to participate in mealtimes with peers. Similarly, a fear of touching objects due to hypersensitivities may interfere with participation in school and social activities. Abnormal responsiveness to sensation may also restrict interests and activities, impacting on play behaviour. For example, peer interactions in the playground may be limited due to excessive fear of typical playground equipment, or due to hypersensitivity to noise, light or being touched.

IDENTIFYING STUDENTS WITH TS

Vocal tics can range from coughing or throat clearing to the involuntary utterance of whole words or phrases. During a tic a person is fully aware of their actions but cannot stop, though they may be able to suppress them temporarily. People with TS are of normal or even higher intelligence but may also have educational difficulties due to trying to overcome the urge to tic – to 'suppress', which effects their concentration levels. If not given appropriate help they can become frustrated, withdrawn or do poorly at school.

The child with TS may feel unable to share their concerns or explain their condition to others. They may find ways to 'suppress' by not speaking or leaving the room suddenly and often. Children with TS do this frequently as a coping mechanism and, if they haven't explained about their TS or it is not disclosed to the educationalists, this may be seen as odd behaviour (Cavanna and Robertson, 2008).

Parents will know that their child has some traits and may be the first to seek a formal diagnosis:

> We knew our child had tics, and suspected Tourette Syndrome; we learnt more about the condition and noticed that despite the fact that our son was intelligent and academically bright, there were areas he was struggling with when in school, because of his tics. After he was formally diagnosed, a plan was agreed by the school and us which was discussed at each subsequent review meeting. We also worked closely with an educational psychologist who was able to identify with our son's condition and this gave us much needed support. This support has continued to work well over the years (parents of TS boy, aged 16).

Many people with TS lead normal lives, with understanding and support. Others find the condition, and people's prejudices about TS, to be an obstacle to school, to learning and in forming peer relationships:

> Growing up with TS was very difficult. I believed I was different from everyone else due to the involuntary symptoms. I often felt unloved and unwanted by family and friends and felt that I was being a hindrance to the rest of my family. I was very self conscious about my condition especially when all I wanted to do was fit in with my peers … I was often very paranoid at everything and everyone around me and at times felt very alone (Davidson, 2010).

Students with TS may:

- have poor concentration in class;
- have problems with organizing themselves;
- be slow producing their work;
- have poor handwriting skills, although computer skills are very good;
- become anxious with change or different routine, especially when unexpected;
- have low self-esteem through negative experiences;
- have poor social skills due to isolation;
- stay away from school rather than endure bullying or exclusion;
- try to suppress their tics; and
- have unexpected absences during class.

EFFECTIVE INTERVENTIONS, SUPPORT AND ACCOMMODATING CHILDREN AND YOUNG PEOPLE WITH TS

Children will be more prone to changeable tics and outbursts when changing classes or schools, or feeling insecure in a given situation. They will be more likely to change tics or manifest vocal tics if they are nervous or afraid. A record of their TS and, more importantly, a note of the types of tics they show, updated when new tics appear, would assist in the educationalist's role of accommodating the needs of the TS child. When asked, many teenagers with TS will say that the worst part of their syndrome while at high school is bullying or mimicking.

The child should have a support mechanism around them that allows for communication, support and mentoring in regard to bullying or feelings of isolation. A useful approach is to provide a time when the child or young person can explain their condition to their peers – in a safe and sociable setting, such as in a personal and social development class. Reviewing this approach with the child will be helpful, making adaptations that are flexible to the situation as it stands – as TS can vary and change in constancy, the approach will need to take into account the person's current condition. Many such classroom adaptations will benefit the entire class. Be creative and implement awareness discussions about TS for all students, which will create less stress in the end. For example, giving the child the option of flexible outlines and due dates will help them plan their work and give them structure during a particularly 'ticcy' time. A consistent dialogue with carers/parents will help the child to adapt to school schedules and can help keep constancy in attendance, thus helping the child to feel confident.

Strategies such as allowing the child to leave the classroom – even to deliver a note or go on an errand – will help distract them and give them a reason to be absent during a time when it is evident they would prefer to leave the room. Otherwise, giving the child 'time out' and the ability to leave the room when they need to will help lessen the stress they might otherwise feel during a ticcing session. Some personal favourites for reducing anxiety include sitting the child next to a door in the classroom as they feel they can easily leave the room if the tics become too severe, or sitting them by a window where they may feel less restricted.

Children tend to aquire strategies to adapt to school life: 'I often sit tapping my fingers and tapping my foot which for me helps to alleviate the tics and gives me something to concentrate on', says one child. The child will respond well to being left alone to tic or being allowed to leave the place they are in with minimum fuss: 'My self-confidence goes up and down like a yo-yo and tends to be increased when I have good friends and lots of support around me,' says a young person with motor and vocal tics. 'Having constant reassurance helps tremendously and, of course, being given lots of positive feedback about achievements,' explains another.

It is clear that, with the understanding of classmates and tutors, a young person with TS will feel encouraged to tell their peers about their condition and explain its symptoms, causes and how they can help. In many such cases, the child then tics less in the classroom because their anxieties are lessened, in terms of being less lonely and isolated, and in terms of being allowed to tic, in respect of the knowledge that they will not be punished: 'I find having somewhere quiet to go and gather myself is very helpful.'

The best and most effective coping mechanism that has been identified by youngsters with TS is having the understanding of and being shown patience from others around you, whether that is a tutor or a peer. Having an open and honest dialogue about how the child may feel in different situations helps others to understand what they are going through and therefore encourages them and gives them reassurance.

Pre-planning, letting the child know about any future changes in the school day and encouraging other pupils to ignore tics can assist the child in dealing with their TS when in class. Differences between home setting, where life is fairly static and the child feels safe, often show in the performance given by the child in terms of work done in school. Homework may be excellent but classwork may not demonstrate the same level of concentration or intellect. However, the opposite may also be true in some cases: 'I often find that I can't concentrate on homework when I get home as I am so tired at the end of the school day.'

Youngsters can often feel overwhelmed with either the list of instructions they need to follow, because of their concentrating on suppressing a tic, or indeed with the difficulty of processing information adequately. Some youngsters can then appear to be either disorganized or demotivated, or may be obsessive with having everything organized 'just so' – but this can be counterproductive because of the time that obsession make take. Help, such as written instructions/sheets being made available to the child, can assist greatly with this. If the member of staff ensures that the child has understood all that is required, this is also very useful: 'I wish the teacher would slow down as I can't take in everything he says and I miss what I am supposed to do.'

If writing or reading is slow, poor or erratic, then access to a computer, Alpha Smart and a reader/scribe has proved exceptionally beneficial: 'I knew what I wanted to say in my English exam but I was worried about writing it down without making a mess, then I would get stressed and tic, which just made things worse.' Exams and tests can be challenging for anyone, but for someone with TS they are even more stressful. Apart from the symptoms they have that may interfere with their performance, they also worry about how they may disturb their peers. It is important to establish how best to deal with this and have prior discussions as to what suits all. It may be necessary for someone to have their own room for an exam or a base with fewer people there. It is also important that extra time is allowed for tests or exams.

Some interventions which have worked include the following:

- Allowing for the movement and noise of tics/compulsions.
- Ignoring the tics (remember, not all tics are visible or audible).
- Using distraction tactics, a reason for the child to be able to leave the room – and giving 'time out'.
- Identifying their strengths and weaknesses to instil confidence and address problems.
- Using written instructions to help with organizational skills and technology aids where necessary.
- Being clear about the expectations of both the teacher and the child; allow for flexibility.
- Being patient. Try not to take inappropriate vocal tics personally, and keep a sense of humour.

And, finally, ensure that all teachers, especially substitute teachers, teaching assistants and outside trainers, are continually aware of the condition and are well acquainted with the child in question.

It is important to understand that the transition to school, and also between lessons, can be very difficult for the student with TS. The creation of a safe atmosphere and patient perseverance from the teacher will pay dividends.

As the child progresses through school their teachers are always changing and, in some cases, information is not always fully discharged from teacher to teacher. It may then be up to the child or their parents to ensure that this is done, and often assumptions are made that the child's condition is known to all. Some cases have become acute by the time it is discovered that the child's condition has been the root of their behaviour, by which time there has been distress to the child, the parent and within the classroom setting itself. This is where full knowledge of the condition and how it manifests in a particular child will make for a supportive, nurturing approach. Regular reviews and communication should include parents and guardians. Some have used 'personal passports' to profile the progress of the child, which are regularly updated by mutual agreement.

CURRENT ISSUES

Raising awareness about the condition is a key to assisting practitioners in understanding the condition and making appropriate support available, and in allowing for the person with the TS and their families to be able to explain the condition to others. The ability to explain and allow for the condition varies from school to school, and particularly at primary-school level, where disruptive behaviour has more of an impact. Some schools prefer to leave it to the parents to resolve what they see as 'problems' with TS. Yet practice shows that the school is the best place to explain the condition so that teachers and pupils can resolve a way forward. A view that all experiences should be positive also makes that approach a truthful one.

Therefore, rather than respond to the behaviours with a set of standard approaches, the school and those who support children with different needs could help by taking the approach that the TS is there to stay and should be managed rather than punished or ignored – that the condition is involuntary, and the child is not able to react in a different manner, nor was their intention to be disruptive. Assuring a policy of openness and honesty, sharing and constant review will create a climate in which the child will feel safe.

John Davidson (2010) has explained that, when he was a lonely 16-year-old boy with severe TS, he was too scared to venture outside and face people. His uncontrollable outbursts and violent body jerks denied him a normal life during his school and college years:

A BBC documentary about me when I was 16 changed my life tremendously due to the public awareness it created.

I felt that people now believe I'm not just a nutter and that I was a decent kid who unfortunately has this misunderstood condition. I then had the confidence to walk down the street without feeling I was being watched and laughed at.

Most importantly it put TS out there and has encouraged other people to go get a diagnosis and has allowed me to make many friends over the years.

While attention difficulties are a challenge for teachers, tics are the most overwhelming element of TS in a classroom. If this is labelled as antisocial behaviour and there are incidents between the student, peers and the teacher, the culmination of this could be exclusion and a negative experience for all. The most negative experience felt by the person with TS – disruption and being singled out – will make them more anxious and less likely to do well in class.

The most common issues are that a child is not believed when they explain that they have TS, and a parent has to intervene. In some cases, the parent has been held to blame for the perceived bad behaviours of their child, which negates an effort by the parent and child to gain understanding and support for the condition. Some families have reached a review meeting stage with no agreement on either side, and the child has become more isolated as a result.

An issue arises when substitute or probationary teachers are in place. If they are not aware of the condition or of the child having the condition, the 'status quo' which may have worked well enough can be disrupted. We have cases of children being excluded by such in strange situations, and the child being confused at what was a safe haven becoming an unknown quantity. A recent case showed that a probationary teacher thought that TS was one tic, and that being for life. They did not believe the child with TS and exclusion was threatened. Once the usual teacher was alerted, all was clear. A lack of accurate and wider knowledge and understanding about the syndrome has been identified as the main cause of concern for children in school (http://www.schoolbehavior.com/disorders/tourettes-syndrome/).

PRACTICE, PROVISION AND POLICY

Many young people with TS have tried relaxation exercises at home, have attended cognitive therapy and take medication to alleviate the tics and the OCD. However, it is clear that this does not 'cure' TS, which is inherent in the person who has the condition. The honest, truthful approach in explaining the condition to those around the child, and to help the child to manage their learning despite the need to tic, has worked well in many cases. Where the child has been scolded, excluded or the school does not acknowledge the existence of the condition, many problems have arisen, which exacerbates the anxiety for the teacher, parents and other children in the class.

Where the school has taken the approach to treat the child as they would a 'naughty' child, the situation arises where neither the child nor or their teacher benefits from any exchanges arising from what are regarded as incidents rather than a consequence of TS. In order that a resolution is reached, parents, and teaching staff should share their knowledge of how the TS manifests in their pupils, and share that with the class and with other practitioners.

It is known that such knowledge works well although, in some instances when the knowledge or understanding is not shared or passed on during changes in the schooling, the situation can reverse and the child can be excluded through no fault of their own. A constant approach, building on the facts about the condition and the child who has it, and working with the family and the child's cohorts to gain support and understanding, will allow the child to flourish in the classroom. This is very important in the early years, as the child will then become confident about school, which should help them in their further schooling and higher education.

Understanding TS in schools and colleges is of paramount importance if children and young people are to feel integrated and safe. Many institutions have instigated a policy on the treatment of children with TS and have recognized that, due to its nature and complexity (manifesting a range of behaviours), 'record keeping with respect to children with TS is critical to a uniform approach'(Woods *et al.*, 2008).

It is also crucial that teachers recognize that the behaviours shown by children and young people with TS are involuntary and that they are usually concentrating hard on trying to suppress or mask their tics, and that review meetings begin at an early stage. Many parents are already traumatized by the impact of TS on their children's lives and may have other siblings in the spectrum. A sympathetic approach at review meetings will address any rift in understanding and set the scene for mutual acceptance. It is particularly critical that substitute teachers or teachers who are new to the child are given a full briefing and speak to the child, their carers and families before making any assumptions about the child's behaviour.

A parent said:

> Once we had spoken to the head and the teaching staff about their having training on Tourette Syndrome in the school, they went ahead with a programme of awareness raising and it brought a lot more support and understanding for our son.

Including the facts about TS in the training for in-service days and raising awareness of the condition will assist in the management of the condition and in an appreciation of what the child has to endure. Creating the right environment and engendering understanding from all who encounter the child while at school are essential to help them attain a good education and to do well in their future life.

 Case Study

Connor, aged 11, was missing school because he was unhappy with the classroom setting. He couldn't concentrate and his teacher was excluding him for 'disruptive behaviour'. Connor's mother knew his TS traits and had explained his condition to his peers and his teachers, so was mystified when he suddenly stopped going to school. It transpired that, as Connor moved up a class, his new teacher didn't comprehend his condition and had been punishing Connor for bad behaviour. Connor and his mother, fearing long-term exclusion, asked to meet with all his teachers to come up with a management plan. It was evident from this that Connor's TS was of a complexity that wasn't within the knowledge base of the school at that time. After this was declared it was noted that his OCD and his sensory deprivation were major triggers for his main tics. He was moved near the door in class and allowed 'time out' if his tics built up. A safe place was made for him to go to. All his teachers were made aware, and he was asked to do a special class about his TS traits. He started back at school and, feeling safer, he ticced less during class because he didn't have to think about constantly suppressing his urge to tic and, consequently, his concentration levels went up.

Discussion Points

In response to children whose behaviour is attributable to TS traits, the practitioner might seek out the support and help of self-help organizations, such as Tourette Scotland, Tourettes Syndrome Association Ireland or Tourettes Action (UK). They can be provided with skills sets, toolkits and up-to-date research, plus some management techniques. The practitioner could use their knowledge of the family, who are acutely aware of what the condition is like for their child at all times, to devise a joint plan that suits all.

SUMMARY

- This chapter has identified the traits that make up the condition of TS, which can be more complex and integrated with other spectrum conditions than may be evident to those who have not come across the condition previously.
- Discussions with the person living with the condition and their carers can give an insight into how it feels to live with the condition.
- Children, in particular, are at risk of low attainment, exclusion and isolation at a time when they need to be given better chances.
- The interventions described here are known to be effective and can be developed further by the practitioner.

Further Reading

Carroll, A. and Robertson, M. (2000) *Tourette Syndrome – A Practical Guide for Teachers, Parents and Carers*. London: David Fulton.

Cavanna, A. and Robertson, M. (2008) *Tourette Syndrome*: *The Facts*. New York, NY: Oxford University Press.

Cohen, B. and Wysocky, L. (2005) *Front of the Class – How Tourette Syndrome Made me the Teacher I Never Had*. Acton, MA: VanderWyk & Burnham.

Fabulous Films (1989) *John's Not Mad* (DVD; www.fabulousfilms.co.uk). A documentary on John Davidson and his experience of growing up with TS.

Kutscher, M.L. *et al.* (2005) *Kids in the Syndrome*: *Mix of ADHD, LD, Asperger's, Tourette's, Bipolar, and More! The One Stop Guide for Parents, Teachers, and Other Professionals*. London: Jessica Kingsley.

McKinlay, B.D. (2007) *Nix the Tics*. Calgary, Alberta: Freelance Communications.

Woods, D. *et al.* (2008a) *Managing Tourette Syndrome*: *A Behavioral Intervention for Children and Adults (Therapist Guide)*. New York, NY: Oxford University Press.

Woods, D. *et al.* (2008b) *Managing Tourette Syndrome: A Parent's Guide*. New York, NY: Oxford University Press.

Useful Websites

www.goodschoolsguide.co.uk/sen
www.nhs.uk/conditions/Tourette-syndrome
www.patient.co.uk
www.tourettes-action.org.uk
www.tourettescotland.org

References

Cavanna, A. and Robertson, M. (2008) *Tourette Syndrome: The Facts*. New York, NY: Oxford University Press.

Davidson, J. (2010) '"The Boy Cant Help It": BBC Films and Tourette Scotland web interview' (http://www.tourettescotland.org/information/johninterview.aspx).

Woods, D. *et al.* (2008) *Managing Tourette Syndrome: A Behavioral Intervention for Children and Adults (Therapist Guide)*. New York, NY: Oxford University Press.

Part IV

WORKING TOGETHER

19

THE ROLE AND PERSPECTIVES OF PRACTITIONER EDUCATIONAL PSYCHOLOGISTS

Kevin Woods

Learning objectives

This chapter will help readers to:

- understand the origins and development of the role of the practitioner educational psychologist (EP) in relation to special educational needs (SEN);
- appreciate the current contributions by EPs to the education, development and well-being of children and young people with SEN across different settings; and
- explore the issues shaping the future development of the EP's role.

ORIGINS AND DEVELOPMENT OF THE ROLE

It is often acknowledged that what an EP[1] does may not be entirely clear to those who have not worked within, or closely alongside, the profession (Frederickson and Miller, 2008; Fallon *et al.*, 2010). The reasons for this lack of clarity are examined in the final section of this chapter, but the imperative here is to outline what EPs do and how that role has developed. Squires and Farrell (2007) identify two public concerns which prompted the appointment of the first EP by London County Council in 1913. First, the need to place children appropriately within the available educational provision, which then included newly emerging special schools; this task was previously carried out by medical officers lacking in the necessary psychological and educational knowledge. Second, the need to address concerns from schoolteachers about children showing social, emotional or behavioural difficulties, who were not achieving their academic potential. By the early 1920s, several other local authorities had also employed EPs to assist with these two functions, with further appointments supported by the proliferation of 'child guidance clinics' which were established to help understand and prevent juvenile misbehaviour (Wooldridge, 1994). Further stimulation to the growth of the profession of educational psychology arose from the following:

- The Education Act 1944's stipulation that local education authorities[2] provide suitable education for children who were deemed 'subnormal', 'maladjusted' or 'physically handicapped', which required expansion of capacity to understand the needs of children who appeared to be developing differently.

- The 1968 Department for Education and Science (DfES) Summerfield report, which recommended that there should be a publicly appointed EP for every 10,000 school-age children.
- The Education Acts 1981 and 1996 which laid down responsibilities of local education authorities for the processes of assessment and monitoring of children's SEN. These Acts necessitated increases in local authority capacity to support school staff in their provision for SEN and required local authorities to seek in complex cases formal advice on a child's SEN from an EP.

The most recent data show that there are 3,946 registered EPs in the UK (HPC, 2011).

Although the historical background may seem remote from the detail and context of present-day descriptions of the EP's role (cf. Norwich, 2000a, 2000b; SEED, 2002; Stobie, 2002a, 2002b; Farrell *et al.*, 2006), it can be seen that the historical overview on the functional development of the role provides a clear and relevant insight to *what* EPs fundamentally do (i.e. their broad institutional function; cf. Rowan and Miskel, 1999), which is to:

- provide, more or less formally, expert assessment of children's and young people's needs and linking this to patterns of educational provision[3] and placement (summative function/role); and
- support actively the development of provisions for children and young people that are appropriate to their needs and which improve outcomes for them (formative function/role).

The historical view also locates the origins of practitioner educational psychology within areas currently identified with SEN (i.e. learning difficulties; physical difficulties; social, emotional and behavioural difficulties), though the role has now expanded to include a wide range of groups of vulnerable or marginalized children and young people who may receive input from children's services (Farrell *et al.*, 2006). Notably, Frederickson and Miller (2008) highlight the relevance of the historical perspective on the EP's role by identifying similarities between the role of the first-appointed EP and the role as defined by local authority educational psychology services in the twenty-first century.

With the core institutional functions of the EP role identified, it is interesting to consider why, in particular, it is a professional *psychologist* that is employed to fulfil these institutional functions; indeed, the distinctive contribution of the EP has been frequently debated (Norwich, 2000b; Ashton and Roberts, 2006; Cameron, 2006; Farrell *et al.*, 2006). However, arguing that the issue of distinctive contribution is a judgement more for the service user (e.g. local authority) rather than the service provider, Fallon *et al.* (2010: 4) provide a useful elaboration upon the EP's role with the following definition:

> what EPs actually do appears to have been reasonably clearly articulated: EPs are fundamentally scientist practitioners who utilise, for the benefit of children and young people, psychological skills, knowledge and understanding through the functions of consultation, assessment, intervention, research and training, at organisational, group and individual level across educational, care and community settings, with a variety of role partners.

The notion of scientist practitioners drawing upon and applying knowledge and skills from the discipline of psychology has developed as a central and remarkably simple response to current conceptualizations of the EP's role and contribution (Lane and Corrie, 2006; Frederickson and Miller, 2008). From this perspective it can be seen how one could, in the same terms, query the distinctive contribution of a professional teacher to education, of a professional social worker to safeguarding children or of a medic to health care, since the functions of all these professionals could be replaced, *to some degree*, by a worker not qualified in the particular applied discipline.

Interestingly, the route to developing the EP's professional skills set has changed relatively recently. Up until 2006, all EPs were psychology graduates, trained and experienced as teachers who had also completed a one-year masters programme of training in applied educational psychology. From 2007, the requirement for work as a schoolteacher was changed to experience of direct work with children and young people within educational, care or community settings, and the masters programmes were replaced by three-year full-time doctorate programmes in applied educational and child psychology (BPS, 2010b). This restructuring of initial professional training reflects a broadening of the EP's role beyond the education sector towards service delivery across integrated children's services/trusts, including social-care or primary health-care settings (Farrell *et al.*, 2006; Fallon *et al.*, 2010). Currently, the British Psychological Society (BPS) specifies the curricula for both undergraduate (bachelors) and professional training (doctorate) degrees undertaken by those who train to work as EPs (BPS, 2010a, 2010b), which are summarized in Boxes 19.1 and 19.2 respectively.

Box 19.1   Summary of undergraduate curriculum for training as an EP

Biological psychology

To include:

- biological bases of behaviour
- hormones and behaviour
- behavioural genetics
- neuroimaging
- neuropsychology
- socio-biology
- evolutionary psychology

Cognitive psychology

To include:

- attention, learning
- perception
- memory
- thinking
- language
- consciousness
- cognitive neuro-psychology

Individual differences

To include:

- psychological testing
- personality
- intelligence
- cognitive style
- emotion
- motivation
- mood
- mental health (including social, biological and cognitive processes)
- gender and ethnicity

Social psychology

To include:

- social cognition
- attribution
- attitudes
- group processes and intergroup relations
- close relationships
- social constructionism

(Continued)

(Continued)

Developmental psychology

To include:

- childhood
- adolescence
- lifespan development
- development of attachment
- social relations
- cognitive and language development
- social and cultural contexts of development

Conceptual and historical issues in psychology

To include:

- psychology as a science
- social and cultural construction of psychology
- conceptual and historical paradigms and models
- political and ethical issues

Research methods

To include:

- qualitative and quantitative methods
- research design
- statistical analyses
- an empirical project

Source: BPS (2010a).

Box 19.2   Summary of postgraduate curriculum for training as an EP

Core professional skills

To include how to:

- assess, formulate and intervene psychologically
- demonstrate self-awareness as a reflective psychological practitioner
- exercise duty of care to safeguard children
- maintain effective working relationships with role partners
- engage young people and their carers as active participants
- apply research evidence to practice
- self-organize effectively
- communicate psychological insights effectively
- have effective interpersonal, reporting and recording skills

Practice of applied educational psychologists

To include how to:

- practise within psychological models and frameworks
- formulate interventions applying psychological knowledge and skills
- support national and local initiatives

- work at levels of the individual, family, organization, local authority
- interpret assessment with respect to client needs and intervention possibilities
- apply therapeutic skills
- act preventively to support psychological wellbeing
- work consultatively and within multidisciplinary groups

Personal and professional standards and values

To include understanding how to:

- adhere to the British Psychological Society code of ethics and conduct
- take account of differences and diversity upon life opportunities
- engage proactively and reflectively with continuing professional development and professional supervision
- work with autonomy within an awareness of the limits of one's own competence
- develop strategies to deal with the emotional and physical impact of the work

Application of evaluation, research and inquiry

To include skills to:

- plan and conduct high-quality and ethical research, which is both critical and self-critical
- understand different philosophies of knowledge
- evaluate the effectiveness of interventions to inform evidence-based practice
- work with others in research activities and support local authorities in conducting high-quality research

Source: BPS (2010b).

The respective curricula outlined in Boxes 19.1 and 19.2 show a marked and complementary shift from 'pure' psychological knowledge and skills at the undergraduate level, to applied/contextualized psychological skills and understanding at the postgraduate level. In addition, the postgraduate training programme, which statutorily must be approved by the Health Professions Council, incorporates approximately 300 days of fieldwork practice, which is structured by specialist university-based academic/professional EPs, and supervised by trained fieldwork supervisor EPs within frontline psychological services. Commonly, entrants to postgraduate practitioner educational psychology training have at least two years' work experience in roles such as schoolteachers, teaching assistants, learning support assistants, assistant educational psychologists, assistant clinical psychologists or residential social workers. This combination of requirements for further/ higher-level study and targeted work experience means that even the most direct route to training as an EP would span ten years. Making comparisons with the much shorter initial professional training routes for other professional groups such as social workers and teachers, the question might be asked whether the EP's role requires this extent of initial training, and whether other models (e.g. apprenticeship) might be more economically feasible or attractive to potential entrants to the profession. As it stands, however, the breadth and depth of training do provide to local authorities, schools and families a very flexible, expert resource, which may ultimately be more cost efficient.

For example, in a period of contraction within children's services, a range of specialist services might need to be rationalized. A single EP, who is trained to provide services across learning, behavioural, communication and physical/sensory domains of child development, can work at the levels of the individual child, whole school or a whole organization, and in relation to both statutory and non-statutory functions (Farrell *et al.*, 2006). From an organizational perspective, then, the EP can cover a range of work that might otherwise require several other specialist professionals (e.g. positive behaviour manager, learning support teacher, assessment officer), in much the same way as might a medical general practitioner within a health centre, and so the extensive initial professional training of an EP could be seen to represent relatively good value for money.

Having summarized what EPs do and how they are prepared for that role, the next section of this chapter gives examples of how they carry out their work at different levels and in different settings.

EPs' CONTRIBUTIONS TO THE EDUCATION, DEVELOPMENT AND WELLBEING OF CHILDREN AND YOUNG PEOPLE WITH SEN

Recent reviews of the role of the EP have identified the wide range of their professional activities at individual, group and organizational levels, which contribute to the education, development or wellbeing of children and young people (SEED, 2002; Farrell *et al.*, 2006); each level is considered in the next sections of this chapter. Notably, Woods *et al.* (2009) identify two further dimensions to the work of EPs:

- The reactive/preventive dimension.
- The focus dimension, to indicate whether the work is aimed at universal, targeted or specialized levels[4] (cf. also Fallon et al., 2010).

Given the focus here upon SEN, work by EPs at targeted and specialized levels will be considered.

EP SEN work at individual level

Farrell *et al.* (2006) report the majority of EP work with SEN to be focused at the individual level, with almost half of this relating to children/young people's social, emotional or behavioural needs. Within the case examples cited, Farrell *et al.* (2006: 27) clearly identify both the EP's summative and formative core functions:

one educational psychologist provided a detailed account of the contribution she made to the assessment of a preschool child with complex learning difficulties and of how her key role in this process helped the child transfer to an appropriate school;

The headteacher of a nursery school stated that the educational psychologist provides support to the staff in ensuring that the needs of the child are met.

In respect of the EP's supportive (formative) role, Barrett *et al.* (2002) developed and trialled a framework, grounded in psychological theory and scientific research and referenced to current educational guidance and provision (see Box 19.3), to be used in supporting teachers, teaching assistants and parents, to develop targeted support for children with literacy learning difficulties.

Box 19.3 'Framework of enquiry for monitoring literacy learning'

1 *Nature of noticing that leads to adjustments*: What kinds of observations and adjustments take place in the classroom? What is the range of school-based approaches, both formal and informal, for monitoring the progress of individual children?
2 *Confidence and perception*: How are teachers incorporating their observations on how children are learning in order to make adaptations accordingly?
3 *Inclusive teaching methods:* How is teaching being tailored to individual needs within inclusive group and class settings?
4 *Mastery learning principles in teacher adjustments*: How are teachers providing opportunities for each child to consolidate their learning at word level? How does assessment continuity and progression work?
5 *Monitoring and motivation*: How are the children themselves involved in the monitoring of their own word level progress?
6 *Working together*: How is information about teaching and progress communicated between all those involved for the benefit of the pupil? How is progress defined?

Source: Reproduced from Barrett *et al.* (2002).

Barrett *et al.* (2002) exemplify the use of the framework with reference to case examples from their own educational psychology practice, which illustrates how support for the individual child with SEN can fit within targeted group support within the mainstream classroom. Subsequently, the DfES (2004b) incorporated the authors' concept of 'noticing and adjusting' into its nationally published guidance on meeting the needs of students with dyslexia.

Further detailed examples of EPs' work fulfilling a formative function with students with SEN are given by Eccles and Pitchford (1997) and Miller (2008a). Eccles and Pitchford (1997) describe and evaluate an intervention using functional behavioural analysis with a 6-year-old boy in a primary school. The psychologists outline strategies within five main areas, summarized in Box 19.4.

Box 19.4   A functional approach to helping a boy with behaviour problems

1 *Analysis*: What do the boy's communications indicate about his needs and his communication skills? What is the boy's view of what is happening and why? What can be independently observed about what the boy is doing in different situations and the reactions this elicits (i.e. 'baseline data')?

2 *Ecological strategies*: Modification of physical, instructional and interpersonal environments in order to minimise likelihood of occurrence of problems; for example, teaching optimal peer reactions to the boy's disruptions.

3 *Positive programming*: Teaching the boy helpful: general skills (e.g. reading); functionally equivalent skills (e.g. boy going to sit on a cushion when 'upset'); coping and tolerance skills (e.g. when it is the boy's turn, he is asked to wait for just ten seconds whilst the teacher completes an urgent task – 'just let me write this down before I forget').

4 *Direct treatment*: Strategies, such as Differential Reinforcement of Low Rates of Responding (DLR), derived from psychological learning theories such as operant conditioning; for example, the boy receives smiley face stickers for request compliance that can be traded in for tangible benefits.

5 *Reactive strategies*: Devise a plan to put in place for those inevitable points when the preventive strategies are not effective, so that the boy's teachers can react calmly, confidently and optimally, e.g. provide specific feedback on what is unacceptable in the boy's behaviour, its effects and the required behaviour.

Source: From Eccles and Pitchford (1997).

Miller (2008a) presents a psychological analysis and intervention for a 14-year-old boy experiencing 'school phobia'. He explores several theoretically plausible hypotheses around the case, including separation anxiety, omnipotent self-perception, classical conditioning of a specific school-focused anxiety and social anxiety. Miller (2008a) outlines the evidence base for 'rapid response' to school phobia, combined with elements of cognitive behaviour therapy (CBT). The educational psychologist's intervention plan for the boy considered individual, school and family factors and incorporated elements such as the following:

• Clarifying with the boy's parents the reality of the local authority's legal and policy position with regard to school refusal (i.e. that legal action was unlikely where a reintegration plan had been made).

• Solution-focused brief therapy interviews with the boy and his parents.

• A review with school staff of possible bullying of the boy.

• Communication of the reintegration plan to all the other professionals working with the boy.

• Home tuition arranged on an interim basis strictly as part of the reintegration plan.

• Reintegration to school commencing through attendance at after-school art classes, initially with support of home tutor, following which the boy elected to return to school full time.

Miller (2008a) observes the wider therapeutic benefit of EPs' successful work with individual children, such as those who are refusing to attend school, in developing coping skills which may be transferred to other areas of life besides school.

In respect of their summative function, EPs have a central role in providing psychological advice for local authority statutory assessments of SEN for children and young people (HMG, 1996), as well as the related activities of reviews of local authority statements of SEN and SEN tribunals in respect of individual children/young people. The Association of Educational Psychologists (AEP, 2009) provides guidance on the EP's role in preparing statutory advice to children's services authorities. In this guidance, the AEP (2009) outlines the inter-related purposes, nature, principles and core components of the educational psychologist's advice on a child's SEN (see the summary in Box 19.5).

Box 19.5   Purpose, nature, principles and core components of the educational psychologist's statutory advice to children's services authorities

Purpose

- Define the educational and psychological barriers to learning faced by the child
- Advise the local authority about strategies that might help to overcome such barriers
- Ensure effective progression towards the five Every Child Matters outcomes (be safe, stay healthy, enjoy and achieve, make a positive contribution, be economically active) (DfES, 2004a)

Nature

- Find solutions to barriers or problems through hypothesis testing
- Determine the current state of affairs
- Formulate specific desired outcomes
- Generate possible intervention strategies
- Test out one or more intervention strategies through the proposed intervention
- Close links between assessment data and intervention

Principles

- Child's view gathered directly by the educational psychologist
- Communication and consultation with people who have frequent direct contact with the child
- Direct observation carried out by the educational psychologist
- Individual assessment carried out by the educational psychologist
- Discussion and collaboration with other professionals (e.g. speech therapists, paediatrician)
- Evidence from intervention over a period of time

(Continued)

(Continued)

Core components

- Background to the case to include significant developmental, family or cultural factors and sources of information used in the assessment by the psychologist
- Description of the child to include physical, sensory, medical, cognitive, social, emotional, language functioning; child's feelings and attitudes; educational and psychological barriers faced by the child; outcomes of previous interventions
- Summary of objectives of future provision and the required strategies to include methods and approaches, organizational arrangements, support of professional groups, monitoring arrangements

Source: AEP (2009).

In addition, the AEP (2009) emphasizes the EP's paramount duty of care to the child when making recommendations or giving advice to overcome barriers to learning. The child is the psychologist's client, whereas the local authority, as commissioner of the child assessment, is the psychologist's customer. This duty of care to the child is placed above the EP's responsibilities to the local authority employer, and the psychologist's advice should therefore not be influenced by considerations such as local authority financial or other constraints. An important theme throughout the AEP (2009) guidance on psychological assessment is the adoption of an 'interactionist' paradigm, which runs counter to enduring positivist philosophies that assume the psychologist's assessment would aim to 'diagnose' what is 'wrong with' the child and recommend an appropriate 'treatment' plan (cf. Bronfenbrenner and Morris, 2006; Frederickson and Miller, 2008):

> The focus of concern (the functioning of the child) should not be separated from the analysis of the interactions between the child and the context or environment (family, peers, teachers, classroom setting or community) (AEP, 2009: 5).

The Division of Educational and Child Psychology of the BPS (1999: 2) also provides general guidelines on psychological assessment and extends the interactionist perspective towards social constructionist considerations of ethics, politics, personal values and equality of opportunity: 'The purpose of the [psychological] assessment is to generate understanding of what is happening, who is concerned, why it is a problem and what can be done to make a difference to the situation'.

Alongside the summative role assumed in local authority statutory SEN assessments, EPs often act as independent expert witnesses to the courts, carrying out assessments of children and/or their parents or carers (e.g. JSA, 2011). In these assessments, which often involve children with some social, emotional, behavioural or learning needs, the EP receives a set of very specific questions ('instructions') with respect to the case of a particular child or children, and is required to form a psychological opinion on those questions to assist the court in reaching decisions on the issues under consideration (e.g. whether residential education placement is appropriate, whether developmental delay is likely to have been caused by parenting). This area of work is highly specialized, requiring additional training and supervision in legal processes and the presentation of psychological evidence in court.

EP SEN work at group level

Farrell *et al.* (2006) identified a wide range of EPs' successful work with groups of children, school staff and parents, including the following:

- Training for parents in the management of children's behaviour difficulties, autistic spectrum disorder, procedures and provision for SEN.
- Training for school staff in the use of specialist techniques, such as social stories, precision teaching, learning styles, challenging behaviour.
- Groupwork with children/young people on anger management or cognitive behavioural problem-solving.
- Research in relation to targeted groups in school such as those with social and emotional learning needs or those who are looked after by the local authority.

More recently, the Children's Workforce Development Council (CWDC) (2010) provides several examples of EPs' innovative and successful work with groups of children and professionals, including:

- a project providing booster classes and support at home for targeted groups of nursery-aged children who are finding it difficult to cope with the demands of nursery; and
- a support group for parents of children with autistic spectrum conditions.

In addition, successful group work is also reported by EPs themselves (Burton, 2006; Apter *et al.*, 2010). For example, Apter *et al.* (2010) sampled behavioural difficulties in class groups across the UK and found a positive correlation between student on-task behaviour and teacher verbal approval for desired social behaviour, suggesting that this teacher behaviour may to some extent mitigate social and behavioural difficulties.

EP SEN work at organizational level

Though it is widely acknowledged that work at an organization level requires an understanding of organizational processes (Argyris, 1999; Stoker, 2000; Weick, 2001), there are numerous examples of EPs working across organizations to improve outcomes for children and young people with SEN (e.g. Farrell *et al.*, 2006; Woods *et al.*, 2009; CWDC, 2010). For example, Woods *et al.* (2009) report four case studies of educational psychologists who have developed provision for child protection and safeguarding across whole local authorities with particular reference to children with social and communication difficulties and those with significant disabilities. In each case, a specialist educational psychologist co-ordinated developments in policy, practice and training spanning several years. The features associated with the success of these organizational developments included the educational psychologist's knowledge of normal and different child development, understanding of the educational context and professional roles within it, and the ability to manage different groups of professionals and processes over a period of time. Farrell *et al.* (2006: 101) made similar observations in relation to educational psychologists' work at organizational level:

> Typically EPs have a detailed knowledge of the range of resources that exists in and outside the local authority, the procedures that are needed in order for pupils to access these, and of the role and function of other professional groups who work in the local authority ... This knowledge is used to help agencies work together and to 'oil the wheels' of joint working and decision making. It also places EPs in an excellent position to work with others in identifying gaps in services for children and in the planning and evaluation of new initiatives.

Having considered examples of EPs' SEN-related work at individual, group and organizational levels, the final section of this chapter briefly considers current issues within the future development of the EP role.

FUTURE ROLE OF EPs IN RELATION TO SEN

Though the focus of this chapter is upon EPs' roles in relation to children and young people with SEN, there is recognition of the considerable evidence of their contribution to education at universal level, leading to benefits across the school-age population (cf. Farrell *et al.*, 2006; Cline, 2008; Miller, 2008b). For example, CWDC (2010) cites the example of an EP who ran meditation sessions in a primary school which were seen to have significant benefits to children's abilities to concentrate and learn. Similarly, Burton *et al.* (2010) report on a participatory project in which classes of children from different schools were trained in research skills and then supported to develop research projects across their schools. Nonetheless, Farrell *et al.* (2006) acknowledge EPs' work to promote achievement and inclusion of children with SEN as being central to their role past and present.

There are, however, seemingly perennial challenges in communicating the value and distinctive contribution of the EP's role within SEN (Farrell *et al.*, 2006; Frederickson and Miller, 2008; Fallon *et al.*, 2010). Baxter and Frederickson (2005) offer some insight to this problem by explaining that EPs work within a 'service business model', in which they most often work for the benefit of children and young people through assessment, consultation and intervention planning, alongside or through other professionals or adults. Indeed the 'giving away' of psychology is a longstanding theme in debates about the EP role (Gillham, 1978; Frederickson and Miller, 2008; Fallon *et al.*, 2010). Within the EP's service business model, Baxter and Frederickson (2005) highlight the challenge to EPs to evaluate clearly the effectiveness of their work in improving outcomes for children and young people, lest their contribution be obscured or, worse still, negated. Though the issue of evaluating impact may be similarly challenging to other professional groups (e.g. health visitors, social workers), the evaluation of the impact of the

EP's work may also be particularly crucial since the EP's work often necessarily involves 'soft' skills of interpersonal facilitation and empowerment, including the use of challenge, which build upon the capacities of the team around the child, but which may seem relatively invisible, intangible or counter-intuitive to others working on behalf of the child (Wood, 1998; Farrell *et al.*, 2006; Frederickson and Miller, 2008; AEP/BPSDECP/ NAPEP, 2009; Fallon *et al.*, 2010). A recent joint report by the leading professional bodies of the EP profession presents a practical framework for the evaluation of educational psychology services which may provide a step to making more tangible the impact of EPs' work (AEP/BPSDECP/NAPEP, 2009).

Accountability for the outcomes of EPs' work for children and young people may become particularly significant in an era of service 'commissioning', underpinned by a principle of providing 'value for money' (Fallon *et al.*, 2010). In addition, there may be concern that a reshaping of statutory frameworks relating to SEN (cf. Lamb, 2009; DfE, 2011) might result in more commissioners, such as local authorities, opting out of employing as many EPs directly. However, Farrell *et al.* (2006) found that a reduction in EPs' statutory work, with concomitant dispersal of responsibilities across a wide range of other services, actually (and perhaps predictably) increased demand for a range of other EP services. Similarly, recent experience of central finance restrictions within local authorities has allowed psychological services, both within and without direct employment of local authorities, to flourish (e.g. EGS, 2011; JSA, 2011; MCC, 2011). Notably, such changes in the way in which psychological services are positioned and commissioned often lead to the development of highly distinctive, specialist services (e.g. assessments for special provisions, mediation services, work with children in care, expert witness work), which in turn are more 'marketable' and less susceptible to being undercut by a better/better-value provider (Fallon *et al.*, 2010). In overview, the question could be asked whether in fact local authority employment of EPs for the purposes of discharging statutory duties has in fact been a restriction to the development and expansion of psychological services rather than a foundation for them.

However, directly linking EPs to several individual commissioners, possibly for individual pieces of work, throws into sharp focus the EP's strong ethical responsibilities, including the aforementioned paramount duty of care to the child (AEP, 2009). The conduct, ethics and performance of all EPs are statutorily regulated by the Health Professions Council (HPC, 2008) and EPs' initial professional training includes development of understanding about ethics within professional practice (see Box 19.2). Fourteen 'standards' set by the Health Professions Council (HPC, 2008) include the requirements to act 'in the best interests of service users' and 'with honesty and integrity'. Such standards will be paramount to EPs in those inevitable circumstances where there may be challenge to, or dissonance with, commissioners' views or expectations: for example, where a teacher's request for a specific assessment approach as part of commissioned work with a young person is deemed inappropriate by the EP; or where an EP's research to evaluate a commissioner's favoured intervention suggests that the intervention is relatively ineffective.

Furthermore, while EPs will act honestly and in the best interests of the service user, accepting that this could sometimes possibly affect the likelihood of future commissions of work, there may also be an issue relating to equality of access to EP services for children and young people, as some schools or settings might choose not to 'buy in' EP services which challenge preferred ways of working. It is suggested that although this may be challenging to some EP practitioners' notions of a public service ethic of equality of opportunity, this issue is essentially a political and personal one, rather than one relating to ethical professional practice (Wilson, 1994; BPS and DECP, 1999).

SUMMARY

- EPs have two core institutional roles: a formative role in which they actively support the development of provisions for children and young people; and a summative role in which they link specialized assessments of children and young people to available provisions.
- Though EPs do work at a universal level, and with other groups of potentially vulnerable or marginalized children, work with children with SEN continues to be a significant part of their role.
- EPs have completed extensive postgraduate training in applied psychological knowledge, understanding and skills, which complement their undergraduate psychology studies.
- Once qualified, EPs engage in a wide variety of work with, and on behalf of, children and young people with SEN at individual, group and organizational levels.
- Challenges for the future development of the EP role are the development of the means of evaluating the impact of their work for children and young people with SEN, and the management of the possible transition to an increased variety of commissioners of their work.

Further Reading

Association of Educational Psychologists, British Psychological Society Division of Educational and Child Psychology and National Association of Principal Educational Psychologists (AEP/BPSDECP/NAPEP) (2009) *The Evaluation of Educational Psychology Services in the Light of Outcomes for Children: A Report from a Joint Working Group.* Durham: AEP.

Cameron, R.J. (2006) 'Educational psychology: the distinctive contribution', *Educational Psychology in Practice*, 22: 289–304.

Children's Workforce Development Council (CWDC) (2010) *Leading Change: Educational Psychologists Showcase their Innovative Work.* Leeds: CWDC.

Farrell, P., Woods, K., Lewis, S., Rooney, S., Squires, G. and O'Conner, M. (2006) *Function and Contribution of Educational Psychologists in light of the 'Every Child Matters: Change for Children' Agenda.* London: DfES.

Frederickson, N. and Miller, A. (2008) 'What do educational psychologists do?', in N. Frederickson *et al.* (eds) *Educational Psychology.* London: Hodder Education.

Useful Websites

Association of Educational Psychologists www.aep.org
British Psychological Society www.bps.org.uk
Children's Workforce Development Council www.cwdc.org.uk
Department for Education www.dfe.gov.uk
Health Professions Council www.hpc-uk.org

Notes

1 The term 'practitioner educational psychologist' indicates those professionals statutorily registered with the UK Health Professions Council as 'practitioner psychologists' in the 'educational' division and thereby being the sole persons eligible to identify themselves to members of the public as practitioner educational psychologists. The term is comparable with that of 'school psychologist' in the USA, where the term 'educational psychologist' most commonly refers to an academic psychologist who researches within the field of education and pedagogy (Jimmerson and Oakland, 2007).

2 In England and Wales the terms 'local education authority', 'local authority' or 'children's services' encompass the state-mandated and funded education service (at county, borough, district or city level).

3 With the inception of integrated children's services (Children Act 2004), educational psychologists are increasingly working within social care and health provision as well as educational provision.

4 Service work at 'universal level' aims to benefit all children without additional needs; work at 'targeted level' aims to benefit children with additional needs; work at 'specialized level' aims to benefit children with complex additional needs. Universal, targeted and specialized levels of intervention in the UK correspond to core, supplemental and individual levels of intervention in the USA.

References

Apter, B., Arnold, C. and Swinson, J. (2010) 'A mass observation study of student and teacher behavior in British primary classrooms', *Educational Psychology in Practice*, 26: 151–72.

Argyris, C. (1999) *On Organisational Learning* (2nd edn). Oxford: Blackwell.

Ashton, R. and Roberts, E. (2006) 'What is valuable and unique about the educational psychologist?', *Educational Psychology in Practice*, 22: 111–24.

Association of Educational Psychologists (AEP) (2009) *Guidance to Educational Psychologists in Preparing Statutory Advice to Children's Services Authorities*. Durham: AEP.

Association of Educational Psychologists, British Psychological Society Division of Educational and Child Psychology and National Association of Principal Educational Psychologists

(AEP/BPSDECP/NAPEP) (2009) *The Evaluation of Educational Psychology Services in the Light of Outcomes for Children: A Report from a Joint Working Group*. Durham: AEP.

Barrett, M., Reason, R., Regan, R., Rooney, S., Williams, C., Woods, K. and Stothard, J. (2002) 'Co-researching the concept of "noticing and adjusting" in monitoring literacy learning', *Educational Psychology in Practice*, 18: 297–312.

Baxter, J. and Frederickson, N. (2005) 'Every Child Matters: can educational psychology contribute to radical reform?', *Educational Psychology in Practice*, 21: 87–102.

British Psychological Society (BPS) and Division of Educational and Child Psychology (DECP) (1999) *Framework for Psychological Assessment and Intervention*. Leicester: BPS (DECP).

British Psychological Society (BPS) (2010a) *Guidance for Undergraduate and Conversion Degree Programmes*. Leicester: British Psychological Society.

British Psychological Society (BPS) (2010b) *Guidance for Educational Psychology Programmes in England, Northern Ireland and Wales*. Leicester: BPS.

Brofenbrenner, U. and Morris, P.A. (2006) 'The bio-ecological model of human development', in R.M. Learner and W. Damon (eds). *Handbook of Child Psychology*. Vol.1. *Theoretical Models of Human Development* (6th edn) Hoboken, NJ: Wiley.

Burton, D., Smith, M. and Woods, K. (2010) 'Working with teachers to promote children's participation through pupil-led research', *Educational Psychology in Practice*, 26: 91–104.

Burton, S. (2006) '"Over to you": group work to help students avoid school exclusion', *Educational Psychology in Practice*, 22: 215–36.

Cameron, R.J. (2006) 'Educational psychology: the distinctive contribution', *Educational Psychology in Practice*, 22: 289–304.

Children's Workforce Development Council (CWDC) (2010) *Leading Change: Educational Psychologists Showcase their Innovative Work. Leeds:* CWDC.

Cline, T. (2008) 'Effective communication in school: do teachers and students talk the same language?', in N. Frederickson *et al.* (eds) *Educational Psychology*. London: Hodder Education.

Department for Education (DfE) (2011) *Support and Aspiration – a New Approach to Special Educational Needs and Disability*. London: DfE.

Department for Education and Science (DES) (1968) *Psychologists in the Education Services*. London: DES.

Department for Education and Skills (DfES) (2004a) *Every Child Matters: Change for Children*. London: HMSO.

Department for Education and Skills (DfES) (2004b) *A Framework for Understanding Dyslexia*. Nottingham: DfES Publications.

Eccles, C. and Pitchford, M. (1997) 'Understanding and helping a boy with problems: a functional approach to behaviour problems', *Educational Psychology in Practice*, 13: 115–21.

Educational Guidance Service (EGS) (2011) *The Educational Guidance Service*. Retrieved 8 March from www.egs.org.uk.

Fallon, K., Woods, K. and Rooney, S. (2010) 'A discussion of the developing role of educational psychologists within children's services', *Educational Psychology in Practice*, 26: 1–24.

Farrell, P., Woods, K., Lewis, S., Rooney, S., Squires, G. and O'Conner, M. (2006) *Function and Contribution of Educational Psychologists in light of the 'Every Child Matters: Change for Children' Agenda*. London: DfES.

Frederickson, N. and Miller, A. (2008) 'What do educational Psychologists do?', in N. Frederickson *et al.* (eds) *Educational Psychology*. London: Hodder Education.

Gillham, B. (1978) *Reconstructing Educational Psychology*. London: Croom Helm.

Health Professions Council (HPC) (2008) *Standards of Conduct, Performance and Ethics*. London: Health Professions Council.

Health Professions Council (HPC) (2011) 'Profession and modality data – practitioner psychologists.' *Personal email communication to the author, 23 February.*

HMG (1996) *Education Act 1996*. London: HMSO.

Jimmerson, S.R. and Oakland, T. (2007) 'School psychology in the United States and England', in S.R. Jimmerson *et al.* (eds) *The Handbook of International School Psychology*. London: Sage.

JSA Psychology (2011) *The child psychologists in family law*. Retrieved 28 February from: www. jsapsychology.co.uk.

Lamb, B. (2009) *Special Educational Needs and Parental Confidence*. Nottingham: DCSF Publications.

Lane, D.A. and Corrie, S. (2006) *The Modern Scientist Practitioner: A Guide to Practice in Psychology*. Hove: Routledge.

Manchester City Council (MCC) (2011) *Trading Local Authority Education Services to Schools – Manchester's Model. Manchester*: MCC.

Miller, A. (2008a) 'School phobia and school refusal: coping with life by coping with school?', in N. Frederickson *et al.* (eds) *Educational Psychology*. London: Hodder Education.

Miller, A. (2008b) 'Raising educational achievement: what can instructional psychology contribute?', in N. Frederickson, *et al.* (eds) *Educational Psychology*. London: Hodder *et al.* (eds) Education.

Miller, A. and Frederickson, N. (2006) 'Generalizable findings and idiographic problems: struggles and successes for educational psychologists as scientist-practitioners', in D.A. Lane and S. Corrie (eds) *The Modern Scientist Practitioner: A guide to Practice in Psychology*. Hove: Routledge.

Norwich, B. (2000a) *Education and Psychology in Interaction: Working with Uncertainty in Interconnected Fields*. London: Routledge.

Norwich, B. (2000b) 'Educational psychology and special educational needs: how they relate and where is the relationship going?', *Educational and Child Psychology*, 17: 5–15.

Rowan, B. and Miskel, C.G. (1999) 'Institutional theory and the study of educational organizations', in J. Murphy and K.S. Louis (eds) *Handbook of Research on Educational Administration* (2nd edn). San Francisco, CA: Jossey-Bass.

Scottish Executive Education Department (SEED) (2002) *Review of Provision of Educational Psychology Services in Scotland*. Edinburgh: SSED.

Squires, G. and Farrell, P. (2007) 'Educational psychology in England and Wales', in S.R. Jimmerson *et al.* (eds) *The Handbook of International School Psychology*. London: Sage.

Stobie, I. (2002a) 'Processes of change and continuity in educational psychology. Part 1', *Educational Psychology in Practice*, 18: 203–12.

Stobie, I. (2002b) 'Processes of change and continuity in educational psychology. Part 2', *Educational Psychology in Practice*, 18: 213–37.

Stoker, R. (2000) 'The sixth discipline of the learning organization – understanding the psychology of individual constructs and the organization (or PICTO)', *Educational and Child Psychology*, 17: 76–85.

Weick, K.E. (2001) *Making Sense of the Organisation*. Oxford: Blackwell.

Wilson, J.E. (1994) 'Is there a difference between professional and personal development for a practising psychologist?', *Educational and Child Psychology*, 11: 70–83.

Wooldridge, A. (1994) *Measuring the Mind: Education and Psychology in England c. 1860–c. 1990*. Cambridge: Cambridge University Press.

Wood, A. (1998) 'OK then: what do EPs do?', *Special Children*, May: 11–13.

Woods, K., Bond, C., Farrell, P., Humphrey, N. and Tyldesley, K. (2009) *The Role of Educational Psychology in the Safeguarding of Children in the UK*. Durham: AEP.

20 THE ASSESSMENT OF CHILDREN AND YOUNG PEOPLE – THE LEGAL ISSUES

John Friel

Learning outcomes

This chapter will help readers to:

- explore the relevant legislation in relation to special educational needs;
- understand the legal definitions of a learning difficulty and the appropriate provision, the rights of appeal and tribunals, and the implications of the Equality Act 2010 and case law;
- understand the role of the psychologist, definitions of independent expert witness and the rules of tribunals.

INTRODUCTION TO THE LEGAL STRUCTURE

The relevant legislation in relation to special educational needs can be found in the Education Act 1996 as amended. However, a green paper is in the process of being issued by the government. It is not clear whether this will result in any new substantial changes. The most recent amendments were made in the Education and Inspections Act 2006, which included in s. 13A a duty to promote high standards and the fulfilment of potential. It also includes a duty on local education authorities to promote the fulfilment of every child concerned in their areas to their educational potential.

By virtue of s. 312 of the 1996 Act a child has special educational needs if they have a learning difficulty which calls for special educational provision to be made for them. A child is now defined up to the age of 20, as a result of the 2006 Act. Also by virtue of s. 312, subject to certain exceptions, a child has a learning difficulty if they have significantly greater difficulty in learning than the majority of children of their age, or a disability which prevents or hinders them from making use of educational facilities of a kind generally provided for children of their age in schools within the area of the local authority or, if under compulsory school age, are likely to have such difficulties. Special educational provision is defined by s. 312(4) and it is provision additional to or otherwise different from the educational provision made for children of their age in schools maintained by the LEA.

There can be, and has been, considerable debate as to what educational provision is. The Court of Appeal in *Bromley* v. *The SENT* (2000 Education Law Reports at p. 260) accepted that many needs, considered to be medical or practical care needs and which cover a wide spectrum of potential areas, could fall within the definition of educational provision. In this respect the Children Act 2004 requirements also come into play and, in *W* v. *Leeds* (2005 ELR at p. 617), the Court of Appeal pointed out that there was a general duty to approach these cases not as a separate department but to look at the child's overall needs, whether or not they were classified as educational or purely social needs. In a later case, overall cost (i.e. health, education and care) was held to be relevant.

The Act presupposes that children with special needs but without a statement be educated in mainstream school (see s. 316) and that parents can insist on a mainstream school unless the placement of a child in a mainstream school interferes with the provision of efficient education for other children; it does not take into account the efficient use of resources in such circumstances.

For children with special needs, there is a right of choice under Schedule 27 of the Act, additional to the duty to educate in a mainstream school and irrespective under s. 316A. However, the system under Schedule 27 is different from the s. 316 system which comes in afterwards: s. 316A as it currently stands limits the effect of parental choice under Schedule 27 in that a local authority under Schedule 27 can rely on the efficient use of resources, but s. 316 then knocks that out. It is a complicated way of saying that, where there is a statement, the parents can now insist on a mainstream school, unless the child would disrupt the education of other children in the classroom.

Section 317 creates a general duty on the headteacher and governing body to provide for children with special needs not under a statement. The *Code of Practice on Special Educational Needs* made as a result of s. 313 describes the relevance and nature of intervention at School Action and School Action Plus, the two stages of intervention before a Statement of Special Educational Needs.

If the child requires a statement, s. 324 governs the making of statements, requiring the authority to make and maintain the statement. The statement specifies:

- the needs;
- the provision to meet the needs; and
- the school or institution or otherwise at which such provision will be made.

RIGHTS OF APPEAL

Parents have a right of appeal to the tribunal under the statutory provisions:

- where the council refuses to assess a child's needs;
- where the council refuses to make a statement following an assessment;
- against the contents of a statement;
- where the parents seeks a change of a particular type of school under Schedule 27; or
- in relation to the decision to cease to maintain a statement.

As a result of the President's Practice Direction given in 1994, the tribunal looks at the child's needs at the date of the hearing, whether they have improved or not on the basis of the information available to the tribunal at the date of the hearing, not at an earlier date.

DISABILITY DISCRIMINATION/EQUALITY ACT 2010

The Disability Discrimination Act 1995, as a result of amendments made in 2001, entered the area of education. It is now replaced by the Equality Act. In law, the Equality Act provisions impose a duty on the responsible body not to discriminate against the disabled person:

- in arrangements made for determining admission to a school as a pupil;
- in the terms in which a pupil is admitted;
- by refusing to accept an application; or
- in a very important provision generally, namely, the provision of education or associated services offered to or provided to a pupil.

There is an additional duty to ensure that pupils are not substantially disadvantaged. The responsible body is normally the school or institution but can, where there are residential duties or joint responsibility, be the local education authority.

Being a new definition, the Equality Act will affect new case law but, as the previous *Code of Practice on Disability Discrimination* points out, children with special educational needs will often be disabled but won't necessarily be disabled as defined under the Act. However, a recent decision by the Employment Appeal Tribunal, which has the equivalent status at least to the High Court, has certainly widened the prospective scope of what is thought to be a disability. It found that a senior police officer who required concessions in exams fell within the definition of disability. The Equality Act alters the scope of the rights of disabled persons.

The twin concepts of disability and disabled persons are central to the operation of disability discrimination law. Someone who can satisfy the definition of a disabled person within the meaning of the Act can enjoy the protection of its framework. The disabled person is defined as a person who has a disability. The person has a disability if they have a physical or mental impairment which has a substantial and long-term adverse effect on their ability to carry out normal day-to-day activities (see Schedule 1 to the Act). These provisions are supplemented in some areas by regulations.

The apparent intention of the 1995 Act was to create a commonsense definition of disability and to avoid vagueness. The 2010 Act is much clearer (see s. 6, band 14). In general, issues arising under the Equality Act and eventually determined by a tribunal, employer or institution of education are as follows:

- Does the claimant have an impairment?
- Does the impairment have an adverse effect on the ability to carry out normal day-to-day activities?

- Is the adverse effect substantial?
- Is the adverse effect long term?

The definition in the 1995 Act was amended recently so that it was less rigid and not dependent, for example, on World Health Organization definitions or, alternatively, on *International Classification of Diseases* (ICD) 10 criteria. It should be remembered that the World Health Organization (in its 1980 clarification of impairment, disability and handicap) defined impairment as 'any loss or abnormality of psychological, physiological or anatomical structure or function'.

In relation to the schedule of the 1995 Act which gave guidance on carrying out day-to-day activities, the following are referred to as being impaired:

- mobility;
- manual dexterity;
- physical co-ordination;
- continence;
- the ability to lift, carry or otherwise move everyday objects;
- speech, hearing or eye sight;
- memory or the ability to concentrate, learn or understand; and
- the perception of the risk of physical danger.

This is still unhelpful.

It is also clear that it is the effect on the particular person and not on people generally that matters. In *Goodwin* v. *The Patent Office* (1999 IRLR at p. 4), the Employment Appeal Tribunal pointed out that the Act was concerned with an impairment on a person's ability to carry out activities. The fact that that person could carry out such activities does not mean that his ability to carry them out has not been impaired. It is not the doing of the act which is the focus of attention but the ability to do or not do the act. The focus of the act is on what cannot be done or what can only be done with difficulty rather than what can generally be done by the person.

In *Paterson* v. *The Commissioner of the Police for the Metropolis* (Employment Appeal Tribunal), in dealing with the definition of disability, the tribunal made it much clearer as to what a disability was. The tribunal applied the decision of the European Court case of *Chachon Navas* v. *Eurest* (2007 All ER (EC) 59). In essence, although Mr Patterson's disability was described as mild, even by the psychologist whose evidence was accepted, it was decided that he was clearly disabled. Carrying out an assessment or an examination was properly to be described as a normal day-to-day activity. The tribunal pointed out that, moreover, the act of reading and comprehension was itself a normal day-to-day activity. That gave meaning to day-to-day activities by also encompassing those which were relevant to participation in professional life. As the effect of a disability such as dyslexia might adversely affect promotion prospects, this hinders professional life. A proper basis for establishing a disadvantage was to compare the effect on the individual of the disability in how they carried out an activity with someone who carried out the activity not suffering from the impairment. If the difference was more than the kind of difference one might expect, taking a cross-section of the population, then it would be substantial whether or not it was described as mild or medium, etc. Concessions in exams were deemed sufficient.

It is a defence to show that:

- it was not known that the person was disabled (s. 15);
- the responsible body could not reasonably be expected to know that the person was disabled (s. 15);
- the failure to take a step was attributable to the lack of knowledge; or
- the actions taken were justified.

INVOLVEMENT OF PSYCHOLOGISTS

In relation to special educational needs, psychologists working for local authorities or other similar bodies will generally be involved in the following:

- Providing reports on the initial assessment or at some later stage when the case is being reassessed for the purpose of deciding whether a statement should be made or not.
- Following up on such reports and advising the school generally by regular visits, where appropriate.
- When an appeal is taking place, providing an initial report or looking at the case overall. They will also look at the state of the case generally once an appeal has been lodged and at all the information exchanged after the case statement period.
- Providing independent reports for an appeal which is being contemplated by parents; looking at the child's needs, progress and the effectiveness of provision; and advising on the aspects of the case.
- Looking at, from either side, the proposed schools and the framework of the proposed provision (i.e. special units and some other provision away from the school).
- Providing reports on the above.
- Sometimes commenting on the evidence used as part of an appeal which has produced a new view or a new light on the case.

Those providing reports and giving evidence should remember that the statutory test is generally what is appropriate. To be added to this is 'probably', although the courts have not yet worked this out: what is appropriate to the child's potential? Thus, the fact that the parents don't agree is not on its own a reason why the statement and the provision proposed or used are not working. There must be hard evidence as to why a particular statement or a particular provision is not effective.

Most, if not all, psychologists deal with local authorities. A recent article by Ireland (2008) outlines the whole situation, from the point of view of a psychologist, in an extremely cogent manner. Local authority psychologists are principally asked to provide reports which may be used in the Special Educational Needs and Disability Tribunal (SENDIST) and, more rarely, in the Family Court. The SENDIST is now part of an overall tribunal service. This reform has affected all tribunals in England in particular, and it makes them much more formal than they were before. As a result, the tribunal looks to establish the same approach as an expert witness takes in other jurisdictions. In these circumstances, whether the expert witness is acting as an independent expert or is acting as defined, at least initially, as a professional witness (i.e. a witness employed by a particular party; Ireland, 2008), the tribunal will expect the same standard of competence as shown and required in the Civil Procedure Rules.

The Civil Procedure Rules have not been fully applied yet in the tribunal. One reason for it is that, although it wished to do so, the SENDIST does not have before it a situation similar to a Family Court. In a Family Court, there is funding so that the parties can obtain Legal Aid for work with an expert witnesses, even if the court imposes such a witness upon them. In the SENDIST there are no such funds, and the idea of a single expert or an imposed expert has been dropped due to the fact that it is only the local authority who can be guaranteed to have employed psychologists and has access to other experts. This would mean that the process would be one-sided and therefore technically unfair. Thus, the SENDIST process remains less court-like and will remain less court-like at least for the immediate future.

An important issue not referred to by Ireland (2008) is that the expert witness, as required by the Civil Procedure Rules, should, at the end of the report, set out a short statement signed by the expert, demonstrating they appreciate that they owe a duty to the court or the tribunal in this case and that they understand that that is their duty. In other words, their report is not one-sided and slanted. Ireland's warning, in particular, that experts should stay within their own area of expertise and defer to other professionals if needed is important.

The difference between an independent expert witness and a professional witness is not so clear in the SENDIST, but it is likely to become more significant in time: a professional witness differs mainly from an expert witness in that they are employed as a represented party and are therefore not independently instructed. In court proceedings, professional witnesses are technically there to give factual evidence, but this does not apply in the SENDIST.

Further, the SENDIST proceedings are less formal than the court. There isn't the same emphasis on examination in chief and cross-examination as explained by Ireland. However, the formality of such proceedings varies enormously. Tribunal proceedings are informal, but some can appear more like a court. However, the tribunal itself is expert and can ask a number of very searching questions indeed. The fact that it is not a court does not mean that the competence and expertise of the tribunal and those before it should be underestimated.

TRIBUNAL RULES – THE NEW SYSTEM: FURTHER ASSESSMENTS/FURTHER REPORTS

The new system envisages that the tribunal can order an assessment of a child. This is because it is considered that one party should be given adequate access to the child or that some exceptional reason may arise why an assessment is deemed necessary.

The tribunal and its practice directions do not really address Family Court considerations. Family Court case law and rules only allow the examination of a child in certain circumstances. There must be a specific reason to do so, not that simply someone has not seen the child or someone has left the authority's employment. The Family Court criteria (which obviously should apply and are likely to be applied by the higher courts in the SENDIST) require that there should be a specific object or reason for an assessment and that it is carried out in a professional and competent manner.

However, children who are competent to make a decision can themselves object and refuse. If they are competent to make a decision, they can also limit the experts' access or testing. This is therefore not quite so simple as the tribunal making an order. Further, there is likely to be detailed legal argument on this issue.

If there is a specific reason to request a further assessment, this should be clearly defined and set out, and what is intended to be done. It should also be further remembered that the fact that the particular party to the proceedings wants an assessment and a psychologist agrees to carry it out may not comply with the psychologist's professional duties as recognized by the British Psychological Society. Once orders are made to impose assessments and the assessments are carried out in a manner the parents object to, then there are likely to be further complaints to the British Psychological Society.

While the Family Courts will obviously be familiar with abuse and child protection issues, this is not the case with the SENDIST or disability discrimination. If there is a claim of fault on the parents and if the parents do not see any good reason why their child should be assessed or do not want to assist an authority to do something they object to, the result is likely to be the professional themselves facing difficulties. This is a new rule, however, which has not been thought out nor its effects considered.

THE NEW SYSTEM

Because the new tribunal system is currently being worked out, is only explained in very brief detail here. It matches the old system in the following ways:

- There should to be a rapid appeal, normally within two months.
- It expects, but does not require, expert evidence to be given on behalf of the parents.
- It expects the authority to justify its position and explain it, both in a written response and before the tribunal.
- The Tribunal will manage the case, which includes giving directions. Those directions may include suggestions that children are assessed. However, it may not be thought to be a good idea by either one or both parties, and directions proposed should be subject to serious consideration and thought.
- The tribunal will expect some form of case statement and a working document to be produced and worked on by both parties. The case statement will be individual to the parties; the working document will be required in good time – namely, two weeks before the hearing.
- Hearings are likely to be longer and possibly more complex as more witnesses may be available to give evidence than under the previous system, which limited witnesses.

From the point of view of an authority, and equally from the point of view that independent reports are simply bought, can we justify this position? Has the child made adequate progress? Do we or did we know the full extent of the child's needs? If not, how do we meet them now?

Giving evidence in the tribunal is less stressful than in a court. In special educational cases, and this extends to disability discrimination but not to the same degree, the tribunal regards matters as an informed business discussion. It normally goes through matters on an issue-by-issue basis and, although some chairs of tribunals and lawyers attempt to treat it like a court, this is rarely the case. That type of approach does not normally happen.

SUMMARY

- Disability discrimination cases almost always involve the questions: is there a disability? Does this meet the requirements set out for impairment or not?
- The psychologist giving evidence may be asked to consider whether the actions taken in a particular case are reasonable and in accordance with teaching standards or with other professional standards.
- The questions in disability discrimination cases are like those in an employment tribunal and are likely to be more aggressive than those in a special educational needs case.
- If a psychologist is examining appropriate interventions, this could well involve a substantial amount of records as well as witness statements.
- Any report that is provided must be very carefully considered.

Further Reading

The main, current relevant material that is essential reading is as follows:

Bielanska, C. with Scolding, F. (2006) *Health and Social Care Handbook*. London: Law Society.

Clements, L. (2000) *Community Care and the Law* (2nd edn). London: Legal Action Group.

Department for Educational Skills (2001 England/2004 Wales) *Code of Practice on Special Educational Needs* (English: https://www.education.gov.uk/publications/eOrderingDownload/DfES%200581%20200MIG2228.pdf; Welsh: http://wales.gov.uk/topics/educationandskills/publications/guidance/specialeduneedscop/?lang=en).

Human Rights Committee (2010) *Code of Practice for Schools, Equality Act* (http://www.equality-humanrights.com/uploaded_files/EqualityAct/draft_code_of_practice_schools_eng_wales.pdf).

Ireland, J. (2008) 'Psychologists as witnesses: background and good practice in the delivery of evidence', *Educational Psychologists in Practice*, 24: 115–27.

McManus, J.R. (2004) *Education in the Courts*. Bristol: Jordans.

Oliver, S. (2007) *Special Education and the Law*. Bristol: Jordans.

References

Ireland, J. (2008) 'Psychologists as witnesses: background and good practice in the delivery of evidence', *Educational Psychologists in Practice*, 24: 115–27.

WHO (1980) *International Classification of Impairments, Disabilities and Handicaps (ICIDH)* (http://www3.who.int/icf/icftemplate.cfm).

21 SEN: PARENTS' PERSPECTIVES

Adrienne Papendorf, Lindsay Peer, Gavin Reid and Susan Strachan

INTRODUCTION BY GAVIN REID

The field of special educational needs (SEN) can be a confusing one for professionals but can be fraught for parents. All the contributors to this chapter are parents and each has had experiences in SEN and each has had challenges and anxieties as well as positive feelings that their child can do well at school and that the social, emotional and educational needs can be met. This, however, is not always easy and for different categories of special needs different challenges are evident. This of course means that the strategies may have to be different but nevertheless, there are some common experiences and common tips that parents can pass on to others. The purpose of this chapter is to achieve that. By discussing the challenges some parents have eventually experienced hope and encouragement, and this can be the same for many other parents.

A good friend of mine who was a leading force in the development of the Dyslexia Association in Edinburgh and southeast Scotland (Gill Thomson MBE) always told parents at meetings that being 'forearmed is being forewarned'. This was almost like a trademark comment for her and one that was always appreciated by audiences and those who benefited from the support provided by the association. Parents associations can be an excellent source of support – they are initiated by parents for parents and can be invaluable. In my experiences at speaking to and working with parents associations I have found this to be the case. Gill Thomson and I some time ago wrote and presented a paper at the British Dyslexia Association conference (BDA 1994) entitled from 'Pain to Power'. This characterized the journey the association had taken from its inception to one where they had the ear of Parliament and were consulted on education matters. The journey of the British Dyslexia Association is very similar and they today hold a very influential position in the UK in relation to education matters and are regularly consulted by government for advice.

The story has been very similar in other areas of special needs –such as in autistic spectrum disorders and down's syndrome. As a parent of a young man with autism I can appreciate the range of support that is currently available. Although such support was not available when my son was at school it is reassuring to know that there is now a greater awareness of autism than ever before and that interventions are more thoroughly researched and promoted and that much is being done to ensure that young people with autism are now rightly placed alongside their peer group in an inclusive educational and social environment. This of course takes considerable commitment and a great deal of courage from parents to put their trust in the education system and to work collaboratively with others in the hope that their child will benefit in the short and in the long run.

The long term considerations are always uppermost in a parent's mind and it is important that they obtain some reassurance on this as early as possible in their child's school career.

The stories below provide real examples of how parents have had to consider all angles in their child's education and social and emotional development. It is remarkable to consider that few parents choose to have a child with special needs and that few have previous training in the area, yet virtually all in a short time become experts in the area. They have a desire to ensure that children's needs are met and that all children with special needs access their potential and become fulfilled and fulfilling adults and can share this with others in the community. Parents too need to share their experiences and that is exactly the purpose of this chapter.

The examples commence with Susan Strachan who writes about her own family experiences with both her children. Like quite a number of parents Susan is also a professional very much involved in the field of special education and this clearly brings additional insights to the situation and this, in turn, helps others in the same situation who may not have the professional insights shared by Susan. Many of course turn their hand to working in this field when they realize the challenges faced by their child and also realize that they have gathered experiences that can prove invaluable in a professional as well as a parental capacity. I for one was in that situation and it was my experiences as a father of an autistic boy that motivated me to embark on a career in this field.

DYSLEXIA – A PARENT'S PERSPECTIVE BY SUSAN STRACHAN

'I'm sorry Mum, but you know what my brain's like?!' Even at the age of 6 years, Zoe and myself (fortunate enough to be a health professional as well as her mother,) knew that her brain didn't quite work in the way that it should. It was not so much her literacy abilities in those days, but her memory, frustration levels and attention that were the main problems. Having had severely disordered language as a child, (where Zoe had difficulty producing correct sounds in sequence), there was always that worry that school may never be straightforward for her. But even working in a related career to education, it never ceases to amaze me just how hard many of us parents of kids with additional support needs (ASNs) have to fight.

In Zoe's case, this meant not just moving primary school, but also local authority, to ensure that her learning issues were acknowledged and appropriately supported. This was following a learning support teacher from her first school, trying to explain that Zoe could not have dyslexia, as she had demonstrated some good, almost appropriate levels in some test areas. I do appreciate that in this country we have moved away from using discrepancies in learning abilities and avoid using one-off tests to definitively identify dyslexia, but there was no credit given to the fact that this young girl was bright and had spent the first five years of her life fighting to make herself understood (due to her disordered language) and had developed quite effective coping strategies. In fact, the first time a speech and language therapist came to the house only to 'listen' to her language at 2 years, Zoe disappeared and promptly returned, giving her a clock and saying 'bye bye'.

Similar to many ASNs, it can often be a battle to gain recognition of parental concerns, particularly if your child presents very differently between home and school or does not not show any obvious behavioural signs of not coping. How many parents have I, as a young naive professional, initially considered overanxious, too sensitive or neurotic? Fate perhaps has an ironic way of teaching you life's lessons. Here I am now with both my children affected by the 'hidden disability' of dyslexia, (with my son, Adam severely affected). A condition where the name is frequently avoided and that some feel might not even exist? I appreciate that with continual levels of school leavers being described as functionally illiterate, there is an argument for suggesting that it is the way our nonsensical English language is taught that may be more to blame. But I would urge anyone that did have any doubts about whether this complex processing disorder called dyslexia truly exists, to come and spend some time in my house!

Sometimes the pathway to recognition of need for families can seem lengthy, with the common process of 'gathering' information from various sources before developing a comprehensive profile feeling protracted. Luckily for us, both our children received identification of their dyslexic issues early on, unlike some individuals who may cope with the education system until exam time at school or not be 'picked up' until pursuing further education. Although this highlights just how contextual dyslexia can be (in relation to the demand of skills required), it perhaps also emphasises the existence of inconsistent identification processes and conflicting perceptions of dyslexia that contribute to the lack of dyslexia recognition throughout different age levels.

Like so many ASNs, diagnosis or identification of need often still relies on personal or locally agreed interpretations and attitudes. Presently this is being assisted by new developments in Scotland both locally and nationally, including Local Authorities producing Guidelines for Dyslexia, the Scottish Government agreed working definition, the Assessing Dyslexia Toolkit for professionals and several other National legislative documents. As a result, there is an established promotion of inclusion and emphasis on teaching in a dyslexia friendly way as excellent practice. Luckily, our local school also acknowledge the need for targeted, specific teaching and learning to address my son's individual needs.

But I have heard of many families, fights to gain recognition of their child's needs and access to the term 'dyslexia', often finding the use of 'specific learning difficulty' too vague. Some families report lengthy delays until they receive intervention from already stretched psychological services and some parents sceptically suggest a minimisation of their child's presentation, in order to avoid initiation of education paperwork or support. Perhaps when there is more global appreciation of 'Dyslexia as a difference and not a disability' (Mackay, 2005) there will be more freedom to discuss and accommodate for dyslexia more positively.

It is perhaps then no wonder that so many families of dyslexic children feel the need to seek privately funded assessments. We did seek private assessment for our son, not because Adam's dyslexia had not been identified, but to both confirm his intellectual abilities and ensure that his school staff had detailed information and advice from a dyslexia expert about his significant complexities. Across Scotland there seems to be national inconsistencies of dyslexia education and skill development and it is unfortunate that education staff do not have the same access to Government funded dyslexia training as the Rose Report has ensured for the English system.

Acceptance in families of any ASN can be difficult and it is often extended family members (not experiencing it daily) who perhaps do not fully appreciate the continuum of issues and often frustrating presentation of dyslexia. It was after showing my parents a video about a dyslexic young man that they finally began to appreciate that our son's volatile emotions, poor memory and explosive outbursts were all part of this term dyslexia and that he was not a deliberately unruly 7 year old. They now understand both our kids better and even though their dyslexic issues are quite different, my parents try to focus activities around each of their strengths and avidly praise their successes. A good friend of mine who knows both our kids very well, commented (at the end of a joint family holiday) that she hadn't realised even in a non-academic environment just how challenging our life can still be, on a daily basis. She also admitted to not fully appreciating the extent that dyslexia affects their abilities to regulate their emotions and cope with social situations.

For my husband and I it can sometimes be like 'walking on eggshells' to avoid moment to moment conflicts with Adam's reactive angry outbursts. Using a stern voice can be perceived as shouting, enforcing boundaries with him can end in tears or – 'well I didn't know!' For both of them, getting the dynamics of friendships right and coping with not always having their own way is a constant challenge with their peers.

Obviously these areas may be indicative of their age and do not necessarily reflect universal presentation of dyslexia, although I do know of many children and indeed adults who would cite experiences of problems 'fitting in' and coping with relationships. But it does highlight the overlapping of issues with similar ASN conditions (like attention deficit disorder, autism and others mentioned in this book), as well as the influence that dyslexia can have on an individual's personality.

When faced with identification of dyslexia, it is often an immediate reaction to assume that professionals have all the answers and know how to deal with each individual with dyslexia. But as parents we often don't realise how much essential information and expertise we have – 'knowing' the child, not just the common clinical presentation of dyslexia. Unfortunately education professionals do not always utilise family knowledge of personal 'quirks', motivational interests and behavioural management approaches used successfully at home.

Being a professional in an associated field does not provide you with all the answers either. Over the years, I have realised I don't have the natural skills to teach my kids phonics and spelling rules, but at the end of the day I am not a teacher, fundamentally

I am their mother. As Gavin explains, it can give you additional professional insights and the motivation to develop your career in a certain direction, but it does not make you immune from uncertainty and the common feeling of sometimes not being able to see the wood for the trees. Parents pushed to their limits in trying to ensure their child's needs are being met, often have to develop the confidence to take control, use legislation, fight for collaborative working and provide much of the detailed interpretation of who their child is. Again we are perhaps luckier than most, having a proactive, supportive primary school that listens to us and accommodates for Adam's issues. Our home-school communication is invaluable to assist joint planning and consistent working, and a successful home-school relationship relies on a constant process of discussion, monitoring and joint decision making.

Secondary education can be quite different though, as often there are not the same systematic opportunities to regularly 'communicate' with teaching staff (even with an 'open door' policy), there may be differences in teaching styles and there is always that worry about how Zoe's processing abilities and appropriate levels of support will keep up with increasingly challenging coursework. Like many parents, although we may be cursed with natural apprehension about our kids' futures, we also have the powerful advantage of unlimited motivation to ensure everything can be done to help ensure our kids' lives are as happy as they can be!

Our kids know that they are different. Just like Zoe at 6, Adam too has often commented on how he 'just can't help it!' (although we have to be careful that it's never used as an excuse for not trying!). Often they are reminded just how different they are by their peers as well. Both have had brief experiences of bullying, resulting in a dip in their confidence and self-esteem. Frequently it relates more to them feeling different; for example, some time ago when Adam had difficulty playing in the playground because he didn't want to play football and found it difficult to cope with rough play; when Zoe was reluctant to use her laptop in class due to derogatory comments from her peers. Both our kids have always known that they have dyslexia, it has given them a 'reason' for having the learning issues that they have and meant that they don't feel stupid – because they can blame it on their brain, wiring, genetics, whatever… ultimately it means it's not their fault. In our family we have tried to explain that being dyslexic is an integral part of who they are, just like the colour of their eyes. But as they get older, we have tried to develop a greater appreciation, explaining that it is not a static condition like some physical characteristics, but an ever-changing process, a way their brain prefers to learn, which can make some things tricky, but also results in strengths and other positives. For them this definitely includes unorthodox thinking and problem solving. Both are also very creative and visual learners, resulting in Zoe's striking use of colours in her art and Adam's intrinsic desire to build things that interest him from any old junk! The term itself also gives them an identity and encouraging an awareness of famous dyslexics and their successful lives can also be a way of highlighting the potential of their learning difference!

It has taken our family a long time to consider dyslexia as having positives, particularly as it has resulted in severe learning barriers for Adam. We have been through the 'trying to fix or cure it' stage, (at a substantial cost!) realising that one doesn't exist.

We have always known that both our kids were creative and a bit quirky, and we have for a long time worried about where our kids will get to in life. It helps to see how successful many people can be with dyslexia, given the correct tools and self-confidence. Getting them adequate support so they can travel safely through the education system relatively unscathed is always a worry. It is encouraging to see that there are more organizations like oil companies, design firms, engineering firms, etc., purposely seeking to employ dyslexics for their natural creativity and atypical 'outside the box' thinking.

Being a parent of dyslexic kids and the interaction I have had with many other families, has taught me more about working with families than any course or years of professional experience. Commonly, I have found that families go through a process, not just of emotional and psychological acceptance of their child's issues, but often a hard road to success; identification/acknowledgement of needs, educational provision and accommodation and last but certainly not least, ensuring adequate emotional support and confidence. My advice on how to achieve this as best we can as parents is to empower yourself with knowledge (about dyslexia and legislation) as it's the most powerful tool a parent can utilize, develop effective communication/ relationships with involved education staff, focus on your child's interests and strengths and most importantly, never lose sight of them being your son or daughter.

It is only now, having lived with my dyslexic children for 13 and 9 years respectively, that I am realizing as a non-dyslexic parent how important it is for me to teach my kids that although each day can be a challenge for them, there are ways to see the positives about their differences, find ways around potential learning barriers, and fundamentally, help them have the confidence and faith in who they are as individuals.

The Scottish Government agreed working definition (2009):
Dyslexia can be described as a continuum of difficulties in learning to read, write and/ or spell, which persist despite the provision of appropriate learning opportunities. These difficulties often do not reflect an individual's cognitive abilities and may not be typical of performance in other areas.

The impact of dyslexia as a barrier to learning varies in degree according to the learning and teaching environment, as there are often associated difficulties such as:

- auditory and/or visual processing of language-based information
- phonological awareness
- oral language skills and reading fluency
- short-term and working memory
- sequencing and directionality
- number skills
- organisational ability

Motor skills and co-ordination may also be affected.

Case Study

A parent's story (Adrienne Papendorf)

My eyes filled with tears when hearing the words, 'I'm sorry, in spite of all of our support, Chris is not making progress, in fact, he is getting worse.' I had been called in for a meeting with the special educational needs co-ordinator (SENCo) to discuss our 9-year-old son. He had experienced learning difficulties from the start. The small school he was attending had been supportive and offered a lot of assistance, but it was not enough. They knew he was bright, especially verbally, but they could no longer help him. It was put to me that we should be thinking of moving schools. But where do we go? Panic filled me – I knew there was no specific learning difficulties (SpLD) provision locally. And what of the cost – we could no way afford specialist provision. I was on my own; the school had no idea what to suggest.

I stumbled across the CReSTeD website which provides a list of schools specializing in supporting dyslexic children. So began a quest to find a school not too far away, but one with the expertise to help our son. The choice was limited. Most specialist schools are located in rural areas, hours from where we live. They all were horribly expensive. What were we to do?

It was his tutor who suggested to me that we apply for a statement for our son. I remember looking at her open mouthed. I knew anecdotally that getting a statement was virtually impossible these days, especially if your main problem was dyslexia. Chris had already been diagnosed with sensory processing disorder and developmental co-ordination disorder and was receiving therapy through the NHS with an occupational therapist. Our tutor suggested I contact a well-known education psychologist for advice. So began what was to be 22 months of intense anxiety and heartbreak.

We were advised early on to seek legal representation, as we would need expert advice to win our case against the local authority. The process would be long (minimum time 18 months), expensive and stressful and, if things got complicated, we would need to use counsel. They also advised that we would need to produce recent evidence of our child's problems to support our case. This was going to be a big step. My husband and I felt concerned about using lawyers. This was unknown territory for us. The thought of the costs was scary. What if we lost our case? How were we to fund the process? What I had not been prepared for was just how awful the assessment process is. Your child is looked at in minute detail and all their problems are highlighted. We were not expecting the new labels that came with the assessments. And the labels came thick and fast: dyslexia, dyspraxia, sensory processing disorder, attention deficit hyperactivity disorder (ADHD) auditory processing disorder and pragmatic language impairment (an autistic spectrum disorder). This last label was a huge shock and I can remember crying when I understood that our child had autistic traits.

We were advised to have our child looked at by a speech and language therapist (SaLT). We were told many dyslexic children have language problems as well. I went to this assessment confident it would show nothing. Our child had an excellent vocabulary and had spoken well from an early age. Verbal ability was his strength. I had no idea at this stage what a SaLT diagnosed. I did not know what a pragmatic language impairment was. The assessment by the SaLT showed our child to have very high verbal ability but a

(Continued)

(Continued)

significant pragmatic language impairment. It slowly dawned on us that our child's difficulty in having a conversation, in joining in groups, in seeing things from another point of view was not because he was being difficult or contrary; he couldn't help it. This was a recognized condition. It took my husband and I both a long time to accept this last label. I expressed to the lawyers my devastation at all the labels. The brisk reply was, 'labels get you help'.

Yes, labels do get you help, and they gave us understanding. This process of assessments (15 in all including our ones and the local authority-conducted ones) was very upsetting. Reading about your child's problems is a demoralizing experience. However, it made many things so much clearer for us. We began to understand our child better and understood why he couldn't do things. This was a watershed moment for us and if we gain nothing further out of the statementing process we have gained an understanding of our child. This has been invaluable. Yes there was heartbreak realizing just how difficult life was for him, but with time comes acceptance and we find it easier now to deal with the labels.

One of the worst parts of this process was the impact it had on our son and the family as a whole. He found the assessment process very upsetting. Every assessment he had confirmed to him that he had problems and was different from other children. It became so bad at one point that he began to vomit and complain of stomach ache all the time. The all-time low was transferring to our new 'specialist' school. He found settling very hard, and the realization that his problems meant life was going to be different for him. On a bad night he cried and cried and said:

> I am so angry, I hate not being normal. I hate being dyslexic. I just want to be the same as other children. I want to like the same things other children do. Life is so hard, I struggle all the time.

Our other son has suffered. He has had to accept he has a brother with problems who can't go to the same local state school he attends, and his brother is very demanding of our attention which makes him jealous. My husband and I were often preoccupied and busy with paperwork relating to the case. It seemed to occupy our heads all the time. If you go down this route, be prepared for paperwork. I have just put away five full lever-arch files. It is endless. To be able to cope with the process you need to be literate, organized and prepared to devote a lot of time to it. I work part time so could give the case the time it needed. The process itself is not easy. Parents with literacy problems would struggle without assistance. It is also not accessible to people who can't afford the legal representation. I have to say, nobody in their right mind would go through the process unless they had to.

Why did we put ourselves though this? We could just have sent our child to the local state school. We already knew that he couldn't cope in a small private school with lots of help. So he would not cope in a large mainstream school with less help. One friend suggested to me that I needed to accept that my child was not academic. I realized then that she had no idea what this was about – it was not a question of being academic or not. It was a question of gaining literacy skills. All people, academic or not, should have literacy skills. Being unable to read or write properly as an adult is a terrible disability. What would the future hold? What job could our son do? And most importantly, how would he feel about himself? At 9 he already thought he was stupid, different and found life very, very hard. We had to try to get our child the help he needed. He could succeed and do well, if supported in the right way.

As parents we had not realized how difficult the process could become. We needed to visit the school the local authority deemed suitable. Over two visits, we decided we were unhappy with the school and that it would not be the right place for our son.

We finally received a statement without needing to go to court. The final fight was for the funding. We then had our day at the tribunal. This was incredibly stressful for my husband and me. We had no experience of court. We knew there would be lots of people there, a panel of three including a judge, our barrister, an educational psychologist (EP), occupational therapist (OT) and SaLT. The local authority had their own lawyer, OT, SaLT, EP and the head of special needs from the local authority-named school. As a mother I had to give evidence about our child. When asked to speak, I dissolved into tears. I cried out of sadness for our son and at the situation we were in – having to share such intimate information with a room full of strangers, just to get our child the help he needed, while others seemed to be determined that he should not get the type of help we thought vital. It seemed so unfair that we had to go to these lengths.

To make matters worse, our day in court became two, the next available date being two months away. Those intervening months were very hard. We could not move on and our lawyers used the time as a means to get more evidence, a constant reminder of the next hearing. We were warned at the start that the process is costly and more so if your case is complicated. We are at the end now and our total costs are in excess of £40,000. My advice to any other parent who might read this is to choose a school, if at all possible, which will take their child through to 16 or 18. The costs of our case meant we have had to make financial decisions which will have a significant impact in other areas of our lives.

We waited ten days after our hearing for the outcome. It is so good it is all over. It feels as if a weight has been lifted. We understood at the outset that we might lose and were prepared to accept the risk. It has been a long, tiring, stressful experience, but also a journey of growth and understanding. We can now focus on the success our child is experiencing in his specialist school and enjoy seeing his self-esteem being restored. On Friday he came home with an example of his handwriting – beautiful, cursive writing. He could barely write a year ago. How wonderful to see this success. This is why we fought this battle.

DYSLEXIA, GLUE EAR AND HYPER-REACTIVITY – A PARENT'S PERSPECTIVE (LINDSAY PEER)

We give birth to our children, never dreaming that such bright, happy, smiling bundles of joy may grow up to experience difficulties in learning to such a degree that, despite love and support from home, they may develop low self-esteem, demotivation and lack of confidence which, if not handled appropriately, may affect them for life. My 'children', now 32, 30 and 25, were all born with dyslexia to varying degrees and all had 'glue ear' to the extent that they needed grommets surgically inserted. Two children came late into our family – one now aged 29 is severely dyslexic. One of my children went on to become protected by a Statement of Special Educational Needs. One became, as I have described in the literature, a child with 'hyper-reactivity'.

What is Hyper-reactivity?

'Hyper-reactivity' is a term I have cultivated and used for some years now. It describes children who display hyperactive-type behaviours at school and yet are not hyperactive. Medication (e.g. ritalin) does not appear to work for them. Often parents of hyper-reactive children inform me that their children's behaviour is vastly improved during the school holidays. Their children are calmer, they sleep better and they are more confident; they seem to display their strengths rather than focus upon their weaknesses. As soon as the holidays draw to a close, however, tension increase and the hyperactive-type behaviours return.

It is undoubtedly the case that there are many children whose behaviour deteriorates when faced with significant challenges at school; this often worsens at secondary school when faced with large classes, changing rooms, numerous teachers and varying demands. While there are some who become passive and withdraw, there are others who 'act out' and become the class clown or become aggressive, angry and/or over-sensitive. In time they develop lowered self-esteem.

I have seen many hyper-reactive children whose hyperactivity disappears once they are placed at an appropriate school in small classes, with specialist teachers and sometimes therapists. I am not suggesting that all children need to be placed in specialist schools; many do well in mainstream schooling. However it is indeed the case that for those SEN children learning within an inclusive environment, their teachers need to be trained and well resourced if the children are to have a chance of success at school – and ultimately in life. Provision is often sitting a child with a non-trained, kindly teaching assistant; this is for many insufficient.

Children with hyper-reactive behaviours are often highly aware of what is going on around them. They cannot keep up in class, find following instructions challenging and often struggle with their homework; many of them tell me that their teachers talk too fast for them to follow and then they get into trouble for not listening. They recognize that they are constantly in trouble and underachieving academically. They see that their peers who can, for example, handwrite neater or spell better than them, are gaining higher marks than they are – even though they may well have more knowledge; this is indeed very frustrating for them. It is important that their anxieties and frustrations are recognized for what they are and that they receive the support and appropriate teaching that they require so that they make progress academically, socially and emotionally.

What is Glue Ear?

Many children are born with 'glue ear' (i.e. otitis media) which is an inflammation of the middle ear. In a healthy child, an area in the middle ear is filled with air allowing for the flow of sound; when a child has glue ear, it is partially or completely filled with a sticky fluid reducing the transmission of sound and resulting in fluctuating hearing. Due to the loss of good hearing at a young age, in some children it may result in a delay in emerging receptive or expressive language or both. Problems with processing the good-quality sounds necessary for auditory perception and speed of processing are common. It may also become a contributing factor to poor language and literacy development, listening comprehension, academic achievement, attention, concentration, behavioural difficulties and/or other learning difficulties. It affects the development of phonological awareness so common in dyslexia; it may also cause difficulties with balance, including problems such as travel sickness.

Identification of glue ear and/or dyslexia with their overlapping difficulties should be carried out as early as possible to ensure that language and learning are not hindered. A medical diagnosis when young may be seen as a likelihood of language and/or learning difficulties, particularly if family members have difficulties in areas of reading, spelling, writing, speaking or mathematics. The prerequisites for learning (e.g. phonological, language, listening and memory skills development) should be put in place to develop early learning skills as soon as possible. Schools should be informed whenever the child is experiencing fluctuating hearing loss so that they can take the necessary steps (Peer, 2005).

My Children

I was informed by various professionals on several occasions not to expect too much from my children – which as a parent and a teacher at the time was totally unacceptable to me. I felt and still feel that there is no way that any child should do any less well than that of which they are capable or become any less of a person than they can be. All children need the opportunity to grow and become successful, happy and secure young people; if at all possible, they need to have the chances in life to become independent and successful adults. My children were the catalyst for my journey into the world of dyslexia; I am very proud of them all and will never forget their struggles along the way. So where are they now?

M is now a teacher of English as a foreign language to very young children in a school in Frankfurt. She is very concerned about the needs of children with SEN and has worked with adults and children with severe learning disabilities. She is now planning to qualify as a teacher of dyslexic children. She is a sensitive and caring person who works hard on building the self-esteem of children whom she already sees are struggling with learning. Y – the boy I was once told would never learn to read and write – has his masters degree in architecture and is now working his way through his examinations to practise. He has the dyslexic gift of visualization, art and design and worked successfully with the world-renowned Czech architect, Jan Kaplicky, until his untimely death in 2009. Y focuses on bio-climatic architecture. As a volunteer, he has worked with cancer patients and has additionally raised money for the rebuilding of a town in Peru post-earthquake. D achieved her first degree in psychology and is now completing her masters degree in animal welfare. She has a passion for the care and welfare of animals and wishes to develop her skills in changing policy and practice. Like her sister, she is a sensitive and caring person. She wants to change the hearts and minds of those working with, researching on and meeting with animals who by definition cannot speak and legislate for themselves. A became head boy of a specialist dyslexia school. He is now a teacher of autistic children and is additionally developing a business running parties for children. He has taken the skills and strategies he learnt as a schoolboy into his work.

FINAL THOUGHTS

In our working travels around the world as professionals, we have met parents, teachers, psychologists and policy-makers who are all dealing with the same issues – regardless of where they are and who they are. We urge all parents to become as knowledgeable as they possibly can about the SEN experienced by their children. It is undoubtedly the case that the more you know, the better you will be equipped to help your children. We also urge teachers and teaching assistants to acquire as much knowledge as they can – as their attitude and skills in teaching and supporting these children in school are critical. We hope that this book with its excellent contributions from a range of first-rate contributors will help to make this possible.

Further Reading

Assessing Dyslexia Toolkit for Professionals – The Scottish Teacher Education Committee's National Framework for Inclusion http://frameworkforinclusion.org/AssessingDyslexia/

For an introduction to dyslexia:
http://www.dyslexiascotland.org.uk/links-and-resources Dyslexia Scotland information guides.
Reid, G. (2011) *Dyslexia: A Complete Guide for Parents and those who Help them*. Chichester: Wiley.
http://www.dystalk.com/topics/1-dyslexia video clips about dyslexia.

For books explaining dyslexia to young people:
Hultquist, A.M. (2008) *What is Dyslexia? A Book Explaining Dyslexia for Kids and Adults to Use Together*. London: Jessica Kingsley.
http://www.bdadyslexia.org.uk/about–dyslexia/famous-dyslexics.html British Dyslexia Association's list of famous dyslexics.

For strategies to support learners with dyslexia:
Mackay, N. (2006) *Removing Dyslexia as a Barrier to Achievement: The Dyslexia Friendly Schools Toolkit*. Wakefield: SEN Marketing.
Mackay, N. (2011) *Taking the Hell out of Homework: Tips and Techniques for Parents and Home Educators*. Wakefield: SEN Marketing.
Reid, G. and Green S. (2011) *100 Ideas for Supporting Pupils with Dyslexia* (2nd edn). London: Continuum.
http://www.supportingdyslexicpupils.org.uk/ Teaching and secondary subject guides.

For training online:
http://www.icepe.co.uk/ parents and professionals.
www.cpdbytes.com professionals.

For guides to legislation:

www.enquire.org.uk   Scotland.

http://www.scotland.gov.uk/Publications/2008/11/13161112/1

http://www.direct.gov.uk/en/Parents/Schoolslearninganddevelopment/SpecialEducational Needs/index.htm

http://www.education.gov.uk/schools/pupilsupport/sen   UK.

Useful Websites

www.ghotit.com a dyslexia-friendly online spellchecker/text-to-speech facility.

http://www.rsc-ne-scotland.ac.uk/eduapps/mystudybar.php free ICT applications.

http://www.callscotland.org.uk/resources/Quick-Guides/Assets/Downloads/Low-Cost-Software Low-cost-No-cost-Software-Tools-for-People-with-Dyslexia.pdf low-cost software tools.

www.peergordonassociates.co.uk Advice, guidance and assessment.

http://www.scotland.gov.uk/Topics/Education/Schools/welfare/ASL/dyslexia

References

Reid, G. (2009) *Dyslexia: A Practitioner's Handbook* (4th edn). Chichester: Wiley.

Peer, L. (2005) *Glue Ear.* London: David Fulton Publishers.

GLOSSARY

Assistive hearing technology   Equipment used to make spoken language accessible and comfortable for students with hearing loss and includes digital programmable hearing aids, bone-anchored hearing aids, cochlear implants, hybrid cochlear implants, and personal FM systems.

Coprolalia   The involuntary use of obscenities and swear words. This only occurs in about 1 in 10 people with Tourette Syndrome. Note: if this occurs, the person cannot help swearing, and it is not a reflection on their moral character or upbringing.

Disability   A personal attribute or trait that impairs normal everyday function.

Echophenomena   Copying what others say and do.

Engram   Memorized motor patterns used to perform a movement or skills, which are stored in the motor area of the brain.

Executive function   Makes up the higher order cognitive processing responsible for metacognition and behaviour regulation and is closely related to family and school environments and practitioner instruction.

Graphophonic   Based on symbol (letter)/sound correspondences that help readers decode and understand text. Combination of phonic and graphic knowledge used in decoding text.

Literacy   The set of skills which allows an individual to engage fully in society and in learning, through the different forms of language, and the range of texts, which society values and finds useful.

(Learning and Teaching Scotland (2008))

Non obscene socially inappropriate (NOSI) behaviours   Such as saying inappropriate or rude personal comments.

Palilalia   Repeating your own last word or syllable after the end of a sentence.

Psycholinguistic   Relating to the psychology of language.

Pull-out support model   Specialist practitioner withdraws the student from the classroom for direct expert instruction purposes.

Push-in support model   Specialist practitioner working within the classroom performing a variety of roles including team teaching with the classroom teacher, small group discussion with the child with hearing loss and hearing peers, and one-on-one intervention in a quiet area of the classroom.

Scaffolding   Refers to the idea that specialized instructional supports need to be in place in order to best facilitate learning when students are first introduced to a new subject. Scaffolding techniques can include displaying graphics, activating prior knowledge, modelling an activity beforehand, and introducing motivational techniques to stimulate student interest.

Screening   Screening in education can indicate that difficulties are present and that specific help or intervention is required. It is not the same as assessment. Screening can often be done with groups rather than individually.

Socially-constructed disability   Impairment of an individual's everyday function that stems more from barriers within the social environment than from that individual's personal attributes or traits.

INDEX

Added to a page number 'f' denotes a figure, 't' denotes a table, 'g' denotes glossary and 'n' denotes a note.